AMPHIBIAN CONSERVATION

Amphibian Conservation

Edited by Raymond D. Semlitsch | Foreword by David B. Wake

Smithsonian

Books

Washington and

London

Copy Editor: Fran Aitkens
Production Editor: Ruth G. Thomson

Library of Congress Cataloging-in-Publication Data
Amphibian conservation / edited by Raymond D. Semlitsch ; foreword by David B. Wake.
    p.   cm.
    ISBN 1-58834-119-4 (alk. paper)
     1. Amphibian declines. 2. Endangered species. 3. Wildlife conservation. I. Semlitsch, Raymond D.
    QL644.7.A47 2003
    333.95'7216—dc21   2002030485

British Library Cataloging-in-Publication Data available

Manufactured in the United States of America
10 09 08 07 06 05 04 03   5 4 3 2 1

⊗ The paper used in this publication meets the minimum requirements of the American National
Standard for Information Sciences — Permanence of Paper for Printed Library Materials
ANSI Z39.48-1984.

CONTENTS

FOREWORD

The fact that amphibians are in trouble around the world was slowly and painfully made clear over a period of about 20 years. My own awareness of the problem dates to experiences of students in my laboratory who had difficulty locating frog populations in the Sierra Nevada in places where I *knew* they occurred. David Green was a postdoctorate fellow in my group in the early 1980s. David was an experienced frog biologist, so when he too had difficulty finding anurans—in this instance toads—I became concerned. We went together to places where anurans had earlier been abundant and found almost none. However, I work on salamanders and for the most part they remained abundant, so I did not become overly alarmed at first. Then I began to hear rumors and anecdotes from others. I began having trouble finding salamanders even in Costa Rica, and it was clear that frogs were far less common than in previous years. Plethodontid salamanders became hard to find in Mexico and were virtually absent in areas where they once were common. Other scientists were having similar experiences, but we were not communicating with each other very effectively. A few cases of declines have been documented (Hayes and Jennings 1986; Heyer et al. 1988; Weygoldt 1989), but most of the information was anecdotal. The First World Congress of Herpetology in Canterbury, England, in the fall of 1989, offered an opportunity for workers from around the world to compare notes. What emerged profoundly shocked me. Australian workers were finding declines of many upland tropical species and thought that some species might have gone extinct. The two stomach-brooding frogs disappeared from protected sites. Research in Costa Rica suggested that some dramatic declines had taken place in the Monteverde Cloud Forest Reserve and at least one species, the golden toad (*Bufo periglenes*), had disappeared. Other species had disappeared locally. Problems had been detected in many other parts of the world as well, and most of us were perplexed, not drawing conclusions, but simply asking questions.

Much happened in the few months from fall 1989 to spring 1990. With Harold Morowitz, I organized and moderated a workshop sponsored by the National Research Council at Irvine, California, in February 1990. The results served to highlight what we did not know and the workshop itself attracted a great deal of media attention. From that point to the present, much attention has been directed to the problem of amphibian declines and the causes for them. Although most participants felt that there was, indeed, something to be explained (e.g., Blaustein and Wake 1990; Vitt et al. 1990), naturally there were many skeptics. Despite reports of declines that began to appear in the literature (as opposed to simple discussions or reports at meetings), such as Richards et al. (1993), there was little solid research supporting the suggestion that amphibians in general were in decline. A 12-year study of four amphibian species monitored daily in a protected area in South Carolina showed that there were great fluctuations from year to year and emphasized how difficult it would be without long-term studies to distinguish natural fluctuations from declines (Pechmann et al. 1991). Fortunately, a number of monitoring studies were initiated in the wake of the early alarm calls.

I think of the early 1990s as a time of confusion and concern. On one hand, some individuals had direct field experience with amphibians that had declined or disappeared, whereas many biologists were unable to discern any long-term trend in the populations they had been studying and did not see a problem. This period is best summarized in the contentious articles that appeared in the journal *Herpetologica* (e.g., Pechmann and Wilbur 1994; Blaustein 1995).

Because I was one who had personally witnessed declines, I always felt there was something to be explained, and I could also understand the skepticism of others, which unfortunately sometimes was manifested in questions about the quality of science or the field abilities of the observers. Recently there has been a shift in the opinion of herpetologists in general, and in retrospect I believe that it occurred after publication of two landmark papers. The first paper showed that amphibians were in steep decline in Yosemite National Park (Drost and Fellers 1996) and the second documented the decline and disappearance of many species of frogs from the famous Monteverde Cloud Forest Reserve in Costa Rica (Pounds et al. 1997). By that time, we knew that frogs were disappearing from other protected areas, such as national parks in the United States (Fellers and Drost 1993; Drost and Fellers 1996) and Australia (McDonald, 1990). These disappearances were especially alarming because everyone knows that habitat destruction is the major factor in loss of biodiversity and that could be ruled out. What was so compelling about the new papers was the nature of the sampling (thorough, and in the case of Pounds et al. 1997, over a 5-year period) against a background of knowledge of amphibian diversity and abundance in the past. Now we know that amphibian declines may have started much earlier than the events of the 1980s that spurred the current interest (Houlahan et al. 2000).

Since 1996, many advances have occurred, both in the research community and in the funding of research. The clear demonstration of declines and disappearances in protected areas demands that explanations other than habitat destruction be explored, and I am gratified that so much progress has been made in identifying diverse potential explanations. There is no "smoking gun" that I can perceive. Rather, the list of threats has grown so long that one has to be surprised that so many species continue to appear to be doing well. As I write, several categories of threat are known that were basically not considered at all during the early days of interest in amphibian declines. A chytrid fungus that has negative effects on amphibians has been implicated in declines of frogs in Middle America, Australia, and other regions (e.g., Berger et al. 1998). This discovery has spurred much research, ranging from field and laboratory studies to ecological and epidemiological modeling. Deformed amphibians have been found in many areas, often in high densities (Johnson et al. 2002). These deformations range from mild, such as a bifurcated digit, to extreme, such as multiple complete legs or even no hind limbs at all. Although parasitic infestations of a trematode seem to be the primary causative factor, it is unclear whether parasites are present at higher than historic levels or if there are ecological reasons why parasites are so dense at present. Or are amphibians more susceptible to parasitization than in the past? These deformities often affect survival and reproductive performance severely, but their role in amphibian declines remains unclear. Residues from pesticides and herbicides are associated with more subtle but still major deformities of reproductive and other organs (Hayes et al. 2002), and such residues have been implicated in declines (Davidson et al. 2001). The existence of synergistic interactions, between ultraviolet-B radiation and pathogens, for example (Kiesecker et al. 2001a), means that simple explanations will always be viewed with some skepticism. Doubtless other findings will change our perspective on the nature of the problem in general.

This book is a vivid demonstration of the progress that has been made in the past decade and bears witness to the current high level of attention amphibian declines are receiving. The quality and quantity of research in amphibian biology have increased, and results to date are impressive. The authors and the editor of this volume have served us well in summarizing what is known today and what they believe we will need to know to develop effective amphibian conservation strategies. The community of amphibian biologists has dramatically increased in size, and the scope of research has enlarged as well, as is manifest in the chapters in this book. But there have also been unanticipated benefits of the renewed research effort. Resource development has progressed rapidly, and we now have such online resources as Amphibia-Web (available online at http://elib.cs.berkeley.edu/aw/) and Amphibian Species of the World (http://research.amnh.org/cgi-bin/herpetology/amphibia). The community in general is now far better equipped to conduct ground-breaking research and we can expect many substantial products in the near future.

Another unanticipated outcome of the focus on amphibians has been many more people in the field, looking for amphibians. Of course this activity is also the result of focused research on biodiversity inventories throughout the world. In 1985, I was delighted to hold in my hand the wonderful summary of amphibian species of the world (Frost 1985), compiled as a result of the cooperation of amphibian biologists throughout the world. That book includes 4,003 species and we had every expectation that discovery of new species was about done. How wrong we were! According to AmphibiaWeb, we now count 4,726 species of frogs alone, plus 506 salamanders and 159 caecilians (the numbers change weekly), or an increase of more than 35% since 1985. It is ironic that as many amphibians decline and even go extinct (our latest rough estimate is that about 125 species are severely threatened or have gone extinct recently; see AmphibiaWeb), the total number of species known continues to increase (Hanken 1999).

The fate of many amphibian populations is surely extinction as habitat destruction directly associated with the astonishingly rapid growth of human populations increases. But amphibians are survivors, having passed through the end-Cretaceous extinction relatively intact, for example, and one hopes they will survive us as well. In the meantime, I hope that our continued investigations will inform future activities as we move from an age of discovery to one of husbandry, for increasingly it is clear that the fate of at least most vertebrates on this planet will be in our hands.

David B. Wake
Berkeley, California
23 April 2002

ACKNOWLEDGMENTS

I thank the many students I have had the pleasure of knowing, teaching, and learning from over the years and who have helped me formulate many of the ideas presented here. I thank my mentors Whit Gibbons, Jim Spotila, and Henry Wilbur who instilled in me a great love for amphibians and taught me how to study their biology. Their words and deeds inspired me to develop this book. I thank especially the reviewers of each chapter for their thoughtful comments and suggestions and timely responses: Ronn Altig, Kimberly Andrews, Val Beasley, Gayle Birchfield, Russ Bodie, Michelle Boone, David Bradford, Phillip deMaynadier, Maureen Donnelly, Meaghan Doyle, Christine Geist, Whit Gibbons, James Gibbs, Xavier Glaudas, David M. Green, Tracy Green, Robert Hay, Robert Inger, Pieter Johnson, Lee Kats, Mike Lannoo, Hugh Lefcort, Karen Lips, Joyce Longcore, Vince Marshall, Nathan Mills, Matt Parris, Jim Petranka, George Rabb, Chad Rittenhouse, Betsie Rothermel, Chris Rowe, Travis Ryan, Rich Seigel, Meg Stewart, Hartwell Welsh, and Lucas Wilkinson. I thank Vincent Burke of Smithsonian Books for his encouragement and help in this project. I also thank J. David for teaching release time to work on this project. Last, I am grateful to my wife, Malissa, and children, John Harper and Sarah Margaret, for allowing me the time to focus on this project. Preparation of the manuscripts was partially supported by grants from U.S. Environmental Protection Agency (827095-01), U.S. National Science Foundation (DEB 99 03761), and U.S. Geological Survey (01CRAG0007).

1

INTRODUCTION

General Threats to Amphibians

RAYMOND D. SEMLITSCH

> All ethics so far evolved rest upon a single premise: that the individual is a member of a community of interdependent parts. His instincts prompt him to compete for his place in the community, but his ethics prompt him also to cooperate (perhaps in order that there may be a place to compete for).
>
> The land ethic simply enlarges the boundaries of the community to include soils, waters, plants, and animals, or collectively: the land.
>
> This sounds simple: do we not already sing our love for and obligation to the land of the free and the home of the brave? Yes, but just what and who do we love? Certainly not the soil, which we are sending helter-skelter downriver. Certainly not the waters, which we assume have no function except to turn turbines, float barges, and carry off sewage. Certainly not the plants, of which we exterminate whole communities without batting an eye. Certainly not the animals, of which we have already extirpated many of the largest and most beautiful species. A land ethic of course cannot prevent the alteration, management, and use of these "resources," but it does affirm their right to continued existence, and, at least in spots, their continued existence in a natural state.
>
> In short, a land ethic changes the role of *Homo sapiens* from conqueror of the land-community to plain member and citizen of it. It implies respect for his fellow-members, and also respect for the community as such. *A Sand County Almanac*, Aldo Leopold, 1949

CENTRAL ISSUES

Amphibians, like many other groups of organisms, are facing worldwide population declines, range contractions, and even species extinctions. It is imperative that conservation action be taken to reverse this trend and maintain amphibian diversity. The goals of conservation biology are to understand the structure and function of natural ecological systems in the face of a growing human population and then to apply that knowledge to maintain their diversity. Understanding past, present, and future threats to amphibians and how those threats disrupt natural processes is critical to finding solutions and conserving amphibian diversity. Further, knowing the basic ecology, behavior, and evolutionary history is necessary to understanding the natural functioning of amphibian systems. A summary of our current knowledge concerning the biology of amphibians and the threats they face is an essential starting point.

INTRODUCTION

Over the past two decades, amphibians have been the focus of increasing concern in the scientific literature and popular press because of numerous reports of population declines, range constrictions, and extinctions. Recent analysis of data on 157 species from 37 countries and 8 regions of the world suggests that amphibians have declined on a global scale (Houlahan et al. 2000). In the United States alone, 27 species are listed as threatened or endangered (Table 1.1). Current evidence indicates that the declines appear to be related to effects at local, regional, and possibly global scales (e.g., Halliday 1998; Wake 1998; Alford and Richards 1999). Although most biologists agree that local habitat destruction (filling and draining of wetlands, clearing of forests, channelization of streams, creation and maintenance of impoundments) is the major factor causing declines, recent evidence suggests that other factors (such as disease and pathogens, global climate change, invasive species, chemical contamination, and commercial trade) are real threats (reviewed in Blaustein et al. 1994a; Dodd 1997; Berger et al. 1998; Lips 1998; Wake 1998; Alford and Richards 1999; Carey et al. 1999). There is also concern that because some amphibian populations naturally undergo wide fluctuations in number, they may be especially sensitive to stochastic events, whether natural or anthropogenic (e.g., Berven 1990; Pechmann et al. 1991). Further, there is growing evidence that any of these factors can be synergistic, allowing subtle or undetectable effects of any single factor to be exacerbated to harmful levels by another factor (e.g., chemical contamination and predation; Relyea and Mills 2001). In combination, these factors may result in reduced viability of populations, setting the stage for potential extinctions. This is perhaps one reason why obvious causes of decline have not been detected in most cases. Therefore, it is essential to summarize the knowledge accumulated and to develop potential solutions to conserve amphibian diversity in the face of continuing economic development and a growing human population.

Why are amphibians worthy of large-scale conservation efforts? First, as Aldo Leopold so boldly stated in 1949, all organisms have an ethical right to existence on this planet we share. Second, with a potential sensitivity to habitat alteration and pollution, amphibians may serve as indicators of overall environmental health (e.g., Vitt et al. 1990). Third, in terms of ecosystem function, the abundance of amphibians in

Table 1.1

Amphibians protected and proposed for protection under the U.S. Endangered Species Act during 2001

Year Listed	Status[a]	Order[b]	Scientific Name	Common Name
1967	E	U	*Ambystoma macrodactylum croceum*	Santa Cruz long-toed salamander
1967	E	U	*Typhlomolge rathbuni*	Texas blind salamander
1970	E	A	*Bufo houstonensis*	Houston toad
1973	E	U	*Batrachoseps aridus*	Desert slender salamander
1976	T	U	*Phaeognathus hubrichti*	Red Hills salamander
1977	T	A	*Eleutherodactylus jasperi*	Golden coqui
1977	T[c]	A	*Hyla andersonii*	Pine barrens treefrog
1980	T	U	*Eurycea nana*	San Marcos salamander
1984	E	A	*Bufo hemiophrys baxteri*	Wyoming toad
1987	T	A	*Peltophryne lemur*	Puerto Rican crested toad
1989	E	U	*Plethodon shenandoah*	Shenandoah salamander
1989	T	U	*Plethodon nettingi*	Cheat Mountain salamander
1994	E	A	*Bufo microscaphus californicus*	Arroyo toad
1996	T	A	*Rana aurora draytonii*	California red-legged frog
1997	E	U	*Eurycea sosorum*	Barton Springs salamander
1997	E	U	*Ambystoma tigrinum stebbinsi*	Sonoran tiger salamander
1997	T	A	*Eleutherodactylus cooki*	Guajon
1999	T	U	*Ambystoma cingulatum*	Flatwoods salamander
2000	E	U	*Ambystoma californiense*	California tiger salamander
2001	PE	A	*Rana capito sevosa*	Mississippi gopher frog
2001	PE	A	*Rana muscosa*	Mountain yellow-legged frog
2001	PT	A	*Rana chiricahuensis*	Chiricahua leopard frog
2001	C	A	*Rana luteiventris*	Columbia spotted frog
2001	C	A	*Rana pretiosa*	Oregon spotted frog
2001	E	U	*Ambystoma californiense*	California tiger salamander
2001	C	A	*Bufo boreas boreas*	Boreal toad
2001	C	U	*Necturus alabamensis*	Black warrior waterdog

[a]Status under the Endangered Species Act: E = Endangered, T = Threatened, PE = Proposed Endangered, PT = Proposed Threatened, C = Candidate for Listing.

[b]Order: U = Urodela (Caudata; salamander), A = Anura (Salientia; frog, toad).

[c]Species listed in 1977 but delisted in 1983.

some regions (e.g., Burton and Likens 1975; Petranka 1998), their direct effects on nutrient flux (e.g., Seale 1980), and their function as nutrient vectors connecting aquatic and terrestrial environments through emigration and immigration processes (R. D. Semlitsch, unpublished data) suggest that they play an important role in forest and aquatic ecosystem dynamics.

Why is now a good time to publish a book like this? I see two major reasons to discuss amphibian conservation issues at this time. The first relates to the attention amphibians now receive from the public and scientific community. This attention has spawned new questions and concerns about conservation planning and management that need to be answered and discussed. Second, much new research and knowledge, both basic and applied, have come to light in the past few years. We are now at a point where change must be effected to save the remaining amphibian diversity, and solutions must be readily available.

Yet, how do we proceed? What is the conceptual framework on which the conservation of amphibians is based? Sure, there are organizations that advocate the conservation of amphibians and are actively organizing stakeholders and developing partnerships for monitoring and research. These groups will serve as highly effective instruments for facilitating change. But these groups clearly rely on biologists to reveal critical issues and prioritize research, management, and education goals. The chapters in this book are organized to present the current view of major amphibian conservation threats and our state of knowledge. My hope is that such knowledge can be used to focus the efforts of conservation organizations. The principles on which to base conservation efforts emerge from each chapter, particularly where authors discuss potential solutions and priorities. Other principles for conservation are discussed in the last two chapters, in which solutions for better integration of land use and management are discussed.

However, the framework will not end here; rather, I hope more detail will follow after readers can contemplate what is known and what is needed, thereby stimulating innovative plans of action, and refining a conservation framework. In addition, it is important to consider the basic ecological and conservation principles that guide efforts in other taxa. Much can be learned from conservation efforts that have worked or failed with other species.

Although the chapters in this book are not organized strictly around Meffe and Carroll's (1997) three underlying paradigms for conservation biology (evolutionary change, dynamic ecology, and human presence), these factors should be kept in mind while reading each chapter. Essentially, these paradigms suggest that we must understand first the evolutionary history of amphibians, which includes phylogenetic history, biogeographic patterns, taxonomic differences, adaptations, and the potential for future evolutionary change. Next, we need to understand the processes that underlie the ecology of amphibians, such as environmental limitations, population growth and regulation, community structure, and metapopulation dynamics. And, perhaps most importantly, humans must be included in any conservation solution. Understanding the social, political, and economic pressures and attitudes that affect resource use and thus our ability to manage and restore the critical habitat needed by amphibians is a key component for effective conservation. Filling gaps in our knowledge based on Meffe and Carroll's paradigms should become a research priority.

Each chapter in this book is written by a senior author and collaborators who have many years of experience working with amphibians and are dedicated to developing conservation solutions. Within the limited space of this book, I want readers to gain an appreciation of the diversity of amphibians in the world. To do this, several chapters are devoted to identifying general biological, biogeographical, and life history differences that may determine which threats are most critical and necessitate different solutions for pond-breeding, stream-breeding, and terrestrial amphibians. Most of the chapters focus in detail on the six major threats (habitat destruction and alteration, disease and pathogens, global climate change, invasive species, chemical contamination, and commercial trade) identified by the Partners in Amphibian and Reptile Conservation (PARC) during their organizational meeting in Atlanta, Georgia, in June 1998. One chapter is devoted to the difficulty of detecting population declines and the use of null models. Next, because social, political, and economic factors play a significant role in conservation issues, several chapters deal with the complex interplay of social attitudes, economic and other values of amphibians, and land-use practices affecting amphibians. Finally, because our ultimate goal is to provide a conceptual framework for the conservation and management of amphibians, a final chapter deals with integrating our current knowledge into a set of essential elements to guide conservation efforts.

Each chapter begins with a statement of the central issues to focus the reader on the important findings, problems, patterns, or questions for each topic. The authors then review the state of knowledge, provide examples, and discuss patterns and mechanisms related to that topic. Each chapter ends with a statement of the potential solutions or suggestions for designing solutions. These may or may not be testable hypotheses or even practical solutions for the most part, but the ideas presented will leave readers with approaches to contemplate and some concrete actions to take, regardless of interest or focus (i.e., research, management, education, or regulation).

WHY ARE WE LOSING AMPHIBIANS?

Habitat Destruction and Alteration

Most amphibians depend on both aquatic and terrestrial habitats to complete their life cycle. Conservation of these habitats at local population and landscape levels is critical to maintaining viable populations and regional diversity. However, both habitats have been heavily affected by human use, and these effects are likely the primary cause of reported species declines (Blaustein et al. 1994a; Dodd 1997; Alford and Richards 1999). Major land-use practices affecting amphibian habitats include agriculture, silviculture, industry, and urban development. These practices are often associated with the filling and draining of wetlands that serve as amphibian breeding sites, removal of trees or natural vegetation in upland habitats used for feeding and as refuges by adults, or alteration of the hydrodynamics of stream and river ecosystems that affect natural functioning and the ability of the ecosystems to support viable populations.

Global Climate Change

Global climate changes caused by the accumulation of greenhouse gases and reduction of the ozone layer are now being linked to species declines. This raises serious questions about the future of amphibians in areas of high vulnerability, particularly species with specialized habitat requirements. Two factors of primary concern have been identified: alteration of rainfall and temperature patterns, and increases in ultraviolet (UV-B) radiation. The increase in frequency and severity of El Niño–southern oscillation events is likely associated with amphibian declines and has been closely related to negative effects on diverse fauna worldwide (e.g., bird communities, Grant and Grant 1996; reef fish assemblages, Holbrook and Schmitt 1996). Also, increases in temperature and UV-B radiation are likely to interact with other factors, such as disease and chemical contamination (e.g., Zaga et al. 1998; Davidson et al. 2001).

Chemical Contamination

Many amphibians encounter chemical contamination in both terrestrial and aquatic environments. Chemicals applied to agricultural fields, golf courses, and forests may directly expose terrestrial juveniles and adults to harmful levels of herbicides, insecticides, and fertilizers. Furthermore, because aquatic environments are the ultimate sink for most chemical contaminants regardless of their source (e.g., agriculture or industry, Anderson and D'Apollonia 1978), all aquatic stages of amphibians are likely exposed. In addition, new evidence suggests that airborne contaminants may be affecting amphibian populations in pristine and montane regions that do not receive direct application (e.g., Davidson et al. 2001; Sparling et al. 2001). Last, research on chemical effects is also exploring sublethal reproductive effects that may have important implications for population persistence (Hayes et al. 2002).

Disease and Pathogens

Some amphibian mass mortality events reported in relatively pristine areas of the world have now been linked to infectious diseases (reviewed in Carey et al. 1999). This suggests that pathogens are responsible for declines of some species (e.g., Carey 1993; Laurance et al. 1996; Berger et al. 1998; Lips 1998). Two primary pathogens that appear to be involved are now the current focus of attention: a parasitic chytrid fungus and an iridovirus. What makes both these pathogens so significant to conservation issues is that they can interact with other factors and likely have enhanced susceptibility of various species or populations to other threats.

Invasive Species

Numerous concerns have been raised about the negative effects of invasive species on native amphibians. Of particular concern are the stocking of predatory game fish, range expansion and introduction of American bullfrogs (*Rana catesbeiana*), and the introduction of exotic species such as cane toads (*Bufo marinus*) and Cuban treefrogs (*Osteopilus septentrionalis*; Dodd 1997). Fish have been considered the most critical and widespread problem because they can be both competitors and predators of amphibians, especially on aquatic larvae (e.g., Bradford et al. 1993; Knapp and Mathews 2000; Pilliod and Peterson 2000). It is now believed that fish can also act as vectors for disease.

Commercial Exploitation

The commercial trade in amphibians is a great concern for natural populations and communities for several reasons. First, the direct impact of commercial or illegal collecting may remove a large portion of breeding adults and reduce the capacity of populations to sustain themselves. Second, the reintroduction of wild-collected or captive-reared amphibians (intentionally or accidentally) into natural populations may expose native animals to diseases or pathogens not present in the region (e.g., fish fungus, Blaustein et al. 1994b).

POTENTIAL SOLUTIONS

Interdisciplinary approaches that include social, political, and economic components have been necessary to solve conservation problems in other groups of organisms and must therefore be considered in approaches to help conserve amphibians. Further, looking beyond the local population or ecosystem level to regional or even global scales will be necessary for many of the threats that cross political or geographic boundaries. Many solutions will necessitate international involvement of all stakeholders, including the exchange of information on education, research, and management. Finally, although we can learn much from past efforts to conserve other vertebrate groups (e.g., birds), amphibians have unique physiological, morphological, behavioral, and ecological features that will necessitate different and innovative solutions. The subsequent chapters of this book detail the features of amphibians that are different from other vertebrates and what is necessary to begin solving conservation problems.

2

CONSERVATION OF POND-BREEDING AMPHIBIANS

RAYMOND D. SEMLITSCH

CENTRAL ISSUES

Amphibians that use temporary ponds and pools usually possess a complex life cycle with two morphological stages that require the use of aquatic habitats for reproduction and larval growth and terrestrial habitats for growth to maturation and dispersal. These two habitats are therefore biologically linked and cannot be managed separately. Because of the ephemeral and stochastic nature of most ponds, amphibians face unique stressors and possess adaptive features to cope with these transient environments. In addition, because temporary ponds or wetlands are physically isolated, they can often be completely surrounded by human disturbance (e.g., agricultural fields, urban or industrial areas). The amphibians using these habitats often experience additional anthropogenic stress that can exacerbate inherent natural environmental factors (e.g., pond drying) and can be isolated from neighboring source populations by unsuitable habitat that lies between them. The transient nature of their breeding habitat, the influences of surrounding land-use practices, and the interaction of natural and anthropogenic stressors has likely led to the decline of many species.

IMPORTANCE AND LIFE HISTORY OF POND-BREEDING AMPHIBIANS

Pond-breeding amphibians are defined as species that use lentic aquatic habitats (defined as static, calm, or slow-moving water) for some part of their life cycle. It is difficult to determine the number of species of amphibians that use lentic aquatic habitats for some aspect of their life cycle. Part of the problem is that the natural history of many species is unknown or poorly understood, especially in the tropics. In addition, many species use pools of water so small (e.g., tree holes, bromeliads) as to not be recognized as typical aquatic habitats, or they may use backwater pools along slow-moving streams, or they may be facultative in their use of lentic and sometimes lotic aquatic habitats (defined as fast-running water, such as streams or rivers) that are low-gradient. However, if some type of lentic aquatic habitat is a required part of a species' life cycle, such as for oviposition or larval development or both, then as many as 60 to 80% of the estimated 5,421 species of amphibians can be placed in this category (including Caudata, Gymnophiona, and Anura; D. Frost, American Museum of Natural History, personal communication). Pond-breeding amphibians occur in all regions of the world where other amphibians are found. In some regions, pond-breeding species are common in the landscape (e.g., on the coastal plain of the southeastern United States, all 31 species of anurans use ponds; Martof et al. 1980); thus they can be a dominant group of amphibians with unique features important to consider in conservation efforts.

Pond-breeding amphibians can play three important ecosystem roles: (1) Larval anurans are consumers of primary production in the form of periphyton and phytoplankton, and larval caudates are consumers of secondary production in the form of zooplankton and aquatic insects in aquatic environments. On land, all amphibians consume small invertebrates often not available to other vertebrate groups. (2) Pond-breeding amphibians comprise a large amount of protein biomass that is readily available in the food chain (e.g., snakes, birds, mammals). (3) Pond-breeding amphibians serve as nutrient vectors connecting aquatic and terrestrial environments through emigration and immigration processes.

Although a few species are permanently aquatic (e.g., sirens, amphiuma), most species require both aquatic and terrestrial environments to complete their life cycle, a unique feature of this group of amphibians among vertebrates. Neither of these habitats are optional if the species is to persist. The transition between the two environments is typically marked by metamorphosis that developmentally provides a change in morphology, physiology, ecology, and behavior. This biphasic life cycle is often referred to as a complex life cycle, in contrast to those species with a simple life cycle, such as those that undergo direct development as in the genus *Plethodon* (Wilbur 1980; see Chapter 4, this volume). Most amphibians with complex life cycles spend egg and larval development time in temporary ponds; this is most typical of temperate species (Figure 2.1). In some cases, however, only the larvae develop in ponds (e.g., foam or leaf-nesting tropical species that oviposit on vegetation above pools, after which hatching tadpoles drop into aquatic habitats).

Much is known about the behavior, ecology, and evolution of the aquatic larval stage. The length of time larvae remain in aquatic habitats is quite variable and is

Lifetime home range

Aquatic

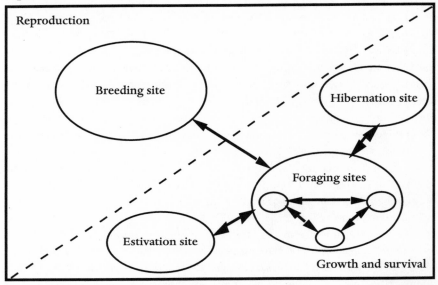

Figure 2.1. Diagram of habitat, function, and life history stage for pond-breeding amphibians with complex life cycles. Hibernation sites may be totally terrestrial or aquatic in some cases (see text).

generally thought to be an adaptation to exploit resource-rich but ephemeral aquatic habitats (Wassersug 1975). Generally, individuals that remain in the aquatic environment longer reach a larger size at metamorphosis and achieve a greater portion of their final adult size (Wilbur and Collins 1973; Werner 1986). Larger size at metamorphosis is associated with increased fitness of adults (e.g., Smith 1987; Semlitsch et al. 1988; Berven 1990). Conversely, in some predator-rich or highly ephemeral aquatic habitats, rapid larvae development and metamorphosis increases survival, but often at the expense of reduced body size (e.g., Smith 1983; Travis et al. 1985a, 1985b; Newman 1988a, 1988b). Time to and size at metamorphosis are both considered highly adaptive traits that are subjected to strong environmentally dependent selection. Thus, selection has caused significant divergence in required habitats of many species. These habitats range from fast-drying desert and vernal pools to large permanent wetlands.

Much less is known about the terrestrial stage of most amphibians. However, we do know that most species spend the majority of their life on land where they grow and reach reproductive maturity after 2 to 3 years. Most metamorphosed juveniles remain near their natal ponds, but some disperse and later become faithful breeders at new sites. Local breeding populations probably remain within 100 to 200 m of the breeding pond, but dispersing individuals may move several thousand meters.

NATURAL PROCESSES AFFECTING POPULATIONS AND COMMUNITIES

Population Dynamics and Regulation

The persistence of a local population is obviously dependent on adequate reproduction to replace individuals that die and therefore to maintain the adult breeding population. Larval growth and development to metamorphosis, which can be affected by many environmental factors, are thought to be critical for recruiting new breeding adults into the population.

The use of the aquatic habitat varies among species and depends on their species-specific larval period and varying environmental quality of the habitat (e.g., food and temperature). Length of habitat use can range from just 12 days for spadefoots (*Scaphiopus* sp.) to 1 to 2 years for American bullfrogs (*Rana catesbeiana;* personal observation). Because of high larval densities (e.g., up to 4,000 per square meter for anurans; Woodward 1982; Petranka 1989) and species diversity (e.g., ponds in the southern United States may have more than 20 species; Wiest 1982; Dodd 1992; Semlitsch et al. 1996; Scott and Bufalino 1997) in many ponds, density-dependent and species interactions are likely to be important for regulation of natural larval populations and communities (Wilbur 1980; Pechmann 1994). Field studies have demonstrated a strong negative effect of density on growth and survival of larvae, with consequent carryover effects on maturation (Smith 1983; Petranka and Sih 1986; Petranka 1989; Scott 1990, 1994; Van Buskirk and Smith 1991). These studies indicate that as larval density increases, larvae grow more slowly, larval period increases, and fewer individuals reach metamorphosis (less than 5% of larvae normally metamorphose; Herreid and Kinney 1966; Licht 1974; Semlitsch 1987).

High growth rates enable tadpoles to metamorphose quickly to escape death in drying ephemeral ponds (Smith 1983; Semlitsch 1987; Newman 1988a, 1988b), to escape aquatic predators (Smith 1983; Woodward 1983; Travis et al. 1985a, 1985b), or to maximize size at metamorphosis in more permanent ponds (Wilbur and Collins 1973). Large size at metamorphosis can also result in better physiological and locomotor performance in the terrestrial environment (Pough and Kamel 1984; Goater et al. 1993), higher juvenile survival, earlier first reproduction, and larger size at first breeding (Berven and Gill 1983; Smith 1987; Semlitsch et al. 1988; Berven 1990). In most species, successful larval development to metamorphosis in natural aquatic habitats is affected by the interaction of multiple factors, typically related to pond drying, competition for food, and predation.

The hydroperiod of a wetland is the length of time it continuously holds water and therefore provides aquatic habitat for amphibian larvae. Temporary wetlands usually fill and dry at least once annually, whereas more permanent wetlands may only dry once or twice a decade. Statistically, hydroperiod length is continuously distributed among wetlands across landscapes and within wetlands through time. Long-term studies have shown that variation in the amount and timing of rainfall among years affects pond hydroperiods, which in turn affects the production of metamorphosing juveniles (e.g., Pechmann et al. 1991; Semlitsch et al. 1996). More rainfall usually results in longer pond hydroperiods (i.e., producing longer growing seasons), allowing more individuals of a species to reach metamorphosis. However, maintaining ponds with extremely long hydroperiods also is detrimental to successful metamorphosis of most amphibian species. Ponds with hydroperiods of more than 2 years (e.g., farm ponds) can accumulate a diverse array of aquatic predators, including invertebrates, aquatic salamanders, and, most seriously, fish. In fact, even short-hydroperiod ponds close to rivers, streams, canals, and drainage ditches that flood seasonally may allow fish to colonize each year. Only a small subset of amphibian species can coexist with fish because they possess antipredator behaviors and skin toxins (e.g., American bullfrog; southern cricket frog, *Acris gryllus;* green treefrog, *Hyla cinerea;* green frog, *Rana clamitans*). Most amphibians are eliminated by predatory fish (e.g., Heyer et al. 1975; Bradford 1989; Hecnar and M'Closkey 1997b).

Amphibian species display different larval periods and thus are differentially favored by hydroperiod length. Once a pond is colonized by adults, success depends on synchrony between the annual availability of water (i.e., time of filling, hydroperiod length) and the timing of reproduction to maximize the growing period of the larvae. After successful reproduction, species' characteristics, such as larval food requirements, temperature tolerance, susceptibility to predation, and minimum length of the larval period, interact to determine larval success along the gradient of pond hydroperiods.

In general, success at the population level is believed to be determined primarily by the number and quality of metamorphosing larvae leaving a pond and thus the number recruited into the terrestrial adult population. Biodiversity persists in a given area because each species, under the right conditions, periodically produces large numbers of metamorphosing juveniles (e.g., Gill 1978; Semlitsch 1983; Pechmann et al. 1989; Berven 1990; Semlitsch et al. 1996). Different species usually are successful in different years. This is in sharp contrast to the constant low-level reproductive success every year exhibited by most mammals and birds. This characteristic of amphibian populations means that multiple years of reproductive failure due to unfavorable aquatic conditions, such as rapid pond drying or fish predation, can result in decline and eventual extinction of species in a given area (Semlitsch et al. 1996). Because breeding adults have a strong preference to return to natal ponds (e.g., Oldham 1966; Breden 1987; Berven and Grudzien 1990), metamorphosing juveniles are likely the primary dispersal stage (sensu Gill 1978). A high rate of successful metamorphosis is critical to maintain local populations, reestablish extirpated populations, and establish new populations.

Community Structure and Regulation

The structure of amphibian communities is strongly influenced by the hydroperiod of wetland habitats (e.g., Pechmann et al. 1989; Semlitsch et al. 1996). Species characteristics such as physiological tolerances and life history requirements determine the use of ponds. A critical factor like pond drying that varies annually within and among ponds may be viewed as a disturbance for larval amphibians, as larvae may be killed if the site dries before metamorphosis can occur. Likewise, increased water permanence also negatively affects larval amphibians by allowing many predators, especially fish, to persist. Heyer et al. (1975) and Wilbur (1980, 1984) suggested that extremely temporary ponds (<30 days) or permanent ponds (>1 year) are used by fewer species of amphibians than ponds with intermediate hydroperiods (e.g., among all semipermanent or seasonal palustrine wetlands, e.g., Types 1, 2, 3, 6, 7, 8 of Cowardin et al. 1979). However, a diversity of hydroperiods are necessary to maximize species diversity.

Predation and competition interact within pond hydroperiod in communities of pond-breeding amphibians (Morin 1981, 1983; Smith 1983; Wilbur 1987; Semlitsch et al. 1996; Skelly 1996; Wellborn et al. 1996). Because all salamanders (larval and adult) are carnivorous and frequently occur in high densities, they can exert strong predation pressure on amphibian communities (e.g., Morin 1981), especially small, herbivorous anuran tadpoles. Salamanders can maintain populations only in ponds with long hydroperiods. Predatory fish generally occupy permanent ponds (e.g., deepwater and permanently flooded lacustrine wetlands, e.g., Types 4 and 5 of Cowardin et al. 1979) and occasionally they colonize seasonal wetlands where they remain until the next drying cycle. Predatory fish can reduce or completely eliminate small vulnerable salamanders and anuran larvae and other amphibians without effective skin secretions or behaviors that deter predators (e.g., Kats et al. 1988; Lawler 1989; Hews 1995; Kats and Dill 1998). Thus, local and regional distribution of amphibians can be strongly influenced by the presence of predatory fish (e.g., Petranka 1983; Woodward 1983; Bradford 1989; Bradford and Graber 1993; Bronmark and Edenhamm 1994; Skelly 1996; Tyler et al. 1998a, 1998b; Azevedo-Ramos et al. 1999).

In ponds with short hydroperiods that lack predatory fish or salamanders, some anuran species breed in one or two nights and produce large numbers of fast-developing larvae that compete for limited food through exploitative and interference competition, sometimes even switching from herbivory to carnivory and cannibalism (e.g.,

Collins and Cheek 1983; Newman 1989; Pfennig 1990). Interspecific competition for food reduces growth and developmental rates and increases length of the larval period, and hence vulnerability to desiccation (Semlitsch 1987; Wilbur 1987; Wilbur and Fauth 1990).

Complex interactions between predation and competition have been experimentally demonstrated in artificial ponds. For example, Morin (1981) showed that in the absence of salamander predators, some anuran species whose larvae forage efficiently can outcompete other species and dominate in numbers of metamorphs. In the presence of predators, however, competitively superior species may be preferentially eaten, allowing other competitively inferior species to increase in relative abundance. Wilbur (1987) also demonstrated that predation can ameliorate the effects of competition at high densities by removing larvae from the community and lowering effective density, thereby allowing survivors to grow more rapidly and metamorphose before ponds dry. Thus, regulation of community structure within an amphibian pond occurs through the predictable interaction of hydroperiod, competition, and predation (sensu Wellborn et al. 1996).

Spatial and temporal variation in the physiochemical and hydrological characteristics of ponds due to climatic conditions, habitat succession, and anthropogenic disturbance usually produces a mosaic of habitats available to amphibians (Semlitsch et al. 1996; Skelly et al. 1999; Werner and Glennemeier 1999). Pond hydroperiods vary tremendously, even in undisturbed regions. Different species do well in different years, depending on pond hydroperiod. The eastern tiger salamander (*Ambystoma t. tigrinum;* Figure 2.2) with a long larval period can produce metamorphs only in years when a pond fills during the breeding season and does not dry for 3 to 4 months (Semlitsch 1983). Also, it is known that some anuran species (eastern spadefoot, *Scaphiopus holbrookii;* eastern narrow-mouth toad, *Gastrophryne carolinensis;* pine woods treefrog, *Hyla femoralis*) produce large numbers of metamorphs only after a pond dries completely and refills later in the season, thereby eliminating all competitors and predators (Pechmann et al. 1989; Semlitsch et al. 1996).

It is important to note, however, that maintaining ponds with hydroperiods that are too long is also not conducive to successful metamorphosis in most species. Ponds with long hydroperiod years accumulate a diverse array of aquatic insect predators and aquatic salamanders and are available for colonization by fish. In fact, some ponds may be close to rivers, streams, canals, and drainage ditches that flood seasonally, allowing fish to colonize ponds most years. Thus, pond drying is a natural process that eliminates or reduces predation on larval amphibians and can be used as an effective management technique. An effective management plan must maintain or restore an array of natural ponds that vary in hydroperiod from perhaps 30 days to 1 to 2 years to ensure that all local species have sites where the probability of reproductive success is high, even in extremely dry or wet years.

Figure 2.2. Eastern tiger salamander, *Ambystoma t. tigrinum*. (Photo by David Scott, Savannah River Ecology Laboratory)

Metapopulation Dynamics

A metapopulation is a set of local populations (number or density may vary with landscape or region) connected by processes of migration, gene flow, extinction, and colonization. Two primary factors control amphibian metapopulation dynamics: (1) the number or density of individuals dispersing among ponds, and (2) the density and distribution of wetlands in the landscape that determine dispersal distances and the probability of successfully reaching ponds (Hanski and Gilpin 1991b; Sjogren 1991; Gibbs 1993; Travis 1994; Semlitsch 2000a, 2000b; Marsh and Trenham 2001).

Once larvae metamorphose and leave the aquatic habitat, the majority live in the surrounding terrestrial habitat (usually within a few hundred meters; e.g., Madison 1997; Semlitsch 1998) but some disperse to new sites (e.g., Breden 1987). Ecological connectance is critical to maintaining amphibian metapopulations. Alteration and loss of wetlands reduces the total number or density of ponds where amphibians can reproduce and successfully recruit metamorphosing juveniles into the breeding population. Further, reducing the number of wetlands reduces the total number of individual amphibians available to found new populations or to reestablish extirpated populations. Because small seasonal pools and temporary ponds (<4.0 ha) are the most numerous type of wetland in many natural landscapes (Gibbs 1993; Semlitsch and Bodie 1998), their loss especially reduces the number of "source" populations. Small, temporary wetlands often have higher species diversity and produce more metamorphosing juveniles than either ephemeral pools or permanent ponds (Pechmann et al. 1989; Semlitsch et al. 1996; Snodgrass et al. 2000). Any failure to protect small wetlands can result in loss of source breeding ponds from the landscape. However, even in the "best" breeding ponds that are undisturbed by agriculture or development, reproductive failure occurs in many years due to other factors such as low rainfall. For a small, isolated wetland (1.0 ha) in South Carolina protected for more than 30 years, we estimated annual reproductive failure rates of 42 to 56% for 13 species over a 16-year period (Semlitsch et al. 1996). Frequent reproductive failure in local amphibian populations due to drought has been observed in other areas as well (Dodd 1993, 1995). It is also known that ponds acting as sources for recolonization in some years may be sinks in subsequent years. After producing large numbers of dispersing juveniles for several years, pond condition in terms of primary productivity or buildup of predators and parasites can decline (Gill 1978). However, extinction risks are buffered by metapopulations, that is, by maintaining the network of total ponds and the connecting habitats between them. Any human threat that adds to the probability of metamorphic failure (e.g., pond ditching, fish introductions) and disrupts this dispersal process (e.g., fragmentation, clearcuts, roads) will further increase the probability of local population declines and extinctions.

In addition to recruitment failures, reductions in pond density also change the spatial configuration of remaining ponds and can hinder dispersal processes. Reduced pond density increases the distance between neighboring ponds, thereby affecting critical recolonization processes (Brown and Kodric-Brown 1977; Gill 1978; Pulliam 1988; Gibbs 1993; Semlitsch and Bodie 1998). For example, simulated wetland loss on a natural landscape causes an exponential increase in interpond distance or isolation (Gibbs 1993; Semlitsch and Bodie 1998), and the chance of rescuing amphibian populations from extinction decreases (e.g., Sjogren 1991; Skelly et al. 1999). This adverse effect is critical because most individual amphibians cannot migrate long distances due to physiological limitations of water loss (Spotila 1972), and most adults return to "home" ponds, usually after migrating no more than 200 to 300 m to foraging or overwintering habitats (Semlitsch 1998). Genetic dispersal distance for wood frog (*Rana sylvatica*) populations averages only 1,126 m, suggesting that migration and gene flow are near zero beyond this (Berven and Grudzien 1990). Semlitsch and Bodie (1998) demonstrated in South Carolina that the loss of all natural wetlands less than 4.0 ha in size (a typical wetland protection threshold for regulators) would increase the nearest-wetland distance from 471 to 1,633 m. This distance is likely many times farther than can be traversed by most species within a generation. Thus, the loss or alteration of wetlands could severely impede rescue and recolonization processes and place populations of amphibians in remaining wetlands at increased probabilities of extinction (Gibbs 1993; Travis 1994; Marsh and Trenham 2001).

MAJOR THREATS TO POND-BREEDING AMPHIBIANS AND POTENTIAL SOLUTIONS

Destruction and Alteration of Aquatic Habitats

Habitat loss and alteration is considered to be the most significant threat to pond-breeding species. Wetland regulations have historically been biased against small, isolated wetlands, precisely those used by pond-breeding amphibians. Current regulations (via U.S. Army Corps of Engineers Permit 404) to protect small wetlands (<4.0 ha) are still inadequate for maintaining the biodiversity of amphibians. Why is there a bias against protecting small isolated wetlands? The primary issue seems to revolve around the question of whether small wetlands are expendable. Too often, decision-makers assume that because a wetland is small or ephemeral, it is unimportant or less valuable than a large wetland (i.e., >4.0 ha). A fundamental reason for this assumption has been the lack of biologically relevant data on the value of wetlands for amphibians. This situation is changing, however, with adequate biological information demonstrating the value of small wetlands for maintaining biodiversity (e.g., Wiest 1982; Moler and Franz 1987; Dodd 1992; Gibbs, 1993; Semlitsch and Bodie 1998).

The density and frequency distribution of wetlands is critical to understanding the biological importance of small wetlands. This information addresses how common they are in the landscape, how frequently they might be encountered, and how often they are colonized by amphibians. Analyses of natural wetland abundance using isolated depression wetlands known as Carolina bays on the southeastern Atlantic Coastal Plain of South Carolina revealed a density of $0.476/km^2$ (Semlitsch and Bodie 1998). A similar analysis of natural wetlands in Maine revealed a slightly higher but similar density of $0.59/km^2$ (Gibbs 1993). Semlitsch and Bodie (1998) also showed that 46.4% of all Carolina bay wetlands were 1.2 ha or smaller, and 87.3% were 4.0 ha or smaller. Thus, in these apparently undisturbed landscapes, wetlands are close together and most frequently small.

Small wetlands also house rich biodiversity. During a 16-year monitoring study at a Carolina bay (0.5 ha) known as Rainbow Bay, we documented 27 species of anurans and caudates (Semlitsch et al. 1996), one of the highest species diversities known for amphibians in this region. The study also recorded the breeding activity of 41,776 females and the production of 216,251 metamorphosing juveniles during the 16-year period (Semlitsch et al. 1996). Monitoring studies of other small wetlands for shorter periods in the same area have yielded similar numbers of amphibian species: Sun Bay (0.5 ha), 22 species (Gibbons and Semlitsch 1981); Karen's Pond (0.08 ha), 19 species; Risher Pond (1.1 ha), 18 species (Gibbons and Bennett 1974); Ginger's Bay (1.0 ha), 20 species; Squirrel Bay (0.5 ha), 21 species (D. Scott, Savannah River Ecology Laboratory, personal communication). Small wetlands may also harbor rare and endemic species with narrow habitat requirements, such as pine barrens treefrogs (*Hyla an-*

dersonii) or flatwoods salamanders (*Ambystoma cingulatum*). These results suggest that the levels of species richness found at Rainbow Bay are not uncommon for the area, and when combined with other studies from the southern United States (e.g., Wiest 1982; Dodd 1992), indicate that small wetlands contain high levels of diversity.

The less obvious consequence of a bias against small isolated wetlands lies in potential changes to the metapopulation dynamics of the remaining wetlands. The loss or alteration of any wetland, large or small, reduces the total number of sites where pond-breeding amphibians can reproduce and successfully recruit juveniles into the breeding population. These juveniles serve as dispersers for adjacent populations. For amphibians, the loss of small wetlands, in particular, may reduce the number of "source" populations because juvenile recruitment is higher at sites with intermediate hydroperiods that favor periodic drying (Pechmann et al. 1989). Thus, the loss of small wetlands could be detrimental to "rescue" (= recolonization) effects through a reduction in the number of dispersing juveniles. Along with the detrimental effects caused by the direct loss of wetlands as breeding habitat, regional fauna likely will also suffer indirect effects through reduced recolonization after local population extinction (for a potential example in the western United States; see Drost and Fellers 1996).

It is apparent that small isolated wetlands are not expendable if our conservation goal is to maintain present levels of biodiversity. At the very least, based on available data, regulations should protect wetlands as small as 0.2 ha until additional results are available to directly compare diversity across a range of wetland sizes. It is actually philosophically reasonable to place the burden of proof on land developers to demonstrate that small wetlands are expendable. Equally important, regulatory agencies should scrutinize applications for the presence of small wetlands and the potential for harboring rare and endemic species before issuing permits that result in their loss. Furthermore, to protect ecological connectance and source–sink dynamics of species populations, I strongly advocate that wetland legislation focus not only on size but also on local and regional wetland distribution. Current mitigation practices that are used to "offset" the loss of wetlands, such as "wetland banking," by equating the total area of many lost small wetlands (20 wetlands of 1.0 ha) to an equivalent area of one large 20-ha mitigation wetland, ignore critical source–sink processes. Such practices are contrary to what is biologically essential and hence weaken conservation efforts for pond-breeding amphibians.

Destruction and Alteration of Terrestrial Habitats

Terrestrial habitat adjacent to wetlands also is important because it serves as habitat for many amphibians to carry out life history functions, and therefore, ultimately is essential for maintaining diversity. Although the importance of this core habitat is quite clear to biologists working on amphibians, terms used to define this habitat, as well as regulations to protect it, are very unclear (Semlitsch and Jensen 2001). A conundrum for natural resource managers is created because, although the adjacent terrestrial habitat is core habitat for a vast array of species, this habitat is defined in the literature by the terms "buffer zone" or "buffer strip," which denotes its primary use as a protective habitat for aquatic resources (i.e., drinking water, fisheries), rather than as necessary habitat for species. Unfortunately, natural resource managers are left using a guideline that was not designed to protect the core habitat of amphibian species or to maintain biodiversity explicitly.

To make matters worse, although this core habitat should be managed for two purposes—protecting water resources and conserving biodiversity—only water protection receives U.S. federal oversight (via the Clean Water Act). Maintaining biodiversity has minimal, if any, enforceable regulations to oversee criteria or implementation—especially associated with isolated wetlands—unless endangered species are present (e.g., Semlitsch 1998). Further, the criteria for setting the size or width of terrestrial habitats to protect each function are different. Water resource protection is based primarily on siltation rates and contaminant levels within aquatic habitats; protection of biodiversity is based on use of the terrestrial habitat by species for life history functions such as feeding, mating, nesting, and overwintering.

It is not surprising that the terrestrial ecology of amphibians is often underappreciated or overlooked by managers and conservationists. Many pond-breeding amphibians are highly fossorial and are therefore infrequently seen in terrestrial habitats. Observations and studies of these animals are consequently concentrated at the ponds where they are readily found at certain times, rather than in terrestrial habitats where detection is extremely difficult, yet where much of their life history occurs. Because the aquatic and terrestrial habitats of semiaquatic species are explicitly linked by life cycle functions, they are both core habitats and cannot be managed separately (Semlitsch 2000a).

I propose that a stratified scheme of three zones should be used to protect terrestrial habitats: a first terrestrial zone immediately adjacent to the aquatic habitat, designed to buffer the core aquatic habitat and protect water resources; continuous with the first, a second terrestrial zone to encompass the core terrestrial habitat defined by species use; and a third outer zone that serves to buffer the core terrestrial habitat from surrounding land-use practices (see Semlitsch and Jensen 2001). For example, forest edge effects (e.g., more sunlight and wind, drier soils, invasive species, predators) that result from a variety of land-use practices vary greatly, but the physical effects commonly extend into natural habitats a mean of 50 m (reviewed in Murcia 1995). Reducing edge effects would require additional area or a zone of protection around core habitat, for example, 50 m added to the distances provided for core habitat (Semlitsch 1998).

Chemical Contamination in Aquatic and Terrestrial Environments

The biological link between toxicological studies and conservation lies in effects that disrupt the natural regulation of species populations and community structure. Seldom have population declines been directly linked to chemical contamination alone (but see Davidson et al. 2001). Part of the problem is that only severe contamination is visible (because it usually results in mass mortality). In the absence of mass mortality, a more realistic biological view of chemical threats is that variation in natural environmental factors interacts with anthropogenic stressors, such as sublethal levels of chemicals, to cause local or regional declines of amphibian populations as have been reported in the literature. When considering how chemical contamination can disrupt natural processes, it is important to recognize that pond-breeding amphibians exhibit complex life cycles, with aquatic larval stages for growth and development and terrestrial adult stages for reproduction and dispersal (Wilbur 1980). Also, because regulation of populations most likely occurs in the aquatic larval stage and direct application or runoff of chemicals can find their way into aquatic habitats, chemicals can affect critical regulatory processes of amphibians.

Metamorphosis from the aquatic larval habitat to the terrestrial environment is the critical step for individuals to be recruited into the breeding adult population, with growth and development leading to metamorphosis being extremely sensitive to most environmental factors. Any factor, biotic or abiotic, that impedes the process of metamorphosis and that can interact with the presence of chemical contaminants reduces juvenile recruitment and the probability of species persistence. Further, understanding how chemicals affect species attributes leading to successful metamorphosis and how the attributes of one species interact with those of competitors or predators is critical to understanding how community processes can be disrupted. What is also important to understand is that in natural populations of amphibians, only 3 to 5% of all offspring produced annually ever reach metamorphosis, and the production of any metamorphs from year to year is episodic (Semlitsch et al. 1996). Thus, anthropogenic stress from chemical contamination may be enough to reduce recruitment even further in those years where metamorphs are produced, or to increase the time interval between bouts of successful recruitment. Either effect could lead to species declines and local extinctions if adult reproductive lifespan is short or chemical contamination is long-term.

Another problem with chemical contamination that needs to be understood is the relative role of direct versus indirect effects of chemicals, especially at the community or ecosystem level. Indirect effects are responses of species or components of a community or ecosystem that are not a result of direct exposure of the amphibians to chemical contamination. They may be obvious or be so far removed as to affect species many steps further up or down the food chain. In a simple example, a herbicide reduces algal and periphyton productivity, which in turn reduces the available food, thereby slowing growth rate of anuran tadpoles that are present well after the chemical degrades or dissipates. Summer-breeding anurans might experience such indirect effects when a herbicide is applied in early spring before planting or when chemicals enter the aquatic environment during snow melt. In another example, an insecticide reduces the zooplankton but has no effect on the algal or periphyton community (e.g., carbaryl; Fairchild et al. 1992). Predators such as newts (*Notophthalmus;* Figure 2.3) might enter the aquatic environment after the chemical dissipates but would be negatively affected by the reduced zooplankton food supply that can cause two potential indirect effects: (1) a negative effect on anuran prey because of increased predation pressure by newts during the time tadpoles are below gape limitations of the newts, or (2) facilitation of the anuran prey because of enhanced phytoplankton food supply through reduced competition with zooplankton when tadpoles are above gape limitations of newts (Boone and Semlitsch 2002; Mills and Semlitsch 2002). If indirect effects on the ecosystem as a whole are not revealed, conservation efforts may miss subtle and hidden threats of chemicals and will be ineffective in solving the problem of declining populations and in maintaining biodiversity of amphibians.

Figure 2.3. Red-spotted newts (*Notophthalmus v. viridescens*). (Photo by David Scott, Savannah River Ecology Laboratory)

Fish Invasions (Natural, Stocking)

Only a few amphibian species can truly coexist with fish because they possess anti-predator behaviors and skin toxins (e.g., American bullfrog; cricket frog; green frog; green treefrog). Most amphibians are quickly and thoroughly eliminated by predatory fish (e.g., Bradford 1989; Hecnar and M'Closkey 1997b). Management plans should be focused on eliminating avenues of colonization by fish, such as drainage ditches that connect fish-inhabited areas (streams or rivers) with amphibian breeding ponds. Also, ponds with hydroperiods of more than 2 years (e.g., farm ponds, reservoirs) can accumulate a diverse array of aquatic predators, including invertebrates, aquatic salamanders, and fish. In fact, even short-hydroperiod ponds close to rivers, streams, canals, and drainage ditches that flood seasonally may allow fish to colonize most years. Restoring the natural drying process in wetlands can work effectively to eliminate fish if they do invade. Deliberately manipulating pond drying can eliminate other nonnative species such as exotic fish or bullfrog larvae (nonnative in some regions such as the western United States and Europe) and would promote successful metamorphosis of native species. Management decisions such as constructing or maintaining impoundments or canals and ditches that are connected to rivers and used to enhance fisheries or waterfowl may be in conflict with the needs of many amphibians. Creative solutions such as designing topographic landscape features that "filter" or prevent larval fish from reaching wetlands located at greater distances from the river may need to be tested. Finally, a major cause of fish invasion is active stocking of game fish on public and private lands. Such practices must be modified to eliminate blanket stocking in all ponds and wetlands, and the philosophy of managers must be changed to deemphasize fish-centered aquatic communities.

Ecological Connectance among Populations

The movement and survival of individuals in the terrestrial environment is the critical component that ensures successful dispersal and recolonization within metapopulations and serves to connect local populations. Practices that diminish the quality of terrestrial habitat (i.e., reduced canopy cover, coarse woody debris, and leaf litter) or quantity of terrestrial habitat around wetlands should be eliminated or minimized. Also, practices that fragment natural vegetation and create unsuitable habitat between adjacent wetlands (e.g., agricultural fields and pastures) should be considered harmful. Further, it is thought that maintaining corridors of natural vegetation between wetlands may increase the probability of dispersal (an issue of much debate; Saunders and Hobbs 1991; Puth and Wilson 2001). Although few data are available on the dispersal of amphibians through terrestrial habitats, a study in a forested landscape of the northeastern United States indicated that dispersing juveniles of some species avoid open powerline rights-of-way (deMaynadier and Hunter 1999). Recent results comparing three species of dispersing juveniles (spotted salamander,

Ambystoma maculatum; small-mouthed salamander, *A. texanum;* American toad, *Bufo americanus*) in the midwestern United States suggest that most but not all species avoid moving through open field habitats (Rothermel and Semlitsch 2002). Further, highly fragmented landscapes that isolate ponds at distances of more than 1.0 km can result in the lack of recolonization and the absence of species in the landscape (Laan and Verboom 1990). Thus, management plans that maintain continuous natural vegetation for dispersal adjacent to wetlands, and ideally between neighboring wetlands, could help maintain metapopulation dynamics of amphibians. In addition, restoration of the metapopulation landscape—that is, the natural density and spatial configuration of wetlands (e.g., 0.476/km^2 in South Carolina, Semlitsch and Bodie 1998; 0.59/km^2 in Maine, Gibbs 1993; >1.0/km^2 in New York, Gibbs 2000)—is critical for broad-scale maintenance of amphibians. However, to increase wetland density, it may be necessary to develop new small artificial wetlands in place of those degraded or lost to land-use practices. These small wetlands can act as "stepping stones" to help increase connectivity among extant species populations and potentially promote recolonization. Creative borrowing of soil to construct small (0.2–1.0 ha), multishape, shallow (0.5–1.0 m deep) basins and placement of soil to build adjacent mounds can create a diversity of wetland and upland habitats for amphibians (Stratman 2001). However, caution must be used when creating new wetlands to mimic the periodic drying cycle of natural small wetlands and not to create wetlands with permanent hydroperiods (Pechmann et al. 2001).

CONCLUSIONS

Conserving a diversity of aquatic habitats that vary in their hydroperiod and surrounding terrestrial habitat is an important solution to maintaining pond-breeding species in the world. Equally important is the ecological connectance of these local populations to ensure dispersal and recolonization in the face of natural or anthropogenic-induced local extinction. Achieving this is not a simple task, given the ever-increasing demands of a growing human population and consequent land use. However, incorporating the critical elements for managing amphibians into existing reserve systems and conservation areas, resolving conflicts in management practices between amphibians and other species (e.g., game species), and conserving new areas that represent especially high species diversity may go a long way to maintaining this unique group of animals for future generations to enjoy.

ACKNOWLEDGMENTS
I thank Russ Bodie, Michelle Boone, and Nathan Mills for thoughtful comments and suggestions on the manuscript. I also thank John David for time to work on this project. Preparation of the manuscript was partially supported by grants from U.S. Environmental Protection Agency (827095-01), U.S. National Science Foundation (DEB 99 03761), and U.S. Geological Survey (01CRAG0007).

3

CONSERVATION OF NORTH AMERICAN STREAM AMPHIBIANS

PAUL STEPHEN CORN, R. BRUCE BURY, AND ERIN J. HYDE

CENTRAL ISSUES

Concern over the status of amphibians is international in scope (Wake 1991; Houlahan et al. 2000). Although the issue has a long history (Bury 1999), interest in it among both scientists and the public has greatly increased since the formation of the Declining Amphibian Populations Task Force in 1990 by the International Union for the Conservation of Nature (IUCN) Species Survival Commission. There is now considerable evidence that many amphibian species in various parts of the world are in decline (Dodd 1997; Alford and Richards 1999; Corn 2000). Declines appear to be most severe in western North America, Central America, and Australia. The stresses and assaults on amphibian populations are diverse, and some are better understood than others. Experimental evidence for causes of amphibian declines is scarce, and most studies have employed a correlative approach. Factors with the best supporting data include habitat destruction and alteration, disease, introduced predators, and contaminants (Corn 2000; Linder et al., in press). However, the effects of these factors may involve complex interactions and may depend on geography and species.

The recent spate of amphibian declines stimulated concerns that stressors operating globally, such as increasing ultraviolet radiation or global warming, might be responsible (Blaustein and Wake 1990). However, studies increasingly identify different causes in specific cases, and global stressors are not readily apparent (e.g., Carey et al. 2001). The search for common causes of amphibian decline has been elusive and complex because amphibians are an evolutionarily diverse group with complicated life histories and a wide range of habitats. No single factor is likely to affect most species in the same manner. This is no less true for species that breed or dwell in lotic habitats (seeps, streams, and rivers) than the more typical lentic habitats (ponds, lakes).

About one-third of the 265 (or so) species of amphibians north of Mexico can be considered as stream amphibians—those associated with lotic (flowing) water during part of their life history. Most of these species require lotic water for breeding and life as aquatic larvae or adults and the rest are associated with lotic habitats (e.g., are most abundant in adjacent riparian zones). Regarding amphibian decline issues, stream amphibians have received much less attention than lentic-breeding, or even terrestrial species (not including Central American anurans associated with streams, see Chapter 5, this volume). Potentially there are several reasons for this. Fewer recent declines of stream species have been documented, but this may be partly a perceptual problem. Lotic-breeding anurans and salamanders occur at discrete points on the landscape, often in large numbers, and their disappearance is more obvious and easier to document than is the decline of cryptic animals in a continuous riparian habitat. It may also be that declines of stream species have been more gradual and are often associated with long-term habitat alteration (e.g., Welsh 1990).

In the United States, timber harvest in both the Southeast and the Pacific Northwest have altered stream habitats and decreased many amphibian populations. Pollution of rivers and streams in the east is a significant threat to aquatic salamanders. For example, acid precipitation and acid mine drainage are known to damage stream faunas (Gore 1983; Driscoll et al. 2001). In this chapter, we will discuss these and other factors that affect the status and conservation of stream amphibians. First, however, we will survey the diversity, distribution, ecology, and life history of stream amphibians in North America.

MAJOR GROUPS OF STREAM AMPHIBIANS

Stream amphibians in North America occupy the freshwater continuum (Vannote et al. 1980; Welsh et al. 2000) from seeps and headwaters to higher-order streams and large rivers. The largest group of North American stream amphibians (a subgroup of the salamander family Plethodontidae) includes brook (*Eurycea*), dusky (*Desmognathus*), and spring (*Gyrinophillus*) salamanders, and others. These stream salamanders with gilled aquatic larvae and aquatic or semiterrestrial adults are found in headwaters and small to midsized streams. The geographic diversity of this group radiates from the southern Appalachian Mountains, but includes most of the eastern United States and several central and midwestern states. In the Pacific Northwest, several endemic species of salamanders (giant, *Dicamptodon*, torrent, *Rhyacotriton*) and tailed frogs (*Ascaphus*) are also well adapted to life in cascading headwater streams. A few members of the woodland salamanders (*Plethodon*) in the Pacific Northwest do not require lotic water for reproduction but are strongly associated with streamside habitat.

The perennibranchiate *Eurycea* of central Texas comprise a large and poorly understood group of stream and troglobitic salamanders characterized by high levels of endemism, low population sizes, restricted ranges, irregular hydrology, and proximity to urban areas. This group has unique conservation and management concerns, and include the only federally protected stream salamanders (Barton Springs salamander, *Eurycea sosorum;* Texas blind salamander, *E. rathbuni;* and San Marcos salamander, *E. nana*).

Several large-bodied salamanders inhabit larger rivers of the eastern United States, including permanently aquatic salamanders in four families (Cryptobranchidae, Proteidae, Amphiumidae, and Sirenidae). A few anurans both in southeastern United States and on the West Coast use lotic waters as breeding habitat. In the Southwest, species of both *Rana* and *Bufo* use small streams, probably because lentic habitats are scarce. Newts (Salamandridae) on the West Coast breed in a variety of waters, including the slower parts of larger streams.

The cool, wet forests of the Pacific Northwest and the Appalachian Mountains are two of the major centers of evolution of living amphibians (Duellman and Sweet 1999), but there are considerable differences in diversity between the two regions. In the Appalachian and Ozark mountains and forests of the East and Southeast, about 47 species from 8 genera of lungless salamanders (Plethodontidae) are the dominant vertebrates of small streams and other lotic waters, such as springs, seeps, and caves (Petranka 1998; Crother 2000). Phylogenetic relationships among genera of aquatic plethodontids are poorly understood (Wake 1993). Speciation within the genus *Plethodon* dates from at least the Pliocene (2 to 10 million years ago; Highton 1995).

In the Pacific Northwest, species in three endemic families breed and live in flowing water: torrent salamanders (Rhyacotritonidae), Pacific giant salamanders (Dicamptodontidae), and tailed frogs (Ascaphidae). Until 20 years ago, *Ascaphus, Dicamptodon,* and *Rhyacotriton* were considered monotypic genera. Although molecular techniques have revealed considerable variation within these genera, only 10 species are recognized (Crother 2000; Nielson et al. 2001). This lower species diversity is not the result of a more recent adaptive radiation. Inland lineages of *Ascaphus* and *Dicamptodon* diverged from coastal lineages at the end of the Miocene or beginning of the Pliocene (Nielson et al. 2001), and speciation among the coastal forms of *Dicamptodon* and *Rhyacotriton* occurred during the Pliocene (Good and Wake 1992).

ECOLOGICAL RELATIONSHIPS OF STREAM AMPHIBIANS

Stream amphibians are important components of riparian and aquatic ecosystems. Hairston (1987) estimated that the biomass of aquatic and terrestrial plethodontids in the southern Appalachians was greater than all other vertebrate predators combined. Bury et al. (1991) reported that stream amphibians in the Pacific Northwest were an order of magnitude more abundant than salmonid fish. Estimates of the abundance of stream amphibians are variable, but local densities can be very high. In

North Carolina, Bruce (1995) recorded densities of seal salamanders (*Desmognathus monticola*) of up to $3.5/m^2$, and Allegheny Mountain dusky salamander (*D. ochrophaeus*) densities have been estimated at $7/m^2$ (Tilley 1980) and up to $41/m^2$ on a wet rock face (Huheey and Brandon 1973). Nussbaum and Tait (1977) found densities of southern torrent (*Rhyacotriton variegatus*) and Cascades torrent (*R. cascadae*) salamander larvae to be $12.9/m^2$ and $41.2/m^2$, respectively, in two small streams in Oregon. Welsh and Lind (1992) reported $14/m^2$ for southern torrent salamanders in a northern California stream. Corn and Bury (1989) found the total density of stream species averaged about $3.7/m^2$ in Oregon streams unaffected by logging. These large abundances are ecologically significant. Stream amphibians are often the dominant predators in small streams, and most of these species are, in turn, prey for larger vertebrates (e.g., snakes, birds, shrews, small carnivores). Because the adults in many of these species have semiterrestrial habits, significant energy may be transported from aquatic to terrestrial environments. The effects of the input of terrestrial energy into streams has been a major theme in freshwater ecology, but the reverse pathway has been largely ignored, although there are ecosystems where energy flow out of streams is extremely important (Willson et al. 1998).

Stream salamanders have provided material for extensive studies of community and behavioral ecology. In the east, community interactions are complex in dusky salamanders (*Desmognathus*), with at least 11 unique combinations of *Desmognathus* species occurring in streams in the Appalachians (Hairston 1987). *Desmognathus* are often distributed along a moisture gradient with the smallest-sized species (e.g., Allegheny Mountain and northern, *Desmognathus fuscus,* dusky salamanders) in more upland areas, slightly larger salamanders (e.g., seal salamanders) in water margins and shallow water, and the largest species, the black-bellied salamander (*D. quadramaculatus*), in the deepest and fastest water. Southerland (1986) found that excluding seal salamanders from a community changed the substrate use by other species. This partitioning of habitat may result from inter- and intraspecific resource competition, predation, or both. Competition alone is inadequate to explain distribution of *Desmognathus* species, because the distribution of species does not correlate well with body size (Hairston 1980). For example, small body size necessarily increases evaporative water loss, but the smallest species is the most terrestrial. Camp and Lee (1996) found few salamanders in the stomach contents of the large-sized black-bellied salamander, suggesting that predation might not be the driving force behind salamander distribution. Despite strong habitat preference among species, access to both terrestrial and aquatic habitats may be important for homeostasis.

Stream species separate ecologically not only on a moisture gradient perpendicular to the water, but occurrence and abundance of amphibians change along the stream continuum from the uppermost ends of watersheds (seeps and headwater streams) downstream to larger waters with more open canopies.

In the Pacific Northwest, several species are adapted to cascading streams in mature forest with closed canopies that maintain the cool temperatures required for embryonic and larval development. Rocky seeps and the margins of headwater streams are occupied by one species of *Aneides* (H. H. Welsh, U.S. Forest Service, Redwood Sciences Laboratory, Arcata, CA, unpublished data), one of three species of *Plethodon*, and one of the four *Rhyacotriton*. Torrent salamanders also occur on the bottoms of headwater streams, along with one of the two species of *Ascaphus* and one or two species of *Dicamptodon*. Pacific giant (*D. tenebrosus*) and Cope's giant (*D. copei*) salamanders are sympatric near Mount Rainier and along the Columbia River in Washington and Oregon, but congeners of stream amphibians in the Northwest otherwise have allopatric distributions. *Ascaphus* occur in headwaters and higher-order streams (generally less than 2-m wide), but on occasion are found in larger waters, perhaps being swept downstream in seasonal flooding. *Dicamptodon* occur from headwaters to larger streams, including warmer streams in more open forests. *Dicamptodon* and *Ascaphus* co-occur with trout and salmon in some larger waters. In large streams and rivers, backwaters and pools with slow water are breeding habitat for foothill yellow-legged frogs (*Rana boylii*), red-legged frogs (*R. aurora*), western toads (*Bufo boreas*), and Pacific newts (*Taricha* spp.). Foothill yellow-legged frogs are restricted to these habitats, but the other species can be considered riparian associates and breed in lotic sites, when available.

In the Southeast, there is higher species diversity, with greater sympatry among closely related species. Competition and predation have led to greater subdivision on the perpendicular moisture gradient, but there are similarities to the Pacific Northwest along the stream continuum. There is no eastern analog to tailed frogs, but dusky (*Desmognathus*) and brook (*Eurycea*) salamanders occur in seeps and headwaters and are replaced by larger plethodontids (species of *Gyrinophilus* and *Pseudotriton*) in larger, forested streams. Large, open streams and rivers with a rocky substrate are home to hellbenders (*Cryptobranchus alleganiensis*), and slower portions of larger waters are home to varied large aquatic salamanders (*Siren, Amphiuma*) and river frogs (*Rana heckscheri*). The causes of habitat segregation of salamanders across the moisture gradient have received considerable attention, but the reasons for separation of amphibians along the stream continuum are poorly documented. Predation is probably a major factor. Several species are restricted to headwaters with cold, cascading waters and few or no fishes. Progressing downstream, the canopy is increasingly open, stream temperature rises, volume of water increases, and velocity slows. Predaceous fish dominate these habitats and the amphibians that occur there tend to be large predators (*Cryptobranchus, Dicamptodon*).

The Edwards Plateau and Balcones Escarpment region of Texas is home to several endemic species of *Eurycea* that occupy springs and lotic waters in caves (Hillis et al. 2001; Petranka 1998). These include the federally protected San Marcos, Texas (*Eurycea neotenes*), and Texas blind salamanders, the only stream salamanders listed as threatened or endangered. These species occupy habitats that are often inaccessible, which has resulted in a dearth of knowledge about their ecology, natural history, and systematics. Several species have only recently been recognized (Hillis et al. 2001). Many of these species have highly restricted distributions consisting of a few springs at a single location (Petranka 1998).

THREATS TO STREAM AMPHIBIANS

Stream species are subject to the same threats as other amphibians, mainly habitat alteration, pollution, introduced predators, disease, and the future effects of climate change. However, the effects of only a few of these threats on stream amphibians have been studied in any detail. Here, we examine the effects of habitat alteration by timber harvest, pollution from acidification, and briefly discuss other factors that have been identified.

Timber Harvest

Because the majority of stream amphibians occur in forested landscapes, timber harvest and related road building is the primary agent of habitat alteration. The effects of logging on stream species have been studied most intensively in the Pacific Northwest.

Headwater streams are required habitat for several species of stream amphibians endemic to the Pacific Northwest because these taxa require cool temperatures and permanent waters. Removal of canopy or streamside vegetation by logging or upslope activities such as road development creates immediate changes in stream habitats. The initial impact of clearcut logging increases insolation and raises stream temperatures, thereby increasing microbial respiration, primary production, invertebrate consumers, and populations of invertebrate and vertebrate predators. Stream amphibians may be susceptible physiologically to increased temperatures. For example, tailed frog larvae prefer temperatures below 22°C (deVlaming and Bury 1970), and the abundance of southern torrent salamanders is limited by water temperature (Welsh and Lind 1996).

Logging may also result in long-term alteration of the stream habitat. Streams in natural forests are rocky (gravels, cobble, and boulders), which provide vital cover for stream amphibians. The presence of large, downed wood in streams also provides energy input to the stream ecosystem. Streams in logged areas suffer increased sedimentation, which degrades amphibian habitat by reducing availability of cover sites (Corn and Bury 1989; Welsh and Ollivier 1998; Dupuis and Steventon 1999). However, this effect is influenced by topography and geology. Increasing stream gradient results in greater flushing of sediments, which may mitigate inputs from logging. Hall et al. (1978) studied headwater streams in the Cascade Mountains in central Oregon and found that when the stream gradient was more than 9%, there was a higher density of Pacific giant salamanders in streams traversing clearcuts than in streams in old-growth forest. The nature of the bedrock underlying drainages also is important in determining the severity of sedimentation. Wilkins and Peterson (2000) surveyed stream amphibians on heavily logged private forests in southwestern Washington. As have other researchers, they found greater abundance of all species as the gradient increased. But they also found that amphibians were less abundant (*Dicamptodon* spp.) or absent (tailed frogs) in drainages underlain by sedimentary rock than in drainages underlain by basalt. Elsewhere, in streams unaffected by logging in Olympic National Park in Washington (Adams and Bury 2002) and Prairie Creek Redwoods State Park in California (Welsh and Ollivier 1998), amphibians were abundant in streams with sedimentary bedrock.

Stream amphibian populations in the Pacific Northwest are reduced in landscapes dominated by logging (Corn and Bury 1989; Welsh and Lind 1996; Dupuis and Steventon 1999). Because most forests that support amphibians have been logged in the last 50 years, Corn (1994) hypothesized that regional populations of stream amphibians are much lower than before European settlement. Whether this has resulted in local extinctions of any species is unknown, but there is concern for the status of tailed frogs and species of torrent salamanders. Comparisons of the abundance of tailed frogs and the southern torrent salamander in Redwood National Park and in commercial timberlands revealed significant reduction or elimination of both species in streams in logged areas (Welsh et al. 2000). Although a petition to list the southern torrent salamander as a Federal threatened species was denied because of lack of evidence, the torrent salamanders are the northwestern species most sensitive to the effects of logging. These salamanders are likely to be extirpated from some streams in logged areas, and recovery of populations may take decades (Bury and Corn 1988b; B. Bury and D. Major, U.S. Geological Survey, Forest and Rangeland Ecosystem Science Center, Corvallis, OR, unpublished).

In the eastern United States, timber harvest is also a major factor altering forest habitats. Petranka (1993) estimated that clearcuts in western North Carolina reduced forest salamanders in mature stands by as much as 75 to 80%, including at least five species with aquatic larvae that use forest streams. Ash and Bruce (1994) criticized the magnitude of these conclusions, but the disappearance of salamanders from clearcuts was undisputed. Ford et al. (2002) found that abundance and diversity of salamanders, including stream species, were positively related to stand age, stand size, and amount of nearby habitat in cove hardwood stands in the southern Appalachians, suggesting that salamanders in this habitat are vulnerable to logging.

Acidification

Most research on the effects of acid conditions on amphibians has examined pond-breeding species. Although amphibians, particularly their embryos, are vulnerable to acidification, the effect on populations is uncertain. There is no convincing evidence that the decline of any species can be attributed to acidification (Rowe and Freda

2000). Still, acid conditions, either directly or through interactions with other ions and toxic metals, have multiple negative effects on amphibians, including direct mortality, increased rates of deformity, and reduced rates of growth and development (Rowe and Freda 2000). A significant percentage of stream habitats in the eastern United States have been acidified or are vulnerable to acidification (Herlihy et al. 1993), indicating a potentially serious threat to conservation of stream amphibians.

Acidification is not considered a threat to western amphibians, but streams in the east are subject to acidification from a variety of sources. The mid-Atlantic states, particularly the northern Appalachian Mountains, receive some of the highest amounts of atmospheric deposition of sulfate and nitrate ions (Driscoll et al. 2001). Streams are also acidified when Anakeesta rock formations are exposed to air by mining, road construction, or landslides, resulting in oxidation and leaching of toxic amounts of sulfuric acid and various metals (Kucken et al. 1994). Another pathway for stream acidification is defoliation of forests by insect pests, such as gypsy moth caterpillars (*Lymantria dispar*), which results in inputs of excess nitrogen into surface waters (Eshleman et al. 1998). Vulnerability of streams to acidification is largely based on geology. Streams in watersheds with carbonate (limestone) or crystalline (basalt or granite) bedrock have high acid neutralizing capacity (ANC). Watersheds underlain by siliciclastic (noncarbonate sedimentary) bedrock have streams with low ANC and are vulnerable to acidification (Herlihy et al. 1993) that is chronic (permanent reduction in ANC and pH) or episodic (reductions in ANC and pH following storms or snowmelt).

Acidification from mine drainage and exposure of Anakeesta rock has occurred in several thousand kilometers of streams in the Appalachians, with severe effects on salamanders and other organisms (Gore 1983; Kucken et at. 1994). The effects on salamanders of acidification from atmospheric deposition are more difficult to demonstrate. Chronic and episodic acidification has affected a large percentage of Appalachian streams in areas with sensitive geology, and native fish diversity has been significantly reduced (Heard et al. 1997; Bulger et al. 2000). Although few studies have been done on stream salamanders, we would expect that larvae might suffer mortality from acidic episodes, but the semiterrestrial adults could move out of the stream to avoid temporary acid conditions. Responses of salamanders to acidification, particularly episodic acidification, are likely to be complex.

Introduced Species

Nonnative species, as either predators or competitors, can threaten the survival of stream amphibians. The top predators in small streams are often salamanders, which may be unable to deal with the introduction of predaceous fish, either native or nonnative. Brook trout (*Salvelinus fontinalis*) have negative effects on survival and growth of spring salamanders (*Gyrinophilus porphyriticus*) and northern two-lined salamanders (*Eurycea bislineata*), and significantly reduce diversity of salamanders in Appalachian streams (Resetarits 1997). The streamside salamander (*Ambystoma barbouri*) is one of the few species of *Ambystoma* to breed in flowing water, using pools in intermittent streams that are free of fish. Salamander larvae often become prey when they drift downstream into pools or reaches containing predatory green sunfish (*Lepomis cyanellus*). Surviving larvae alter their behavior, remaining more under rocks in shallow water than in deeper open water (Sih et al. 1992).

Crayfish (*Procambarus clarkii*) native to the southeastern United States have been introduced widely in the West. These aggressive predators are suspected of contributing to declines of ranid frogs in the Southwest. Gamradt et al. (1997) observed that *P. clarkii* attacked adult California newts (*Taricha torosa*) in experimental cages and, when crayfish colonized a stream in southern California, newts reproduction failed. The American bullfrog (*Rana catesbeiana*), another eastern species that has been widely introduced in the West, has long been implicated in declines of native western frogs. Kupferberg (1997) documented that reaches of the Eel River drainage in northern California invaded by bullfrogs have a significantly reduced abundance of foothill yellow-legged frogs. Competition experiments resulted in reduced survival and growth of foothill yellow-legged frog tadpoles in the presence of bullfrog tadpoles.

Other Threats

Water pollution is a major problem for large salamanders in eastern rivers (Petranka 1998). The eastern hellbender (*Cryptobranchus alleganiensis*) is scarce or absent in drainages that have received acid mine drainage, industrial effluents, or inadequately treated urban sewage (Gates et al. 1985). Davidson et al. (in press) analyzed a number of factors involved with declines of amphibians in California. The disappearance of foothill yellow-legged frogs and other species from previously documented locations was correlated with the amount of agricultural land upwind of the sites. This suggests that aerial transport of agricultural chemicals may be a factor in these declines.

Alteration in the hydrology of free-flowing rivers caused by construction of dams and other water projects may have serious effects on stream amphibians. For example, Lind et al. (1996) found that habitat for foothill yellow-legged frogs was reduced by 95% for 40 miles below a dam on the Trinity River in California. In some years, water releases designed to benefit endangered salmon were ill timed for frogs and resulted in the washing away of egg masses and young larvae. In the Edwards Plateau of Texas, alteration of groundwater hydrology may have devastating effects on endemic *Eurycea*. This unique assemblage of salamanders occurs in a region undergoing rapid population growth and associated urban development that may put several species at risk of extinction. In 1951, a streambed excavation discovered a new stream species (blanco blind salamander, *Eurycea robusta*). Only four individuals were found and the species has not been detected since (Potter and Sweet 1981).

Global climate change has been suggested as the cause of declines of anurans in

Central America (Pounds et al. 1999) and episodic mortality of western toad (*Bufo boreas*) eggs in Oregon (Kiesecker et al. 2001a), but it has not yet been implicated as affecting the status of stream species in North America. However, amphibians are vulnerable to the effects of climate change because of their dependence on water for breeding and the relationships between temperature and amphibian growth and development (Ovaska 1997). The future effects of climate change may be severe. During the twenty-first century, climate models based on increasing atmospheric carbon-dioxide concentrations predict warming over the United States of between 2.8 and 5°C, reduced snow cover, reduced soil moisture, and more frequent extreme precipitation events (MacCracken et al. 2001). Decreased soil moisture and increased summer temperatures could affect stream amphibians in many ways (Donnelly and Crump 1998). It is likely that terrestrial habitat and prey populations will be reduced. Reduced stream flow during summer will reduce aquatic habitat and duration of remaining pools, especially in headwater streams that are primary habitat for many amphibians. Conversely, increased frequency of storm events will increase flooding, which is a major cause of catastrophic mortality among stream species (Kupferberg 1996).

The pathogenic chytrid fungus (*Batrachochytrium dendrobatidis*) has been associated with declines of frogs throughout the world and may be at least the proximate cause of amphibian declines that lack another plausible explanation (Berger et al. 1998; Bosch et al. 2001; Muths et al., in press). The chytrid fungus has not yet been reported in stream species in North America, but it is potentially a serious threat.

Fire has considerable potential to cause habitat change, but the effects of fire on amphibians are only recently receiving attention. Direct mortality of aquatic and wetland-associated life stages of amphibians may be low where wet areas (e.g., riparian zones) provide suitable refugia from fire (Vogl 1973), but terrestrial life stages in uplands may experience much higher mortality associated with the direct and indirect (e.g., prey availability, shelter, microclimate) effects of fire (Russell et al. 1999). Further, physical and biological changes in adjacent uplands may influence biota in riparian zones through changes in hydrology and water chemistry in the streams.

POTENTIAL SOLUTIONS AND CONSERVATION STRATEGIES

Adopting a Landscape Perspective

To effectively conserve stream amphibians, we need to identify threats to amphibians and offer potential solutions with a landscape perspective that address the diversity and interactions of organisms along the stream continuum. Most requirements for riparian protection have only included fish-bearing, larger streams while ignoring seeps, intermittent streams, and permanent headwater streams that are home to significant amphibian populations. These "feeder" sites intimately affect downstream water chemistry, hydrology, and biota. Research and management must address conservation issues at all levels of the stream continuum.

Some current logging regulations include prescriptions to protect headwaters and adjacent riparian buffer zones. In California, Diller and Wallace (1996) predicted that these regulations would be sufficient to protect populations of the southern torrent salamander in logged landscapes. Welsh and Lind (1996) criticized this conclusion, suggesting that the regulations are not sufficient to protect the microclimatic conditions required for survival of headwater amphibians, particularly at inland locations that are warmer and drier than the coastal sites studied by Diller and Wallace (see also Welsh et al. 2000). Thornburgh et al. (2000) provided further analysis of the California regulations, which are among the most restrictive of state forest practices, concluding that they are inadequate to protect headwater riparian habitats, particularly because they are biased toward larger, fish-bearing streams and that there is no long-term protection from sedimentation resulting from perturbations (e.g., failure of logging roads). Wilkins and Peterson (2000) suggested that streams in drainages with unconsolidated, erodible bedrock (e.g., more recent marine deposits) are poor habitat for stream amphibians and could receive lower priority for protection. On the contrary, streams with this lithology in unlogged forests harbor abundant amphibian populations, indicating that such streams are highly vulnerable to sedimentation from logging activities and may require higher levels of protection (Adams and Bury 2002; Welsh and Ollivier 1998).

Stream conservation efforts must also address the diverse life histories of stream amphibians. In many cases, we lack data about the movement patterns, dispersal abilities, and landscape-level needs of stream amphibians necessary for effective conservation. For example, current protection of tailed frog streams is based on the habitat needs of larvae (MoF and MELP 1995). However, because forest harvest or other human alterations may remove potential dispersal corridors, research on the overland movement patterns of adult stream amphibians is needed. Although we know a considerable amount about the life history of a few species (e.g., desmognathine salamanders), basic life history data are lacking for most stream amphibians. Demographic modeling could be used to predict the responses of stream amphibians to habitat alteration or climate change, but in many cases the necessary data are not yet available. For most stream amphibians, we have only rudimentary knowledge of their reproductive ecology (even clutch sizes), diet, growth rates, physiological tolerances, and, in particular, habitat requirements.

Clean Air Act and Reductions in Sulfate Deposition

The Clean Air Act of 1970 and Amendments (CAAA) have resulted in significant reductions of sulfate emissions from coal-fired power plants (Driscoll et al. 2001). However, deposition of sulfate and nitrate anions during the past 150 years caused significant depletion of base cations in forest soils, which now limits the buffering capacity of the soil. This means that even modest inputs of acid anions today can result in acidification of surface waters, and recovery of aquatic and terrestrial systems will require several decades, even if additional proposed reductions in power plant emissions occur (Driscoll et al. 2001). Bulger et al. (2000) predicted that sulfate deposition needs to be reduced by more than 70% to result in recovery of acidified trout streams in Virginia. A further complication is that nitrate deposition has significant sources other than power plants (e.g., automobile emissions) and has not been significantly reduced since implementation of the CAAA (Driscoll et al. 2001). High nitrate deposition will prevent or limit ecosystem recovery, even if emissions from power plants continue to be reduced. As with logging issues, the emphasis on acidification damage and recovery has been on larger, fish-bearing streams. The threats to stream amphibians from acidification remain more a hypothesis than a proven fact, and research is still needed.

Changing Forestry Practices

Historic clearcut logging over large areas has likely fragmented local populations of stream amphibians, and continued timber harvest at these sites may further deplete remaining populations. However, the response of amphibians to logging is complex; it can be mitigated somewhat by the retention of the microhabitats and dispersal routes required by amphibians. For upland species or life stages, this means retaining coarse woody debris and some canopy, as well as reducing the amount of soil disturbance. For larvae and stream life, the primary prescriptions are to retain a buffer strip or riparian reserve of uncut trees along streams, to reduce or eliminate entry by machinery into riparian zones, and to reduce the number of stream crossings by new logging roads (deMaynadier and Hunter 1995; Dupuis and Steventon 1999). We must yet determine the effectiveness and cost efficiency of buffer zones along streams and of leaving uncut timber upstream to protect aquatic organisms.

Fire

Almost nothing is known about the responses of amphibians to fire and fire management, including fire retarding chemicals and site preparation techniques. Because several amphibian species in the mountainous regions of the western United States are declining, understanding the effects of fire on amphibians and amphibian habitats is increasingly important. Several studies are starting on the topic, but are few compared to the vast landscape occupied by stream amphibians. Amphibian populations should respond positively to increased productivity (periphyton growth) when canopies are open, but they are also sensitive to changes in water velocity, temperature, chemistry, substrate size, and sedimentation that result from perturbations and loss of forest canopies.

Special Habitats

Ultimately, conservation of stream amphibians depends on conservation of habitat. Conservation efforts should emphasize specialized habitats: seeps, headwater streams, and riparian zones. These habitats are relatively small, patchily distributed on the landscape, and extremely vulnerable to disruption. For example, the recently discovered diversity of *Eurycea* in springs and caves in Texas may be threatened by greater demands on groundwater supplies from a growing human population. The effect of altered hydrology on stream amphibians is another topic that needs research. Information necessary to improve the protection of specialized habitats can help ensure the conservation of a large proportion of stream species.

4

CONSERVATION OF TERRESTRIAL SALAMANDERS WITH DIRECT DEVELOPMENT

RICHARD L. WYMAN

CENTRAL ISSUES

Salamanders with direct development are cryptic, mostly fossorial, and little appreciated by the public, but they are often the most abundant vertebrates in many areas of their range. Direct development means that the species do not have a larval stage; the young hatch as miniature adults. Salamanders with direct development belong to the family Plethodontidae, which includes approximately 27 genera and 240 species (Petranka 1998). The species in this family are lungless and possess nasolabial grooves. Two subfamilies have been described based on skeletal and musculature attributes: Desmognathinae and Plethodontinae. Three species of Desmognathinae have direct development. The Plethodontinae have been subdivided into three tribes. Species in the tribe Hemidactyliini have aquatic larvae; species in the tribes Plethodontini and Bolitoglossini have direct development. Two species of plethodontids are found in Europe and the remainder in North, Central, and South America. In this chapter, I focus on the species with direct development in the United States and Canada because more information is available on them (Petranka 1998). Much less is known of the life history, ecology, and population status of Central and South American species. About 56 species with direct development occur in the United States and Canada. Work currently underway on the genetics of several species complexes will no doubt increase this number (Petranka 1998; Wake and Jakusch 2000).

An overview of these 56 species reveals several trends that affect their conservation status. The first challenge to the conservation of this group results from a lack of a clear understanding of the goals of conservation. For several species, especially in the southeastern United States, some authors report no change in abundance in single or several locations over many years. Simultaneously other authors, viewing the same species over its entire range, report that many demes and populations have been lost to habitat destruction (urban sprawl, forestry practices). Clearly it is possible for one species to have locally abundant and stable populations and yet be declining throughout its range. This fact raises two concerns when thinking about the goals of the conservation of these species: Are we seeking only to preserve some representatives of the species, or are we seeking to preserve the functional role of these species in the ecosystem throughout their range? Furthermore, are we also concerned with preserving the full evolutionary potential of the species throughout its range? There does not appear to be a clear consensus on these issues among biologists or in society.

A second challenge to conservation of this group results from a lack of knowledge about the biology, ecology, life history, and status of populations and species. A somewhat crude analysis presented below reveals that we do not know enough about 43% of the species to determine whether or not we should be concerned. This is especially true for many of the recently described species. There is a need for herpetologists to study the natural history and population status of these species.

This overview, although limited to the United States and Canada, suggests several generalities about salamanders with direct development. There appears to have been no mysterious disappearances like those reported for frogs and toads in the western United States, Central and South America, and Australia. The six species classified here as stable share some characteristics. They tend to be widely distributed and are habitat generalists. Four species (desert slender salamander, *Batrachoseps major aridus;* Red Hills salamander, *Phaeognathus hubrichti;* Cheat Mountain salamander, *Plethodon nettingi;* and Shenandoah salamander, *Plethodon shenandoah*) are Federally listed and protected by law. These species and those reported to be in need of protection have small ranges, exist as relicts, have narrow habitat requirements, or have some combination of these characteristics.

As indicated in other chapters, amphibians possess a suite of characteristics that may make them sensitive indicators of environmental change. These same physiological characteristics may also present problems for their conservation. Because salamanders of this group are lungless, they must respire through the epidermis and lining of the buccopharyngeal region. These epithelial membranes must therefore be kept moist to allow for the transport of oxygen molecules across the epithelium. Thus, provision of moist habitats throughout their life cycle is another challenge to conservation of this group. This group may also be threatened by changes in precipitation and temperature patterns predicted to occur due to increased greenhouse gases in the atmosphere (Wetherald 1991).

Recent studies of genetic variation in several species have revealed that what was previously considered to be one or two species are in fact species complexes made up of several semispecies, sibling, or sister species. These salamanders show marked genetic variation with strong tendencies for regional differentiation, and management plans should assure that their unique genetic diversity is preserved. Another challenge to conservation of these salamanders results from the contrast between preserving a single widely distributed species (presumably also a habitat generalist) to preserving several or many species with more restricted distributions and habitat requirements.

A specific challenge to conservation of this group is forestry practices. Twenty-six species have been shown or are suggested to be adversely affected by intensive forest management (such as clearcutting), but are less affected or not at all by more selective forestry practices. The problem here is that we do not know where the division lies between too intensive management practices and ones that will preserve these species and their ecological roles.

Invasive species are an emerging threat to this group. In the northeastern United States, the beech bark disease, the gypsy moth, and earthworms are invaders that have the potential to alter forest ecosystem-level processes to the detriment of terrestrial salamanders.

These salamanders may be important in influencing the cycling of nutrients (e.g., carbon and nitrogen) and the ability of the forest to provide ecosystem services important to humans. Knowledge of the role of salamanders in ecosystem function could be used to tell the public why conservation of plethodontid salamanders is important.

LIFE HISTORY, BEHAVIOR, AND ECOLOGY

In this section, I describe this group in general terms; of course, any one species may differ from the general pattern. For more detailed information, consult Petranka (1998) and Bruce et al. (2000).

Table 4.1 summarizes information from the literature on the status of terrestrial salamanders with direct development in the United States and Canada. I assigned "Status" categories that express what I gleaned from the literature. Some categories are straightforward, such as "federally listed." Other categories are not as easy to interpret. For instance, "uncertain" means that I could not determine the status of these species with the literature available. I assigned "should be protected" and "rare" when an author reported these. "Stable/declining" indicates that at least one author reported the population as stable and another reported loss of demes and populations throughout the species range. For "causes of concern," I relied on the published reports and Petranka (1998).

Plethodontid salamanders inhabit a wide range of mainly forested habitat types. Many species inhabit the forest floor of deciduous forests and a few species appear to be specialist in coniferous forests. The presence of rocks, talus, large woody debris, and old rotten logs is frequently mentioned as important to plethodontid salamanders (Wells and Wells 1976). These microhabitats function as sites to which the salamanders retreat when surface conditions become harsh. Females also use these micro-

Table 4.1

Summary of conservation information from published literature on salamanders with direct development in the United States

Taxon	Status[a]	Habitat	Cause of Concern	Reference
Desmognathinae				
Desmognathus aeneus	1	Seepages in forests	Forestry practices, disjunct populations	Petranka 1998
D. wrighti	1	Mature forests	Spruce dieback, forestry practices	Petranka 1998
Phaeognathus hubrichti	2	Cool, moist ravines	Forestry practices, restricted habitat	Dodd 1989, 1991
Plethodontinae				
Bolitoglossini				
Batrachoseps aridus	2	Desert canyon	One small population	Bury et al. 1980; Stebbins 1985
B. attenuatus	1	Old-growth forests	Probably a species complex	Welsh and Lind 1988, 1991
B. campi	3	Spring-fed desert canyons	Restricted habitat and range	Petranka 1998
B. incognatus	4	Mixed evergreen forests	Very little known	Jockusch et al. 2001
B. gabrieli	3	Forested talus	Very restricted range (~1 ha)	Petranka 1998
B. gavilanensis	1	Mixed evergreen forests	Very little known	Jockusch et al. 2001
B. luciae	1	Mixed evergreen forests	Very little known	Jockusch et al. 2001
B. minor	1	Moist canyons	Very little known	Jockusch et al. 2001
B. nigriventris	1	Oak forest	Very little known	Petranka 1998
B. pacificus complex	5	Various	Probably a species complex	Petranka 1998
B. simatus	6	Forests of Kern River	Restricted range, very little known	Petranka 1998
B. stebbinsi	3	Moist canyons	Restricted habitat and range	Petranka 1998
B. wrighti	1	Old-growth forests, rotten logs	Forestry practices	Bury and Corn 1988a; Gilbert and Allwine 1991
Hydromantes brunus	7	Limestone cliffs and talus	Restricted habitat and range	Petranka 1998
H. platycephalus	1	Rock outcrops and talus	Collecting by herpetologists	Petranka 1998
H. shastae	1	Caves, cliff faces	Very little known	Petranka 1998
Plethodontini				
Aneides aeneus complex	1	Forested rock outcrops	Restricted habitat	Snyder 1991
A. ferreus	1	Old growth forests, rotten logs	Forestry practices	Corn and Bury 1991

Table 4.1 continued

Taxon	Status[a]	Habitat	Cause of Concern	Reference
A. flavipunctatus	7	Coastal moist forests	Forestry practices	Petranka 1998
A. hardii	1	Old growth forests, rotten logs	Forestry practices, restricted range	Scott and Ramotnik 1992
A. lugubris	8	Oak forests	Forestry practice, restricted habitat	Petranka 1998
Ensatina eschscholtzii	5	Various	Species complex	Corn and Bury 1991
Plethodon aureolus	1	Forests	Restricted range, very little known	Petranka 1998
P. caddoensis	1	Forests, talus, rock outcrops	Restricted range, very little known	Petranka 1998
P. cinereus	5	Mesic forests	Soil acidification, forestry practices	Wyman and Hawksley-Lescault 1987
P. dorsalis complex	9	Mesic forests	Habitat destruction, forestry practices	Petranka 1998
P. dunni	5	Mesic forests	Forestry practices	Corn and Bury 1991
P. electromorphus	1	Deciduous Forests	Newly described species	Highton 1999
P. elongatus	9	Coastal moist forests	Forestry practices in drier habitats	Welsh and Lind 1988, 1991
P. glutinosis complex	9	Mature hard-wood forests	Forestry practices	Petranka et al. 1993
P. hoffmani	9	Mature hard-wood forests	Habitat destruction, forestry practices	Petranka 1998
P. hubrichti	1	Mesic forests	Forestry practices, restricted range	Kramer et al. 1993
P. idahoensis	3	Wet rocky conifer forest	Restricted habitat	Groves et al. 1996
P. jordani complex	9	Mesic forests	Forestry practices	Ash 1988; Petranka et al. 1993, 1994
P. kentucki	9	Mesic forests	Forestry practices	Petranka 1998
P. larselli	8	Old-growth forests with talus	Forestry practices	Aubry et al. 1987
P. neomexicanus	1	Forested canyons	Very little known	Petranka 1998
P. nettingi	2	Red spruce/yellow birch forest	Restricted habitat	Petranka 1998
P. oconaluftee	5	Mature forests	Forestry practices	Hairston and Wiley 1993
P. ouachitae	9	Forested talus	Forestry practices	Petranka 1998

Continued on next page

Table 4.1 continued

Taxon	Status[a]	Habitat	Cause of Concern	Reference
P. petraeus	1	Cave mouths/ rock outcrops	Very restricted range	Petranka 1998
P. punctatus	1	Forests with rocks	Forestry practices, restricted range	Buhlmann et al. 1988
P. richmondi	1	Forests with rocks	Habitat destruction, forestry practices	Petranka 1998
P. serratus	1	Mesic forests with rocks	Habitat destruction, forestry practices	Camp 1986
P. shenandoah	2	Forested talus	Restricted range and habitat	Jaeger 1980a; Petranka 1998
P. stormi	7	Forested talus	Restricted range and habitat	Petranka 1998
P. vandykei	3	Mesic rocky conifer forests	Restricted habitat, forestry practices	Welsh 1990
P. vehiculum	5	Forests	None	Aubry and Hall 1991; Corn and Bury 1991
P. virginia	1	Forests	Newly described species	Highton 1999
P. websteri	9	Hardwood forests with rocks	Forestry practices	Petranka 1998
P. wehrlei	3	Forested hillsides	Forestry practices, isolated populations	Petranka 1998
P. welleri	3	Spruce fir forests	Spruce dieback, restricted habitat	Petranka 1998
P. yonahlossee	1	Hardwood forests	Forestry practices	Petranka et al. 1993, 1994

[a]Status: 1 = uncertain; 2 = federally listed; 3 = should be protected; 4 = very little known; 5 = stable; 6 = protected in California; 7 = rare; 8 = declining; 9 = stable or declining.

habitats for oviposition and brooding. Perhaps the most unusual microhabitat requirement in this group is the use of holes in oak trees for reproduction by the arboreal salamander (*Aneides lugubris;* Stebbins 1951).

Courtship and internal fertilization of ova are followed by a period of one to several months of ova development. Fecundity is generally low (i.e., tens of eggs). Females then deposit a cluster of eggs in a small chamber underground, in a rock crevice, or under or in a rotting log. The eastern red-backed salamander (*Plethodon cinereus*) female wraps her body around the eggs and remains with the eggs for a month until they hatch. This behavior apparently provides the eggs with some factor that aids development; young with females present grow more quickly than those without females (Highton and Savage 1961). Females may also protect the eggs from predators. After a month, the eggs hatch into miniature adults. Almost nothing is known about the ecology of young-of-the-year terrestrial plethodontids (but see Maglia 1996), and this is another important area where research is needed.

The timing of breeding, gestation, and oviposition by these salamanders differs in eastern and western United States and Central America (Houck 1977; Duellman and Trueb 1986; Herbeck and Semlitsch 2000). In the eastern United States, surface activity occurs from spring to fall (in nondrought years), with courtship in either spring or fall. In the southern United States, salamanders may be active during the winter. Oviposition occurs in midsummer and egg attendance by females continues until mid- to late summer. In the western United States, salamanders tend to be active on the surface during the spring, fall, and winter, but move underground during the hot, dry summer. Courtship occurs throughout the active period. Egg laying and attendance of eggs by females occur in summer when females are below the surface. In Central America, salamanders are active and court year-round. Egg laying occurs in late fall and females attend eggs throughout the winter and spring. These patterns may make some of these species vulnerable to the changes in temperature and precipitation regimes that are predicted by general circulation models to occur as greenhouse gases continue to accumulate in the atmosphere (Wetherald 1991).

In the eastern red-backed salamander, adult males reproduce at three years and females at four. Females in the south of the species range reproduce every year, whereas those in the north reproduce every other year (Sayler 1966; Nagel 1977). There is some anecdotal evidence that females remain with the young after they hatch.

Competition has been documented frequently and extensively in this group (Jaeger 1970, 1972, 1980a; Fraser 1976; Pauley 1978; Hairston 1980; Marvin 1998; Camp 1999; Mathis and Britzke 1999). Jaeger and colleagues have published extensively on the behavior of the eastern red-backed salamander. Both adult males and females are territorial (Lang and Jaeger 2000) and appear to defend retreat sites. Pheromones produced by postcloacal glands appear to aide in the identification of individuals in the eastern red-backed salamander and other species (Anthony 1993; Jaeger and Gabor 1993).

Stomach content analyses have revealed that many species are euryphagic (Bishop 1943; Jaeger 1972; Petranka 1998). They appear to eat any palatable invertebrate that will fit into their mouths. Some plethodontids may be cannibalistic or prey on smaller species. Distribution in a habitat is related to soil moisture (Heatwole 1962; Jaeger 1971; Grover 2000,), soil pH (Wyman and Hawksley-Lescault 1987; Wyman and Jancola 1992), litter and humus depth, forest age, and downed woody debris (Petranka 1998; Moore et al. 2001). Terrestrial salamanders with direct development can reach high densities in appropriate habitats. For instance, eastern red-backed salamanders reach densities of $4/m^2$ in Virginia (Jaeger 1980b), $0.9/m^2$ in Michigan hardwoods (Heatwole 1962), $0.5/m^2$ in hardwoods of New York (Wyman 1988), and $0.3/m^2$ in the Hubbard Brook Experimental Forest of New Hampshire (Burton and Likens 1975). Petranka and Murray (2001) report that removal sampling along streamsides revealed $1.8/m^2$. The eastern red-backed salamander appears to be able to regulate the abundance of some litter invertebrates, which indirectly affects leaf litter decomposition (Wyman 1998).

SAMPLING

Sampling of abundance is critical to determining the conservation status of a species. Terrestrial salamanders may be sampled by time-constrained searching of the forest floor, including rocks and logs; area-constrained searching (also called hand searching of quadrats); pit fall traps; night-time visual searches; and searching under boards previously placed in the habitat to attract salamanders. Any of these relative estimations of abundance can be supplemented with marking of salamanders and subsequent recapture to estimate absolute population size. The smaller plethodontids are difficult to mark effectively. Most studies in northeastern United States have found that searches conducted in the spring and fall locate more individuals and species than those conducted in the summer. Because salamanders may retreat below ground when forest floor conditions are dry, and because some portion of the salamander population is usually below ground, absolute density estimates are difficult to obtain. However, time-constrained searches and the searching of quadrats, when conducted over years and in wet weather in the spring or fall, result in estimates of salamanders on the forest floor surface that are remarkably consistent over many years (Welsh and Droege 2001).

Some recent work with cover boards placed on the forest floor suggests that they may be useful for qualitative sampling of relative abundances (deGraaf and Yamasaki 1992). It is difficult to know whether the boards attract surplus salamanders (those without adequate territories) or cause those with territories to abandon them for the boards. A recent study suggests that relative abundance indices based on surface catches are valid indices of changes in absolute population size (Smith and Petranka 2000).

HABITAT DESTRUCTION, FRAGMENTATION, LANDSCAPE-SCALE POLLUTION, AND GLOBAL CHANGE

Habitat loss due to outright destruction, fragmentation, forestry practices, and pollution are chiefly responsible for the loss of salamander habitat (Table 4.1). Areas dominated by human activity, such as highways, shopping centers, housing developments, agricultural land, and other intensive land use, make poor salamander habitat. The remaining land with relatively intact vegetation (natural and plantations) and less intensive land use is the focus of the following discussion. First, however, it should be recognized that at one time much of eastern United States was covered with old-growth forest that was removed by the late 1800s. Some of this previously forested landscape has been reforested, but trees and the forest floor are still relatively young (i.e., less than 100 years old). We do not know if salamander abundances have fully returned—or if they can return—to levels of the pre-European colonization era.

Forestry Practices

Timber harvesting by clearcutting results in the loss of salamanders in the clearcut area for many species (Table 4.1; Dupuis et al. 1995; deMaynadier and Hunter 1995; Ash 1997; Grialou et al. 2000). There is debate about whether salamanders are killed or move to more favorable habitat after timbering (Ash and Bruce 1994; Petranka 1994). However, if the area surrounding a clearcut previously had intact salamander populations at stable densities, then the fate of displaced salamanders may be indirect and entail death due to competition, predation, and lack of suitable microhabitat. Selective cutting has been shown to have less effect than clearcutting (Messere and Ducey 1998; Brooks 1999). Messere and Ducey (1998) found that, at least in the year after selective cutting of single trees, the abundance of eastern red-backed salamanders was unaffected. A difficulty with these studies is that they provide information on relative abundance and usually cannot inform us about population changes or about the ecological or evolutionary potential of the salamanders that remain; we do not know how large a population of salamanders must be to provide normal ecological and evolutionary functions into the future.

During searches of forest floors over many years (Wyman 1988; Wyman and Jancola 1992), I realized that very few young-of-the-year eastern red-backed salamanders were ever encountered. Far fewer occur than would be needed to maintain the relatively stable populations of adults on the forest floor. When we did find young-of-the-year, they were frequently associated with the rotting remains of trees lying within the soil. If this type of nursery log is required for the development and survival of yearling plethodontids, then long-term forestry practices that eliminate this kind of microhabitat may need to be modified. Large logs, rotten logs, and coarse woody debris have been mentioned repeatedly as being important for many species of terrestrial salamanders with direct development and should not be overlooked. There is some evidence that underground woody debris may play a role in chelating toxic iron and aluminum ions at low soil pH and may provide nontoxic sites for the development of young salamanders (Appendix Table 1 in Frisbie and Wyman 1992). More research is needed on whether buried logs influence the cycling of iron and aluminum on a landscape scale. Another factor that may adversely affect salamander populations is habitat fragmentation caused by road building, although very little experimental work on the effects of roads has been done (but see Wyman 1991). The presence of roads has also been shown to result in reduced abundance of salamanders near them, possibly because roads represent psychological barriers to salamanders (deMaynadier and Hunter 2000).

Several recent studies have suggested that invasive species may adversely affect terrestrial salamanders. Introduced tree diseases (e.g., beech bark disease; Houston 1994) and pests (gypsy moth; Petranka 1998) may alter forest structure and ecosystem processes to an extent that may threaten this group. Much more research is needed in this area. For instance, does the loss of beech trees, which have relatively recalcitrant leaves, degrade salamander habitat when they are replaced by species such as sugar maple with more easily decomposed leaves? Does the drying of the forest floor after defoliation by gypsy moth larvae adversely affect salamander populations in the area? Does the presence of introduced, large earthworms (*Lumbricus terrestris*) in the northeastern United States adversely affect salamander populations? These worms cannot be consumed by small plethodons and the worms remove large quantities of litter that is, indirectly, the source of salamander food.

Landscape-Scale Pollution

We know that larval and aquatic amphibians appear to be particularly susceptible to pollution such as acidification because they have a relatively thin epidermis that lacks a well-developed cornified layer (Dunson et al. 1992) and they take up ions through their epidermis from their aquatic surroundings (Freda and Dunson 1985). The effect of such pollutants on terrestrial salamanders is less well known. In this section, I discuss the work of my colleagues and I on the effects of terrestrial soil acidity on the eastern red-backed salamander. It is not known if the response of eastern red-backed salamanders to acidic soils is predictive of the response of other terrestrial plethodontid and nonplethodontid salamanders, but it is likely.

Sulfuric and nitric acids produced during combustion of fossil fuels fall to the ground in rain and snow and as dry material. These acids may accelerate the acidification of soils, alter the dynamics of ion balance in soils, and lower the final equilibrium pH (Tomlinson 1990). Soil acidification is a complex process involving changes in a number of chemical relationships within soils (Tomlinson 1990). Soil pH ranges from about 8 to 3 and reflects the nature of the minerals present, biological activity, and deposition of atmospheric chemicals. As H^+ enters the soil, the ions react with minerals and release cations. There are a series of buffering ranges in soils where different cations predominate. In the greater Catskill region, the lower three buffering ranges are of interest: the exchange buffering range (pH 5.5 to 4.2), the aluminum buffering range (pH 4.2 to 3.8), and the iron buffering range (pH <3.8). It may be important that our work has shown that both amphibian density and species richness fall when the pH is below 3.8 (Wyman and Jancola 1992).

Soils can be moved through these buffering ranges as the dominant ions are leached due to the accumulated deposition of acid anions and changes in the rate of chemical weathering of the parent rock. In the aluminum and iron buffering ranges, ions of these chemicals dominate the exchange sites on colloidal surfaces. This leads to the electrochemical leaching of other cations that have lower valences (e.g., Na^+) as negatively charged anions move out of the soil carrying these anions with them. Cations with small atomic weight and low valence are least attracted to soil exchange sites and leach first and faster than larger, higher-valence ions. Thus, in soils of low pH, deficiencies of sodium (and other ions) may develop. Similar deficiencies in calcium and magnesium have been implicated in the decline of trees in Europe (Tomlinson 1990).

Amphibians in aquatic habitats are sensitive to acidification, and this sensitivity appears to be linked to the loss of sodium ions through the epidermis (Freda and Dunson 1985). Through systematic searching of 1-m-square quadrats at 17 sites in New York, Wyman (1988) found a correlation between soil pH and the density and distribution of several amphibian species (Wyman and Hawksley-Lescault 1987; Wyman and Jancola 1992). Eastern red-backed salamanders were found in approximately 60% of quadrats with a pH of at least 3.8. Below this pH, only about 6% of quadrats contained salamanders. The distributions of the northern two-lined salamander (*Eurycea bislineata*), the northern dusky salamander (*Desmognathus fuscus*), and the Allegheny Mountain dusky salamander (*D. ochrophaeus*) were also skewed away from low pH soils. On the other hand, the distribution of the red eft of the red-spotted newt (*Notophthalmus v. viridescens*) did not appear to be influenced by soil acidity. Although correlation cannot be used to demonstrate causation, these data are consistent with the hypothesis that low soil acidity limits the distribution of three species. The density of amphibians and species diversity were also positively correlated with soil pH for the 17 sites investigated (Wyman and Jancola 1992).

These results led us to investigate the ionic balance of these species in a series of laboratory and field experiments (Frisbie and Wyman 1991, 1992, 1995). It is known that amphibian larvae, when in acidic water, lose sodium through their epidermis (Freda and Dunson 1985). Sodium is a vital intercellular ion important for cellular homeostasis and electrical signal generation along nerves and muscles. We wanted to determine if sodium balance was altered in a similar manner in terrestrial stages. Individual animals were injected with radioactive sodium and placed on substrates with buffered pHs of 3, 3.5, 4, 4.5, and 5. The concentration of sodium remaining in the animals was determined at 24 hours and 48 hours. A sodium efflux rate constant was calculated using the slope of the line of decreasing concentration over time. In eastern red-backed salamanders, the efflux rate constant was significantly higher at pH 3 and 3.5 than at higher pHs. In the northern two-lined salamander and Allegheny Mountain dusky salamander, the efflux rate constant was higher at pH 3. The opposite occurred with the red-spotted newt: the rate was lower at pH 3 and 3.5 than at other pHs. These data support the hypothesis that sodium balance may be disrupted in salamanders on low-pH substrates. There is evidence that soils at higher elevations in the Catskills are being affected by acidic deposition (Lovett et al. 1999).

Frisbie and Wyman (1991) showed that salamanders living on acidic substrates lose sodium more quickly, contain less body water, and lose mass more quickly than salamanders on less acidic substrates. The combined effects of living on soils with reduced sodium content and an increased rate of sodium loss may result in a disruption of sodium balance in salamanders. We suggest that the disruption of sodium balance in adult terrestrial amphibians is responsible for the absence of salamanders on low-pH soils. Of course the balance of other essential ions may also be disrupted. In addition, the forest interior may be fragmented because of low soil pH and may act as a barrier to dispersal.

Global Climate Change

Climatologists use general circulation models as tools to predict the consequences of altering the chemical composition of the earth's atmosphere (Wetherald 1991). These models suggest that changes in the yearly pattern of precipitation may occur, with most continental interiors in the northern hemisphere receiving less precipitation in the growing season and more in the winter. This could result in an increased frequency and intensity of summer-time droughts. Terrestrial salamanders may be particularly vulnerable to this kind of change, both because of the dryness itself and because of changes in soil chemistry associated with drying. These models also predict a general warming. The result is that high-elevation habitats may shrink or be eliminated from mountaintops (Peters 1991). Salamanders currently living in high-elevation sites may be the first to experience these effects, especially species with highly restricted ranges (e.g., the pygmy salamander, *Desmognathus wrighti,* and Weller's salamander, *Plethodon welleri*).

There appears to be a synergistic interaction between drought and soil acidity. Wyman (1991) reported on the results of monitoring soil acidity in deciduous and coniferous forests during the drought of 1988–1989. I found that as soil dried (determined as soil suction in microbars), the soil acidified. The effect differed among forest types; some forests showed the effect during the spring or summer and others during the fall. Soils in the spruce forests fell below the previously identified limiting pH of 3.8 during all three seasons studied. Few red-backed salamanders are found in spruce forests. The decrease of soil pH with drying occurred in all forest types, resulting in soil conditions that may threaten terrestrial salamanders with simultaneously reduced soil sodium concentrations, increased rate of the loss of sodium through the epidermis, increased body water loss, and drier soil.

Genetic Structure

A large literature has accumulated recently on the genetics of the plethodontid salamanders because of the identification of many complexes containing many new semi- and sibling species (Highton 1995, 1999; Wake and Jakusch 2000). For example, in the western United States the plethodons are divided into four semispecies complexes, each containing two species. In the eastern United States, the small plethodons are divided into three semispecies complexes containing a total of 13 species, and the larger species in the northern slimy salamander (*Plethodon glutinosis*) semispecies complex are divided into three complexes with 23 species. These new subdivisions of what were previously classified as one or two species present an interesting problem for conservation of this group for several reasons.

First, because these species have only recently been recognized, little is known about their individual ecologies, habitats, population sizes, demographies, and behaviors. This makes it difficult to know their conservation status. Second, these species were not previously recognized because the members of any one group of species are morphological similar. A few species have specific characteristics that can be used to identify them in the field, but most do not. Others may be identified by their location, but this can be misleading. This makes it difficult for field workers to easily determine which species they have found and complicates studies of their ecology and population status. Third, because the ranges of many of the species are apparently restricted, it can be predicted that their populations will be relatively small and have less genetic variability than the more widely distributed ones. It is not known what the consequences are in salamanders of long-term inbreeding in small populations. Further, the presence of at least 140 contact zones where once previously isolated species ranges are now in contact provides the potential for hybridization (Highton et al. 1989; Highton 1995). These hybrid zones will make determining the status of the species population size extremely difficult. Members of these semispecies complexes show significant genetic differentiation, but usually lack reproductive barriers and freely interbreed in zones of contact. Although this will invariably result in disagreement about the number of species in a group, the fact remains that salamanders show marked genetic variation with strong tendencies for regional differentiation. These regional groups deserve taxonomic recognition, and management plans should ensure that their unique genetic diversity is assured.

Fragmentation of habitats is hypothesized to isolate salamanders into smaller population sizes with the potential to reduce genetic variation in the isolates. However, in the only study to date to test this prediction, Gibbs (1998c), studying genetic variation in the eastern red-backed salamander, found little loss of variation in more isolated populations. This may be because the fragmentation of the habitats is a relatively recent occurrence (i.e., 100 years).

Lastly, with such interesting examples of evolution in progress, the hybridization of threatened species may result in contentious legal battles (such as in the Florida panther, which is genetically distinct from western United States forms, but contains some shared alleles through hybridization).

POTENTIAL SOLUTIONS

Because these salamanders occur at high densities in many forested habitats, they may play a role in regulating some forest floor processes (Burton and Likens 1975; Wyman 1998). In field experiments, I found that the presence of eastern red-backed salamanders indirectly slowed leaf litter decomposition. The salamanders prey heavily on leaf litter fragmenters, which results in a reduced rate of colonization of leaf litter by decomposers. Because the eastern red-backed salamander is ubiquitous and often very dense, the slowing of decomposition may have consequences for carbon cycling. That is, habitats with healthy salamander populations may sequester more carbon than those without. More recent research has shown that the salamanders eat invertebrates that would eat the higher quality portion (lower carbon:nitrogen ratio) of the leaf first. By reducing the abundance of these invertebrates, leaves remaining in the presence of salamanders also hold more nitrogen. Thus salamander predation appears to influence carbon and nitrogen cycling. I provide preliminary calculations that suggest the amount of carbon stored on the forest floor due to salamander predation could be as high as 0.4 gigatons in New York State (Wyman 1998). There are far too many simplifying assumptions in this calculation to place much trust in the magnitude of the estimate, but it is interesting that predation by salamanders on forest floor invertebrates appears to modulate both the carbon and nitrogen cycles. Additional research should be conducted to confirm or refute this finding, because if confirmed, the fact would be very important in communicating, to the public and policymakers, the importance of amphibians to ecosystem and human health.

Conservation activities generally focus on species that are already in trouble—species that have a high probability of becoming extinct. Although this approach is important for those species, it leaves all other species vulnerable to the rapid and continuous loss of habitat and hence to the loss of demes and populations. Thus, private undisturbed forested land is not protected, only so-called unique habitats (e.g., wetlands) or those containing endangered forms. As mentioned earlier, we do not know what size a population must be to preserve its ecological function and evolutionary potential. Research should attempt to determine the magnitude of the effect of salamander communities in the ecosystems they inhabit, because their activity may influence ecosystem services important to humans.

I believe that another significant and contentious problem facing the conservation of terrestrial salamander species with direct development is caused by a difference in perspective of researchers regarding the status of the species studied. Some researchers have studied a few species from a limited number of sites for long periods and report little or no changes in density. Other researchers working at sites throughout the range of the same species record the loss of demes and populations due to urban sprawl and intensively managed hardwood stands and conifer plantations. The latter workers conclude that the species is declining. Both groups are correct. I have had this experience with the eastern red-backed salamander, being at times in one camp and at times in the other. As suggested earlier, the difference may be due to the different goals held by the two groups of researchers. The two questions I asked at the beginning of this chapter can be answered in the affirmative. Yes, we should strive to protect individual populations of these salamanders and, by doing so throughout the range of the species, we also protect their ecological role and evolutionary potential. I attempt to offer some suggestions for achieving these goals.

More care must be exercised in differentiating and clarifying the terms *relative abundance, density, population size,* and *population status.* These terms are often used too casually. This is particularly unfortunate for discussions of plethodontid sala-manders because they do show simultaneously stable local populations and shrink-ing ranges. In addition, we should identify as our goal the perpetuation of the role of the species in its ecosystem throughout its range and not just at a few last strong-holds. It is a relatively easy task to preserve populations on a single parcel of land for some time to come. It is an entirely different matter to ensure that these plethodon-tid species will be able to fulfill their role in ecosystem processes in forested ecosys-tems in perpetuity. It is also a much more difficult problem to ensure the evolution-ary potential of the group. For instance, it may be important to preserve disjunct populations and those at the edge of a species' geographic range where genetic differ-entiation may be greatest.

Today many species exist as fragmented populations within human-dominated landscapes and, as such, may be considered to be metapopulations (Gill 1978). Yet very little attention has been directed toward what this may mean for all but a few species (Gibbs 1998b). The theory that demes and populations of these salamanders may be viewed as islands and that island biogeography theory (MacArthur and Wil-son 1967) offers a useful tool to aide in their conservation must be investigated.

Any species that currently exists in one or a few isolated localities needs to be pro-tected now. Managers responsible for these habitats should take the actions needed to ensure protection. Specialized habitat types in forests (moist seeps, rocky out-crops, talus slopes, large rotten logs) need to be protected now. For species that have been recently described, it is urgent that studies be undertaken to determine their status. Once the status is determined, work can focus on those most in need of pro-tection. Clearly herpetologists and their students should refrain from removing indi-viduals and making collections of any species even suspected of experiencing a prob-lem. For most species, it is likely that sufficient material already exists in university and museum collections.

The species complexes that have been identified will present particularly vexing problems for conservation. Evolutionary biologists, although well-meaning, have in-advertently prepared a minefield through which conservation biologists will have to march. I can hear the politically charged question now: "Is this a species or not?" Re-member that our goal should be the protection of the ecological roles and evolu-tionary potential of the ecosystem, including semispecies, sibling species, sister spe-cies, full species, and all other representations of evolution in action.

Clearcutting over large areas and in short cycles is detrimental to the long-term survival of many species of plethodontid salamanders (Table 4.1). A few species (e.g., the ensatina, *Ensatina eschscholtzii*) seem to tolerate intensive forestry practices, but most do not. It is not known even for a single species how intensively a forestry program can be applied before the species ceases to perform its role in the ecosystem or begins to lose its potential to evolve. More research and thinking is needed on these aspects of the conservation of terrestrial salamanders. We need active forestry to provide wood products to help sustain society, and simultaneously we need to assure the continued existence and function of the species in those forests. Research questions include the following: Is it true that populations of salamanders exist as source / sink metapopulations? If so, then should forestry practices be concentrated in sink areas? Are source and sink areas stable or do they reverse function over time? Should harvest rotation times be managed to aid the reestablishment of healthy salamander populations? In the area of ecological economics, we need to determine the cost of the loss of ecosystem services when forestland is cleared, so this cost can be taken into consideration during decisionmaking.

Because terrestrial salamanders with direct development may help forests provide essential ecosystem services to humans, their well-being should be monitored. A national monitoring effort should be launched to help conserve these species and their ecological roles and evolutionary potential.

ACKNOWLEDGMENTS

I thank Carolyn Barker, Marilyn Wyman, the book editor Ray Semlitsch, and an anonymous reviewer for helpful comments on the manuscript. I am especially indebted to J. W. Petranka for his wonderful book, *Salamanders of the United States and Canada*. My work and writing of this paper have been supported in part by grants from the USDA National Research Initiative Competitive Grant Program, National Science Foundation, Bay Foundation, the Sweet Water Trust, and the E. N. Huyck Preserve.

5

CONSERVATION OF AMPHIBIANS IN THE NEW WORLD TROPICS

MARTHA L. CRUMP

CENTRAL ISSUES

This chapter is restricted geographically to the New World tropics. The tropics lie within about 2,500 km north and 2,500 km south of the equator, bounded by two imaginary lines, the Tropic of Cancer on the north and the Tropic of Capricorn on the south. The western hemisphere is also known as the New World. The New World tropics therefore include the Caribbean, Mexico, Central America, and South America down to northern Chile, Argentina, Paraguay, and southern Brazil. Everything north of the Tropic of Cancer is the North Temperate Zone and everything south of the Tropic of Capricorn is the South Temperate Zone.

Why does conservation of amphibians in the New World tropics deserve its own chapter? The answer is simple: the number of species—or species richness—in the tropics is much higher than in the temperate zones, and the New World tropics is the most species-rich region of the world. There are an estimated 2,281 species of amphibians in the New World tropics (2,013 anurans, 188 salamanders, and 80 caecilians), versus a mere 241 species (90 anurans, 151 salamanders) in the North Temperate Zone (calculated from Duellman 1999b). Consider the following tropical–North Temperate comparisons of anurans to emphasize this difference. Ecuador and the state of Colorado are about the same area. Whereas Ecuador boasts approximately 393 species of frogs, Colorado has 17. Costa Rica is home to 123 species of frogs; Florida, with nearly three times the area, has 23. Many areas in the New World tropics are considered to be biodiversity "hotspots" (see Chapter 6, this volume): for example, the tropical Andes, Caribbean, Brazil's Atlantic Forest, Mesoamerica, and the Chocó-Darien regions of Colombia and western Ecuador. The tropical Andes has the highest amphibian species richness of any of the hotspot areas: 830 species, 604 of which are endemic to the region. Based on diversity alone, the New World tropics deserves special attention and merits intensive conservation efforts for amphibians.

We have reason to be concerned about the status of amphibians in the New World tropics because of widespread reports of population declines (Young et al. 2001). Many of these declines have occurred at high elevations, in relatively undisturbed areas, and many declines involve species associated with streams (Lips and Donnelly 2002). In some cases, the cause of the decline remains a mystery. A pathogenic, aquatic chytrid fungus is thought to be responsible for mass mortality of frogs at high elevations in Puerto Rico, Costa Rica, Panama, and Ecuador (Carey et al. 1999). How quickly this pathogen will spread or where it will occur next is anyone's guess. Habitat destruction is probably the major cause of amphibian population declines worldwide. Lowland rain forests and high-elevation cloud forests in the New World tropics are being cut down and fragmented at an unprecedented rate. Additional threats to tropical amphibians include climatic factors such as prolonged droughts, as well as commercial exploitation, invasive species, and chemical contamination. The prognosis is indeed sad if we do not take conservation action, because the world is destined to lose considerable biodiversity.

To take conservation action we must devote more time, energy, and resources to the study of tropical amphibians. Population parameters of tropical amphibians are less well understood than those of temperate species. In part this disparity is due to less awareness of and appreciation for amphibians in the tropics. Many fewer biologists work in the tropics, especially in relation to the number of known species of amphibians. Logistics are often difficult, in part because much of the landscape is inaccessible due to a lack of roads or because roads are impassable during much of the year. Some areas of South America have never been surveyed for amphibians. We lack a good understanding of distribution patterns for most tropical amphibians. Furthermore, there is considerable taxonomic confusion, and many species have yet to be described. Nearly 50% of the recognized species of amphibians from the Andes, and more than 67% of the species of amphibians in the Guiana highlands, were described within the past two decades (Duellman 1999a). Another problem is that funding for tropical amphibian research is difficult to obtain, especially for nationals in the region.

For conservation efforts to be successful, however, we need more than increased research effort. We need the support of the people on whose land the animals live. The local people must appreciate amphibians and want to protect them. These people need to be empowered with knowledge and responsibility to become an integral part of any conservation initiative. Finally, because conservation measures will work only if critical habitat is protected, local people must support such efforts.

The goals of this chapter are to examine the status of amphibians in the New World tropics, to look for possible associations between declining species and the characteristics of their natural history, to describe the threats to these animals and causes for their declines, and to suggest potential solutions for their conservation.

Ideally, I would include all three amphibian orders in my discussion. Caecilians are pantropical in distribution and are certainly well-represented in the New World. Unfortunately, however, next to nothing is known concerning the status of their populations. Although salamanders are most abundant in North America and Eurasia, members of one family, Plethodontidae, have invaded the Neotropics to southern Brazil and central Bolivia. Again, however, we know very little concerning the status of these populations. Thus, I will focus mainly on anurans in this chapter.

STATUS OF ANURAN POPULATIONS IN THE NEW WORLD TROPICS

Three relatively undisturbed low-elevation sites studied in South America have no reported amphibian declines: Cuzco Amazonico, Peru; Madre de Dios, Peru; and Reserva Florestal Adolpho Ducke, Amazonas, Brazil (Duellman 1995; Middleton et al. 2001). Anuran populations in lowland central Panama are fluctuating, but no general decline has been observed (Ibáñez 1999). No doubt many other assemblages of tropical anurans remain healthy to date. In some cases, populations of a given species have been reported as declining from high elevations, but remaining stable at low elevations. Such is the case with the Puerto Rican coqui (*Eleutherodactylus coqui*; Joglar and Burrows 1996). Likewise, the bromeliad frog, *Hyla bromeliacia*, a treefrog that breeds in bromeliads, has declined at high elevations in Guatemala, but populations seem stable at low elevations (Campbell 1998). Unfortunately, however, these seemingly healthy populations and assemblages may be the exceptions.

From the primary literature, issues of *Froglog*, personal communications, and personal observations, I compiled a list of 106 species of anurans for which at least some populations have been reported as declining or have disappeared from the New World tropics. Some species with restricted distributions, such as golden toads (*Bufo periglenes;* Figure 5.1) and some *Colostethus* and *Atelopus*, are thought to be extinct from throughout their ranges. This number of 106 is approximately 5% of the known fauna in the region. In contrast, populations of at least 30 species of anurans (~33% of the known fauna) have declined from the New World North Temperate Zone. Rather than suggesting that tropical anurans are not in trouble, the data reveal the incompleteness of our knowledge of tropical declines. Indeed, recent reviews and analyses of the global decline of amphibians barely mention examples from Latin America (e.g., Alford and Richards 1999; Houlahan et al. 2000). We just do not know much about the status of populations in Latin America nor the mechanisms responsible for the observed declines. With this caveat in mind, I offer the following description of the status of anurans in the New World tropics.

Representatives of at least seven families have declined in the New World tropics (Table 5.1). A relevant question is whether some families have been affected more

Figure 5.1. Male golden toad, *Bufo periglenes,* now believed to be extinct. (Photo by M. L. Crump)

than would be expected based on chance alone. For example, there are 162 species of bufonids in the New World tropics. With a 5% overall anuran decline, based on chance alone we would expect 8 species of bufonids to be declining. Reports reveal that at least 29 species are in decline. A χ^2 test for heterogeneity reveals that some families have been affected more than expected, based on their representation in the tropics ($\chi^2 = 63.0$, df $= 6$, $p < 0.001$; Figure 5.2). A comparable analysis of the 30 declining species from the New World North Temperate Zone (6 bufonids, 17 ranids, 4 hylids, 2 pelobatids, and 1 ascaphid) likewise reveals that some families have been more strongly affected than expected based on their representation ($\chi^2 = 17.9$, df $= 3$, p <0.001; Figure 5.2).

Most of the declines of tropical anurans that are not caused by habitat destruction have occurred at high elevations in relatively undisturbed areas (Lips and Donnelly 2002). Populations of leptodactylids, hylids, and bufonids in tropical cloud forests and other high-elevation forests in Costa Rica, Panama, and the Caribbean have drastically declined or disappeared (Joglar and Burrows 1996; Pounds et al. 1997; Lips 1998, 1999). In South America, most declines have occurred at high elevations in the Andes. For example, many *Atelopus* (Bufonidae) have declined from high elevations in the Andes of Venezuela (La Marca and Reinthaler 1991; La Marca and Lotters 1997). In Ecuador, populations of at least 26 species of anurans have declined or the species has disappeared entirely; most of these are from high elevations (Ron and Merino 2000).

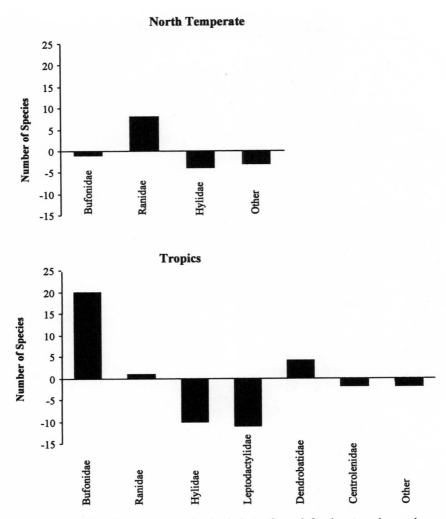

Figure 5.2. Number of species reported to be declining for each family, minus the number expected to be declining. Expected values come from a χ^2 test for heterogeneity, based on the overall rate of decline and the number of species per family in that region. Bars above the line indicate families that are declining more than expected; bars below the line indicate families that are declining less than expected. Other = the remaining families combined found in the region. In the North Temperate zone, six "other" declines were expected; the three observed declines are two Pelobatidae and one Ascaphidae. In the tropics, three "other" declines were expected; the one observed decline is one Microhylidae.

Table 5.1

Taxonomic distribution of declining anurans from the New World tropics

Family	Total No. Species[a]	No. Species Declining	Percentage Declining
Bufonidae	162	29	18
Centrolenidae	122	4	3
Dendrobatidae	179	13	7
Hylidae	553	19	3
Leptodactylidae	908	37	4
Microhylidae	42	1	2
Ranidae	33	3	9

[a]Totals add up to 1,999 species; the remaining 14 of the 2,013 species in the New World tropics belong to families not reported to be declining.

In general, tropical species have smaller distributional ranges than do temperate species (Arita et al. 1997). Many tropical amphibians are found only in one mountain range, in one watershed, or along one river. This high endemism in the tropics translates into considerable concern for the conservation of amphibians, because restricted species are more prone to extinction than are widespread ones (MacArthur and Wilson 1967). With fewer populations, a restricted species is less able to recolonize an area once local animals have gone extinct. Of 81 declining species for which I could categorize their geographic distribution, 69% have restricted distributions of less than 50,000 km^2 (Table 5.2).

ASSOCIATION OF DECLINES WITH NATURAL HISTORY CHARACTERISTICS

In contrast to the North Temperate Zone where 53% of the declining anurans are semiaquatic (mostly *Rana*), 59% of the tropical declining anurans are terrestrial and another 31% are arboreal; only 4% are semiaquatic, and 6% are aquatic (Table 5.2). This disparity reflects a basic difference between temperate and tropical species: a much larger percentage of tropical species are terrestrial or arboreal. Nonetheless, 61% of the tropical declining species are associated with running water. Most of these species use running water for breeding (see below), but some of the *Eleuthero-dactylus* are only found in riparian forest near streams.

A major difference between tropical and temperate anurans is their modes of reproduction and associated life history characteristics (Crump 1974). Most North Temperate anurans have aquatic eggs and tadpoles. Many tropical species have specialized ways of breeding that allow for independence of aquatic environments. In the tropics, many species have parental care or nonaquatic eggs whose embryos de-

Table 5.2

Characteristics of declining anurans of the New World tropics

Declining Characteristic	No. Species in Dataset[a]	No. Species Declining	Percentage Declining
Geographic distribution[b]	81		
Restricted		56	69
Widespread		25	31
Associated with running water	84		
Yes		51	61
No		33	39
Habitat	90		
Aquatic		5	6
Semiaquatic		4	4
Terrestrial		53	59
Arboreal		28	31
Development pattern	105		
Larval		78	74
Direct		27	26
Clutch size	82		
<50 eggs		44	54
50–200 eggs		5	6
201–1,000 eggs		29	35
>1,000 eggs		4	5
Site of egg deposition	99		
Running water		33	33
Still water		17	17
Land/vegetation		45	45
Bromeliad/tree hole		2	2
Ovoviviparous/female's pouch		2	2
Site of larval development	68		
Running water		43	63
Still water		18	26
Land		2	3
Bromeliad/tree hole		5	7

[a]Datasets are incomplete; a complete dataset would be 106 species.

[b]Restricted = occurs in an area less than 50,000 km²; all others are widespread.

velop into miniature froglets within the capsule without going through an aquatic larval stage (direct development). Most temperate species have large clutches of small eggs, whereas many tropical species have small clutches of large eggs. Is there any association between declining species in the tropics and their life history characteristics?

Whereas all of the North Temperate declining anurans have aquatic eggs and tadpoles, only 74% of the tropical declining species have larval development (Table 5.2).

Most North Temperate declining species have large clutches (>1,000 eggs). In contrast, many of the declining species in the tropics have either small clutches (<50 eggs) or medium to large clutches (201–1,000 eggs). Again, this reflects a basic difference between the faunas mentioned above. Many declining species are associated with running water, both in the North Temperate Zone and in the tropics. In the North Temperate Zone, more than half of the declining species deposit their eggs in running water, and the tadpoles develop there. In the tropics, many declining species deposit their eggs out of water, and then the larvae develop in running water. Many of these are hylids or centrolenids, which deposit their eggs on vegetation above streams, and the tadpoles develop in the water below. Others are *Colostethus*, which lay their eggs on land, and then a parent transports the tadpoles to a stream. Among the declining tropical frogs, a large contingent (mainly *Atelopus* and some hylid tree-frogs) deposit their eggs in running water and the larvae develop there. In the New World tropics, more than 60% of the declining species are associated with running water, and most of these occur at high elevations.

Using the literature and in some cases "best guesses" on my part, I tallied the total number of anuran species represented in the New World tropics for each of the three main reproductive modes: mode 1, eggs deposited in water, aquatic larvae (1,029 species); mode 2, eggs deposited out of water, aquatic larvae (413 species); mode 3, neither eggs nor free-swimming larvae in water (571 species). I then tallied the number of declining species for each mode of reproduction: mode 1, 52 declining species; mode 2, 21 declining species; and mode 3, 30 declining species. These numbers are almost identical to the expected values from a χ^2 test of heterogeneity, based on an overall rate of 5% decline ($\chi^2 = 0.033$, df = 2, not significant). Thus, it appears that declines are independent of mode of reproduction.

THREATS TO AMPHIBIANS IN THE NEW WORLD TROPICS

The threats to amphibians in the New World tropics are the same as the threats to temperate amphibians. These threats are the mechanisms (or causes) of declines and disappearances. The six main threats considered here are habitat loss and alteration, climatic factors, pathogens and disease, overexploitation, introduced species, and chemical contamination.

Habitat Loss and Alteration

Deforestation in the New World tropics is occurring at an alarming rate. The reasons include logging and mining operations, petroleum extraction, road construction, hydroelectric dams, agriculture and livestock grazing, and housing developments. In Central America and the Caribbean, Costa Rica, El Salvador, Haiti, and Jamaica are the countries with the highest percentages of remaining forest being cut down (World Resources Institute 2000). In fact, Jamaica's net annual rate of deforestation, 7.5%, is the highest in the world (World Resources Institute 2000). In South America, Bolivia, Ecuador, Paraguay, and Venezuela have the highest rates of deforestation (World Resources Institute 2000; Figure 5.3).

Habitat loss and alteration (degradation or modification) are probably the leading causes of amphibian declines in the tropics, as in the temperate zone (Pechmann and Wilbur 1994; Blaustein and Wake 1995). Hedges (1999) stated: "At the population level, virtually all West Indian amphibians presumably have declined substantially as a consequence of deforestation and the resulting loss of habitat." The percentage of amphibian species affected by habitat loss and alteration is no doubt less in Central and South America, but nonetheless substantial. Curiously, we lack quantitative data on the effect of habitat loss and alteration on amphibians.

Effects on the resident animals include more than simply loss of trees and leaf litter substrate. Habitat fragmentation may restrict movements of amphibians within their home ranges and ultimately reduce the potential for recolonization. When populations become isolated and when the number of individuals per population is reduced, potential for inbreeding is increased and demographic structure may change, leading to less successful reproduction. Furthermore, many species of amphibians have complex habitat requirements related to their complex life cycles. Species that are aquatic and terrestrial during different life history phases require a mosaic of

Figure 5.3. Swath bulldozed through rainforest in eastern Ecuador for a road leading to major oil fields. (Photo by M. L. Crump)

habitats and must migrate between suitable sites. Habitat fragmentation, whether by roads, agriculture, or housing developments, often makes this impossible.

Other devastating effects of deforestation are felt at the edge of the forest (Murcia 1995). These "edge effects" can penetrate hundreds of meters into the forest and exert influence on the converted land as well. Changes in predators, competitors, vegetation structure, and wind, moisture, and temperature conditions may alter habitat quality significantly. Direct-developing species such as plethodontid salamanders and *Eleutherodactylus* may be especially affected by habitat alteration because the increased insolation reduces availability of moist sites for egg deposition and subsequent development (Pearman 1997; Schlaepfer and Gavin 2001; personal observation).

Loss of a given area of habitat in the tropics may be more likely to result in population declines and species extinctions than in the temperate zones because many tropical species have restricted distributions. Loss of habitat may wipe out a substantial part of a population, making reproduction less successful and recolonization next to impossible. The same area loss in the temperate zone may be less disastrous because, in general, species have more widespread distributions (Arita et al. 1997).

Climatic Factors

Climate change and associated factors such as increased levels of ultraviolet B (UV-B) radiation and drought can affect tropical amphibians adversely. In general, montane regions in the New World tropics have experienced increasingly warmer temperatures and decreased cloud cover over the past two decades (Still et al. 1999; Middleton et al. 2001). Furthermore, the elevation at which freezing occurs in tropical mountains rose about 110 m from 1970 to the late 1980s, most likely related to increased tropical sea surface temperatures (Diaz and Graham 1996). What are the possible effects of global warming for amphibians?

Four aspects of predicted climate change may affect amphibians: increased temperature, increased length of the dry season, decreased soil moisture, and increased variability of rainfall among years (Donnelly and Crump 1998). The effects may be direct or indirect. The most drastic direct effect of increased temperatures and drought is death. Other direct effects may be changes in individual growth rates, reproductive output, life spans, breeding periodicity, activity patterns, and use of microhabitat. A major indirect effect is stress. Once an amphibian is stressed, it may be immunosuppressed and thus more susceptible to pathogens and disease. Warmer and drier climatic conditions may provide more optimal habitat for pathogens or may increase vulnerability of amphibians to these pathogens (Carey et al. 1999, 2001). Another effect of climate change is that population densities of invertebrate prey may be reduced. All of the preceding effects work on the individual level, but populations will be affected because of changes in birth, death, immigration, and emigration rates. Ultimately, changes in the dynamics of populations will have repercussions at the community and ecosystem levels.

A prolonged drought in the Monteverde region of Costa Rica's Cordillera de Tilarán may be partly responsible for the disappearance of golden toads (*Bufo periglenes*) and harlequin frogs (*Atelopus varius*) (Crump et al. 1992; Pounds and Crump 1994). Eighteen other species (for a total of 20 of 50 species of anurans present in the area) declined or disappeared from the area beginning in 1987 (Pounds et al. 1997). Analyses of rainfall and temperature patterns suggest that these amphibian population crashes, as well as reductions in the populations and changes in distribution patterns of some birds and reptiles, are associated with patterns and amount of mist during the dry season (Pounds et al. 1999). Atmospheric warming associated with rising sea surface temperatures over the past two decades has raised the level of the cloud base, resulting in less mist in the cloud forest surrounding Monteverde (Still et al. 1999).

Another aspect of climate change that may affect amphibians is increased levels of UV-B radiation reaching the earth's surface. Many tropical anurans lay their eggs in shallow water where embryonic stages and tadpoles may be exposed to harmful rays. In paramo and other high montane regions, many species are diurnal and spend much of the day exposed to sunlight. In the high Andes of Ecuador, the species that have disappeared generally are those that lay their eggs in water (*Atelopus*, *Colostethus*). In contrast, those that do not lay their eggs in water (e.g., *Eleutherodactylus*, which lays terrestrial eggs protected under leaf litter or other cover; and *Gastrotheca*, which broods eggs in dorsal pouches) have not disappeared. Have levels of UV-B radiation increased in the New World tropics? Middleton et al. (2001) found significant increases in UV-B radiation at all 11 sites in Central America examined, and smaller but still significant increases at five of nine sites in South America; the other four sites in South America were at lower elevations. Although the correlation exists, it is too early to conclude that exposure to increased UV-B radiation is the direct cause for tropical amphibian population declines.

Pathogens and Disease

Pathogens and disease have been identified as mechanisms of amphibian declines in the New World tropics, the best known being a chytrid fungus belonging to the genus *Batrachochytrium*. To date, it is thought to be responsible for declines of frogs in Puerto Rico, Costa Rica, Panama, and Ecuador (Berger et al. 1998; Carey et al. 1999; Lips 1999). It has affected frogs primarily at elevations above 500 m, and its known targets have included *Atelopus* and *Bufo* (Bufonidae), *Cochranella* (Centrolenidae), *Gastrotheca* (Hylidae), and *Eleutherodactylus* and *Telmatobius* (Leptodactylidae). This pathogen could have devastating effects on the amphibian fauna of the New World tropics. Duellman (2001) predicted that even if the chytrid infestations are restricted to frogs living at elevations above 500 m, approximately 85% of the Middle American species of treefrogs (Hylidae) could be affected. A possible 91 species could disappear, as well as most populations of an additional 25 species.

Overexploitation

Frogs are collected for the zoo and pet trade, for human consumption, for folk remedies, and for biological study. Although frogs are thought to be declining from overcollection in many areas in the New World tropics, we lack quantitative data. In Michoacán, Mexico, the Patzcuaro frog (*Rana dunni*), a large endemic frog, is declining due to commercial harvesting (Díaz 1999). Anecdotal reports suggest that *Telmatobius* has declined from areas in Peru and Bolivia because of extensive collecting for human consumption. Scientists often argue that what they remove from the wild is miniscule compared to collection for the pet trade or for food. In fact, many argue that no species of amphibian is known to be threatened by scientific collecting efforts (e.g., Duellman 1999b). Although it is likely true that scientific collecting is responsible for a very small fraction of amphibians removed from the wild, we all need to be more cautious than ever not to put additional stress on wild populations.

Introduced Species

Introduced invasive species, especially trout and American bullfrogs (*Rana catesbeiana*), have likely caused amphibian declines in the tropics. Introduced trout may be responsible for anuran declines in Central America and along the Andes mountains in South America, for example affecting *Atelopus* in Venezuela (La Marca and Reinthaler 1991). In some cases these invasive species act as direct predators on amphibians, in other instances they are competitors. As humans invade the forest, they often bring their domesticated animals with them. Pigs and goats further destroy the habitat, and some, such as cats, are predators on amphibians. In the West Indies, introduced predators such as mongoose, feral cats, and black rats may be responsible for anuran population declines, even in undisturbed forest (Hedges, 1993, 1999). Introduced cane toads (*Bufo marinus*) and American bullfrogs may have a negative impact in that region as well.

Another potential problem with introduced species is that they may carry diseases. For example, the chytrid fungus has been identified from bullfrogs raised on a frog farm in Uruguay. If any of those infected animals escape into the wild, apparently a common occurrence on frog farms, native frogs may soon be affected.

Chemical Contamination

Agrochemicals, including fertilizers and pesticides, are used extensively in the tropics (Castillo et al. 1997). Many pollutants are airborne, carried long distances by wind currents or deposited as acid rain or fog (Eklund et al. 1997). Others, such as those from mining operations, are dumped directly into streams where they render the water toxic for amphibian eggs. Likewise, toxic chemicals from pesticides and fertilizers become concentrated in runoff from agricultural fields and end up in roadside ditches where amphibians breed. Unfortunately, there is little regulation of potential environmental contaminants in the New World tropics.

Chemical contamination has likely taken a large toll on tropical amphibians. Chemicals may damage amphibians' delicate skin, which is critical in gas exchange. Chemicals may kill directly, or they may exert indirect effects such as increasing amphibians' susceptibility to pathogens. Even the most "pristine" areas are not immune to contaminants. Consider the following examples. The Caribbean region, Central America, and northern South America receive large quantities of contaminants from Africa (Stallard 2001). Extensive fires in Africa and South America from the burning of vegetation as part of deforestation efforts send out bioactive gases that contaminate the Neotropics (Stallard 2001). Widespread and indiscriminate use of insecticides to eradicate the Mediterranean fruit fly and help control the Africanized honey bee in Central America have probably been detrimental to amphibians (Campbell 1999). Direct-developing *Eleutherodactylus* are becoming scarce in coffee fincas in El Salvador, likely because of increasing use of pesticides (M. Santana, Northern Arizona University, personal communication).

Different Reactions to Changes

Although the threats to amphibians are the same as those operating in the temperate zone, I suspect that amphibians in the tropics may react differently to some of these threats. Depending on the threat, tropical amphibians may be more or less vulnerable. For example, two consequences of habitat alteration may be that amphibians are more exposed to the wind and sun, increasing vulnerability to desiccation, and breeding sites are lost. Tropical species might be affected more by a given level of disturbance for two reasons. First, because tropical species are normally exposed to a narrower range of moisture and temperature conditions, their tolerance levels may be narrower and they may be less able to acclimate to change caused by habitat alteration (Feder 1978). Second, tropical species might be less able to cope with sudden loss of ponds, swamps, and water-filled ditches because most species breed at local sites rather than migrating long distances in search of breeding sites (personal observation).

POTENTIAL SOLUTIONS

Conservation issues and solutions for the tropics often differ from those in temperate areas (Janzen 1994; Lips and Donnelly 2002). Part of the difference is that the tropics house more total species, more geographically restricted species, and more rare species. Beyond that, I see four major challenges to conservation efforts for tropical amphibians. One challenge is the widespread apathy of local people regarding these animals. Admittedly, many people in temperate areas do not care about amphibians, but in my experience the level of apathy is worse in the tropics. Another challenge is biologists' ignorance of the basic natural history, distribution patterns, and population status of tropical amphibians, as discussed in this chapter. A third challenge is that to preserve amphibians, we must protect habitat in the face of ever-increasing demands on the environment by growing human populations burdened by poverty. A fourth challenge is the general lack of funds available in developing countries in the New World tropics for conservation efforts.

Potential solutions for the conservation of tropical amphibians fall under three themes: education, research, and habitat protection. To accomplish effective conservation, we need to encourage collaboration and communication among biologists (Young et al. 2001). Ultimately, we must search for conservation solutions that can be implemented fairly easily and with modest or low-level funding.

Education

Because one of the most critical challenges to conservation of tropical amphibians is public apathy, we need to increase local awareness of these animals. An effective vehicle would be an international conference in Latin America sponsored by a prominent nongovernmental organization such as the World Wildlife Fund, Conservation International, or the Wildlife Conservation Society. Delegates from each country in the New World tropics would be invited: scientists, natural resources managers, politicians, teachers, anyone interested in conservation of amphibians. Focusing on sharing critical problems and potential solutions, the conference would heighten concern for amphibians and the ecological impacts of human activities on the habitats of these animals. Such an initiative would help break down the barrier of isolation that is so deeply felt by Latin American countries, and would provide an opportunity to learn from each other.

Perhaps such a conference is "pie-in-the-sky." Realistically, most of us must work on a more local level. Regardless of the scale, for a conservation program to be effective, it must integrate the needs of the local people with habitat and species protection. Just because the conservation biologist believes that protection is the "right" thing to do does not mean that his or her wishes will be carried out. Lectures do not work; collaboration does. First and foremost, the conservation biologist must establish rapport with the community of people on whose land the conservation concern exists. An ideal way of doing this is by offering a community-wide workshop for sharing ideas about the conservation concern and the fate of the landscape (Feinsinger 2001; personal observation). By becoming involved first-hand, community leaders, local politicians, and members of regulatory and planning boards are more likely to become strong advocates. Acting as a facilitator, the biologist can increase awareness among the local people of the need for conservation efforts by emphasizing the importance of amphibians in the ecosystem. The biologist can provide background concerning the nature and extent of declining populations of amphibians. By encouraging the participants to express the hope that their landscape will remain intact for their children and grandchildren, the biologist can stress respect for the environment and protection of resources needed by amphibians.

Once local people understand the significance of the conservation effort, collaboration can begin. Through additional workshops, community members can be taught the basic natural history of amphibians, how to identify species, and surveying and monitoring techniques (see Heyer et al. 1994; Lips et al. 2001 for techniques applicable for monitoring studies in the tropics). In my experience, these "parabiologists" become indispensable assistants, spreading the word about the value of amphibians to others in the community. Some carry out their own long-term monitoring studies and provide valuable information on the status of populations. Community members may initiate their own projects, such as digging breeding sites where former ponds have been destroyed, or helping migrating animals cross roads. Once locals see that they can make a difference, they will.

Research

To conserve amphibians, we must expand research efforts, ideally through international collaboration between researchers from Europe and North America and those from Latin America. We need to better understand patterns of geographic distribution, population demography, and annual fluctuations in population density, habitat use, feeding ecology, and reproductive behavior and life history patterns. We also need to increase monitoring efforts to determine the status of species and the causes of population declines. We need laboratory experimental research designed to investigate physiological tolerances and the effects of drought on pathogens such as the chytrid fungus and on amphibian immune defenses (Carey et al. 2001).

As indicated earlier, we know very little about the impact of collecting on populations of tropical amphibians. If research suggests that populations are being negatively affected by collecting activities, those species should be considered for national protection and CITES regulation. The decision must be made by weighing all of the alternatives, however, because regulations sometimes impede our ability to better understand the animals. Campbell (1999) expressed this dilemma as follows: "Of what possible consequence is it to protect species of tropical amphibians, of which we know very little of their ecology or population characteristics, from a handful of scientists that might want to study them, when they receive no protection from the lay human population within the country?" Most conservation biologists argue that we need voucher specimens to document biodiversity, because without documentation, we will be left with questions and uncertainties.

Habitat Protection

Conservation of tropical amphibians cannot be effected without extensive habitat protection. Rates of habitat destruction need to be drastically reduced. More land needs to be preserved, and we need to better protect these areas. Watersheds are especially critical areas for preservation. We need to stress preservation of ecosystems, both aquatic and terrestrial, over protection of local populations of individual species. Buffer zones need to be established around protected areas. We must ensure that appropriate habitat exists for animals to migrate between protected areas for recolonization to be possible. Finally, wherever possible, critical habitats need to be restored.

As of 1992, about 5.5% of the land area in South America was protected in the form of biosphere reserves, national parks and reserves, and national and private ecological reserves (Barzetti 1993). We need more protected areas in the Andes where species richness and endemism is especially high. Duellman (1999a) argued that because many amphibians at high elevations have restricted distributions, for protection of the greatest number of amphibians in montane regions, we need more small protected areas rather than a few large ones. On the other hand, protection of widespread species at lower elevations may require preservation of large areas to maintain metapopulations.

So, how does one argue for more protected land when land is so crucial for the well-being of humans in the tropics? First, conservation biologists must advocate balance between preservation of land and economic development. That said, ethically if a conservation biologist sets out to advise local people not to destroy their land, he or she must suggest (and help implement) alternative sources of income. Habitat preservation must be of economic value to locals for it to work. We must educate—in a nonthreatening way—policy makers and government officials of the importance of amphibian conservation within the wider framework of ecosystem preservation. But we also need to focus considerable effort at the local level, because the locals are the ones who take pride in their landscape.

CONCLUSIONS

As the highest diversity region in the world for amphibians, the New World tropics deserve more conservation effort than they currently receive. Populations of many species are declining in high-elevation areas, and undoubtedly many species are strongly affected by deforestation and habitat alteration in the lowlands. Declines appear to be independent of mode of reproduction. Many species affected are associated with streams or have terrestrial, direct-developing eggs, suggesting that whatever the cause, it is affecting ecologically diverse amphibians. Only by involving local people can we hope to conserve tropical amphibians. We need to expand collaborative efforts with Latin Americans in the areas of education, research, and habitat protection.

When I think about the outbreaks of chytrid fungus, and the demands on the land by ever-increasing human populations just striving to survive, I am pessimistic about the future of tropical amphibians. But when I think about the highly motivated and dedicated young conservation biologists now active in their native countries, I become optimistic.

ACKNOWLEDGMENTS
I thank Ray Semlitsch and two anonymous reviewers for helpful comments and suggestions on the manuscript.

6

CONSERVATION OF AMPHIBIANS IN THE OLD WORLD TROPICS

Defining Unique Problems Associated with Regional Fauna

JEAN-MARC HERO AND LUKE P. SHOO

The Old World region (the world excluding the Americas) includes a diverse array of amphibian faunas, zoogeographic regions, biogeographic histories, varied times of human occupation, and anthropogenic threats. The Old and New World regions have similar familial diversity (27 families each), with more endemic lineages of Anura (18 families, 12 endemic) in the Old World balanced by more endemic lineages of Caudata (9 salamander families, 5 endemic) in the New World (Duellman 1999b). Caecilians are evenly distributed with 4 families (3 endemic) in the Old World and 3 families (2 endemic) in the New World (Duellman 1999b). Higher generic diversity (58% of amphibian genera) is found in the Old World (Duellman 1999b). Species diversity in the Old and New Worlds is roughly equal for Anura, whereas species diversity of Gymnophiona and Caudata is lower in the Old World (Duellman 1999b). Higher species diversity in the New World is attributable to large radiations within the leptodactylids (mostly within the genus *Eleutherodactylus*), centrolenids, dendrobatids, and plethodontids. Although six anuran, four caudate, and one gymnophionan families are shared by both the Old and New Worlds, only three have greater species diversity in the Old World: Microhylidae, Ranidae, and Salamandridae. The most specious families in the Old World include the Ranidae (575 spp.), Microhylidae (276 spp.), Rhacophoridae (223 spp. plus 200 recently discovered in Sri Lanka), Hyperoliidae (210 spp.), Hylidae (161 spp.), and Myobatrachidae (122 spp.) (Pethiyagoda and Manamendra-Arachchi 1998; Duellman 1999b).

Amphibian biodiversity and threats to biodiversity are not uniformly distributed over latitudinal and altitudinal gradients. Biodiversity is concentrated in tropical lowlands, where habitat is fast disappearing through broad-scale developmental projects involving wide-scale deforestation for agricultural and infrastructure developments (e.g., dam construction). Amphibian biodiversity is further threatened by unexplained declines in intact forest areas, predominantly at high altitudes (Richards et al. 1994; Campbell 1999). Suggested causes of these declines include synergistic effects of emerging infectious disease, changing weather patterns, and increased ultraviolet radiation (Campbell 1999; Pounds 2001). Temperate regions are well studied and have relatively low diversity. Because most habitats have been greatly modified, conservation action is focused on the restoration and rehabilitation of amphibian habitats. The distribution of research and resources does not appear to correspond to the distribution of biodiversity and threats.

In this chapter, we examine the distribution of amphibian biodiversity in the Old World, the immediate anthropogenic threats of deforestation and large-scale developments, and the role of protected areas in amphibian conservation. We also examine the unexplained amphibian declines recorded in high-altitude populations where no direct anthropogenic influences are evident. Then we discuss the distribution of research and resources to address the issues of biodiversity loss. Although many of the problems (and solutions) are not unique to amphibians or to the Old World, these issues are discussed from an Old World perspective.

Solutions at the regional scale include identifying and protecting species-rich habitats and geographically restricted species, monitoring and mitigating habitat loss within countries, and identifying and monitoring amphibian species susceptible to extinction (threatened species and stream-breeding amphibians at higher altitudes). Scientists and government and nongovernmental agencies must collaborate globally to improve research training and provide resources for developing countries. Integrated catchment management will ensure the integrity of individual watersheds that are providing protection at local and regional scales, while multinational collaboration and scientific communication play an important role in finding solutions for the effective management and conservation of amphibians at national and international levels.

CENTRAL ISSUES

Amphibian Biodiversity, Habitat Loss, and Protected Areas

Biodiversity hotspots (defined as exceptional concentrations of species or endemism or both) that are undergoing exceptional habitat loss or are poorly protected are a useful tool for setting priorities for conservation and management (Mittermeier et al. 1998; Myers et al. 2000). In this section, we examine areas of high amphibian biodiversity and the extent of habitat loss and habitat protection within them. Duellman (1999b) identified 43 areas of the world as having significantly high amphibian species richness, high endemism, or both. Six additional amphibian biodiversity hot-spots (areas with more than 50 species, more than 30 endemic species, or both) are identified (the Congo basin, Sri Lanka, the Philippines, Sulawesi and Lesser Sunda Islands, Brazil's Cerrado, and the central Amazon basin) for a total of 49 (Figure 6.1a). High species richness and endemism in the Old World are associated with large island and montane habitats (Duellman 1999b). Within biogeographic regions, amphibian diversity is broadly associated with broken topography (montane regions separated

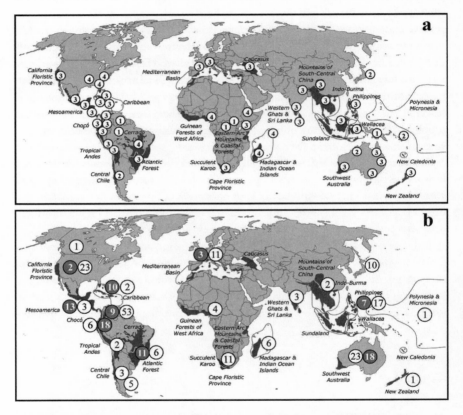

Figure 6.1. Amphibian biodiversity and conservation in the Old and New worlds. (a) Amphibian biodiversity hotspots. Each circle represents a region of significant species richness and/or endemism (modified from Duellman 1999b). Numbers represent conservation priority as follows: 1 = poorly protected major wilderness areas; 2 = poorly protected forested areas; 3 = well protected, heavily deforested areas; and 4 = poorly protected heavily deforested areas. (b) Threatened amphibians. Dark circles = number of species Extinct, Missing, or Critically Endangered. White circles = number of species listed as Endangered or Vulnerable (IUCN 2000; AmphibiaWeb, Watch List 2002; Hero 2001). Background map of biodiversity hotspots (dark-shaded areas) reprinted with permission from Conservation International, see Myers et al. 2000).

by lowlands and islands separated by oceans), altitudinal gradients, climate (principally rainfall), and vegetation associations (Inger 1999; Poynton 1999; Tyler 1999).

Latitudinal Gradients in Species Richness and Endemism   Amphibian biodiversity in the Old and New Worlds is concentrated in a number of hotspots (Figure 6.1a). Most hotspots are in the tropics (37), and the remainder (11) are in subtropical areas. These hotspots generally overlap with the 25 biodiversity hotspots for endemic plants and vertebrates identified by Myers et al. (2000), although 14 sites with high amphibian diversity do not. Three areas of high amphibian biodiversity (New Guinea, the Congolian Forest, and parts of Amazonia) have been identified as "major wilderness areas" (Myers et al. 2000), but are included here as hotspots because protection is low (<25% of remaining forest protected).

About 80% of the amphibian species in the Old World (more than 1,700 of 2,213 species in Duellman 1999b) occur in 13 of these hotspots, including Sundaland, Madagascar, Indo-Burma, the Philippines, south-central China, West African forests, Western Ghats of India, Sri Lanka, Wallacea, Eastern Arc and coastal forests of Tanzania and Kenya, the Congo, New Guinea, and northeastern Australia.

Altitudinal Gradients in Species Richness and Endemism   Examination of available data on species richness along altitudinal gradients in Borneo, Cameroon, Australia, Ecuador, and the West Indies (Figure 6.2a) shows that amphibian diversity is strongly mediated by altitude, with species richness generally highest at low altitudes (100–1,000 m) and decreasing with increasing altitude in montane areas (>1,000 m). The observation that higher altitudes support fewer species than low altitudes is broadly consistent with general patterns reported elsewhere for vertebrates (Rahbek 1995). These patterns of species distribution highlight the importance of protecting remaining lowland areas to maximize the conservation of amphibian species richness. Although species richness is highest at low altitudes (<1,000 m), it is important to consider species composition. Endemism may be higher at high altitudes (Figure 6.2b) and thus protection of high-altitude endemics is also important to conserve overall species diversity.

Habitat Loss   Deforestation rates documented to define global biodiversity hotspots are from Myers et al. (2000) and deforestation rates compiled by the UNEP World Conservation Monitoring Center (2001). Perhaps the most striking difference between Old and New World areas is the higher proportion of original forest remaining and of forest in protected areas in the New World. In most regions of the Old World, either less than 25% of the original forest remains or less than 25% of the remaining forest is protected, or both. It should also be noted that the major wilderness areas of New Guinea and the Congo fall within the "hotspot" definition because of the low level of remaining forest protection (10.8% and 6.5%, respectively).

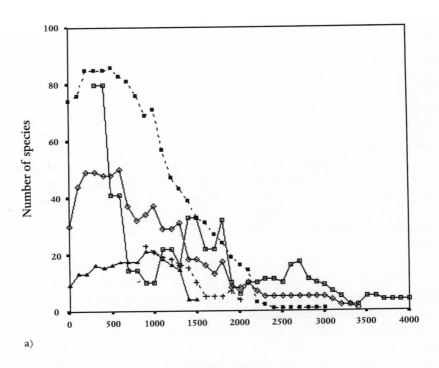

a)

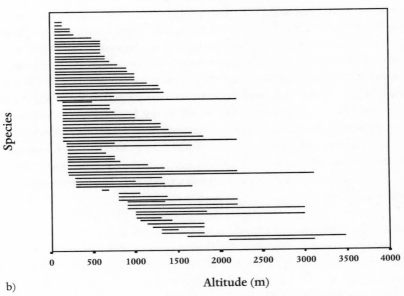

b)

Figure 6.2. Altitudinal gradients in amphibian biodiversity. (a) Altitudinal gradient in species richness of amphibian fauna of northwestern Borneo (open diamonds, Inger and Stuebing 1992), Cameroon (cross, Hofer et al. 1999), northeast Australia (closed triangles, McDonald 1992), Equador (open square, Duellman 1978, 1979), and West Indies (closed square, Hedges 1999). (b) Altitudinal distributions of 71 frog species from Borneo (Inger and Stuebing 1992).

It cannot be overstated that habitat loss is the principal threat to biodiversity, and that halting deforestation is the greatest challenge for conservation biologists in the twenty-first century. Humans currently appropriate more than a third of the production of terrestrial ecosystems and about half of the usable fresh waters on earth (Tilman et al. 2001), causing extensive habitat degradation and fragmentation. Land alteration for agriculture is a major cause of global habitat destruction and fragmentation (Laurance 2001; Tilman et al. 2001). Deforestation for agriculture is projected to rise sharply over the next 50 years, with approximately one billion hectares of natural forest to be converted to agriculture, including more than a third of remaining tropical and temperate forests, savannas, and grasslands (Laurance 2001; Tilman et al. 2001). Loss of habitat and fragmentation is also associated with major forestry concessions and large-scale developments (e.g., an estimated 60% of the world's large river basins are highly or moderately fragmented by dams; World Commission on Dams 2000).

Extensive deforestation is continuing in both developed and developing countries throughout the tropical regions of the world. It is extremely difficult to halt because the development of agriculture and infrastructure is seen as the first crucial step toward economic development and the reduction of poverty and food insecurity (Alexandratos 1999). Coastal lowlands are particularly vulnerable because of the concentration of human activities (i.e., direct threats of urban development and intensive agriculture). Subsequent changes in species composition result in biotic homogenization: forest-adapted species are replaced by a small number of species that thrive in human-altered habitats (McKinney and Lockwood 1999).

Although the relationship between altitude and habitat loss has not been examined on a global scale, extensive clearing is generally more widespread in lowland tropical areas, although clearing in upland areas is also continuing. A study in Southeast Asia indicates that lowland forests have been cleared extensively, whereas montane forests are less affected (Brooks et al. 1999). These estimates of deforestation indicate that 75% of montane forest (above 1,000 m) remained, compared with only 49% of the lowland forest. Extensive deforestation and fragmentation of lowland tropical forests has occurred throughout the Old World tropics. Similar threats are expected in the remaining biodiversity hotspots (especially the two "wilderness areas" of New Guinea and the Congo).

Protected Areas   Most Old World countries have established conservation areas that afford varying levels of protection. Few areas have adequate protection of existing forests, except for some regions where the small amount of original forest remaining (<11%) is largely incorporated in protected areas (e.g., Indo Burma, southwestern Australia, Sri Lanka, and Kenya). Areas of major concern in the Old World (<25% of remaining forests protected) include Madagascar, West African forests, East Africa, Japan, Congo, Ethiopia, India, Sri Lanka, Indo-Burma, China, Sundaland, Papua New

Guinea, the Solomon Islands, and Australia. Hotspots can be grouped into four categories (Figure 6.1a) depending on the degree of habitat loss and level of protection of remaining forest as follows:

- Poorly protected major wilderness areas ($>$100,000 km^2) where more than 60% of original forest remains, of which less than 25% is protected (Congo, West Papua, and Papua New Guinea).
- Poorly protected forested areas where more than 25% of original forest remains, of which less than 25% is protected (Japan, Australia).
- Well-protected, heavily deforested areas where less than 25% of original forest remains, of which more than 25% is protected (Mediterranean basin, Eastern Arc of Tanzania and Kenya, Cape region of South Africa, Indo-Burma, Malaysia, Philippines, Sundaland including Borneo, Wallacea including Sulawesi and the Molucca Islands, southwestern Australia, south-central China, Western Ghats, Sri Lanka, and New Zealand).
- Poorly protected, heavily deforested areas where less than 25% of original forest remains, of which less than 25% is protected (Madagascar, West African forests, Ethiopian highlands).

Within hotspots, the degree to which protected areas afford conservation to amphibians is dependent on whether representative habitats and breeding sites are incorporated. Common widespread (nonthreatened) frog species are habitat generalists found in either closed wet forests (e.g., rainforest) or in open habitats (e.g., open forests, savanna and desert areas), or both, and have extensive geographic ranges. In contrast, most threatened amphibian species are regional endemics, restricted to specific vegetation types (e.g., rainforest, heath, or montane habitats) that are associated with altitudinal and climatic gradients (Williams and Hero 1998, 2001). Species that are habitat specialists produce most of the regional variability in frog diversity (Williams and Hero 2001), and their protection is pivotal for conservation of regional biodiversity. For example, threatened frog species in Australia are habitat specialists (Table 6.1) that can be broadly classified into three groups: wet forest, stream-breeding species from upland areas (above 300 m); isolated wetland species (e.g., species associated with coastal heath vegetation); and species restricted to montane habitats (above 1,000 m).

Specific attention to the protection of amphibian breeding habitats is lacking, although amphibian breeding sites are included incidentally in larger protected areas. The larval stages of most amphibian species are adapted to and often use only one of four generalized breeding habitats: (1) terrestrial habitats with either direct development within the leaf litter or aquatic development in arboreal tree hollows and pitcher plants (note this group is generally dependent on wet forest types, i.e., rainforest endemics), (2) permanent swamps and ponds, (3) semipermanent or ephemeral ponds and swamps, and (4) stream and riparian habitats. Species distributions are

Table 6.1

Breeding habitats and potential threats to listed Australian amphibians (data from Hero 2001)

IUCN-GAA[a] Categories	No. of Species	Breeding Habitat[b]			No. of Species Linked to Potential Cause of Decline					
		WS	IW	M	Restricted Geographic Range[c]	Habitat Modification	Introduced Fish Species	Emerging Diseases	Global Change	Unknown
Extinct	3	3	—	—	3	—	—	—	—	3
Critically endangered	14	8	2	4	6	3	3	4	2	12
Endangered	8	6	2	—	1	3	1	7	—	5
Vulnerable	15	2	9	4	7	8	—	3	—	1
Near threatened	4	3	1	—	1	2	—	1	—	1
Total	44	22	14	8	18	16	4	15	2	22

Note: Some species are recorded as having several potential threats.

[a]IUCN = International Union for the Conservation of Nature, Global Amphibian Assessment.

[b]Breeding habitats: WS = wet forest stream, IW = isolated wetland, M = montane.

[c]Range of less than 1,500 km^2.

strongly influenced by the presence or absence of fish and invertebrate predators, and few species will breed in more than two of these habitat types (Hero et al. 1998, 2001). Common (nonthreatened), widespread species will sometimes use three of these breeding habitats (e.g., cane toad larvae are found in breeding habitats 2, 3, and 4; Evans et al. 1996), whereas threatened species usually breed in only one of these habitats.

Protection of freshwater biodiversity has been neglected in favor of protecting terrestrial environments that sustain the more charismatic taxa such as mammals and birds (Kottelat and Whitten 1996). Wetland conservation efforts (i.e., Ramsar Convention) have focused on "major" or extensive wetland areas at the expense of smaller ephemeral wetlands (Kottelat and Whitten 1996; Semlitsch and Bodie 1998; Snodgrass et al. 2000). Most large wetlands typically support hardy amphibian species that are of little conservation interest (with the notable exception of species limited to patches of heath vegetation in the Cape Region of South Africa, southwestern Australia, and coastal eastern Australia). Threatened frog species tend to breed in small ephemeral ponds and wetlands (that are often too small to be identified as important in legislation; Semlitsch and Bodie 1998; Snodgrass et al. 2000), or in streams and associated habitats, or are restricted to montane habitats above 1,000 m (see Table 6.1).

Unexplained Amphibian Declines and Declines Associated with Disease

Amphibian declines in the New World have received considerable attention (Kiesecker et al. 2001a; Pounds 2001) but few amphibian extinctions or declines have been reported in the Old World tropics (Inger 1999; Poynton 1999), with the notable exception of widespread declines in eastern Australia (Campbell 1999, Alford and Richards 1999) and Spain (Bosch et al. 2001). In Australia, 8 species have mysteriously disappeared (despite active searching) and a further 14 species have declined for unknown reasons (Campbell 1999; Hero 2001).

In recent years, amphibian populations have declined and disappeared suddenly from relatively undisturbed, high-altitude areas throughout the world (Richards et al. 1994; Alford and Richards 1999; Pounds 2001). The cause of these declines has been the subject of conjecture. In 1998 a chytrid fungus (*Batrachochytrium dendrobatidis*) was found to have lethal effects on amphibians (Berger et al. 1998) and was proposed as the potential cause for the unexplained amphibian declines in northern Australia and Central America. Since 1998, several massive die-offs have been associated with the disease in Central America (Lips 1999), Spain (Bosch et al. 2001), and North America (Carey 2000). Chytrid fungus has now been located in a number of countries throughout the world (Speare and Berger 2000b). In the Old World, massive die-offs associated with the chytrid fungus have been observed in Australia and New Zealand (Berger et al. 1998; Speare and Berger 2000b). In Europe (principally Germany) the chytrid fungus has been found in captive populations of 15 species of Anura and 4 species of salamander (Speare and Berger 2000b), but the first outbreak of chytridiomycosis in wild populations of the common midwife toad (*Alytes obstet-ricans*) was only recently reported from Spain (Bosch et al. 2001). Chytridiomycosis has been reported in Kenya and captive populations from South Africa, although amphibian population declines have not been reported there. There have been no reports of chytridiomycosis from Asia.

In Australia, chytridiomycosis has been documented in 46 frog species (more than 20% of Australian species; Speare and Berger 2000a), 15 of which are currently listed as threatened (Table 6.1; Hero 2001). Twelve of these species are either extinct or on the verge of extinction, having suffered dramatic population declines throughout their range (Hero 2001). These data demonstrate that many species have been exposed to chytrid fungus, which is now known to be geographically and altitudinally widespread throughout Australia (Speare and Berger 2000b). A current investigation of unexplained frog declines at high altitude areas of eastern Australia (above 300 m) has established that species most susceptible to decline have an aquatic stage in the life cycle, small numbers of ovarian eggs, and restricted geographic ranges (approximately the extent of occurrence; Williams and Hero 1998; J.-M. Hero, S. Williams, and W. Magnusson, Griffith University, Australia, unpublished data).

The chytrid fungus is now recognized as an emerging infectious disease and a direct or proximate cause of deaths associated with population declines (Berger et al. 1998; Daszak et al. 1999). However, it is not yet clear whether the chytridiomycosis outbreaks are the result of either an epidemic associated with a novel introduced pathogen or the increased prevalence of an existing pathogen (Berger et al. 1998; Daszak et al. 2000), but both may be associated with a weakening of amphibian immune systems (Berger et al. 1998; Carey 2000). Other die-offs have been associated with the fungus *Basidiobolus ranarum* (the bacteria associated with "red leg" disease) and *Ranavirus*, but the declines associated with the chytrid fungus in relatively undisturbed habitats appear unprecedented in recent history (Carey 2000).

Changes in the global environment have been proposed as the ultimate or indirect cause of the disease outbreaks (Kiesecker et al. 2001a; Pounds 2001). Determining the links between the chytrid disease as a direct or proximate cause and environmental change as an indirect or ultimate cause of population declines poses a substantial problem that is perhaps one of the most important issues associated with the conservation of amphibians throughout the world.

Distribution of Research and Resources

Amphibian conservation is currently monitored internationally by the Declining Amphibian Population Task Force (DAPTF) and the Species Survival Commission of the International Union for the Conservation of Nature (IUCN). The IUCN Global Amphibian Assessment process lists threatened species as vulnerable, endangered, critically endangered, or extinct. Despite the range of serious threats to amphibians, only 95 Old World amphibian species are currently recognized by the IUCN as threatened (<5% of all amphibian species, Figure 6.1b). Most of these are listed in Australia (26%), the Philippines (23%), the Mediterranean (14%), Japan (10.5%), South Africa (10%), and Madagascar (6%) (Hilton-Taylor 2000).

Poorly protected regions with high biodiversity (such as the Sundaland, south-central China, West African forests, Congo, New Guinea, Sulawesi, and Sri Lanka) have few if any species listed as threatened. This situation is likely to change with improved knowledge of population trends and diversity of amphibian species in tropical areas. In recognition of this shortfall, the IUCN initiated a Global Amphibian Assessment, beginning in 2001, to update national listings.

Most amphibian research has been conducted in developed countries with relatively low biodiversity and where large-scale habitat loss has occurred (e.g., Australia, Europe, and the United States). In contrast, limited research is executed in developing countries in tropical regions (Sodhi and Liow 2000) that contain the bulk of amphibian biodiversity. Clearly, research and resources do not correspond to biodiversity and the level of threat, and there is an urgent need for expanding current research and resources for conservation in tropical areas of the Old World.

POTENTIAL SOLUTIONS

Amphibian Biodiversity and Habitat Loss

Large-scale extinction of amphibian species is expected to occur in most regions as a result of habitat loss, which emphasizes the urgent need to halt habitat loss and, wherever possible, to expand or establish new protected areas. Management and conservation agencies should explore causes of deforestation (e.g., poverty and traditional land-use practices, broad-scale agricultural initiatives, changes in technology, large-scale forestry concessions, and large-scale development projects) and impediments to establishing and adequately managing protected areas. Independent international scientific committees should closely monitor the environmental impacts of developments and establish programs to promote more ecologically sustainable agriculture, water supply, and power, including regionally appropriate education, incentives, and legal restrictions (Tilman et al. 2001).

Amphibian Biodiversity and Protected Areas

Catchments rather than political boundaries should govern the selection and management of protected areas. The catchment is the smallest natural unit of the landscape that combines terrestrial and aquatic ecosystems (Hornung and Reynolds 1995) and is the basic unit for management on any scale in most terrestrial biomes (Magnusson 2001). Integrated catchment management provides for protection of water quality and connectivity of habitat patches within and between watersheds. This is achieved by establishing protected areas in the upper catchments of watersheds (first- to third-order streams; Strahler 1957) and protecting riparian zones along larger, higher-order streams. Many local communities include catchment management as part of traditional ecological knowledge (Berkes et al. 2000; Das 2001). Conservation of watersheds by local communities is enhanced through effective management of regional and national river systems. Movement and translocation of both native and introduced amphibians and fishes across catchments should be discouraged—and, where possible, prevented—to maintain the integrity of watersheds (Kupferberg 1997; Gillespie and Hero 1999). Exclusion of major agricultural and infrastructure developments from entire catchments could be achieved through national and international agreements to preserve a subset of riverine and aquatic ecosystems in their natural state.

Priorities for the establishment of new protected areas and expansion and management of existing protected areas should be directed at hotspots of amphibian biodiversity. This includes addressing the needs of the most threatened hotspots (Category 4) while, at the same time, preventing the remaining hotspots (categories 1, 2, and 3) from falling into a higher threat category. Wilderness areas and hotspots with more than 25% of original forest remaining (categories 1 and 2) offer excellent potential for amphibian conservation and a unique opportunity to undertake effective planning based on integrated catchment management before development. In well-protected, heavily deforested areas (Category 3), restoration and rehabilitation of terrestrial and freshwater habitats and riparian corridors should be initiated to link remaining habitats and protect threatened species. Loss of habitat and lack of protection seriously threatens amphibians in poorly protected, heavily deforested areas (Category 4). Urgent conservation measures are needed to identify and halt sources of habitat destruction and to protect remaining vegetation. Integrated catchment management strategies and restoration should be considered for determining priorities and long-term action. Finally, to conserve the full complement of amphibian diversity and geographically restricted endemic species, protected areas should aim to incorporate ecological gradients (Smith et al. 2001), vegetation types, and breeding habitats that are poorly represented in existing protected areas. This could be achieved by protecting areas spread across altitudinal gradients, targeting geographically restricted vegetation types, and incorporating a diverse range of amphibian breeding habitats.

Unexplained Amphibians Declines

Threats to amphibians are compounded by unexplained declines recorded in high-altitude populations where direct anthropogenic impacts are not always evident (Table 6.1). Interdisciplinary research teams should focus on examining the potential links between disease as a direct or proximate cause and environmental change as an indirect and ultimate cause of population declines. Unexplained declines in Australia, Spain, and throughout the New World suggest that emerging infectious diseases may be partially responsible. As a preventative measure to stop the accidental introduction of chytrid fungus and other amphibian diseases into new areas (particularly African and Asian countries), legislation should be enacted globally to restrict all movements (importation and translocation within and between countries) of both native and introduced amphibian and fish species. Monitoring of species susceptible to decline (species occurring at high altitudes, having an aquatic stage in their life history, low fecundity, and small geographic range) should be initiated in African and Asian countries where declines have not been reported to date. Where severe population declines have been observed, recovery programs (focusing on in situ management) for threatened species should be established.

Distribution of Research and Resources

Distribution of research and resources needs to correspond to the distribution of biodiversity and threats. Training of in-country professionals (Pimm et al. 2001) and building local capacity is vital to promote conservation in developing countries and requires educational and financial support for local scientists (Sodhi and Liow 2000). Training and capacity building could be enhanced by (1) international funds to provide a network of grants to support collaborative multinational research projects in developing countries; (2) short-term intensive courses for graduate students from developing countries; (3) international funds to provide graduate scholarships for students from developing countries to study overseas, based on field work in their country of origin; and (4) increased accessibility to journals and conferences. An international scientific group, leveraged from government and international agencies through private sector involvement (Pimm et al. 2001), should coordinate funding. Funding should give priority to helping local scientists to identify the gaps in knowledge about the diversity and distribution of amphibians, and to identify and mitigate threatening processes within each country.

To facilitate and coordinate the conservation initiatives outlined above, we propose establishing a global network of Amphibian Research and Conservation Centers in biodiversity hotspots with significant species richness or endemism, or both. Each center would (1) coordinate training for local scientists; (2) document species diversity, abundance, and endemism; (3) map the distribution of species at the regional scale and focus conservation efforts in areas of high species richness and endemism; (4) identify threatened and geographically restricted species and set priorities for conservation and protection; (5) study the ecology of threatened species to assist management agencies; (6) monitor threatened species and habitat loss across ecological, latitudinal, and altitudinal gradients; (7) restore habitats and fragmented

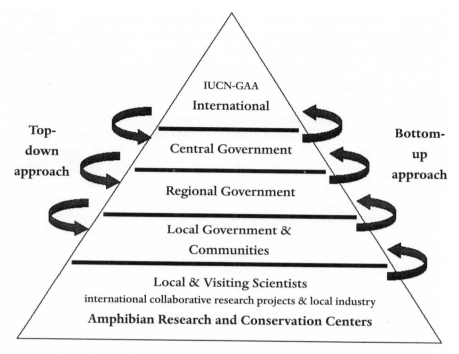

Figure 6.3. Graphical representation of amphibian research and conservation centers through bottom-up (research and information) and top-down (legislation) approaches to management and conservation.

landscapes; and (8) provide information to local communities and government agencies to promote effective amphibian conservation. These centers could be attached to existing centers such as the Centers for Biodiversity Conservation recently established by Conservation International and funded through the Moore Foundation.

Conservation is contingent on effective communication between scientists, local communities, managers, and political decision-makers at all levels of government (Young and Gunningham 1997). Conservation requires a bottom-up approach in which local and regional governments identify and protect locally significant species, combined with a top-down approach in which national government agencies identify and protect species threatened at the national scale (Figure 6.3). Once local scientists identify important biological resources within watersheds, local communities will be empowered to protect those resources (a bottom-up approach). Integrated catchment management and reserve protection must be coordinated at the regional (state) scale to identify biodiversity hotspots and gaps in scientific knowledge and expertise. Conserving the biodiversity of each and every nation is critically important to that nation's survival (Mittermeier et al. 1998) and national legislation (a top-down approach) is an essential component of any overall conservation strategy. The IUCN Global Amphibian Assessment currently in progress will monitor this process and assist in identifying weaknesses in the global conservation strategy.

ACKNOWLEDGMENTS
Thanks to Ilse Kiessling, Michael Cunningham, and colleagues at the Fourth World Congress of Herpetology for discussion on the content for this chapter, Clare Morrison for assistance in the collation of data, and Naomi Doak for freeing up some of our time. Thanks to Ed Meyer, Bill Magnusson, and Naomi Doak who provided valuable comments on early drafts, and Ray Semlitsch, Robert Inger, Ilse Kiessling, and an anonymous reviewer for comments on the submitted draft. Special thanks to Penny Langhammer from Conservation International for providing valuable mapping assistance.

7

NATURAL POPULATION FLUCTUATIONS AND HUMAN INFLUENCES

Null Models and Interactions

JOSEPH H. K. PECHMANN

CENTRAL ISSUES

Concerns about declines and disappearances of amphibian populations (Wake and Morowitz 1990; Alford and Richards 1999) have led to an increased emphasis on monitoring populations (e.g., the Amphibian Research and Monitoring Initiative of the U.S. Geological Survey) and resurveying of previously studied populations (e.g., Drost and Fellers 1996; Fisher and Shaffer 1996). The basic data obtained consist of estimates of the number of individuals in a population (or an appropriate correlate, such as the number of egg masses) at a minimum of two time periods (preferably many more). In some cases, especially in broad-scale surveys, presence/absence data are obtained in lieu of counts of individuals. The goals of these efforts are to identify trends in population sizes and distributions and to analyze potential causes of these trends by examining spatial and temporal associations between the trends and the hypothesized causes.

Analyzing population trends necessitates comparing monitoring data to a null model of population dynamics, whether explicit or implicit. For example, population sizes rarely stay exactly the same from one year to the next; they naturally fluctuate up and down, sometimes by several orders of magnitude (Blaustein et al. 1994c; Pechmann and Wilbur 1994). Deciding whether a population is declining therefore requires defining how much change over what time period falls within the range of expected natural variation; that is, invoking a null model of natural population dynamics. Changes that exceed the expected natural variation suggest that there are extrinsic influences such as human activities.

In this chapter, I critically examine four null models that have been used in analyzing declining amphibian populations. I show that the choice of a null model is not as simple and obvious as it might appear, and that different choices may lead to different conclusions. The null models that I examine are (1) the correlation between population size and time averages zero; (2) the ratio of declines to increases is 1:1 for the years a population is studied or across populations; (3) the mean regional and global trends equal zero; and (4) population disappearances are random events that follow a binomial distribution (Pounds et al. 1997).

NULL MODEL 1: THE CORRELATION BETWEEN POPULATION SIZE AND TIME AVERAGES ZERO

Perhaps the simplest and most common null model for analyzing population trends in amphibians and other taxa is that the correlation between population size and time should average zero (e.g., Joglar and Burrowes 1996; Semlitsch et al. 1996). This must be true over some spatial and temporal scales for a population to persist (but not increase). The scales over which the expected trend should be zero, however, depend on the population and metapopulation biology of the species and the pattern of variation in environmental factors affecting the population.

This null model is usually tested by the standard statistical techniques of correlation or regression (either parametric or nonparametric), although, strictly speaking, population census data violate the assumption of these procedures that each data point must be independent (Poole 1972). A statistically significant trend is one where the observed association between population size and year is highly unlikely to occur by chance (usually <5%) if there is no true association, given the magnitude of the trend, the amount of variation in population sizes not explained by the trend (residual variation), and the length of the series. A statistically significant trend is often considered to indicate changes that exceed natural variation, possibly due to human influences on a population. This line of reasoning confuses unexplained (residual) variation in the statistical sense with natural variation in the biological sense. In actuality, statistical significance indicates nothing about the cause of a trend. A statistically significant decline may represent either natural fluctuations or the result of human influences. For example, Semlitsch et al. (1996) argued that natural factors (an extended drought and perhaps increased predation) were responsible for the statistically significant declines in four species studied for 16 years at Rainbow Bay in South Carolina. Populations having highly variable juvenile recruitment, as do many amphibians (including those studied by Semlitsch et al. 1996), may be in decline most of the time between occasional recruitment booms (see Null Model 2). This can result in statistically significant negative correlations between population size and time that are merely part of the natural population dynamics (Alford and Richards 1999).

A natural fluctuation that results in a statistically significant trend may occur if natural variation in population size is increasing over time, because the increase in variation may result in a temporary trend. Variation in population sizes has been observed to increase over time in numerous taxa, even past 100 years in the case of some insects (Connell and Sousa 1983; Pimm and Redfearn 1988; Hanski 1990; Pimm 1991). This means that the longer a population is monitored, the more likely it is that extremely high or extremely low numbers will be observed. Thus, even studies that are decades long may not provide a complete picture of natural fluctuations and may find statistically significant trends due to natural causes (for a full discussion, see Pechmann and Wilbur 1994).

The spatial scale over which the correlation between population size and time equals zero should also be considered. This null model may apply to a metapopulation (set of populations connected by dispersal) more often than to its component populations (Hanski and Simberloff 1997). This is true when individual populations fluctuate asynchronously, as has been suggested for the mountain yellow-legged frog (*Rana muscosa*) before fish stocking (Bradford 1991), and the red-spotted newt (*Notophthalmus v. viridescens*; Gill 1978). Alternatively, "mainland" or "source" populations might subsidize "island" or "sink" populations that would otherwise not be self-sustaining (Hanski and Simberloff 1997). In these situations, the metapopulation is the biologically relevant scale for testing the null model that the correlation between population size and time equals zero.

Although a correlation of zero between population size and time is an inadequate null model of population dynamics, it represents a good starting point. Failure to reject this null model should allay concerns about a population decline, as long as the test has enough statistical power to detect a biologically meaningful change (Hayes and Steidl 1997). Rejection of this null model suggests that cause(s) of the trend should be investigated. An alternative to a statistical test of the null model is to estimate and examine the variance or confidence interval of the trend along with its mean (Dixon et al. 1998). This provides information on how well the data support the null model and whether any support is due to a trend known to be near zero or is due to large uncertainty in the estimate of the trend.

NULL MODEL 2: THE RATIO OF DECLINES TO INCREASES IS 1:1

A correlation between population size and time of zero might suggest that the size of a population increases over as many years as it decreases. This is true, however, only if the increases and decreases are of the same average magnitude. For example, there was no significant overall trend in the number of spawn clumps (indicative of female breeding population size) of the common frog (*Rana temporaria*) at two sites in Switzerland (Worblaufen and Bermoos) over 28 years and 23 years, respectively (Figure 7.1; Meyer et al. 1998). Nonetheless, the population declined over most of the study period at both sites. These extended declines were offset by occasional large increases over short (1–2 year) periods of time (Figure 7.1). There was a significant population decline at a third site, Widi, due to the introduction of goldfish (a tadpole predator) in the late 1980s. Note the difficulty of distinguishing the decline caused by goldfish from natural population fluctuations without the long-term data.

The population dynamics exhibited by the common frog represent a common pattern in amphibians; many populations decrease during more time intervals than they

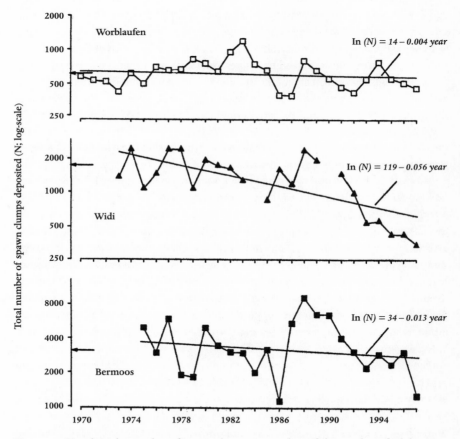

Figure 7.1. Trends in the number of spawn clumps (a correlate of the number of adult females) of *Rana temporaria* at three sites in Switzerland, fit with simple linear regression models. Arrows indicate mean abundances. Goldfish were introduced to Widi in the late 1980s. Mean abundance for Widi was calculated only for 1973 to 1989. (Adapted from Meyer et al. 1998)

increase (Alford and Richards 1999). This may occur if large cohorts of juveniles are produced infrequently. Populations might then increase sharply when recruitment booms occur and decrease the rest (most) of the time (Warner and Chesson 1985). Alford and Richards (1999) argued that this scenario fit the natural history of many amphibians and formulated a null model for amphibian populations that embodied it. Their model is for amphibians having a complex life cycle with an aquatic larval stage that metamorphoses into a terrestrial stage. The model assumes that (1) populations persist and do not increase without limit (i.e., they exhibit no overall trend), (2) survival of aquatic stages varies over several orders of magnitude, and (3) survival of terrestrial stages varies over less than an order of magnitude. These assumptions imply that (1) populations increase rapidly when aquatic survival is high, which happens in few years, (2) populations decrease slowly when aquatic survival is low, which happens in most years, (3) populations decrease during more than 50% of years, and (4) more populations will decrease than increase over any finite time period.

How much more than 50% of the time a single population decreases, and the expected proportion of a group of populations that decreases, depends on the details of the species population biology. Alford and Richards (1999) developed a numerical version of their null model based on data for the cane toad (*Bufo marinus*). Simulated cane toad populations decreased in 56.3% of intervals between years. For a set of cane toad populations, negative linear correlations between log population sizes and years were found in 54.8% of 4-year simulations, increasing to 57.5% of 28-year simulations.

Alford and Richards' (1999) model represents an alternative to the usual null model of a 1:1 ratio of declining to increasing populations commonly applied to amphibians and other taxa. For example, Houlahan et al. (2000) found that 56.6% of 936 amphibian population datasets having nonzero trends were in decline. This ratio differed significantly from 50%, which they interpreted as "quantitative evidence for global amphibian population declines." The 56.6% they observed is strikingly similar to the predictions of Alford and Richards' (1999) null model for cane toads. Applying the cane toad model to Houlahan et al.'s (2000) data would lead to the conclusion that there was no evidence for a global decline. The problem is that the exact proportion of declines predicted applies only to cane toads. It is impossible to calculate a precise ratio for the global dataset using Alford and Richards' approach without knowledge of the population biology of each species (Alford et al. 2001). It may be feasible to come up with a range of approximate null models based on various assumptions about demographics and environmental variation. Comparisons with these alternative models might also lead to different conclusions than comparison with the 1:1 model. Clearly, a 1:1 ratio of declines to increases may not be the most appropriate null model for many amphibian populations, and tests based on it should be avoided except for populations where there is evidence supporting its validity.

NULL MODEL 3: THE MEAN REGIONAL
AND GLOBAL TRENDS EQUAL ZERO

The null model that the correlation between population size and time should equal zero over appropriate spatial and temporal scales suggests that the mean annual change in population size for a set of populations should also equal zero over appropriate scales. Houlahan et al. (2000) applied this null model to a collection of amphibian census data from around the world. The null model was not rejected for the decade 1950 to 1960, but the cumulative global mean trend was significantly negative from 1960 to 1997. Alford et al. (2001) reanalyzed these data using least-squares mean trends rather than simple averages to adjust for the fact that a different set of populations was sampled each year. They found that the adjusted mean global trend was significantly positive from 1964 to 1981 and significantly and increasingly negative from 1990 to 1997 (Figure 7.2). Regional analyses showed significant negative trends during the 1990s in North America and Central and South America and significant positive trends in Asia during this period (Alford et al. 2001).

Although a mean trend of zero across populations is a potentially useful null model, it provides limited insight when applied to all populations at a continental or global scale. Rejection of the null model in these cases is hardly surprising, given the extent to which humans have destroyed, altered, and polluted amphibian habitat. The only surprise was that the global trend did not become negative before 1990 in Alford et al.'s (2001) analysis. This could be an artifact of spatial and temporal variation in sampling intensity and nonrandom selection of populations to monitor (Alford et al. 2001).

Questions about the existence, extent, and causes of global declines in amphibian populations have focused on losses in isolated, seemingly protected, usually high-elevation areas for which human activities are not the obvious culprit, such as the disappearances of the golden toad (*Bufo periglenes*) and other species from the Monteverde Cloud Forest Preserve in Costa Rica (Crump et al. 1992; Pounds et al. 1999; but see Lawton et al. 2001) and the disappearance of gastric brooding frogs (*Rheobatrachis silus* and *R. vitellinus*) from the mountains of eastern Queensland, Australia (Czechura and Ingram 1990; McDonald 1990). These cases suggest the hypothesis that amphibians are being affected by human activities that have global effects, such as climate change, increased ultraviolet radiation, and worldwide spread of nonindigenous pathogens, from which habitat protection provides little defense. Tests for a mean trend of zero would be informative for a representative set of protected high-elevation populations for which there is some expectation that this null hypothesis might be true. Tests that include populations obviously affected by humans may serve to document the biodiversity crisis, but "fail to distinguish between a global decline with global causes and the cumulative effects of local declines with local causes" (Alford et al. 2001).

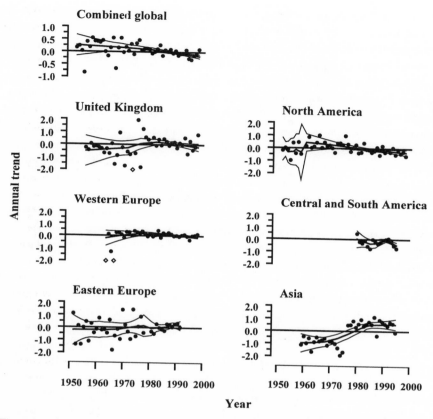

Figure 7.2. Yearly least-squares means of changes in log population sizes for regional and global collections of amphibian census data. Open diamonds indicate data that fall outside the axes. Trend lines are nonparametric regressions; outer lines indicate approximate 95% confidence intervals. (Adapted from Alford et al. 2001)

NULL MODEL 4: POPULATION DISAPPEARANCES ARE RANDOM AND FOLLOW A BINOMIAL DISTRIBUTION

Pounds et al. (1997) developed a null model for the number of amphibian species expected to disappear from an area after a natural disturbance and compared it with the number of disappearances observed in the Monteverde region of Costa Rica from 1987 to 1990. The null model was based on two studies: (1) a 12-year study (1979–1990) of four North American species at a breeding pond (Rainbow Bay) in South Carolina (Pechmann et al. 1991), and (2) a 25-year study (1935–1959) of 15 species in Cleveland County, Oklahoma (Bragg 1960). Population disappearances were associated with droughts in all three studies. Pounds et al. (1997) calculated the average number of disappearances per species per drought, which was 0.089 for Cleveland County and 0.125 for Rainbow Bay. To be conservative, they selected the higher value for their null model, and doubled it to 0.25 to be even more conservative (albeit post hoc). Half of 50 species of anurans were absent from Monteverde in 1990 and had presumably disappeared during a 1987 drought. Assuming that disappearances follow a binomial distribution, the rate was significantly higher than the disappearance rate for the Oklahoma or South Carolina droughts. Pounds et al. (1997) concluded that the disappearances observed at Monteverde exceeded those expected due to natural fluctuations and therefore that other factors such as introduced pathogens or global climate change must be involved (see also Pounds et al. 1999).

The null model proposed by Pounds et al. (1997) makes a number of assumptions. The most fundamental are (1) all natural droughts are equally severe, and (2) the effect of a drought as measured by species disappearance rates does not vary among amphibian assemblages. Together these assumptions imply that the Rainbow Bay and Cleveland County studies are representative of all other places and all other droughts. In my opinion these assumptions are questionable and any null model based on them provides little insight. That being said, no null model is necessary to demonstrate that the disappearance of half the amphibian species from a 30 km² area in nearly a decade is an unusual (and disturbing) event whose causes should be investigated.

POTENTIAL SOLUTIONS

Analyzing population trends may appear to be a simple and straightforward task, but it is not. The problem is often thought of as largely statistical; however, the biggest challenges are biological. The better we understand how amphibian populations normally behave, the better we will be able to recognize deviations from these expectations and know when something may be amiss. Establishing appropriate null models for analyzing population trends requires a thorough understanding of natural population and metapopulation dynamics. This requires long-term studies. Use of simple or inappropriate null models may result in limited or biased insight, as discussed above. The pioneering efforts of Alford and Richards (1999) need to be expanded. However, there are no simple, general models that apply to all amphibian populations.

There is widespread agreement that many amphibian populations have declined or disappeared (Pechmann and Wake 1997; Alford and Richards 1999). Why then should analyzing population trends be a concern? It is because it is important to know which populations have been affected and which have not. This allows us to focus limited resources on conservation and restoration efforts where they are most needed. Also, information on the spatial and temporal patterns of declines and disappearances can be used to help evaluate hypothesized causes (Carey et al. 2001). For example, Davidson et al. (2001) found that disappearances of California red-legged frogs (*Rana aurora draytonii*) were positively associated with elevation, percentage upwind agricultural land use, and local urbanization. Analyses such as theirs depend on being able to distinguish natural fluctuations from declines and disappearances that require other explanations.

There are other challenges in developing null models for amphibian populations. For example, population changes related to climatic variation have traditionally been considered natural fluctuations (e.g., Pechmann et al. 1991; Duellman 1995; Stewart 1995; Semlitsch et al. 1996; Pounds et al. 1997) and hence an appropriate part of null models. Recent work suggests some alternative interpretations. The crash of 19 amphibian populations at Monteverde in 1987 was related to drought, but the drought may have been exacerbated by global warming and lowland deforestation (Pounds et al. 1999; Still et al. 1999; Lawton et al. 2001). In Oregon, precipitation affects the water level in lakes and hence exposure of western toad (*Bufo boreas*) eggs to ultraviolet light, which in turn affects the susceptibility of the eggs to a pathogenic fungus (Kiesecker et al. 2001a). These examples suggest that establishing null models of amphibian population dynamics is complicated by the pervasive influence of humans on the environment and by interactions between the many natural and anthropogenic factors that can affect amphibian population dynamics.

ACKNOWLEDGMENTS
I gratefully acknowledge the intellectual contributions of Phil Dixon, Ross Alford, and Alan Pounds and the financial contributions of the U.S. Department of Energy [Contract #LEQSF (2001-04)RD-A-41], and the Declining Amphibian Populations Task Force toward the development of the ideas discussed in this chapter.

8

HABITAT DESTRUCTION AND ALTERATION

Historical Trends and Future Prospects for Amphibians

C. KENNETH DODD JR. AND LORA L. SMITH

CENTRAL ISSUES

Amphibian life histories are complex and often poorly understood. In addition, the public seems to have a misperception concerning amphibians, equating them most often with wetland habitats. To ensure the survival of amphibians, the biological requirements of all life history stages must be understood on a landscape level, and the public must be presented with accurate knowledge to ensure commitment to their survival. Habitat concepts need to be expanded not only to encompass a multidimensional space over sometimes large landscapes, but also to include the biotic, chemical, and physical factors that affect habitats through time. Historically, amphibian populations have been adversely affected to a great extent, with a tremendous amount of direct habitat loss, alteration, and fragmentation. Although many factors, such as disease, pesticides, and ultraviolet-B light, likely adversely affect amphibians, habitat loss and alteration are probably the most serious causes of current and future amphibian population declines and species extinctions. The biotic integrity of amphibian habitats needs to be ensured.

AMPHIBIANS IN NATURAL LANDSCAPES

Amphibians are found in a great variety of ecosystems, from the rainforests of the tropics to the taiga of central Alaska, and from sea level to above 5,000 m in the Himalayas (Duellman 1999b). They occur not only in humid areas, but also in barren deserts and in dry temperate grasslands. Amphibians are traditionally perceived as associated with wetlands, and this is so for many species. However, a large number of species (e.g., many plethodontid salamanders and leptodactylid frogs) are entirely terrestrial or rarely venture near standing water. Others are in contact with water for only a very brief period in their life cycles. To conserve amphibians, it is first necessary to have a clear understanding of their varied life histories and to identify amphibian habitats.

Knowledge of amphibian habitat requirements becomes exceptionally important in planning for their conservation; requirements change for each species and community. In the discussion that follows, habitat is defined to include the spatial requirements of the species, as well as all other critical physical, chemical, and biotic components of their environment. Habitat thus encompasses biophysical conditions (e.g., the ability of a habitat to retain moisture and relative humidity), chemistry (both soil and atmospheric content, pH, the presence of contaminants), and biotic interactions (predators, prey, disease organisms, intraspecific contact), in addition to the distribution of breeding sites, movement corridors, feeding areas, and refuges from temperature extremes and drought. Only when all of these variables are taken into consideration will amphibian habitat be secure. The variables included in this multidimensional concept of habitat thus constitute the limits within which conservation options become available.

In the sections that follow, we note the complexity of amphibian habitats, document threats to habitats, discuss the fates of amphibians in fragmented habitats, and identify solutions to landscape-level problems affecting these species. Because of space limitations, our focus is on North American ecosystems and their amphibian problems.

Other regions of the world also face substantial threats to amphibian habitats, and from many of the same sources (see e.g., Europe, Beebee 1996; the former Soviet Union, Kuzmin and Dodd 1995; South Africa, Branch 1988; and Australia, Campbell 1999). Certain centers of amphibian biodiversity outside North America are particularly threatened, such as South Africa's Cape peninsula and associated lowlands, the coastal mountain ranges of Kenya and Tanzania, the forests of Sri Lanka, and Australia's southwest lowlands and the rainforests of Queensland. Fully 65% of the world's tropical forests, a source of vast amphibian diversity, have already been lost. The Food and Agriculture Organization (FAO) estimates that 15.2 million hectares of tropical forests, a vast repository of amphibian diversity, were destroyed each year during the 1990s (FAO 2001). Much of the world's amphibian diversity is poorly known, especially in Africa, Australia, and the neotropics, and likely will remain so, particularly as tropical habitats are destroyed.

Spatial Life History of Entirely Terrestrial Amphibians

Many amphibians, such as salamanders of the genus *Plethodon* and frogs of the genus *Eleutherodactylus,* have direct development, that is, their eggs are deposited on land where the young hatch as miniature adults or, as in a few species, they give birth to live young. Such amphibians require humid environments for development and activity, but they rarely if ever are found directly in standing water. Most terrestrial amphibians occupy a two-dimensional surface world, but many species, such as terrestrial salamanders and tropical forest frogs, also frequent subterranean or arboreal habitats. Only a small fraction of their life cycle may be carried out on the ground surface, with much of their lives spent hidden from view.

Animals may move back and forth between subsurface, arboreal, and surface habitats depending on life stage, season, and reproductive condition. Certain habitats are crucial at certain times, such as when eggs are deposited in protective root cavities. In this context, the structure and accessibility of the surface area occupied, the depth and extent of subsurface habitat, and the complexity and availability of the arboreal habitat all serve to define habitat quality. Little is known about subsurface and arboreal activities of amphibians, despite the crucial nature of these habitats, nor about differential habitat requirements of juveniles and adults.

Spatial Life History of Entirely Aquatic Amphibians

Few species of amphibians are confined entirely to water throughout their lives; these include certain poorly known salamanders in eastern North America (*Pseudobranchus, Siren, Amphiuma*), cryptobranchid salamanders (*Andrias, Cryptobranchus*), paedomorphic salamanders (certain newts [*Triturus, Notophthalmus*] and mole salamanders [*Ambystoma*]), cave-dwellers (e.g., the salamanders *Proteus* and *Haideotriton*), and a few aquatic frogs (e.g., *Pipa* of South America). These species almost never leave the water and, like terrestrial species, have a circumscribed two-dimensional habitat on the bottom of the stream or wetland. They also may have a third dimension of importance: depth or habitat preferences within the water column. For species confined to an aquatic existence, the shape of the waterbody defines the spatial shape (e.g., oval as a pond or swamp, or linear as a stream or river) of the habitat. If water levels are affected, the habitat of these species changes, making them particularly vulnerable to even slight modification. When waters recede or vanish, they have nowhere else to go.

For entirely aquatic amphibians, all life history activities occur within the water. However, habitats are not uniform, and certain types of habitats are used at certain times of the year by different life stages. For example, female hellbenders (*Cryptobranchus alleganiensis*) deposit eggs in nests under large flat rocks, which the males guard. After hatching, the larvae burrow down into spaces in the gravel for several years as they grow large enough to avoid predators. Critical components of hellbender habitat thus include both large flat rocks and beds of loose gravel in clear, clean, fast-flowing colder streams, as well as a specialized food source, crayfish.

Spatial Life History When Both Terrestrial and Aquatic Habitats Are Required

In general, the public associates amphibian life history with the biphasic life cycle in which adults move to a waterbody to breed and deposit eggs that then hatch into tadpoles or larvae. After a variable amount of time (from days in spadefoots, *Scaphiopus,* to sometimes years in pond frogs, *Rana* spp.), the larvae metamorphose into juveniles. Juveniles disperse to other semiaquatic (i.e., streamside) or terrestrial habitats, some of which may be hundreds or even thousands of meters from the breeding site. Most of the life cycle is spent in terrestrial habitats, where juveniles and adults feed and find refuge. In colder or dry climates, adults seek shelter in refugia within the uplands, or they may move considerable distances to specific refugia (e.g., wetlands, marshes, or even pond bottoms) to escape the harsh climatic conditions. Little is known about differences in upland habitat use between the sexes or among size classes.

It would seem that amphibians that breed in aquatic habitats but live in terrestrial habitats have the most complex habitat requirements. Each habitat within the terrestrial and aquatic life cycle has both a two- and a three-dimensional component. In addition, movement pathways or corridors must be available between distant aquatic breeding sites and terrestrial habitats. Habitats are used at different times of the year and often by different life history stages, and species are exposed to vastly different sets of physical, chemical, and biotic conditions within their various habitats. The complexity of the overall habitat requirements of these amphibians makes them especially vulnerable to perturbations within their environment. Because of a host of mostly logistic factors (it is hard to track tiny frogs through big habitats or follow salamanders underground), biologists often have scant understanding of terrestrial habitat requirements for most species. Thus, past research and management attention have often focused on breeding sites, which can be delineated, at the expense of terrestrial locations, which may be difficult to identify.

Metapopulations versus Continuous Distribution

Most amphibians are not distributed uniformly within their environments, but instead tend to occur in patches of greater or lesser density within the overall landscape (e.g., Hecnar and M'Closkey 1997a). Many amphibian species exhibit a metapopulation structure, existing as an interconnected series of populations within a larger geographic area. This is particularly true of species that breed in wetlands but mostly live in terrestrial habitats. Some habitats seem to be more important than others; they may be sources for colonization or refugia during harsh environmental conditions. Knowing the population structure of a species is thus critical to understanding how habitat destruction, alteration, and fragmentation affect the species and limit conservation options. To identify species and habitats most susceptible to alteration and fragmentation, it is crucial to identify species with metapopulation structure and to recognize corridors and connections between populations. The protection of a metapopulation needs to include surface, subsurface, arboreal, and even linear habitats (e.g., rivers and streams).

THREATS TO ECOSYSTEMS INHABITED BY AMPHIBIANS

There is a general misperception that the size of the habitat is directly related to its importance for amphibian species richness and diversity. For many species, especially terrestrial species, this is true to some extent on a landscape scale; large tracts of habitat are more likely to contain a diverse assemblage of habitats and thus many amphibian species. However, this is not a universal truism. Small areas on the mountaintops of the southern Appalachians may contain seven or more species of salamanders, and large wetlands (lakes, ponds) may actually contain fewer amphibians than small (<1.5 ha) temporary wetlands (e.g., Dodd 1992). Species composition may overlap only slightly between large and very small wetlands, making the value of size questionable. Habitat loss or alteration on a massive scale can result in devastating losses to amphibian populations, but so can the loss of much smaller and less obvious tracts of habitat.

Another misperception is that regulations are adequate to ensure that no net loss of wetlands occurs. The diverse habitat requirements of amphibians ensures that protecting wetlands alone does not provide protection for an entire amphibian community. Small ephemeral wetlands are nearly universally ignored by planners; they are easily destroyed with no obvious indication of their importance. They are usually seen as minor impediments to urbanization and agriculture. Small wetlands fall through the cracks, just as do other specialized habitats, such as springs, caves, talus slopes, mountain tops, and other unique but sometimes small habitats. The lack of regulation based on size bias certainly contributes to the cumulative loss of amphibian habitats.

Habitat Destruction

Habitat destruction is defined as the complete elimination of a localized or regional ecosystem leading to the total loss of its former biological function. Destruction of amphibian habitats is most dramatically demonstrated when wetlands are drained and filled in or when forests, deserts, and other uplands are paved and converted to parking lots, housing developments, or agricultural fields. In some instances, habitat destruction may be partially reversed, such as when a slash pine plantation is restored to a longleaf pine forest. However, most modern examples of habitat destruction are final, that is, the destroyed habitats will never again function as a natural ecosystem because the logistics, expense, and continued pressure of an expanding human population will make it infeasible. Once extirpated or extinct, species and their complement of genetic diversity cannot be re-created.

Habitat destruction may be far more difficult to recognize than it might initially appear. Ponds or fields heavily contaminated by industrial chemicals or agricultural pesticides might superficially appear fine, even though original species composition and ecosystem function have been completely eliminated. If a farmer plows to the water's edge of a small pond on the North Dakota prairie, the destruction of the surrounding uplands could result in the loss of ecosystem function even though the wetland was spared. Thus, depending on the scale of space and time, there is often a gradient between complete habitat obliteration and the generally perceived lesser impacts of habitat alteration. What may be described as habitat destruction on a local scale might also be described as habitat alteration in a much larger regional context.

Habitat Alteration

Altered habitats are those in which ecosystem function has been adversely affected, although not perhaps totally or permanently. Clearcutting of hardwood trees may severely alter a localized biotic community, but given enough time and sources of new colonizers, the hardwood forest ecosystem may recover. Unlike most habitat destruction, habitat alteration includes more than physical destruction, that is, physical, chemical, and biotic changes may alter habitat conditions to a greater or lesser degree. Habitat alteration also encompasses biophysical changes to an environment, such as when clearcutting opens up remnant forest patches to changes in soil moisture, wind, solar radiation, humidity, and desiccation. Even if forest patches are left, they may be substantially affected beyond the immediate effects of physical habitat change.

A much more insidious effect of landscape-level habitat alteration on amphibians is the piecemeal destruction of large sections of habitat that leave remaining habitats fragmented (Figures 8.1 and 8.2). Amphibians living in small fragments are prone to serious landscape threats, such as edge effects, isolation, barriers to movements, and being confined to small amounts of ever-imperiled remaining habitat. Small populations are also subject to changes in demographic population parameters (e.g., decreased survivorship), genetics (loss of genetic viability), and are more susceptible to stochastic environmental events. Viewed from above, amphibian habitats often appear shredded across the landscape or, in rivers and streams, as a linearly interconnected series of affected and unaffected sections.

Habitat alteration in one location also may have far-reaching effects and lead to habitat destruction in a spatially far-removed location, especially if the habitats are interconnected. For example, any habitat downstream from a disrupted, channelized, dammed, or polluted stream section is affected by what happens upstream and

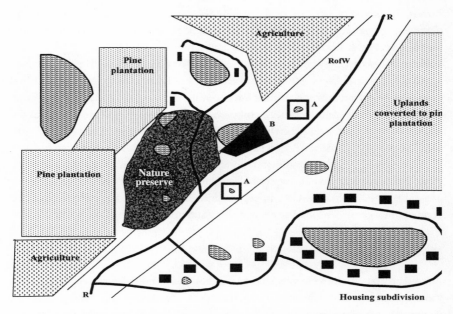

Figure 8.1. Thirteen wetlands are interspersed within a natural uplands habitat. As development begins, a road (R) and its associated right-of-way (RofW) destroy two ponds (A, surrounded by boxes) and partially eliminate a third (B). Surrounding uplands are converted to pine plantations and agricultural fields, both destroying habitats needed by terrestrial species and fragmenting remaining habitats near ponds. A housing development places further impediments to dispersal by eliminating migratory pathways. Although a small nature reserve protects two and a half ponds, it is effectively isolated. Amphibians having a metapopulation structure would have a hard time persisting over a long time period. A diverse species-rich set of communities is thus replaced by a depauperate fragmented assemblage.

within its watershed, no matter how unaffected it may look at a particular point in time. Thus, aquatic salamander larvae living downstream from a strip-mined coalfield or a clearcut stream section might be affected by altered stream flows, increased siltation, chemical pollution, and changes in water temperature. For stream-dwelling species, watershed protection is vital inasmuch as land use drastically affects aquatic biodiversity (Harding et al. 1998).

Other forms of habitat alteration are more subtle, such as the suppression of natural ecosystem processes (e.g., fire in the prairies and in the pine forests of southeastern United States), the alteration of natural processes (e.g., conducting controlled burns in seasons when they do not naturally occur; allowing wetlands to undergo succession; altering flooding regimes and wetland hydroperiods), and the introduction of exotic animals and plants that directly affect amphibians or adversely alter their habitats. Nonindigenous American bullfrogs (*Rana catesbeiana*), for instance,

Figure 8.2. Aerial photograph showing the combined influences of agriculture (top, lower left), silviculture (most of center, in various stages of rotation), and rural development (especially roads) on fragmentation of amphibian habitat. Wetlands in this photograph also have been ditched to allow drainage. In times of high water, predaceous fishes colonize formerly fish-free ponds. The arrow points to the only breeding pond for the striped newt (*Notophthalmus perstriatus*) remaining in this part of south-central Georgia. The riparian corridor of the Alapaha River runs along the left side. Tift and Irwin counties, Georgia. (Aerial photograph courtesy of Georgia Department of Forestry)

feel more at home in the altered urbanizing habitats around Puget Sound than do the native ranid frogs; they also prey on the native frogs. Pollution from acid rain and toxic chemicals is yet another form of habitat alteration.

In summary, assessing the impacts of habitat alteration and destruction on amphibians requires knowledge of spatial (how much area is affected), temporal (long-term versus short-term), habitat (what types are affected), ecosystem (how function is affected), and biotic community (what species are involved and how populations are structured) components. All of these components are important. Each must be evaluated to understand how amphibian habitats have been affected in North America since European colonization.

Changes and Trends in Amphibian Habitat

There are many different assessments of exactly how much habitat loss has occurred—and is occurring—in North America and the Caribbean. Methodology differs among studies (e.g., Landsat images versus aerial photography; some studies employ ground-truthing whereas others do not; habitats may be scored or defined differently; scales of assessment vary; studies only report obvious *physical* alteration), depending on the objectives and the constituencies of the agencies sponsoring the surveys. For these reasons, data from different studies are usually not directly comparable, rarely agree, and may be statistically biased.

As an example, one of the most recent comprehensive attempts to measure wetland changes in the United States was the study by Dahl (2000) for the U.S. Fish and Wildlife Service. Although the study documented substantial decreases in the extent of most natural wetland habitats, impacts on ephemeral wetlands were not included (Dahl, 2000), even though they are crucial for the survival of amphibians and other aquatic or semiaquatic fauna. Likewise, a natural pond may be severely altered by turning it into a retention pond, yet the methodology employed by Dahl (2000) would result in a report of no net loss of wetland extent. Broadly defined concepts of habitat alteration (including physical, chemical, and biotic effects) are not employed in the tabulation of habitat loss. Any figures on habitat destruction and alteration are likely to be underestimates of the actual extent and effect of what is actually occurring. Despite these caveats, the loss and alteration of North American ecosystems, including those required by amphibians, has been extensive and is accelerating (Appendix 8.1).

Terrestrial Habitats

There are approximately 298 million hectares of forested land within the continental United States today, about 66% of the amount present in 1600 (see papers in Mac et al. 1998 for references on the extent of habitat loss cited here and elsewhere in this section). Very little of this forest is old growth, and most areas have been timbered repeatedly. About 124 million hectares of forest have been converted to agriculture and urbanized areas, with 75% of forest clearing for agriculture occurring before the 1920s. Today, croplands constitute roughly 162 million hectares, all converted from forest or grasslands.

Forest losses are not distributed equally throughout the country. In the Northeast, forests were reduced from 90% of the land cover in 1700 to less than 30% in 1900; currently, forests cover about 60% of the landscape. In the Pacific Northwest, however, only about 15% of old-growth Douglas-fir forest remains, and nearly 76% of the old-growth forest on the Olympic Peninsula has been logged since 1940. In the Southeast, only 2% of the original 28.3 million hectares of longleaf pine forests remain on the coastal plain from Virginia to Texas. Although these and other figures of habitat loss are dramatic (Appendix 8.1), they do not reflect the cumulative extent of forest habitat alteration and resulting fragmentation.

Grasslands have fared far worse than forests. Since 1830, 83 to 99% of the tall grass prairie in the Great Plains states and Canadian provinces has disappeared. In mixed grass prairies, losses range from 31% in Texas to 99.9% in Manitoba. Although losses of short grass prairies have not been as dramatic, native species of animals and plants have been extirpated or replaced by nonindigenous species, thus drastically altering community composition and ecosystem function. Although amphibians are not as common in grasslands as in forests, the loss of habitats near wetlands could affect survival. As the prairies have been plowed, so too have the wetlands. Prairie pothole wetlands have been lost at a rate of 1,300 ha per year; Iowa has lost 99% of its prairie wetlands, and other prairie states also show dramatic losses.

Freshwater Wetlands

Wetlands in nearly every part of the country have been drastically altered, from the vernal pools of California, to fragile Southwestern desert oases, to the prairie pot-holes, to Southeastern temporary ponds, to the peat bogs of the Northeast. Especially in areas of water scarcity, habitats have been severely altered, with concomitant but little-documented effects on amphibian communities.

According to Dahl (2000), approximately 40.6 million hectares of freshwater wet-lands remain in the lower 48 U.S. states, with an average net loss of 23,700 ha per year from 1986 to 1997. This rate of loss is less than the rate of wetland loss in previous decades because of federal and state programs designed to minimize wetland loss. The total loss of wetlands from the1980s to 1990s (267,700 ha, or 2.3% per year) was lower than from the 1970s to the 1980s (6.7%). Freshwater emergent wetlands lost 485,800 ha, but shrub wetlands slightly increased in extent. Long-term trends indi-cate that freshwater emergent wetlands have declined 24% since colonial times, but that freshwater forested wetlands sustained the greatest overall loss in area, declining by 4.2 million hectares since the 1950s. Creation of large farm and aquaculture ponds, and mine and urban retention ponds actually increased the "open water pond" cate-gory. As Dahl (2000, p. 69) noted, "these ponds were not equivalent replacement for vegetated wetlands." Deepwater lakes and reservoirs also increased, indicating habi-tat loss to species in areas where these lakes were created. Temporary ponds and other forms of ephemeral wetlands are not included in the figures in Appendix 8.1.

In terms of causes of the wetland loss between 1986 and 1997, urbanization ac-counted for 30%, agriculture 26%, silviculture 23%, and rural development 21%. Of significance to amphibian populations, 55% of the lost wetlands were located in or ad; acent to uplands, 31% adjacent to agriculture, 24% adjacent to silviculture, and 5% adjacent to urbanized areas. Some of these wetlands were adjacent to more than one habitat type; the "upland" category does not mean "areas without human im-pacts." Clearly, the threats to aquatic breeding amphibians, especially those that mi-grate to uplands and have a metapopulation structure, should be evident.

AMPHIBIANS IN FRAGMENTED LANDSCAPES

Immediate Effects

One of the primary effects of fragmentation is the loss of individuals, populations, or even species occurring in the portion of the landscape that is destroyed. Secondarily, as the landscape is fragmented into increasingly smaller pieces, natural linkages between habitat patches are lost and barriers to the natural movements of animals are introduced. Although the effects of fragmentation have been well documented in large, wide-ranging vertebrates, the implications of this phenomenon for amphibian populations are poorly understood. Ecologists have only begun to appreciate the extent to which amphibians move through the landscape. Many species of amphibians exhibit complex life histories, and different life stages may require different habitats that may be widely distributed in space (see above, "Amphibians in Natural Landscapes"). Fragmentation can inhibit movement of individuals between habitats that are needed by different life stages through time. Although many amphibians have an aquatic larval stage, juveniles or adults may inhabit a terrestrial environment some distance from their natal wetland. If the surrounding upland landscape is destroyed or obstacles to movement are constructed (e.g., roads or clearcuts), these species may be unable to complete their life cycle. Most wetlands are afforded some measure of legal protection, at least in the developed world, although the transition zones between uplands and wetlands, and the uplands themselves, are rarely protected.

In addition to the direct mortality often associated with the process of fragmentation, individuals that survive the initial disturbance often face considerable risk in crossing inhospitable or dangerous altered habitats. This issue is likely of particular importance to amphibians because they are typically small-bodied, slow moving, and face unique physiological constraints. Some species (e.g., terrestrial salamanders) are notoriously poor colonizers and many require an intact habitat structure (both subsurface and overstory) to facilitate movement. Although a clearcut or an agricultural field may not appear to be an insurmountable barrier to amphibian movement, most amphibians require a moist environment, rendering dry open areas impassable. Furthermore, individuals may be more exposed to predators in a disturbed environment than in an intact habitat. At best, these altered habitats in a fragmented landscape act as filters to amphibian movement; at worst, they act as completely impenetrable barriers.

According to Brown (2001), in the United States, the area devoted to roads and parking lots covers an estimated 16 million hectares. Roads are one of the least subtle, and perhaps most effective, barriers to animal movements built by humans. Road construction leads not only to the loss of habitat and individuals, but once in place, roads can become a continuous source of mortality, particularly for small vertebrates such

as amphibians (Smith et al., in press). The adverse effects of roads on large vertebrates and biotic integrity in general have been well documented, and there is an increasing body of evidence that roads can have long-term impacts on amphibian populations. Even moderate traffic volumes can cause 100% mortality in migrating toads,
and traffic mortality significantly affects local amphibian density. Road mortality may
be a constant drain on adults that must traverse roads to reach breeding sites from
their overwintering sites. In species such as the federally threatened flatwoods salamander (*Ambystoma cingulatum*), which is already under pressure from habitat loss
and degradation, loss of migrating breeding adults to road mortality could have catastrophic effects on populations and metapopulations.

Roads can also exert a more subtle effect on wildlife populations through a phenomenon termed the "road zone effect" (Forman et al. 1995). Although public roads
and roadsides cover only 1% of the land area in the United States, an estimated 15 to
20% of the country is ecologically affected by roads (Forman and Alexander 1998).
Roadways can act as conduits for nonindigenous species, pollutants, subsidized predators, increased edge effects, and further human development and intrusion into
natural areas.

Long-Term Population Effects

Over time, habitat fragmentation can lead to the loss of genetic diversity in amphibian populations. Small, isolated populations are extremely vulnerable to the accumulation of deleterious mutations and loss of adaptive potential (Lynch 1996). In a
highly fragmented habitat surrounded by an inhospitable landscape, adaptive evolutionary change, rather than emigration, becomes the primary mechanism for responding to local selective pressures. Yet the ability of a population to respond to
these changes may be hampered by the loss of genetic diversity.

An additional long-term effect of fragmentation is the disruption of natural
landscape-level ecological processes. As habitats become fragmented, the altered
surrounding landscape may act as a barrier preventing the spread of natural disturbances such as fire. The elimination of natural disturbances can lead to the degradation of habitat quality for some species, such as the striped newt (*Notophthalmus perstriatus*) and other southeastern sandhill species (Johnson, in press). Small fragments of
habitat may also be subject to edge effects that alter the physical structure and microclimate of the habitat. Along those lines, fragmentation might be expected to exacerbate the impact of climate change on amphibian populations because barriers eliminate migration as a mechanism for coping with environmental change.

The importance of habitat edges is often overlooked in landscape assessment.
Whereas some species prefer edges, others do not cross such landscape boundaries.
Thus, migratory routes and dispersal pathways can be disrupted even without major

habitat destruction. Edges, which expand inversely to the size of habitat fragment (i.e., small isolated habitat patches have a large proportion of habitat affected by the edge), allow increased exposure to certain predators and to habitat-altering biophysical effects, such as increased wind, desiccation, and solar radiation. Edge effects may extend inward many tens of meters; in small habitat patches, virtually the entire fragment may experience edge effects.

Fragmentation also can exert a long-term pressure on the demography of amphibian populations due to the continual loss of particular individuals through direct mortality. Adults on breeding migrations and juveniles exiting wetlands may be particularly vulnerable to mortality. Little is known of the ability of amphibian populations to sustain such losses. However, it seems likely that in species with life stages that must migrate to and from resources, barriers built by humans could have a devastating effect. Populations in fragmented habitats also are more vulnerable to extinction due to random stochastic events, both at a population level (e.g., disease) and as a result of external factors such as weather (e.g., drought).

Large-scale disruption of populations at the landscape level can result in a serious decline in functioning metapopulations. For many populations, survival at a larger regional scale depends on recolonization from other areas. In extreme cases of fragmentation, the possibility of recolonization of empty patches decreases and a species may eventually disappear from a region.

POTENTIAL SOLUTIONS

Habitat Protection of Intact Landscapes

The only way to ensure the preservation of amphibian diversity is to protect intact habitat at the species, community, and regional levels. Efforts must be made to identify, acquire, and actively manage contiguous tracts of habitat, especially to accommodate the metapopulation structure commonly seen in certain amphibians. Historically, land acquisition efforts have focused on the needs of large vertebrates, with the assumption that if large areas were protected, the needs of small vertebrates, such as amphibians, would be met. However, given the highly specific habitat requirements of amphibians with complex life histories, both aquatic and terrestrial, this assumption may not hold true. East of the Rocky Mountains in North America, very few rare or endangered amphibians are found on protected lands. Even when substantial amphibian communities are located on "public" lands, serious threats occur, such as off-road vehicles in wetlands or mechanical site preparation before establishing pine plantations on national forests in the South.

Public and private land acquisition efforts should be focused on maintaining a heterogeneous landscape that includes areas required by all life history stages of amphibians. Conservation organizations traditionally focused on land acquisition should be encouraged to include amphibian communities in their planning. Public and other conservation lands must be managed for the maintenance of all habitats— wetlands, uplands, flowing waters, and ecotones between these habitats. Multiple use of public lands also must not be advanced when the existence of incompatible uses might drive amphibian populations toward extinction. Finally, private landowners should be given inducements to maintain amphibian habitats through conservation easements and tax incentives.

Corridors, Ecopassages, and the Protection of Migratory Routes

Although corridors linking protected areas have been proposed as a solution to population fragmentation, their use by amphibians remains problematic. There has been a tendency to incorporate riparian regions of streams or other waterways as corridors to link protected areas for wildlife without taking into account the often-unique requirements of migrating amphibians. Amphibians often travel long distances in specific directions when moving between aquatic and terrestrial habitats, and corridors must incorporate these natural migratory routes. Effort must be made to identify and protect these routes, or the long-term protection of many species of amphibians will be impossible. When potential corridors are present, natural vegetation in these areas should be maintained and exotic species controlled.

Highly complex and often expensive structures, such as ecopassages that allow animals to travel over or beneath barriers such as roads or railroads, have been used with mixed success. The passages may be used in conjunction with barrier walls a meter or so high with an outward projecting lip to minimize trespass. The long-term effectiveness of these measures in ameliorating direct mortality and habitat fragmentation on amphibian populations remains largely untested, although some preliminary results are promising. In view of the potential application of barrier walls, culverts, and tunnels in many areas where fragmentation already has occurred, further research is needed to determine the types and conditions under which amphibians use them, as well as optimal mechanical design. Tunnels, underpasses, and overpasses are easily incorporated into new road construction or road widening projects (Langton 1989; ALASV 1994; Percsy 1995). The design of ecopassages should address the unique biological needs of amphibians. The passages must be easily navigable by small vertebrates, have a moist substrate, and should not expose the animals to increased risk of predation.

In highway transportation planning, large patches of natural vegetation, major wildlife corridors, riparian zones, and rare or unique habitats and species should be avoided. Efforts should be made to consolidate corridors for motor vehicles, power-lines, cables, and railways. Wherever possible, existing roads through natural areas should be removed or modified to prevent mortality and to allow movement between separated habitat patches.

Wetland and Terrestrial Buffer Zones

The designation of buffer zones around protected areas has been widely applied by natural resource managers and landscape architects, usually to address water quality issues. The habitat needs of amphibians traditionally have not been considered in the design of these zones. Recent studies have shown that buffer zones designed to protect water quality around wetlands are inadequate to meet the needs of the terrestrial life stages of some amphibians; they are simply too small. Buffer zones should be spatially adequate to protect remaining habitat from edge effects as well as provide suitable habitat for migrating amphibians. This will require knowledge of which species are in the community and their terrestrial habitat requirements.

Inasmuch as many species move hundreds or even thousands of meters from breeding sites and that they use different habitats depending on season or life stage, buffer zones may need to be extended from 300 to 1,000 m from a wetland to ensure the survival of its dependent amphibian community. In addition, amphibian habitat use of surrounding uplands may not be uniform. Whereas water quality buffers have been drawn traditionally in a circle around a wetland, amphibians may migrate to some areas more than others, making a circular buffer zone ineffectual. Knowledge of amphibian spatial distribution in surrounding uplands is crucial in landscape planning for community persistence.

Enhancement of Mitigation Sites and Habitat Restoration

Given the broad-scale habitat destruction that has already taken place, it will become increasingly important to design and enhance mitigation sites for amphibians. To be effective, such mitigation efforts must accommodate all life history stages of the amphibians of concern. This tactic may be most appropriate where large tracts of land are reclaimed after large-scale disturbances, such as mining. However, on a smaller scale, it also will be important to recreate specific habitat types within remaining habitat fragments. Where possible, efforts should be made to replace habitats lost to development with some semblance of what was originally present, and in close spatial proximity so that displaced amphibians can find the new habitats.

In many cases it will be necessary to create or attempt to restore specific habitats such as ponds or forests to replace those lost to development. Ponds should be designed based on the habitat requirements of the species of concern. Factors that should be considered in designing artificial ponds include pond placement in relation to terrestrial habitats, hydroperiod, water quality and seasonality, soils, and vegetation. Forest restoration will require a longer time scale than most other efforts, and in many cases it will require a shift in thinking about sustainable use of forest resources. Forests should be restored to native species and management should include the introduction of natural disturbance regimes, such as by introducing controlled burns that mimic natural fire occurrence. Even with the best of intentions, newly created ponds may not mimic the wetland amphibian community they are designed to replace (Pechmann et al. 2001).

The strategies outlined above necessitate a long-term commitment and may require the use of adaptive management to accommodate new information on amphibian life history and genetics. Some attempts to restore wetlands have been successful, particularly in Europe. In other attempts, however, wetlands have been restored but with different physical characteristics that might change community composition. For example, the withdrawal of groundwater for human use has had a significant impact on the hydrology of wetlands in and around urban areas in central Florida. Resource managers have experimented with using groundwater to augment wetlands and restore both species richness and ecosystem function (Means and Franz, in press). Although augmentation may improve the appearance of formerly dry wetlands, changes in water quality may render the wetlands unsuitable for breeding amphibians. The water in most wetlands in the region typically is acidic, whereas water drawn directly from the aquifer has a very high pH. Amphibians requiring acidic conditions for development will not be able to recolonize such restored wetlands. Furthermore, it is prohibitively expensive to manipulate water levels seasonally to mimic a natural hydroperiod. When natural hydroperiods are not followed, augmented wetlands become unsuitable for many amphibian species.

Research

Biologists still lack the knowledge of much of the basic life history required to protect amphibian diversity, and quantitative data on the distribution and abundance of amphibian species are needed for most areas. Even in North America, the amphibians of most national parks and national wildlife refuges have not been adequately sampled. Conservation efforts cannot be prioritized unless biologists and resource managers know which species are present and how they are spatially distributed across the landscape. Much basic information on the life history requirements, conservation genetics, and effects of environmental perturbations on population structure and demography is lacking, making it difficult or impossible to make decisions regarding the acquisition and management of protected areas. Research is needed to determine how to restore and manage altered landscapes for amphibians. Toward this end, efforts should be focused on incorporating a science-based approach when evaluating landscape-level conservation methods and future impacts resulting from land use changes (see references in Appendix 8.2).

SUMMARY

Ultimately, the best way to preserve amphibian populations and to avoid the deleterious effects of habitat destruction, alteration, and fragmentation is to identify important amphibian habitats and to not develop or modify them in the first place. The effects of habitat loss are far more important than habitat fragmentation (Fahrig 1997), which provides us with further incentive to conserve and restore habitats. All mitigation methods are time, labor, and financially expensive. Many techniques are still unproven and must be treated as scientific experiments before being accepted. Unless the rates of habitat loss are ameliorated, other cumulative stresses to amphibian populations will be compounded to the point where biologists will be unable to devise conservation programs to ensure the survival of the world's oldest land-dwelling vertebrates.

ACKNOWLEDGMENTS
We thank Marian Griffey and Russ Hall for their comments on the manuscript. This chapter is a contribution of the U.S. Geological Survey Amphibian Research and Monitoring Initiative.

Appendix 8.1.

Examples of habitat changes that may affect amphibian communities (data from Hedges 1993; Beebee 1996; Mac et al. 1998; and Dahl 2000)

WETLAND HABITATS:

185,400 ha of wetlands lost per year between mid-1950s and mid-1970s.

117,400 ha of wetlands lost per year between mid-1970s and mid-1980s.

155,200 ha of wetlands lost to urbanization and rural development between 1986 and 1997.

70 to 90% loss of wetlands in Connecticut, Maryland, and Ohio between 1780 and 1980.

69% of pocosins of Atlantic Coastal Plain destroyed by 1980.

50% loss of everglades ecosystem by the early 1990s; the remainder greatly altered.

50 to 60% loss of wetland in Alabama between 1780 and 1980.

54% loss of wetlands in Michigan, Minnesota, and Wisconsin.

30 to 36% loss of wetlands in Arizona, New Mexico, and Utah between 1780 and 1980.

91% of vernal pools and wetlands gone from California.

70% loss of ponds in Britain between 1880 and 1980s.

82% of marshlands destroyed in Essex County, England, between 1938 and 1981.

Xenopus gilli has lost 60% of its wetland breeding sites in South Africa due to habitat loss.

STREAM AND RIVER HABITATS

98% of the original 5.2 million kilometers of streams in the continental United States have been seriously affected.

91% of river lengths in lower 48 U.S. states developed by 1988.

33% of hydrological basins in northeastern United States affected by toxics; 63% by excess nutrients.

66% of the riparian forest in the United States has been destroyed.

85 to 98% of riparian forest in Arizona and New Mexico have been destroyed or severely degraded.

TERRESTRIAL HABITATS

0.01% of native grasslands remain in pre-European contact condition.

85 to 98% loss of oldgrowth forest in Blue Ridge and Cumberland Plateau provinces of Tennessee.

69% of Illinois forests present in 1820 are gone today.

60% of old-growth forest on Olympic Peninsula, Washington, is in patches of 40 ha or less.

85% of coastal redwood forest reduced in California.

0.2% of original forest remains on Puerto Rico.

Forest cover is only 13% of Cuba, 10% of the Dominican Republic, 5% of Jamaica, and less than 1% of Haiti because of deforestation.

Appendix 8.2.

Important references regarding amphibian habitat loss, alteration, and fragmentation. Additional information is in the text.

Habitat change benefiting exotic rather than native amphibians: Adams (1999)

Effects of urbanization on amphibians: Delis et al. (1996)

Effects of forestry on amphibians: deMaynadier and Hunter (1995); Lemckert (1999); Waldick et al. (1999)

Habitat threats to amphibians: Dodd (1997)

Ecological processes in complex landscapes: Dunning et al. (1992)

Amphibians and habitat restoration: Gent and Bray (1994); Bray and Gent (1997); Lehtinen and Galatowitsch (2001)

Amphibian movement in relation to edges and barriers: Gibbs (1998b); Schlaepfer and Gavin (2001)

Amphibians and habitat fragmentation: Fahrig and Merriam (1994); Hecnar and M'Closkey (1996); Vos and Stumpel (1996); Gibbs (1998a); Knutson et al. (1999)

Roads and amphibians: Langton (1989); Fahrig et al. (1995); deMaynadier and Hunter (2000); Carr and Fahrig (2001)

Consequences of habitat loss for wetland amphibians: Lehtinen et al. (1999)

Metapopulations and amphibian conservation: Marsh and Trenham (2001)

Effects of agriculture on amphibians: Oldham (1999)

Effects of fragmentation on amphibian genetics: Reh and Seitz (1990); Driscoll (1998)

Amphibians and buffer zones: Dodd and Cade (1998); Semlitsch (1998)

Effects of small wetland loss on amphibians: Semlitsch and Bodie (1998); Gibbs (2000); Semlitsch (2000b)

9

INVASIVE SPECIES AS A GLOBAL PROBLEM

Toward Understanding the Worldwide Decline of Amphibians

JOSEPH M. KIESECKER

CENTRAL ISSUES

The issue of amphibian conservation is obviously complex, especially given current global declines in many amphibian populations. Most scientists are now realizing that a single overriding factor will not explain these global declines. However, the causes that have been hypothesized for amphibian population declines fall into three broad categories of human-induced environmental perturbations: (1) the overexploitation of habitat and resources, (2) pollution, and (3) invasive species (adapted from Coblentz 1990). Issues of habitat and resource overexploitation encompass all forms of habitat destruction, including urbanization, poor mining and logging practices, and excessive harvesting of natural resources. The pollution category incorporates all chemical and radioactive forms of air, water, and soil pollution. Pollutants can act on local (e.g., nutrient runoff and eutrophication), regional (e.g., sulfur dioxide emissions and acid rain), and global (e.g., carbon dioxide emissions and global warming) scales. Invasive species (IS) are those species that have been transported (purposefully or accidentally) into systems where they did not naturally occur. If we contrast these three categories, a few patterns become clear. First, the problems of pollution and habitat loss clearly receive the most attention from the media, the general public, and the scientific community. Second, most problems of pollution and resource use could be halted or even reversed. Difficult as it may be, there is often the possibility of reversing the trends of increased pollution and the overexploitation of habitat and resources. For example, if we modify our energy consumption, carbon dioxide emissions may be reduced and in turn global warming slowed or even reversed. In contrast, at present there is no effective recall of IS. Once they become established, IS are often permanent in ecological time.

113

The seriousness of this permanence is compounded by the fact that we are currently experiencing a massive biotic homogenization of the earth's surface. This homogenization results from the breakdown of biogeographic boundaries that have historically maintained the distinctive flora and fauna found in different regions of the world. In most regions on earth, IS are the first or second most important anthropogenic impact on freshwater ecosystems (U.S. Congress 1993; Naiman et al. 1995; Lodge et al. 2000). Given the strong tie of amphibians to freshwater systems, any attempt to understand amphibian losses will require that we consider the role of IS. However, due to the perception of "amphibian declines" as a global phenomenon, their study is often biased toward the consideration of factors that act on a global scale (i.e., increased ultraviolet-B radiation, global warming). Indeed one of the main impediments in understanding the role of IS in the global decline of amphibian biodiversity has been their lack of recognition as an important global problem. Although the species that cause problems at given locales often differ, the widespread nature of the problem and consistencies of IS impacts on native systems demands that IS be treated as a global issue.

The primary goal of this chapter is to document the impacts of introduced species on amphibian biodiversity. To bring order to the confusing array of interactions between IS and native systems, I have focused on case studies of three invasive taxa: (1) American bullfrogs, (2) predatory fish, namely, brown trout, rainbow trout, and mosquitofish, and (3) cane toads. All of these species are on the International Union for the Conservation of Nature's list of the world's 100 worst invasive alien species. However, our understanding of each of these introductions varies considerably, as do the approaches taken in the study of their interactions with native species. Moreover, there is considerable variation in what might be done to halt and/or reverse the negative effects of each of these introductions. Because IS cannot be studied in isolation from other environmental perturbations, I will focus on the human activities that increase the frequency of introduction, establishment, and impact of introduced species on amphibian biodiversity. I will also discuss the role that IS may play in the spread of diseases that appear to be responsible for widely reported mass mortality events of amphibians. Some recommendations regarding control of the occurrence and effect of IS are included at the end of the chapter.

CASE STUDIES

Bullfrogs

Numerous workers have reported population declines of ranid frogs native to the western United States (e.g., Moyle 1973; Hayes and Jennings 1986; Fisher and Shaffer 1996). Interactions with introduced American bullfrogs (*Rana catesbeiana*) are often invoked as a primary cause for losses of lowland ranids (e.g., Moyle 1973; Bury and Luckenbach 1976). The bullfrog is native to eastern North America, occurring naturally as far west as the Great Plains (Stebbins 1985). Bullfrogs however, have been extensively introduced throughout much of the western United States (Hayes and Jennings 1986). Adult bullfrogs feed on a variety of aquatic prey, including other amphibians (Corse and Metter 1980; Werner et al. 1995; Kiesecker and Blaustein 1998). Bullfrog tadpoles also prey on tadpoles of other amphibian species (e.g., Ehrlich 1979; Kiesecker and Blaustein 1997b). Bullfrogs typically breed from June to August and the larvae take 1 to 3 years to reach metamorphosis (Nussbaum et al. 1983). Thus, the larvae of native species of frogs may be exposed to competition from larger, older bullfrog tadpoles. The specific impacts of bullfrogs on native frog populations are often unclear because at many sites their introduction has occurred simultaneously with habitat modifications and/or the introduction of predatory fish (Hayes and Jennings 1986; Adams 1999; Kiesecker et al. 2001b). However, several recent studies, primarily experimental in nature, have developed a more mechanistic understanding of the impacts bullfrogs can have on native amphibians (Kiesecker and Blaustein 1997b, 1998; Kupferburg 1997; Adams 1999; Kiesecker et al. 2001b).

In the Willamette Valley of Oregon, the impact of bullfrogs on native red-legged frogs (*Rana aurora*) appears to be a complicated mix of direct and indirect interactions (Figure 9.1). These interactions are compounded by habitat modifications that both promote the success of introduced species and intensify interactions between bullfrogs and red-legged frogs. Surveys of 42 historical red-legged frog breeding sites in the Willamette Valley (J. Kiesecker, unpublished data) indicate that red-legged frogs are absent from 69% of their historical sites. A breeding population of bullfrogs is found at 82.7% of the sites now unoccupied by red-legged frogs. One potential reason for red-legged frog declines could be predation and competition from bullfrogs. The presence of larval and adult bullfrogs results in alterations in microhabitat use by red-legged frogs (Kiesecker and Blaustein 1998). These microhabitat shifts make red-legged frogs more susceptible to predation by introduced fish (Kiesecker and Blaustein 1998). Laboratory experiments have shown that tadpoles from populations that are syntopic with bullfrogs employ antipredatory behaviors when presented with chemical cues of either adult or larval bullfrogs (Kiesecker and Blaustein 1997b). In contrast, tadpoles from populations that are allotropic to bullfrogs do not. In field and additional laboratory experimentation these behavioral differences translated into significantly higher rates of predation in tadpoles from allotropic populations (Kiesecker and Blaustein 1997b). Thus, individuals that are unfamiliar with novel introduced predators may not possess adaptations that would prevent a negative encounter.

There are, however, costs associated with these avoidance behaviors (Kiesecker and Blaustein 1998). In large-scale field experiments, red-legged frog tadpoles altered microhabitat use in response to bullfrog presence. These shifts in microhabitat use resulted

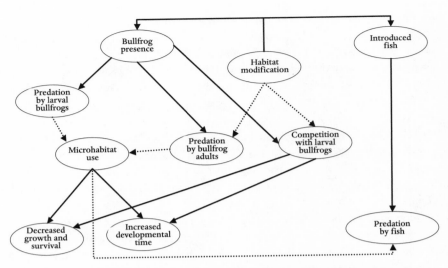

Figure 9.1. Interaction web for impacts of introduced bullfrogs and predatory fishes on red-legged frogs (*Rana aurora*). Arrows represent direct (solid) and indirect (dashed) interactions that have been tested with observational and/or experimental studies (Kiesecker and Blaustein 1997, 1998; Kiesecker et al. 2001b) in Willamette Valley, Oregon. Other direct and indirect interactions are possible but have not been tested.

in decreased growth and development and increased predation by introduced small-mouth bass (*Micropterus dolomieui*). In all experiments, survivorship of red-legged frog tadpoles was only significantly affected when they were exposed to the combined effects of bullfrog larvae and adults, or bullfrog larvae and smallmouth bass. Thus, the interaction between stages (larval/adult) or species (bullfrog/smallmouth bass) produced indirect effects that were greater than when each factor was considered separately.

Habitat modifications appear to play a major role in the interactions described above. In western North America, modification of wetlands frequently benefits introduced bullfrogs and introduced fish (Hayes and Jennings 1986; Richter and Azous 1995; Adams 1999). For example, large, shallow, ephemeral wetlands are commonly converted to smaller permanent ponds (Kentula et al. 1992; Holland et al. 1995; Richter et al. 1997; Adams 1999). These changes provide the conditions needed for successful breeding by bullfrogs. These smaller permanent ponds tend to contain less shallow water and emergent vegetation, and the emergent vegetation is typically clumped along a narrow area at the edge of the pond. Both reducing and clumping vegetation appears to intensify larval competitive interactions between bullfrogs and red-legged frogs (Kiesecker et al. 2001b) and may intensify predation of adult bullfrogs on larval and juvenile red-legged frogs (Kiesecker and Blaustein 1998).

Amphibian losses associated with bullfrog introductions have occurred in other parts of the western United States. For example, Lawler et al. (1999) found that bullfrog tadpoles also had significant negative effects on the growth and survival of larval California red-legged frogs (*Rana aurora draytonii*). Kupferburg (1997) examined the role of larval competition between native foothill yellow-legged frogs (*Rana boylii*) and bullfrogs. Foothill yellow-legged frogs were nearly an order of magnitude less abundant in stream reaches where bullfrogs were established, and bullfrogs also had negative effects on the growth and survival of foothill yellow-legged frogs. Competitive interactions between these species appear to be mediated by bullfrog-induced changes in the algal resources. Bullfrogs have also been introduced into other regions of the world, including parts of Central and South America, Italy, and the Netherlands, where they may have similar effects on other native species (e.g., Albertini and Lanza 1987; Stumpel 1992).

Introduced Predatory Fish

More than 160 species of predatory fish have been introduced in 120 countries worldwide (Welcomme 1988; Minckley and Deacon 1991). In addition, indigenous predatory fish are often translocated within their natural ranges to habitats where they previously did not occur. Thus, the potential of introduced fish to impact amphibian biodiversity is truly global in scale. Here, I will review a few of the numerous studies that incorporate observational or experimental evidence, or both, to demonstrate the negative impacts on amphibians of purposefully introduced predatory fish.

High-elevation lakes in the western United States are of particular concern because most were historically fishless, but many are now stocked for sport fishing purposes with nonnative salmonid fish (rainbow trout, *Oncorhynchus mykiss*, native to western North America; brook trout, *Salvelinus fontinalis*, native to eastern North America; and brown trout, *Salmo trutta*, native to Europe and Asia). Most (>90%) lakes larger than 2 ha and deeper than 3 m have received stocked fish (Bahls 1992).

There is considerable evidence suggesting that salmonid fish introduced into high-elevation lakes and ponds of the Sierra Nevada of California have negative impacts on the mountain yellow-legged frog (*Rana muscosa*). The mountain yellow-legged frog is endemic to the Sierra Nevada Range of California and Nevada. It was historically a common inhabitant of lakes and ponds at elevations of 1,400 to 3,700 m, nearly all of which were naturally fishless. Life-history characteristics of the mountain yellow-legged frog restrict them to bodies of water where the chance of summer drying and winter freezing are reduced (Bradford 1989; Knapp and Matthews 2000). Population declines and disappearances of the mountain yellow-legged frog have been reported from many locations in the Sierra Nevada, including sites within Yosemite, Sequoia, and Kings Canyon national parks, and from several wilderness areas outside these parks (Bradford et al. 1993; Knapp et al. 2001).

Several hypotheses (e.g., acid rain, increased pesticide exposure) have been proposed to explain the declines of the mountain yellow-legged frog. Many of these declines do not appear to be associated with any obvious habitat loss or pattern of land or recreational use (Bradford et al. 1993; Knapp and Matthews 2000). The results of several studies suggest that predation by introduced fishes may have contributed to the declines. In a series of observational studies, Bradford (1989) and Bradford et al. (1998) suggested that the declines of the mountain yellow-legged frog may be the result of tadpole predation by introduced salmonids because of the strong overlap between sites that have successfully received fish and sites that meet the habitat requirements of the mountain yellow-legged frog. In an extensive survey of 1,728 lakes and ponds, Knapp and Matthews (2000) found that the negative effects of fish introduction were evident at three spatial scales: landscape, watershed, and individual waterbody. At the landscape level, a comparison between Kings Canyon National Park and the John Muir Wilderness Area indicated that fish distribution was negatively correlated with the distribution of frogs. Kings Canyon National Park has historically received a lower intensity of fish introductions than the John Muir Wilderness. At the watershed scale, the percentage of total waterbody surface area occupied by fish was a significant predictor of the area occupied by frogs. In individual waterbodies, frogs were three times more likely to be found in fishless than in fish-containing waterbodies.

To some, these data are convincing evidence of the impacts of introduced salmonids on native amphibians. However, a common argument posed against this hypothesis is that sites now occupied by trout are, and always were, poor habitat for amphibians. Nevertheless, many of the surveys adjusted for habitat effects and still found significant influences of introduced fish on amphibian distribution (e.g., Knapp and Matthews 2000). Moreover, recent studies have taken the next step by conducting experimental removals of fish and observing the changes in amphibian communities. In further support of their hypothesis, Knapp and Matthews (1998) removed entire trout populations from select lakes within their study area and have begun to track the recolonization of amphibian populations. Initial evidence suggests that after removal of predatory fish, populations of the mountain yellow-legged frog recover. These results add to the growing body of studies that evaluate the recovery of mountain lake ecosystems after the removal of nonnative fishes (Parker et al. 1996; Frank and Dunlap 1999; Drake and Naiman 2000; Knapp et al. 2001).

Skeptics of the fish stocking hypothesis have asked why declines have occurred only recently, when fish stocking has occurred in these areas since the 1850s. For the declines of the mountain yellow-legged frog, this question of timing is likely a misconception, because researchers noted declines of this species much earlier than the last decade. The observations of Grinnell and Storer (1924) suggest an early start to the declines. During surveys conducted in the Sierra Nevada from 1915 to 1919, these authors reported that larval mountain yellow-legged frogs were absent from lakes containing introduced fish. Thus, the declines reported in the 1980s and 1990s might reflect the remnants of declines that started nearly a century before (Knapp and Matthews 2000). Bradford et al. (1993) suggest a scenario for a time lag between the introduction of predatory fish and population extinction that is consistent with what might be predicted from metapopulation theory (Hanski and Gilpin 1991a, 1991b). Populations are first driven to extinction when introduced fish make the site unsuitable for reproduction. Remaining populations in smaller lakes and ponds that are unable to receive fish are driven to extinction as they become isolated and have a reduced probability of recolonization. Furthermore, these populations may become extinct because of their smaller size, which makes them more susceptible to extinction through stochastic events.

Amphibian losses associated with introduced predatory fish have also been found in other parts of the western United States. For example, Tyler et al. (1998a) linked reductions in larval long-toed salamander (*Ambystoma macrodactylum*) densities to the presence of introduced trout in lakes located in the North Cascades National Park, Washington. However, the effects of introduced fish appear to be mediated by water chemistry. In lakes with a high nitrogen concentration, salamander abundance was higher in lakes without fish. There was, however, no difference in salamander abundance between lakes with and without fish when nitrogen concentration was low. In a laboratory experiment, Tyler et al. (1998b) demonstrated that survivorship and size of long-toed and northwestern salamander (*Ambystoma gracile*) larvae were lower in tanks with trout. Moreover, both species restricted their habitat use in the presence of trout.

A similar situation occurs in parts of Europe (e.g., Spain and Sweden) and Australia where fish have also been stocked into historically fishless waters. In New South Wales, Australia, Gillespie (2001) has suggested that the geographic pattern of spotted treefrog (*Litoria spenceri*) declines may be related to the introduction of brown and rainbow trout. To further support this hypothesis, field experiments were conducted to examine the relative susceptibility of native tadpoles to native and introduced fishes. Results demonstrated that native fishes consumed none or few of the spotted treefrog tadpoles. In contrast, introduced trout significantly reduced survivorship of *L. spenceri* tadpoles, despite the fact that alternative prey and tadpole refugia were available. In the mountains of northern Spain, Brana et al. (1996) found that lakes with introduced fish contained either zero or one species of amphibian, whereas lakes without introduced fish contained three to five species of amphibians. In Sweden, Bronmark and Edenhamn (1994) illustrated the importance of considering fish that are translocated within their natural ranges to habitats where they previously did not occur. They found that the distribution of tree frogs, *Hyla arborea*, was negatively correlated with the presence of fish. Although the fishes in question are native to the area under study, their movement to sites where they did not previously occur had an impact similar to fish introduced from areas outside their normal range. Purposeful introductions offset the joint evolutionary processes that occur between predator and prey, whereby prey evolve morphological structures, chemical repellents, crypsis, and antipredatory behaviors that reduce predation risk (Kats and Dill

1998; Chivers and Smith 1998; Kiesecker et al. 1996). These adaptations appear to be of particular importance for regulating distribution patterns of prey amphibians and predatory fish (Kats et al. 1988). Introduced predators may have particularly strong effects on native prey that do not recognize new predators (Kiesecker and Blaustein 1997b) or do not show appropriate avoidance behaviors (Shave et al. 1994), or when introduced predators have foraging strategies that differ from those of native predators (McIntosh and Townsend 1996).

The purposeful stocking of fish also occurs for reasons other than for recreational sport fishing. For example, mosquitofish (*Gambusia affinis*) are regularly used as a biological control agent of mosquito populations. Mosquitofish are a small poeciliid fish native to the southeastern United States, eastern Mexico, and the Caribbean (Komak and Crossland 2000). Because of its broad abiotic tolerances (Otto 1973) and its effectiveness as a mosquito predator, the mosquitofish has been introduced ubiquitously throughout warm regions of the world. Mosquitofish may consume high densities of mosquito larvae along the banks of streams and ponds, but they also eliminate other invertebrate populations (Hulbert et al. 1972), and recent work has shown that they may have detrimental effects on amphibian populations (Gamradt and Kats 1996; Goodsell and Kats 1999; Komak and Crossland 2000). Gamradt and Kats (1996) compared streams in Los Angeles County that were historically (during the 1980s) known to contain populations of the California newt (*Taricha torosa*) but not populations of introduced predators. They focused on both introduced mosquitofish and introduced crayfish (*Procambarus clarkii*). The crayfish has also been introduced extensively throughout North America and, although it has received little attention from biologists, reports suggest that the spread of *P. clarkii* and other crayfish species has the potential to seriously affect aquatic systems (Lodge et al. 2000). Of the ten streams surveyed by Gamradt and Kats (1996), three contained both or one of the introduced predators, whereas the remaining seven streams contained neither introduced predator. Distribution of the newt was restricted to the seven streams that did not contain introduced predators. Laboratory and field experiments confirmed that both introduced species were effective predators of larval newts and that crayfish were successful predators of eggs as well. In further support of their hypothesis, Gamradt and Kats (1996) and Gamradt et al. (1997) used a natural disturbance to track the population dynamics of newts and introduced predators. In 1995, heavy rains removed crayfish from one of the streams, and the following spring newt egg masses, larvae, and adults were again found in high numbers. In 1996, however, crayfish returned and adult newt populations were reduced by 78%, egg masses were reduced by 89%, and larval newts were totally eliminated.

In Australia, where mosquitofish have been introduced in attempts to control mosquito populations, impacts on native amphibians also appear to be occurring (Komak and Crossland 2000). The truly unsettling aspect of the mosquitofish introductions is that in many cases mosquitofish are distributed by local governmental mosquito control agencies. These same agencies make mosquitofish readily available and free of charge to the general public, often with the assertion that they present no danger and can be distributed freely to any freshwater system (Diamond 1996).

Cane Toads

The cane toad (*Bufo marinus*) is native to tropical parts of the Americas; its range extends from northwestern Mexico to southern Brazil (Zug and Zug 1979). It was introduced into Australia in 1935 as a biocontrol agent of beetle pests of sugar cane (Mungomery 1935). It has failed in this regard and is now considered a pest species. The geographic expansion of the cane toad has been the subject of considerable attention (e.g., Easteal et al. 1985; Sutherst et al. 1995). It now occupies more than 50% of Queensland and a small portion of New South Wales and the Northern Territory (Easteal et al. 1985; Sutherst et al. 1995) and is still spreading. Estimates of the rate of range expansion extend from 1 km per year in northern New South Wales (Easteal et al. 1985; Sutherst et al. 1995) to 27 km per year in northwestern Queensland (Freeland and Martin 1985). Predictions suggest that the cane toad will ultimately colonize areas in at least four of the mainland Australian states or territories (Sutherst et al. 1995).

The cane toad is commonly believed to have a negative impact on native fauna. Despite the entrenchment of this concept in both scientific literature and the popular press, very little quantitative data exists to refute or support this idea. Because of the similarity in life-history and ecology, it has been suggested that native amphibians may experience the most serious impacts from the spread of the cane toad. Despite these claims, few studies have been specifically designed to examine the impacts of the cane toad on native amphibians (but see, Crossland 1997; Crossland and Alford 1998; Crossland and Azevedo-Ramos 1999). Crossland and Alford (1998) demonstrated that cane toad eggs, hatchlings, and tadpoles are toxic to many native aquatic predators. This toxicity may give them a competitive advantage when interacting with nontoxic native species. Additionally, cane toad tadpoles have been shown to compete with native species (Crossland 1997). Crossland and Azevedo-Ramos (1999) have also shown that consumption of larval cane toads by larvae of native amphibian species results in high mortality. The tendency for native Australian tadpoles to avoid consuming larval cane toads when alternative food was available varied widely across species. Consumption of toxic cane toad eggs and hatchlings may explain some of the mass mortality events that have been observed for some native larval amphibians (Crossland and Azevedo-Ramos 1999). To suggest that the cane toad has caused declines of native Australian frogs would require more data than is currently available. Clearly, further research is needed to assess the impacts that the cane toad is having on amphibian populations within the current range and also to assess the effects that the cane toad may have on other amphibian species as their range continues to expand.

Invasive Species as Agents of Disease Dissemination

Disease outbreaks may play an important role in many of the mass mortality events of amphibians that have been widely reported (e.g., Laurance et al. 1996; Berger et al. 1998; Kiesecker et al. 2001a). It has remained unclear whether outbreaks are related to environmental stress or novel pathogens. Given the extensive nature of introducing hatchery-reared fish and the release and spread of many other IS that interact with amphibians, I suggest that IS could be a major vector for diseases that are contributing to amphibian losses.

The mechanisms that enable introduced species to thrive at the expense of native species are often unclear. Competition with or predation by introduced species is frequently proposed to explain losses of native species after the introduction of an exotic species. Rarely are these mechanisms isolated and tested. Moreover, studies that have attempted to examine the mechanisms that underlie the success of exotic species focus primarily on how invaders directly affect particular resident species (Simberloff 1981). In contrast, little is known about indirect effects of introduced species on native communities (e.g., Kiesecker and Blaustein 1998; Nystrum et al. 2001), such as the effect of pathogens carried by IS (Kiesecker et al. 2001c).

In the Pacific Northwest of the United States, massive amphibian embryo mortality is associated with the presence of the oomycete pathogen *Saprolegnia ferax* (Blaustein et al. 1994b; Kiesecker and Blaustein 1997a, 1999). Saprolegniasis is a common disease of fishes, particularly those fish reared in hatcheries (Richards and Pickering 1978). Many of the species introduced into Pacific Northwest lakes (*Salmo* spp., *Salvelinus* spp., and *Oncorhynchus* spp.) are common carriers of *Saprolegnia,* including *S. ferax* (Richards and Pickering 1978). Laboratory experiments have shown that hatchery-reared rainbow trout (*Oncorhynchus mykiss*) can transmit *S. ferax* to developing amphibians and to soil substrate (Kiesecker et al. 2001c). Amphibian embryos exposed to either infected fish or infected soil were more likely to develop *S. ferax* infections and had higher mortality rates than embryos exposed to control conditions (Kiesecker et al. 2001c).

Several other studies have suggested that IS may have been the vector for novel pathogens responsible for recent mass mortality events. In the San Rafael Valley in southern Arizona, populations of the Sonoran tiger salamander (*Ambystoma tigrinum stebbinsi*) have experienced decimating epizootics (Jancovich et al. 1997). An iridovirus (Ambystoma tigrinum virus; ATV) was isolated from diseased tiger salamanders and was determined to be the causative agent involved in these epizootics. Jancovich et al. (1997) speculated that the origin of ATV at their sites may have been introduced fish, bullfrogs, or possibly introduced salamanders that are used as fish bait. However, to date, laboratory tests have failed to transmit ATV to frogs or fish, suggesting that ATV may only infect urodeles (Jancovich et al. 2001).

Pathogens that may infect native amphibians could accompany the spread of the cane toad in Australia. Cane toads are host to a variety of pathogens that could infect native amphibians (e.g., O'Shea et al. 1990; Speare et al. 1997; Thomas et al. 2001). In particular, the pathogenic fungus *Mucor amphiborum* was isolated from both free-ranging cane toads and native green tree frogs (*Litoria caerulea*). It was first described as a pathogen of captive anurans, although it can also kill free-living anurans (Speare et al. 1997). Speare et al. (1997) suggested that the spread of the cane toad may introduce the fungus to new areas and may enable it to become established in the soil, possibly increasing the risk of disease of native amphibians.

Laurance et al. (1996, 1997) postulated that a novel iridovirus, possibly resulting from fish transplanted as part of the international trade in aquarium fish, might be responsible for the mass mortality events of amphibians observed in eastern Australia. They suggested that these mortality events spread northward at a speed of 100 km a year, resulting in an extinction wave. However, Alford and Richards (1997) disputed the evidence for an "extinction wave" and argued that the iridovirus claimed to be the pathogen has not been isolated from moribund frogs, whereas chytrid fungus (*Batrachochytrium dendrobatidis*) has. Regardless of the identity of the pathogen, if it is indeed a novel pathogen, then an IS may serve as an important vector. Furthermore, the chytrid fungus that has been associated with mass mortality events in Australia and Central America has repeatedly been referred to as a novel introduced organism (Berger et al. 1998). Although to date there is no clear evidence that the chytrid is indeed novel or an introduced pathogen, it is interesting to note that IS such as introduced fish are found at sites where disease outbreaks and catastrophic declines of amphibians have been observed (e.g., rainforest of eastern Australia, Laurance et al. 1996; Montane streams of Central and South America, La Marca and Reinthaler 1991). Clearly more work is needed to assess the role of IS as vectors for amphibian disease.

Human-Induced Environmental Change and the Spread of Invasive Species

Successful invasion is the outcome of interactions between IS and properties of the biological community being invaded. Successful IS are those species able to take advantage of the specific opportunities available, which can be greatly increased by disturbance of ecological systems (e.g., Shea and Chesson 2002). Humans often interact with their environment in ways that increase the frequency of introduction, establishment, and effect of IS on native amphibian species. Drawing on recently published reviews (Blaustein and Kiesecker 1997; Kolar and Lodge 2000; Reaser and Blaustein, in press; and Chapters 3, 8, 12, 14, and 15, this volume), we can summarize the nature of several major human-induced environmental changes and assess whether these factors are increasing or decreasing (Table 9.1). We can then estimate the direct effect of each factor on amphibians and, more importantly, estimate how each factor may interact with IS to produce greater impacts on amphibians. For example, a "strong" potential interaction with IS indicates that the environmental change either increases the likelihood that invasion will be successful or exacerbates the effect of IS on native systems.

Although some movement of species would occur without human intervention, human activities greatly increase the rate and spatial scale of species introductions. Human activities directly alter the distribution and abundance of IS through the escape of species that are accidentally transported with other resources. Humans, their vehicles, and their goods are often direct vectors for the movement of IS. Humans are also effective in altering the distribution of IS by intentionally introducing species. IS are introduced for a variety of reasons—as a food source, to enhance stocks for commercial harvesting, for cultural and aesthetic reasons, to enhance leisure activities, and as biocontrol agents to control other IS.

Other human activities have indirectly altered the distribution and abundance of IS through changes in climate or through habitat modifications associated with increased modern agricultural practices and urbanization. For example, habitat modifications associated with urbanization can have negative impacts on amphibians and may also

Table 9.1

Human-induced environmental changes and their effects on amphibians

Environmental Change	Change Trend[a]	Direct Effects on Amphibians	Potential Interaction with Introduced Species
International trade			
Transportation of goods	Increasing	Unknown	Strong
Aquarium pet trade	Increasing	Unknown	Strong
Aquaculture	Increasing	Unknown	Strong
Bait trade	Increasing	Negative	Strong
Climatic change	Possible increase	Negative	Unknown
Atmospheric change			
(e.g., ozone depletion)	Increasing	Negative	Unknown
Purposeful introduction			
(e.g., stocking)	Increasing	Negative	Strong
Habitat modification, agriculture			
Eutrophication	Increasing	Negative	Unknown
Increased pesticide runoff	Increasing	Negative	Unknown
Wetland restructuring	Increasing	Negative	Strong
Habitat modification, urbanization			
Fragmentation	Increasing	Negative	Unknown
Roadway expansion	Increasing	Negative	Strong

[a]Patterns of environmental change may differ from region to region.

facilitate the establishment of IS. Interactions between bullfrogs and red-legged frogs appear to be strongly influenced by habitat modifications (Figure 9.1). Furthermore, evidence suggests that roadway expansion associated with human development speeds the dispersal of many IS, including cane toads (Seabrook and Dettmann 1996). All of these changes are expected to continue; in fact, most of these environmental changes will continue to increase as human populations continue to grow.

POTENTIAL SOLUTIONS

It is unlikely that we will be able to eradicate all species that have already invaded or prevent all future invasions. However, the first step toward recovery is recognizing that there is indeed a problem. Although by no means an exhaustive survey of the impact of IS on amphibians, the case studies discussed in this chapter provide convincing evidence that IS can and do have dramatic effects on amphibians. There is however, considerable variation in the degree of difficulty these introductions pose for halting the problems they create. In the case of introduced predatory fish, reversal of the problem may be accomplished by simply reducing or halting stocking. Early indications suggest that removing fish may allow recolonization and reestablishment of amphibian populations (e.g., Knapp and Matthews 1998; Knapp et al. 2001). Because it may be extremely difficult if not impossible to eradicate cane toads, it remains questionable how amphibian populations will cope with their spread. Clearly, further research is needed to assess the effect they have on amphibian populations. Similarly, it will be difficult to successfully reduce bullfrogs to levels that do not affect native species. However, with a mechanistic understanding of the impacts that IS have on native amphibians, the possibility exists to develop practices that maintain native populations. The studies involving bullfrogs are a case in point.

To date, controlling invasive species has mainly focused on eradicating the exotics or attempting to control their population sizes through the use of biological control agents. Both of these methods have had limited success, and in some cases have resulted in the introduction of additional pest species (Simberloff and Stiling 1996; Henneman and Memmott. 2001). Understanding the context-dependent nature of invasion may allow for the development of strategies to prevent successful invasion and systems that limit the impact of IS. For example, understanding the precise role that habitat modifications play in shifting the balance of interactions in favor of IS may make it possible to create management strategies designed to maintain native species.

It is also clear that the problem of IS extends beyond political boundaries. Thus, attempts to rectify the problem will require cooperation between nations. To that end, representatives of 80 countries, led by the Scientific Committee on Problems in the Environment, The World Conservation Union, and CAB International, established the Global Invasive Species Program (GISP) in 1997 (Mooney 1999; Mooney and

Hobbs 2000). The GISP takes a multidisciplinary approach that includes assessing the status of current IS, developing the ability to predict which species may become serious IS, identifying biological communities that may be at risk from IS, understanding the relationship of global change and IS spread, and developing effective management practices to deal with IS. To date, GISP has made a number of advances including the dissemination of a management toolkit, publication of several books (e.g., Mooney and Hobbs 2000), and a compilation of the world's worst invaders (available online at www.issg.org). Furthermore, its recommendations have led to U.S. Presidential Executive Order 13112, which has established the formation of the National Invasive Species Council and the first ever national invasive species management plan. Initial GISP studies recommend that preventing the introduction of IS is more economical than controlling their spread once establishment has occurred. Thus, development of strategies that will detect and prevent introductions is desirable. Furthermore, many IS have a lag period after introduction when control strategies may be more effective. Thus, resources should be directed to early detection systems and response procedures that can be quickly initiated.

CONCLUSIONS

Researchers and managers cannot disregard invasive species and their impacts on amphibian populations. It is clear that introduced species play an important role in many amphibian declines. Moreover, the impacts that these species have are often exacerbated by and interact with other important environmental changes. Although it is unlikely that a single introduced species (or single factor for that matter) is responsible for all declines, the widespread and consistent impacts of IS require that they be considered in any conservation plan.

Our ability to predict the effects of biotic invasions is still limited. The general result of the many well-intentioned introductions is typically unexpected, and often has deleterious consequences. The need to increase our ability to predict the consequences of invasions and to understand invasion processes has been heightened by the enormous economic and social costs and the growing concern in preventing biodiversity loss. Perhaps the best strategy is to avoid the purposeful introduction of species where possible, to increase our efforts to prevent the accidental introduction of species, and to increase research efforts to understand the invasion process.

ACKNOWLEDGMENTS

Financial support was provided by the National Institutes of Health/National Science Foundation Ecology of Infectious Disease Program (1R01ES11067-01) and by the Department of Biology, Pennsylvania State University. Thanks also to Michael Rubbo, Brooks Hatlen, and Lisa Belden for helpful comments on earlier versions of this manuscript and to Ryan Peterson, Andy Dufresne, and Ellis Boyd Redding for technical assistance.

10
PATHOGENS, INFECTIOUS DISEASE, AND IMMUNE DEFENSES

CYNTHIA CAREY, ALLAN P. PESSIER, AND ANGELA D. PEACE

CENTRAL ISSUES

Habitat destruction, introduction of predators or competitors, and direct application of chemicals to amphibian habitats are generally known causes of amphibian population declines (see other chapters, this volume). These anthropogenic causes could be minimized if amphibian conservation became a high priority for human societies. Many amphibian populations have also severely declined or have even become extinct in relatively undisturbed areas of North America, South America, Europe, Australia, and Central America, where human impacts are not as obvious. In these areas, infectious diseases are now known to be the direct cause of many of the declines. Although disease has always played an important role in the population dynamics of animals and plants (Anderson and May 1986), the unusual features associated with recent mass amphibian die-offs include mortalities on a global scale, the large number of species affected, and the variety of ecosystems in which the die-offs have been observed. Although these epidemics have not yet been proven to have caused extinctions of entire species, they have nonetheless disrupted the demography, genetic structure, and geographic distributions of many species to such an extent that future extinctions are no doubt possible (e.g., Drost and Fellers 1996; Carey et al. 2002b). Neither the emergence of the pathogens responsible for these epidemics, nor the susceptibility of amphibians to these infections is yet attributable to any human disturbances. However, the release of infected animals obtained from biological suppliers, pet traders, and bait shops undoubtedly has contributed to the spread of these pathogens after their emergence.

Outbreaks of infectious disease associated with amphibian declines have recently been reviewed by Carey et al. (1999), Daszak et al. (1999), and Carey (2000). This chapter will briefly summarize the information in these reviews and then highlight new information available since their publication.

PATHOGENS RESPONSIBLE FOR MASS MORTALITIES IN THE WILD AND MODES OF INFECTION

Amphibian skin, digestive tracts, and other surfaces in contact with the environment typically contain a variety of bacteria, fungi, viruses, and parasites (Speare 1990; Cunningham et al. 1996; McAlpine 1997). Some of these organisms may be virulent or opportunistic (able to cause infection only when the defenses of the amphibian are impaired) pathogens, whereas others may have no observable effect on the host or may even participate in mutually beneficial, symbiotic relationships with the host. A compilation of the available information on amphibian pathogens and diseases is available online at http://www.jcu.au/school/phtm/PHTM/frogs.bibliog.htm. Because many potential pathogens are commonly found on external surfaces or internal organs of amphibians, rigorous standards must be met to prove that a specific pathogen is responsible for illness or death of an animal. The minimum standards for proving that a specific pathogen is the culprit include both a complete necropsy, including histopathology, and a culture of the potential pathogen. If, during this process, an entirely novel pathogen is discovered, additional criteria must be met. Identification of a new pathogen must include fulfillment of Koch's postulates, which requires that the pathogen be isolated and purified, and then that healthy animals be exposed to the purified pathogen. When the exposed animals become ill with the same pathological findings as the initial infection, the pathogen must again be isolated and purified from these animals (for an example, see Nichols et al. 2001).

Few of the pathogens found associated with amphibians are known to cause mass mortalities in nature. However, Koch's postulates have recently been fulfilled with two pathogens, a chytrid fungus (*Batrachochytrium dendrobatidis*) and ranaviruses. Both of these pathogens have been shown to cause mass mortalities in amphibian larvae, metamorphosing individuals, and postmetamorphic individuals. Another fungus, *Saprolegnia* (sp.), has been hypothesized to cause some amphibian population declines by killing eggs (cf. Blaustein et al. 1994b; Kiesecker and Blaustein 1995). However, because Koch's postulates have not yet been fulfilled to prove that this fungus is the direct cause of death in these cases, this review will focus exclusively on chytrid and ranavirus pathogens.

Chytridiomycosis

Several outbreaks of infectious diseases in wild amphibians were recorded before the 1970s (see references in Carey et al. 1999). Beginning in the early 1970s, however, widespread mass mortalities of many species were noted in the United States, Canada, Puerto Rico, and Australia (see references in Joglar and Burrowes 1996; Mahony 1996; Carey et al. 1999; Sredl 2000). These unexplained die-offs resulted in serious declines and even extirpations of many populations. For instance, populations of the Wyoming toad (*Bufo baxteri*) declined to such a low level that the few surviving individuals were collected for captive breeding. Western toads (*Bufo boreas*) disappeared throughout 80 to 90% of their former distribution in the Rockies of Colorado and southern Wyoming (see references in Carey et al. 2002b). Remnant populations have not increased in size nor expanded into historically occupied habitats (Carey et al. 2002b). Attempts at reintroduction of captive-reared Wyoming toads or translocation of western toads into historical habitats have been relatively unsuccessful (Carey et al. 2002b), and pathogens must be considered as a likely factor in the poor success of these reintroductions. Mass mortalities are continuing in areas of the American West at this time (Sredl 2000; Muths et al., in press).

Other mass mortalities of amphibians have recently been noted in relatively undisturbed areas of Europe (Bosch et al. 2001), Central America (Lips 1998, 1999), Australia (see references in Daszak et al. 1999; Carey 2000), and South America (Santiago Ron and Merino 2000). A common pattern has been observed in many of these current and historical die-offs: infectious disease is the apparent direct cause of death; most die-offs occur at relatively high altitudes, in cold regions, or during cold weather; metamorphosed individuals are the primary target of the pathogen; populations experience 50 to 100% mortality within 1 to 2 years; mortality is widespread over large geographic regions; and population declines do not occur in all amphibian species within a given habitat (Scott 1993; Carey et al. 1999).

A recently discovered skin disease caused by a fungal pathogen (*Batrachochytrium dendrobatidis*) appears to be the direct cause of many of these unexplained deaths. It was identified first in captive Arizona toads (*Bufo microscaphus*) (Nichols et al. 1996; Pessier et al. 1999) and subsequently in wild amphibians in Central America and Australia (Berger et al. 1998); in this case, Koch's postulates have been fulfilled (Nichols et al. 2001). Chytridiomycosis is now thought to be the direct cause of mass mortalities in a number of amphibian species in Australia, Central America, South America (Ecuador), Europe (Spain), and the United States (Berger et al. 1998; Longcore et al. 1999; Pessier et al. 1999; Santiago Ron and Merino 2000; Bosch et al. 2001). A few museum samples of species such as western toads, northern leopard frogs (*Rana pipiens*), and Yosemite toads (*Bufo canorus*) collected in the western United States during the 1970s have tested positive for this organism (Carey et al. 1999; Green and Sherman 2001). The cause of these historical die-offs cannot be proven conclusively because Koch's postulates cannot be performed on preserved samples and because complete pathological examinations that could rule out other possible pathogens are lacking. The assumption that many mass mortalities in the mid-to-late 1970s and early 1980s were due to *Batrachochytrium* is based both on the presence of the chytrid fungi in museum samples collected at the times of mass mortalities and on the similarities between the patterns of current and historical die-offs (i.e., mortality of metamorphosed individuals, rapid population declines over broad geographic areas, many mortalities in relatively protected areas at high altitudes; Carey 2000).

Some members of the phylum Chytridiomycota break down vegetable matter, chitin, and keratin in aquatic systems, whereas others are parasitic on insects or invertebrates. *Batrachochytrium* is the first known chytrid fungus to be a pathogen of a vertebrate animal (Longcore et al. 1999). The infective stage of this fungus is a motile, asexual reproductive spore that swims with a single posteriorly directed flagellum. Amphibians can be infected by being placed either in water containing zoospores that were taken from agar plates (Nichols et al. 2001) or in water from which infected animals have recently been removed (C. Carey, L. Livo, J. Bruzgul, K. Keuhl, and M. Walling, University of Colorado, unpublished data). After invasion of the keratinocytes into the outer epidermis, the zoospores develop into flask-shaped thalli (zoosporangia) with fine absorptive rhizoids projecting from the thallus. Zoospores are released from the thallus via a discharge tube. The histologically diagnostic features of this chytrid are the formation of colonial or flask-shaped thalli with discharge tubes, zoospores present in the thalli of active infections, and the presence of rhizoids in silver stained sections (Longcore et al. 1999). Infection occurs most frequently in the ventral skin of the pelvic area and on the back legs and toes, but can also occur on the dorsum in severe infections (Pessier et al. 1999). After colonization of the epidermis by zoospores, the epidermal layers become thickened (hyperplastic and hyperkeratotic) in response either to a stimulatory factor secreted by the chytrid or to nonspecific changes in the skin caused by a chytrid infection. Skin inflammation is occasionally observed, but some specimens with severe infections (as determined histologically) do not show external lesions. More details on the clinical signs and microscopic pathology of chytrid infections are available from Pessier et al. (1999), Berger et al. (2000a), and Carey et al. (2002a).

The affinity of *Batrachochytrium* for keratinized cells appears to explain why this pathogen targets metamorphosed individuals. Amphibian eggs, which lack keratin, are not thought to be susceptible to infection, but more study is needed. Tadpole mouthparts, the only tadpole structures that contain keratin, are vulnerable to infection by this chytrid. Infected mouthparts lose their pigment and become deformed. Tubercles on developing hind legs of tadpoles may be susceptible to chytrid infection during metamorphosis. No clinical disease or mortalities of tadpoles have been observed (Fellers et al. 2001), but reduced growth and development have been observed in chytrid-infected tadpoles in mesocosm studies (A. Blaustein, Oregon State University, unpublished data). Tadpoles may carry chytrids through metamorphosis and then die as their newly keratinized skin becomes infected. However, once metamorphosed, individuals of all ages can succumb to this pathogen. Because both newly metamorphosed juveniles and breeding adults are removed from the population by chytrid epidemics, populations decline rapidly. Two hypotheses concerning how this pathogen kills amphibians are currently under examination: (1) the fungus produces a toxin that diffuses through the skin into the blood and causes metabolic disturbances, or (2) hyperkeratosis and hyperplasticity, coupled with other possible changes, disrupt ion and water uptake through the ventral skin.

Thermal (23°C) and pH optima (pH 6.5) for growth of *Batrachochytrium* have been examined in the laboratory (J. L. Longcore, S. Annis, University of Maine, unpublished data). This chytrid is capable of slow growth even below 5°C, which may explain in part why some die-offs associated with this pathogen occur at cold temperatures (Carey 2000). The relationship between the number of days to death and the infectious dose (number of zoospores in the initial exposure), body size, and body temperature has been tested in amphibian models (C. Carey, L. Livo, J. Bruzgul, B. Dixon, K. Keuhl, and M. Walling, University of Colorado, unpublished data), but the relevance of these laboratory results to the interactions among *Batrachochytrium*, its amphibian hosts, and environmental factors in the field has not yet been addressed. Amphibians likely become exposed to zoospores when amphibians congregate during breeding and/or hibernation. Deaths within a population are not synchronous and the demise of the population may take several years. Variation in the timing of deaths within a population may result from differences in individual resistance to infection or behavior, or both. Habitat specializations of some species may also prevent exposure to this chytrid. For instance, stream-dwelling frogs have been dramatically affected by this pathogen in Australia and Central America, but arboreal species, which do not frequent stream habitats, have not suffered population declines (Lips 1998, 1999; Berger et al. 2000b). No obvious patterns in life history traits have emerged: although many tropical rainforest frogs that are vulnerable to this pathogen have restricted ranges and small clutch sizes, those species affected in North America have relatively large clutch sizes and broad geographic ranges (Berger et al. 2000a; Carey et al. 2002b).

Susceptibility to *Batrachochytrium* infection varies among amphibians. Sublethal infections have been found in amphibian populations not known to have recently undergone mass mortalities (J. Longcore, University of Maine, personal communication). American bullfrogs (*Rana catesbeiana*) and tiger salamanders (*Ambystoma tigrinum*) became infected after experimental exposures in the laboratory, but the salamanders have shown the ability to clear the infection and the bullfrogs appear resistant to clinically significant or lethal infections (P. Daszak, Consortium for Conservation Medicine, and E. Davidson, Arizona State University, unpublished data). Some species, such as western chorus frogs (*Pseudacris triseriata*), continue to persist in large numbers in field locations where other amphibians, such as northern leopard frogs and western toads, have become extinct, presumably due to chytrid infections (Carey 1993; Carey et al. 1999). Variations in susceptibility are currently being used to examine the mechanisms of resistance to infection and the possibility that resistant amphibians might serve as reservoir species.

The ability of *Batrachochytrium* to cause near or complete extinction of many populations of amphibians suggests that it has been recently introduced to naïve hosts (Daszak et al. 1999) and that it may have alternative hosts in the environment (R. Speare, Commonwealth Scientific and Industrial Research Organization, Queensland, Australia, personal communication). Whether this fungus has recently emerged as a pathogen or has been present in the environment for some time is unknown. No close genetic relatives have been identified (James et al. 2000). Because experimentally infected amphibians readily succumb to *Batrachochytrium* in laboratory conditions that lack ultraviolet-B light, contaminants, or other potentially stressful factors, no compelling evidence links environmental change to the emergence of this pathogen or its success in killing amphibians (Daszak et al. 1999). Analysis of climatic events in Colorado (United States), northeastern Australia, Costa Rica and Panama found no extreme weather events preceding or concurrent with mass mortalities of amphibians linked to *Batrachochytrium* (Alexander and Eischeid 2001). Although levels of ultraviolet-B have increased since 1979 in locations in Central America in which mortalities due to *Batrachochytrium* have occurred, no evidence yet exists that exposures of amphibians to ultraviolet-B in these localities have increased (Middleton et al. 2001).

At present, several fungicides can be used to successfully treat captive amphibians infected with *Batrachochytrium*, but amphibians in nature will continue to be at risk of infection for the foreseeable future. Whether natural modes of transport of this pathogen across and between continents exist is a subject of debate, but it is likely that humans distribute the pathogen in many ways, including transporting and releasing infected animals into the wild and carrying mud containing *Batrachochytrium* on fishing or hiking boots from one locality to another.

Ranaviruses

Other mass mortalities of both anurans and salamanders have been caused by iridoviruses of the genus *Ranavirus* (Cunningham et al. 1996; Daszak et al. 1999; Hyatt et al. 2000). First recognized in the 1960s, these viruses are now thought to be responsible for die-offs of amphibians on five continents (Jancovich et al. 1997; Daszak et al. 1999; see review of literature in Carey et al. 2002a). Various isolates of *Ranavirus* have been found in fish, reptiles, and amphibians (Hyatt et al. 2000), and several of these viruses can infect both amphibians and fish (Mao et al. 1999). Larval, metamorphosing, and recently metamorphosed amphibians are vulnerable to the virus (Jancovich et al. 1997; Daszak et al. 1999; Carey et al. 2002a).

Ranaviral epizootics are more likely to occur in disturbed or degraded habitats and are more geographically limited than are those attributed to *Batrachochytrium* (Cunningham et al. 1996; Jancovich et al. 1997; Daszak et al. 1999). In some cases, these epidemics appear at high population densities. Although these outbreaks of disease may reduce the population size for a year or more, no evidence yet exists that any populations have become extinct. Extinction may be prevented because breeding adults escape the pond before the epidemic occurs, because not all young of the year may succumb, and/or because immigration from adjacent ponds brings in new, un-infected individuals.

One of the most intensively studied cases of a ranaviral epizootic is the ranaviral infections of tiger salamanders in several areas of North America. During the summer, many of the young (larvae, metamorphosing and newly metamorphosed individuals) die over the span of a few weeks. Deaths may also occur sporadically at other times during the year. During these die-offs, large numbers of floating carcasses can be found in a pond, and living individuals appear disoriented (frequently swimming upside down) and unresponsive and die within a few days of capture (J. Collins, J. Brunner, D. Schock, Arizona State University, unpublished observation).

Ranaviruses probably invade amphibians through the gills, skin, or digestive tract from infected food or feces, direct animal-to-animal contact, or exposure to infectious water (Jancovich et al. 1997). The histological indications of the disease are acute necrosis of hematopoietic and lymphoid tissues, liver, kidneys, muscles, and digestive tract. Death is presumably due to organ failure. Clinical signs of infection range from no visible signs to externally visible hemorrhage (manifested as reddening of the skin or multiple red spots), skin lesions, and/or edema (fluid accumulation within the skin or coelomic cavity). Necrosis of hematopoietic tissues may increase vulnerability of the host to secondary bacterial infections (Cunningham et al. 1996). Because secondary bacterial infections may result in symptoms similar to the amphibian "red-leg" syndrome, a full necropsy, including viral diagnostic tests, is necessary to verify ranavirus infection. Further details regarding methods of identifying ranaviruses are given in Carey et al. (2002a).

Ranaviruses are geographically widely distributed. Because they remain infectious for prolonged periods in the absence of suitable hosts, even under adverse conditions (Daszak et al. 1999), it is probable that they can be spread from place to place on fishing gear. Introduction of invasive species, including fish and infected amphibians, is also a likely mechanism of distribution.

WHY AREN'T IMMUNE DEFENSES AGAINST THESE PATHOGENS PROTECTING AMPHIBIANS?

Amphibians possess sophisticated immune systems that include almost all of the components of mammalian immune systems (Carey et al. 1999). Like those of other vertebrates, amphibian immune systems are divided into two functional categories, innate and adaptive. The innate system provides immediate protection that involves nonspecific elements (i.e., those that can respond to a variety of pathogens), such as antimicrobial peptides, macrophages, neutrophils, natural killer cells, the serum complement system, and the protective secretions and barriers of the skin, digestive tract, and bladder (Carey et al. 1999). The adaptive system, which requires time to be activated after a foreign antigen is detected, includes helper, cytotoxic, and memory T-cells and B-cells, each of which is specialized to respond to only a single antigen. Memory T-cells and antibodies produced by B-cells in response to the first exposure to an antigen provide an enhanced ability to respond to a second exposure and may provide a degree of immunity for a period of time after the first exposure (Carey et al. 1999).

In other vertebrates, immune defenses against viruses include responses from both the innate and adaptive immune systems. Therefore, natural killer cells, nonspecialized cells of the innate immune system, and responses mediated by T- and B-cells would be expected to participate in amphibian immune defenses against viral infection, but experimental data are considerably lacking in this area. It is currently unknown why ranaviruses are so lethal to most amphibians. Perhaps these viruses cause massive tissue destruction before the immune system can mount a successful defense. For example, when tiger salamanders are exposed in the laboratory to the ranavirus Ambystoma tigrinum virus (ATV), death resulted within 7 days (Jancovich et al. 1997), yet a full response of a salamander's adaptive immune system is likely to require more than two weeks, even at optimal temperatures (N. Cohen, University of Rochester, personal communication).

In almost every study to date, the immune system of amphibians infected with *Batrachochytrium dendrobatidis* does not appear to respond to the presence of this fungus in the epidermis. Inflammation, frequently one of the first defensive steps in fighting a pathogen, and recruitment of cellular components of the immune system have not been observed in most necropsies of amphibians succumbing to this pathogen (Pessier et al. 1999). It is unknown at present whether the lack of immune response results from an inability of the immune system to detect the pathogen in the epidermis or from the effects of an inhibitor secreted by the chytrid, or other factors. However, inflammation has been consistently noted in *Batrachochytrium* infections of tiger salamanders, which apparently can clear the infection after exposure (E. Davidson, Arizona State University, personal communication).

Antimicrobial peptides are important innate immune defenses against skin pathogens. These products have received considerable attention recently because of their potential as novel antibiotics. Sympathetic nervous system stimulation causes granular glands to extrude peptides onto the surface of the skin (Nicolas and Mor 1995). These peptides, containing between 10 and 48 amino acid residues, are thought to kill pathogens by lysing their cell membranes. Each species examined to date has a species-specific subset of the approximately 100 peptides that have been characterized in amphibians (Conlon and Kim 2000).

A number of antimicrobial peptides extracted from amphibian skin, including magainin I and II, dermaseptin, and ranalexin, kill *Batrachochytrium*, *Basidiobolus* (an op-

portunistic fungal pathogen of amphibians), and frog virus 3 (a potentially pathogenic iridovirus infecting anurans) (Chinchar et al. 2001; Rollins-Smith et al. 2002b)
in culture. However, none of these same peptides have exhibited any measurable activity against the opportunistic bacterium *Aeromonas hydrophila* (Rollins-Smith et al.
2002b). It is also important to note that the activity of these antimicrobial peptides
against *Batrachochytrium* in culture does not necessarily translate into protection of
the amphibian in nature. For instance, northern leopard frogs produce seven antimicrobial peptides that demonstrate activity in culture against *Batrachochytrium*, yet
these frogs experienced mass die-offs in the 1970s due, apparently, to this disease
(Rollins-Smith et al. 2002a). Environmental factors, such as pH, temperature, ultraviolet-B, or contaminants, may not only affect the activity of a peptide against a pathogen, but also may affect the rate of synthesis, the site of release, and the activation of
antimicrobial peptides.

Some researchers propose that stress caused by sublethal environmental factors is
linked to immunosuppression that could increase the vulnerability of amphibians to
infectious agents (e.g., Carey 1993). Immunosuppression is a poorly defined concept.
It is not clear how many components of the immune defenses need to be impaired,
and to what degree, before an animal becomes vulnerable to an opportunistic pathogen. The concept of immunosuppression typically relates to impairment of the adaptive immune system; little information exists about how environmental factors might
affect the components of the innate immune system. Immunosuppressed individuals would be expected to exhibit a range of opportunistic infections on necropsy;
however, consistent evidence of opportunistic pathogens on individuals heavily infected with chytrid fungi has been lacking (Berger et al. 1998). In contrast, the role of
immunosuppression in ranavirus outbreaks, in which opportunistic infections have
been observed (Cunningham et al. 1996; Jancovich et al. 1997; Daszak et al. 1999),
needs further evaluation.

POTENTIAL SOLUTIONS

Although *Batrachochytrium* and ranaviruses may be transported from place to place
by natural means, including by other animals, humans are also a likely cause of the
spread of these pathogens. The importation of infected amphibians for the pet trade,
the release to the wild of infected animals obtained from biological supply companies, and the use of infected animals as bait has almost certainly spread these pathogens. Some scientific societies, such as the Declining Amphibian Populations Task
Force, have attempted to broadly communicate the need for biologists to sterilize
boots, nets, and other equipment when moving from location to location (for a copy
of the protocol, contact the task force by e-mail at daptf@open.ac.uk), but this information must also be disseminated to the general public, including sports fishers

and hikers. The adoption of new laws preventing trade of amphibians between countries and the release of amphibians from homes, laboratories, or bait shops into the wild is a worthy goal, but unlikely in the near future.

Various programs today use captive breeding and rearing of naturally laid eggs in captivity in an effort to raise amphibians in environments that minimize exposure to pathogens. These approaches, implemented predominantly by zoos and wildlife organizations, can indeed provide a source of healthy amphibians for reintroduction into historical habitats, but they may also have a number of drawbacks (Snyder et al. 1996). Reintroductions of captive-bred animals carry the risk of introducing new pathogens from captivity into the environment (Cunningham 1996). Second, reintroductions are likely to fail if reintroduced animals become infected with the same pathogens that caused historical population declines and extinctions; methods must be developed for detecting the presence of pathogens like *Batrachochytrium* in a proposed reintroduction locality. These problems are currently being addressed via the formulation of protocols by the American Zoo and Aquarium Association.

Australian scientists have been particularly active in addressing issues concerning how to prevent additional outbreaks of *Batrachochytrium* in amphibian populations. Further information is available online at http://www.jcu.edu.au/school/phtm/ PHTM/frogs/ampdis.htm.

ACKNOWLEDGMENTS
Preparation of this review and unpublished data presented in this paper were supported by an Integrated Research Challenges in Environmental Biology grant IBN-9977063 from the National Science Foundation. The authors are indebted to Margie L. Walling and Joyce Longcore for editorial assistance.

11
ECOLOGY AND EVOLUTION
OF INFECTIOUS DISEASE

JAMES P. COLLINS, JESSE L. BRUNNER, VERMA MIERA,
MATTHEW J. PARRIS, DANNA M. SCHOCK,
AND ANDREW STORFER

CENTRAL ISSUES

Two leading challenges in environmental sciences are understanding the causes and consequences of earth's diminishing biodiversity and understanding the ecology and evolution of infectious diseases. At the intersection of these challenges is the global decline of amphibians. Emerging infectious diseases are among the suspected causes of many declines (Daszak et al. 1999; Carey et al. 2002a; Chapter 10, this volume). Emerging infectious diseases are diseases that are newly recognized, novel in a population, or rapidly increasing in incidence, virulence, or geographic range (Daszak et al. 2000). Although infectious diseases are suspected of causing the extinction of some species (McCallum and Dobson 1995), basic epidemiological theory suggests that pathogens are unlikely to cause extinction (Dobson and May 1986). A key to understanding the role of pathogens in amphibian declines is reconciling this discrepancy, which will require understanding pathogen emergence, host susceptibility, and the joint population dynamics of host and pathogen.

Host–pathogen interactions must be understood at several scales—the individual organism, local population, metapopulation, and region—and the outcome at one scale does not extrapolate simply to another. For example, contrary to what we might expect, a pathogen that kills individual hosts rapidly does not invariably drive a population or species to extinction, because a high transmission rate is necessary for pathogens to exert significant population-level effects. In theory, high transmission favors more virulent pathogens, at least as long as the incidence of disease is increasing in the population (Ebert 1999), but as hosts die, population density declines and transmission decreases. Eventually, the host population reaches a low density where transmission ceases; hence, we expect that disease alone will not cause extinction in a one host–one pathogen system.

The chytrid fungus *Batrachochytrium dendrobatidis* and ranaviruses are among the leading suspected causes of many amphibian declines (Daszak et al. 1999; Carey et al. 2002a; and Chapter 10, this volume). Chytrids and ranaviruses have wide host ranges (Appendix 11.1), and our best evidence indicates that they differ in how each affects amphibian population dynamics. Viruses generally cause host populations to fluctuate, whereas declines, even extinctions, attributed to chytridiomycosis are reported from Big Tableland, Queensland, Australia (Berger et al. 1998); Fortuna Forest Reserve, Panama (Berger et al. 1998); Peñalara Natural Park, Spain (Bosch et al. 2001); and Rocky Mountain National Park, Colorado (Muths et al., in press). *B. dendrobatidis* infects 46 of the Australian frog species analyzed to date; 13 species appear to have declined, three are extinct, and many of these occurred at high elevation. Three-quarters of frog species surveyed in Costa Rica and Panama have declined (Lips 1999; Young et al. 2001; Lips and Donnelly 2002); chytrids are associated in almost every instance. Four Central American sites show similar patterns of susceptibility among frog species: the most susceptible species have restricted elevation ranges, large body sizes, and breed in streams (K. Lips, J. Reeve, and L. Witters, Southern Illinois University, unpublished data). Although there are chytrid-associated declines and extinctions, frogs infected with *B. dendrobatidis* also occur at sites without apparent evidence of host population declines in Canada (Quebec: M. Ouellet, personal communication; British Columbia: Raverty and Reynolds 2001) and in the United States (Maine: J. Longcore, University of Maine, personal communication; Georgia: P. Daszak and D. Porter, Consortium for Conservation Medicine, Lamont-Doherty Earth Observatory, Columbia University, personal communication; and Arizona: V. Miera and E. Davidson, Arizona State University, personal observation).

In this chapter, we review amphibian host–pathogen dynamics at the local, metapopulation, and regional scales; Carey and colleagues in Chapter 10 focus on the individual level of analysis. We use two disease models, the tiger salamander–ranavirus system and the amphibian–chytrid system. At each scale we focus on life history variation and genetic variability of hosts and pathogens.

HOST–PATHOGEN DYNAMICS AT THE LOCAL POPULATION SCALE

At the local scale, infected hosts transmit a pathogen to susceptible hosts, which then spread the infection to others before recovering or dying. Depending on conditions, transmission among hosts either causes an epidemic or the disease dissipates. Most simple epidemic models account for disease dynamics at the local scale, and analyses at other levels, especially the metapopulation level, are often extrapolations of the host–pathogen dynamics of local populations. Ranavirus epidemics in tiger sala-manders (*Ambystoma tigrinum*) illustrate host–pathogen dynamics at the local scale.

A breeding pond, marsh, or earthen stock tank is the central point of activity for a tiger salamander population. Eggs are laid in such aquatic habitats in late winter, spring, or summer and develop into quickly growing aquatic larvae that usually metamorphose in the same season. Metamorphosed salamanders overwinter in ter-restrial refugia; some larvae and neotenic adults overwinter in the water (Sexton and Bizer 1978; Collins 1981). In several subspecies, hatchlings may develop into either a typical larva that feeds on invertebrates or a cannibalistic phenotype that preys on in-vertebrates and conspecifics (Collins et al. 1993). Epidemics kill larvae and meta-morphosed animals, and usually occur during late summer or early fall when host densities are high, but after the peak densities (Pfennig et al. 1991; personal observa-tion). *Ambystoma tigrinum* virus (ATV) and the closely related Regina ranavirus (RRV) are virulent pathogens that spread by close contact between infected and sus-ceptible tiger salamanders (Jancovich et al. 1997; Bollinger et al. 1999). The viral life cycle appears to be confined to tiger salamanders—no syntopic alternate hosts are known (Jancovich et al. 2001)—and ATV is infectious for only about 2 weeks outside a host. ATV epidemics progress on a much shorter time scale than larval tiger sala-mander development rates. Infections are generally lethal within 2 or 3 weeks. Sala-mander reproduction and recruitment occurs annually, so within a season, dead or recovered salamanders generally are not replaced with additional susceptible ani-mals. This phenology supports host–pathogen dynamics that result in epidemics. The disease dissipates within a season as fewer and fewer of the original larvae re-main to be infected.

Disease may alter life history trajectories, potentially affecting amphibian fitness components such as timing of and size at metamorphosis (Wilbur and Collins 1973; Alford and Harris 1988). Disease increases risk in aquatic habitats; therefore, selec-tion should favor early metamorphosis by amphibian larvae in ephemeral aquatic habitats. Death need not be caused directly by a pathogen; rather, in an ephemeral pond, a pathogen could slow larval growth and development to the point that host death would result from drying of the aquatic habitat before metamorphosis is pos-sible. This hypothesis was tested by rearing larval salamanders from two areas of Ari-zona (White Mountains and San Rafael Valley) in mesocosms with and without ATV. Survival and growth rates were lowest in viral treatments and in animals from the San Rafael Valley, a region with low genetic variability (Jones et al. 1988; M. Parris, E. Davidson, and J. Collins, University of Memphis, unpublished data). A second lab-oratory study reinforced the result of delayed metamorphosis in disease environ-ments (J. Brunner, D. Schock, J. Collins, and E. Davidson, Arizona State University, unpublished data). However, although infected animals had slower growth rates, they were not exposed to a drying regime. It is possible that larvae in desiccating en-vironments may facultatively reduce their larval period to metamorphose quickly.

Because the experiments thus far have not challenged infected larvae with a desiccating environment, it remains to be tested how larvae respond developmentally to such conditions. Nevertheless, longer larval periods increase the time exposed to aquatic predators, which may have important fitness consequences for salamanders (Wilbur and Collins 1973; Alford and Harris 1988).

How does ATV persist between years? Animals that survive exposure to ATV may harbor transmissible infections for more than six months (J. Brunner, D. Schock, J. Collins, and E. Davidson, Arizona State University, unpublished data). We have also recorded dispersing metamorphosed animals carrying virus at the end of an epidemic, and we have indirect evidence that metamorphosed animals return infected. Persistence between epidemics is apparently due to long-lived, transmissible, sublethal infection; however, we acknowledge the possibility that the virus is sequestered in a still-unidentified, aquatic reservoir. Larvae and metamorphosed animals that survive infection with no clinical signs of disease can transmit infections to naïve individuals seven months after exposure, suggesting that animals with subclinical infections could transmit virus among populations or between years (J. Brunner, D. Schock, J. Collins, and E. Davidson, Arizona State University, unpublished data). The complex salamander life history alone may provide a reservoir (i.e., metamorphosed animals) that explains viral persistence and transmission. Laboratory experiments show that larvae are approximately 10 times more likely to recover from ATV infection than are metamorphosed animals (J. Brunner, D. Schock, J. Collins, and E. Davidson, Arizona State University, unpublished data). Infected, metamorphosed salamanders returning to a pond to breed may reinitiate an epidemic.

Chytrid fungus dynamics differ from viral dynamics in key ways. *Batrachochytrium dendrobatidis* has a wide host range (Appendix 11.1), and may have an independent saprophytic stage. Pathogenicity varies widely by host species, life stage, and environmental conditions. For example, American bullfrogs (*Rana catesbeiana;* E. Davidson, J. Jancovich, Arizona State University, unpublished data) and tiger salamanders (E. Davidson, M. Parris, J. Collins, J. E. Longcore, A. Pessier, J. Brunner, R. Medville, Arizona State University, unpublished data) are resistant carriers, at least in the laboratory; the Australian frog *Litoria caerulea* (White's treefrog) is susceptible in the laboratory (Pessier et al. 1999). Interspecific variation in susceptibility means that host–pathogen dynamics may differ among amphibian community types. An amphibian community with a resistant reservoir host could allow chytridiomycosis to persist in one or more species while driving other susceptible host species to extinction.

Pathogenicity also varies intraspecifically by life stage. Chytrids only infect keratinized epithelial tissue (Fellers et al. 2001). In tadpoles, mouthparts are the only keratinized tissue, whereas in metamorphosed animals keratin is distributed throughout the epidermis. Therefore, frogs with overlapping generations of larval and metamorphosed stages may act as their own pathogen reservoir. There is no evidence that the fungus is lethal in tadpoles, but infected larvae have slower growth and development rates than uninfected larvae. M. Parris, E. Davidson, and J. Collins (University of Memphis, unpublished data) varied intraspecific density, predation, and presence of chytrids in gray treefrog (*Hyla versicolor*; Figure 11.1) larvae in mesocosms. Larvae reared with chytrids were smaller at metamorphosis and had longer larval periods when reared with predators. In a second experiment, F_1 hybrids of plains and southern leopard frogs (*Rana blairi* and *R. sphenocephala*) had smaller body masses at metamorphosis than parents when exposed to chytrids, suggesting disease resistance may be reduced via genetic recombination inherent in hybridization. These experiments indicate that chytrid effects on host life history may be complex and indirect.

Environmental cofactors can significantly alter growth and transmission of a pathogen and/or ability of its host to respond. This is particularly true for external pathogens like chytrid fungi and environmentally sensitive amphibian hosts. For example, different thermal and hydric environments, which tend to cycle together, may affect development of chytridiomycosis. *Litoria chloris* continually exposed to mist, characteristic of natural rainforest habitat in Australia, developed clinical disease and died significantly faster than animals exposed to either continual rain or dry air with access to standing water (R. Alford, James Cook University, unpublished data).

Figure 11.1. Gray treefrog (*Hyla versicolor*). (Photo by David Scott, Savannah River Ecology Laboratory)

Several additional lines of evidence suggest that microenvironment affects infectivity of the chytrid fungus *Batrachochytrium dendrobatidis*. In culture, the fungus grows between 4°C and 28°C, with optimal growth between 15°C and 28°C. Infected western toads (*Bufo boreas*) in Colorado held at either 12°C or 23°C had high mortality, but toads kept on a 5°C/30°C diel temperature regime for 42 days survived, suggesting that a natural daily range of body temperatures could keep the fungus in check (C. Carey, University of Colorado, unpublished data). Thus, frogs that exhibit different basking behaviors may be differentially susceptible to chytrid infection; short periods of high environmental temperature can halt disease progression and may clear animals of chytrid infections (R. Alford, James Cook University, personal communication).

There is no simple, general relationship between ultraviolet (UV)-B radiation and chytridiomycosis in amphibians. UV-B radiation may stress amphibians, making them more susceptible to infection (Carey 1993; Blaustein et al. 1994a). In a multifactorial mesocosm experiment in Oregon, chytrids had no effect on tadpole survivorship; tadpoles exposed to ambient UV-B levels had lower survival than those shielded from UV regardless of chytrid treatment (A. Hatch and A. Blaustein, Oregon State University, unpublished data). UV-B levels have increased about 4% in Central America over the past 20 years (B. Middleton, NASA, unpublished data), but present levels of ambient UV-B may decrease chytrid susceptibility of amphibians in Panama (P. Murphy and K. Lips, Southern Illinois University, unpublished data). Low pH (Harte and Hoffman 1989; Long et al. 1995) and fungal pathogens other than chytrids can also damage amphibians at various life stages (Kiesecker and Blaustein 1995; Berger et al. 1998; Pessier et al. 1999).

HOST–PATHOGEN DYNAMICS AT THE METAPOPULATION SCALE

Naturalists have long known that amphibian population sizes can fluctuate greatly from natural causes. A two- or three-fold increase or decrease in the number of adults from one reproductive season to the next is possible (Wilbur 1980), and even without epidemics, local extinctions are expected. But while a local population, or deme, may go extinct, recolonization from neighboring populations will "rescue" it, and so the regional population size remains relatively stable. However, rare species are statistically more likely to go extinct than common species because rare species generally have some combination of narrow geographic range, specialized habitat, and low abundance (Rabinowitz et al. 1986). Certain life-history traits (e.g., long lifespan, low fecundity, slow development, migratory stages, or complex life cycles) may also make species more vulnerable. K. Lips, J. Reeve, and L. Witters (Southern

Illinois University, unpublished data) found that some amphibian populations in Central America are declining because of ecological factors associated with rarity, although the best predictor was degree of association with stream habitats.

While some amphibian species are exceptions and do not fit the metapopulation pattern (e.g., even pond-breeding amphibians may not necessarily act as metapopulations; Marsh and Trenham 2001), metapopulation models are generally useful for understanding the spatial and temporal dynamics of many amphibian populations. Tiger salamander populations in the western United States are often closely associated with ponds (Collins 1981), and dispersal between breeding sites may be limited by distance such that local ponds/populations are somewhat independent (but see Trenham et al. 2001). In Arizona, we know of local populations that disappear, sometimes for several years, to be recolonized later, and all of the tiger salamander metapopulations that we monitor are apparently stable.

The metapopulation dynamics that maintain these salamander populations could also maintain their pathogens. If an occasional metamorphosed immigrant were infected sublethally by ATV, for example, the metamorph could initiate an epidemic on arrival at a susceptible host population. As noted above, salamanders can harbor transmissible, sublethal infections for more than 6 months. At the end of one fall die-off on the Kaibab Plateau, about 90% of the recently metamorphosed salamanders dispersing from a pond were infected. It is also the case that from the point of view of ATV, since salamanders are a major viral vector, the virus also has a metapopulation structure.

If dispersing amphibians bring pathogens with them, then human alteration of metapopulation structure can alter host–pathogen dynamics. Draining wetlands and similar activities that eliminate aquatic habitats/patches for amphibians increase the probability of metapopulation extinction, but also increase the prevalence of disease among populations such that pathogens go extinct within a local population. Increasing the availability of aquatic habitats, such as new farm ponds and stocktanks, should have the opposite effect. Since the pathogen also exists in this same metapopulation structure, facilitating movement between patches by adding or creating habitats, a common management tool, may make local host populations less independent. Theoretically, this can increase the probability of metapopulation extinction by facilitating the spread of contagious, virulent diseases (Hess 1996). The increased transmission between local populations achieved by easing movement between them might also select for enhanced viral pathogenicity, and increased probability of extirpating all demes.

The metapopulation dynamics of host and pathogen will be overwhelmed when the parasite is a host generalist or has a reservoir, as appears to be the case with chytridiomycosis. Numerous amphibian species are susceptible to infection, but they differ markedly in disease and mortality. The widely distributed American bullfrog

(*Rana catesbeiana*) for example, appears unaffected by chytrid infection so that the prevalence of infections may be very high. Karen Lips found that sentinel, uninfected frogs in Central America contracted lethal infections. The fungus apparently remains viable in the environment, probably in streams, increasing the chance of exposure to the pathogen. Susceptible species, therefore, even though patchily distributed in the landscape, may never be free from exposure to chytrids. Reservoirs are thought to make even metapopulation-level extinction far more likely.

As mentioned previously, the development of lethal chytridiomycosis also depends heavily on abiotic or environmental conditions, such as low temperatures, high moisture, and a nearly neutral pH. These conditions, however, are distributed patchily in space and time, and will conceivably affect disease dynamics among patches. Epidemics associated with chytrids occur in the cooler months in Arizona (Sredl 2000) and at higher, cooler elevations in tropical Australia and Central America where temperatures fall within chytrid tolerance (Berger et al. 1998; Lips 1998, 1999). Declines due to chytridiomycosis are most common at higher elevations in the tropics (Alford et al. 2001; Young et al. 2001). Low-elevation sites have temperatures typically above the limit for chytrid growth (e.g., $>29°C$; Longcore et al. 1999). Cloud forest stream water is often characterized by shaded, low UV conditions, and is consistently buffered between pH 6.8 and 7.5, a range favorable for chytrid growth; chytrid-susceptible anurans are declining in these habitats. Laboratory studies in Panama indicated that high water temperatures, even for short periods, might slow or even allow clearance of chytrid infections. Temperature, pH, and UV-B radiation, acting alone or synergistically, may ultimately determine the degree of chytrid infection in stream anurans (P. Murphy and K. Lips, Southern Illinois University, unpublished data).

Movement of amphibians into patches of habitat that are optimal for growth of chytrids is important for sustaining disease. Lips and colleagues found that mid-elevation populations of the emerald glassfrog (*Centrolene prosoblepon*) at El Copé, Panama, have declined but still persist. Genetic analyses indicate a bias toward up-stream movement and suggest that these populations survive because of migration from downstream sites. Although a means for frog persistence, this recolonization may also provide the transmission necessary for long-term chytrid persistence at the site, and thereby inhibit reestablishment of susceptible species. Immigrants coming from lower elevations may also carry sublethal infections that are expressed as lethal infections when the host reaches a locality with environmental conditions that support disease progression.

The relationship between disease dynamics and metapopulation structure is not well understood. Considerable work is needed to unite the theories for metapopulations, epidemiology, and host–pathogen coevolution in ways that support generalizations and predictions. Relative gene flow rates of pathogens and their hosts, and the resulting population genetic structures, are likely important in determining disease dynamics. These variables influence where and when local adaptation may arise; factors like relative virulence of pathogens and whether diseases are endemic or epidemic are also affected (Gandon et al. 1996; Thrall and Burdon 1997; Gandon and Van Zandt 1998; Otto and Michalakis 1998; Lively 1999).

HOST – PATHOGEN DYNAMICS AT THE REGIONAL SCALE

To understand chytrids and ranaviruses at the regional level, we must understand how they spread and become established. We know that chytrids are in frog populations spanning the United States, but is the distribution of these pathogens continuous with Central American strains (Appendix 11.1)? Amphibian dispersal alone is unlikely to explain pathogen movement on the regional scale, and thus, without the aid of humans or alternative long-distance carriers like birds, we expect the movement of amphibian pathogens between regions to be low. Metapopulations within regions, and regions themselves, should be relatively independent host–pathogen systems. This should result in pathogens from different regions being genetically divergent and locally adapted host–pathogen systems (see below). For example, cannibalistic tiger salamander larvae are rare in the Kaibab Plateau region of northern Arizona where epidemics are common (Pfennig et al. 1991; Jancovich et al. 1997), and cannibals are almost never found in the San Rafael Valley in southern Arizona where epidemics are very common. Cannibalism is most frequent in regions where ranaviral disease is infrequent. Regional variation in epidemics may explain regional variation in occurrence of cannibals because they are more likely to contract disease by eating infected conspecifics.

Despite a priori reasons to expect genetic variability between sites, there are several possible modes of pathogen dispersal that may explain the lack of genetic variability we are finding among virus and chytrid isolates (see below). For example, we are investigating the possibility that birds move sufficient amounts of virus to initiate epidemics in regions separated by thousands of kilometers, as many tiger salamander epidemics occur along migratory bird routes (D. Schock, Arizona State University, personal communication). Game fish such as walleye, which are stocked in many areas, could also act as vectors of salamander viruses on a regional scale (D. Schock, T. Bollinger, and J. Collins, Arizona State University, unpublished data).

Human dispersal of pathogens may have a role in defining the geographic distribution of ranaviruses and chytrids around the world. The pet trade, aquaculture, movement of bait animals, transportation of water and mud, and inadvertent and deliberate movement of species may easily introduce pathogens into naïve populations (Appendix 11.1). Humans moving salamanders, especially as fishing bait, can disperse infected salamanders between normally isolated populations. In the United States, tens of thousands of salamanders are moved between ponds and as far as from Nebraska to Arizona (Collins et al. 1988), and ATV has been isolated from salamanders obtained from a bait supplier in Phoenix, Arizona (A. Storfer, J. Jancovich, D. Schock, and J. Collins, Washington State University, unpublished data).

Genetic variation in host and pathogen can provide important information, such as estimates of time since divergence in pathogens and resulting coevolutionary patterns. About 80 chytrid isolates are now in culture, and 50 are being analyzed with amplified fragment length polymorphisms (James et al. 2000; Bradley et al. 2002). In addition, P. Daszak and D. Porter (University of Georgia, unpublished data) analyzed 613 bases of internally transcribed spacer region portions (ITS1 and ITS2) of 18S and 28S ribosomal DNA and a portion of the 5.8S gene of 39 chytrid strains. There is a maximum of 5% sequence divergence among all isolates (low for fungi) despite their global distribution, and some Australian and Central American chytrid isolates are identical (P. Daszak and D. Porter, Consortium for Conservation Medicine, Lamont-Doherty Earth Observatory, Columbia University, unpublished data). Multilocus sequence typing showed only five variable nucleotides of 5,918 total bases at 10 loci among 32 globally distributed chytrid strains, suggesting recent emergence (E. Morehouse, T. James, A. Ganley, R. Vilgalys, L. Berger, and J. Longcore, Duke University, unpublished data). Collectively, the data support the conclusion that amphibian chytridiomycosis is an emerging infectious disease whose spread was possibly facilitated by humans (Daszak et al. 1999).

Viral phylogeographic analyses also show shallow sequence divergence and likely recent spread. Genome-level comparisons between ATV (J. Jancovich, E. Davidson, N. Parameswaran, J. Mao, V. Chinchar, A. Storfer, J. Collins, and B. Jacobs, Arizona State University, unpublished data) and RRV (Mao et al. 1999) show low sequence divergence at three conserved genetic markers. The major capsid protein shows less than 1% sequence divergence among isolates from Arizona to Saskatchewan and no variation within sites; the methyltransferase gene also shows no variability (J. Jancovich, E. Davidson, N. Parameswaran, J. Mao, V. Chinchar, A. Storfer, J. Collins, and B. Jacobs, Arizona State University, unpublished data). These data suggest that we are investigating several strains of one viral species, and in concert with infected salamanders from bait shops, support the possibility of human-enhanced viral spread (J. Jancovich, E. Davidson, H. Weimann, S. Kumar, J. Collins, A. Storfer, and B. Jacobs, Arizona State University, unpublished data). Despite little genetic differentiation among viral strains, tiger salamanders crossinfected with viral isolates from Arizona, Saskatchewan, and Manitoba differed in survivorship, time to death, and temperature tolerance, providing evidence of local adaptation (D. Schock, Arizona State University, unpublished data). An eIF-2α homolog, one of several genes found during sequencing of ATV and RRV (J. Jancovich, E. Davidson, N. Parameswaran, J. Mao, V. Chinchar, A. Storfer, J. Collins, and B. Jacobs, Arizona State University, unpublished data), is particularly interesting because it modulates host immune response (especially antiapoptosis function) in other viruses. When this homolog was inserted in place of a vaccinia (pox virus) gene, it restored wild-type phenotype (i.e., inhibition of host protein synthesis, coupled with the selective translation of viral mRNAs). These results are the first to suggest that ranaviruses are capable of immune evasion and that their hosts may have an interferon-like activity (B. Jacobs, Arizona State University, unpublished data). Ongoing studies will test the hypothesis that genetic variability in this homolog explains regional variation in viral virulence.

Variation in viral effects on amphibian populations could also be explained by the extent to which viruses and hosts have coevolved. To investigate coevolutionary patterns, A. Storfer (Washington State University, unpublished data) sequenced 900 bp of mtDNA in tiger salamanders from sites with ranavirus epidemics from southern Arizona to southern Canada. Salamanders show little sequence divergence among all sites despite the large geographic area, and the resulting gene genealogy is being reconciled with that of ranavirus isolates from the same regions to test for concordance and local adaptation. Genetic variability in other loci (e.g., MHC) is being investigated to test for a correlation between variation and resistance.

Both viruses and chytrids have shorter generation times than their amphibian hosts, so we expect higher fitness on sympatric versus allopatric hosts. Preliminary support for this prediction comes from cross-infection experiments that exposed tiger salamanders from three widely separated regions in Canada and the United States to ranaviruses collected from the same regions (D. Schock, Arizona State University, unpublished data). As predicted by theory, virus isolates were most effective at evading the defenses of their native host population (estimated by several criteria including percentage of hosts surviving and percentage of hosts sublethally infected), indicating ranavirus isolates are locally adapted. Further, the results of novel host–pathogen pairings were unpredictable; that is, the outcome could not be inferred from knowing how the ranavirus isolate performed in its native host population. Given the increasing ease with which pathogens are moved on a global scale, these findings have important implications for wildlife conservation and epidemiology in general.

POTENTIAL SOLUTIONS

The interaction of environmental factors and population dynamics at the local, metapopulation, and regional levels governs both a pathogen's virulence and its possible emergence as an infectious disease. Amphibians and their pathogens offer ideal, if sometimes unfortunate, cases for studying these forces because there is a continuum from host–parasite coexistence to declines and extinctions of amphibian populations. We have discussed variables that might trigger epidemics and the spread of disease within and among populations. The spatial pattern of habitats dictates dispersal rates among populations, facilitating or slowing an epidemic. Pathogens can alter host life history, and life history stages within the same host may vary in their capacity to serve as a pathogen reservoir. Explaining the emergence and spread of amphibian diseases means understanding the complex interaction of virulence, susceptibility to infection, and the population dynamics of host and pathogen. Each contributes individually and collectively to host–pathogen coexistence or extinction, and each operates at several scales.

Increased education, especially for those involved in protecting and restoring wetlands, is important. If infectious diseases are not considered in habitat conservation, there can be serious, unintended, and unexpected results. The guidelines of the Declining Amphibian Population Task Force (DAPTF) should be followed (available online at http://www.mpm.edu/collect/vertzo/herp/Daptf/fcode_e.html). The possibility of pathogen translocation must be incorporated into legislation and regulations for commercial activities such as the pet trade, bait trade, and aquaculture.

Further research is needed at the scale of the metapopulation. The key questions center on three areas related to how disease affects the likelihood of local population extinction, the probability of successful recolonization, and the source–sink status of subpopulations making up the metapopulation.

1. Dispersal rates and dispersal mechanisms of host and pathogen: How does fidelity to the breeding site vary among species? Are juveniles or adults more likely to disperse? What factors determine dispersal success and disease prevalence of dispersing animals? Will sublethal infections hinder dispersal by reducing the likelihood that infected animals will reach a new site?

2. Effect of disease on local population dynamics: How do epidemics interact with other phenomena (e.g., drought) to affect juvenile recruitment and the likelihood local populations will go extinct? Are there environmental or other factors (e.g., population density) that make some local populations experience epidemics more often than others?

3. Variation in the spatial and temporal patterns of disease outbreaks: Do local populations vary in susceptibility or resistance to disease? Do spatial patterns of disease outbreak vary with distance such that the spread of disease is consistent with transmission by dispersing, infected animals? Or, is the timing and occurrence of new outbreaks independent of epidemics at nearby sites? The latter might suggest human or other modes of disease introduction, or perhaps interactions with other stressors at the local population scale are responsible for epidemics.

The complexity of host–pathogen systems means that solving the problem of how we might minimize or eliminate disease as a contributor to global amphibian declines will not be easy. It seems clear, however, that at the very least we need a much better understanding of how humans might deliberately or inadvertently disperse infected hosts and/or pathogens through commerce—pet trade, bait trade, aquaculture (Appendix 11.1)—and even ecotourism. If we can identify the sources of disease and control pathogen reservoirs, we might forestall the progress of epidemics and prevent susceptible amphibian species from being driven to extinction, perhaps by resistant, carrier species of amphibians. Metapopulation structure offers another way to manage disease. An important element in any effort to restore amphibian populations by constructing or rehabilitating aquatic habitats will be distributing habitats across a landscape in ways that minimize the spread of disease and the evolution of virulent pathogens while still allowing for successful colonization/recolonization of sites (e.g., Hess 1996). Finally, we need a better understanding of the environmental cofactors that might facilitate or inhibit the spread of disease or the susceptibility of amphibians to pathogens. Here again, the complexity of the interactions means that reaching answers and instituting solutions are likely to be difficult, but the alternative—simply watching and describing the loss of amphibian biodiversity—is unacceptable.

ACKNOWLEDGMENTS

An Integrated Research Challenges in Environmental Biology grant (IBN-9977063) and grant DEB-9816645, both from the National Science Foundation, supported preparation of this chapter and much of our published and unpublished research that we discuss.

Appendix 11.1

Host ranges of chytrids and ranaviruses and potential modes of translocating these pathogens on a metapopulation and regional scale.

PATHOGEN: FROG VIRUS 3 (FV3)-LIKE RANAVIRUSES

Known host range (including experimental exposures)

Rana (8 spp.)	Granoff et al. 1965, 1966; Clark et al. 1968; Wolf et al. 1968, 1969; Granoff 1969; Cunningham et al. 1993, 1995, 1996; Drury et al. 1995; Kanachanakhan 1998; Mao et al. 1999; Hyatt et al. 2000; Zhang et al. 2001; Chinchar 2002.
Bufo (3 spp.)	Clark et al. 1968, 1969; Wolf et al. 1968, 1969; Hyatt et al. 1998.
Scaphiopus (1 sp.)	Wolf et al. 1968.
Notophthalmus (1 sp.)	Clark et al. 1968, 1969.

Potential mode of translocation

Aquaculture

Rana grylio is endemic to the United States, but reared for food in several Asian countries. FV3-like viruses caused epidemics in colonies in Hubei, China, highlighting aquaculture's potential role in dispersing ranavirus worldwide (Zhang et al. 1996, 1999, 2001).

The newly discovered tiger frog virus (TFV) is causing epidemics in *Rana tigrina rugulosa*, a cultivated frog endemic to Asia. The molecular sequence of TFV is very similar to that of FV3 (He et al. 2002).

Pet Trade

Researchers in the United Kingdom reported that a virus very similar to FV3 may be responsible for widespread mortality in *Rana temporaria*. FV3 was initially identified and characterized in the United States. Until recently it had not been identified outside of North America. FV3 may have spread to the United Kingdom via infected goldfish imported from the United States. The goldfish are placed in backyard ponds with wild *R. temporaria* (Hyatt et al. 2000; Kirby 2002).

PATHOGEN: AMBYSTOMA TIGRINUM VIRUS – REGINA RANAVIRUS COMPLEX (ATV/RRV) COMPLEX

Known host range (including experimental exposures)

Ambystoma tigrinum	Jancovich et al. 1997, Bollinger et al. 1999
Ambystoma gracile	Jancovich et al. 2001
Notophthalmus viridescens	Jancovich et al. 2001

Potential mode of translocation

Live Bait Trade

Larval tiger salamanders ("waterdogs") are used as live fishing bait in southwestern United States. Larvae are collected from the wild and held in communal tanks until distributed to vendors around the country. Waterdogs are often moved long distances, e.g., Nebraska to Arizona (Collins et al. 1988), suggesting extensive dispersal of virus as well.

PATHOGEN: CHYTRID FUNGUS

Known host range (including experimental exposures)

Ambystomatidae (2 spp.)	Speare and Berger 2000b; E. Davidson et al., Arizona State University, unpublished.
Amphiumidae (1 sp.)	Speare and Berger 2000b.
Bufonidae (9 spp.)	Pessier et al. 1999, Speare and Berger 2000a, 2000b.
Centrolenidae (2 spp.)	Speare and Berger 2000b.
Dendrobatidae (11 spp.)	Speare and Berger 2000b.
Discoglossidae (1 sp.)	Speare and Berger 2000b.
Hylidae (30 spp.)	(Speare and Berger 2000a, 2000b; Pessier et al. 1999; E. Davidson et al., Arizona State University, unpublished; V. Miera, Arizona State University, unpublished.
Leptodactylidae (3 spp.)	Berger et al. 1998, Speare and Berger 2000b.
Microhylidae (1 sp.)	Longcore et al. 1999.
Myobatrachidae (24 spp.)	Speare and Berger 2000a.
Pipidae (2 spp.)	Speare and Berger 2000b; Raverty and Reynolds 2001.
Proteidae (1 sp.)	Speare and Berger 2000b.
Ranidae (11 spp.)	Berger et al. 1998; Speare and Berger 2000b; Sredl 2000; Fellers et al. 2001, Bradley et al. 2002.
Salamandridae (1 sp.)	Speare and Berger 2000b.
Sirenidae (1 sp.)	Speare and Berger 2000b.

Potential mode of translocation

Aquaculture

Rana catesbeiana is introduced widely across the globe. Chytrid-associated mortalities were found in farmed bullfrogs in Uruguay (Mazzoni et al., unpublished)

Pet Trade

Numerous amphibian species are moved around the globe as part of the pet trade. Chytrids are reported from many species moved between continents: *Hymenochirus boettgeri*, imported into Canada from Southeast Asia (Raverty and Reynolds 2001); *Xenopus* imported into the United States from Africa (Reed et al. 2000); numerous amphibian species exported from the Americas, including *Necturus maculosus*, *Siren lacertina*, *Amphiuma tridactylum*, and several dendrobatids (Speare and Berger 2000b). The large and diverse pet trade provides ample opportunity for translocating chytrids quickly across the globe.

Live Bait Trade

Chytrids have been isolated from tiger salamanders. As with ranaviruses, the extensive movement of tiger salamanders for the bait trade presents the opportunity to translocate chytrids on large spatial scales.

12

EFFECTS OF PESTICIDES ON
AMPHIBIAN POPULATIONS

MICHELLE D. BOONE AND CHRISTINE M. BRIDGES

CENTRAL ISSUES

Natural populations and communities are increasingly affected by human activity, including mining, industrialization, and agricultural processes, which amplifies the likelihood of chemical contamination of native plant and animal life. Urban and suburban sprawl, furthermore, coupled with the growing use of pesticides and fertilizers for home use have given rise to an increasingly and much less regulated source of contaminants. The effects of pesticides on amphibians, part of a larger problem of contaminated environments, are the focus of our chapter for several reasons. First, pesticides are intentionally applied in the environment, in contrast to contaminants that occur as a byproduct of industrialization or mining; we therefore have greater control over what pesticides we release into the environment. Second, many of the pesticides in use have widespread application and are believed to have relatively benign effects on nontarget species, but these risks are often not studied at relevant ecological, spatial, or temporal scales. Third, pesticides have modes of action that are well understood in most cases; therefore initial research with amphibians can consider the ramifications of environmental exposure to these chemicals with a general understanding of their mechanisms when physiologies between the pest and nontarget species are similar. Other contaminants can have significant impacts on amphibian populations and have been discussed extensively elsewhere (e.g., Sparling et al. 2000). However, the study of the effects of pesticides, which have known effects on a number of species (especially target species), could aid in a more rapid and thorough investigation of chemical effects on amphibian communities. Further, understanding the effects of pesticides with different modes of action may offer insight for other types of chemical contamination.

Table 12.1

Ninety-six hour LC50 toxicity tests[a] calculated using nonlinear interpolation, moving average, or probit methods

Chemical	Leopard Frog[b]	Boreal Toad[c]	Bluegill Sunfish[d]	Fathead Minnow[e]	Rainbow Trout[e]
4-nonylphenol (ug/l)	0.34 (0.31−0.37)	0.12 (0.09−0.15)	—	0.27	0.19
Carbaryl (mg/l)	8.4 (7.4−9.6)	12.31 (10.3−14.7)	6.2	5.21	1.88
Copper (mg/l)	0.23 (0.21−0.25)	0.12 (0.07−0.18)	7.3	0.47	0.88
PCP[f] (mg/l)	0.14 (0.12−0.17)	0.37 (0.25−0.42)	0.192	0.25	0.16
Permethrin (ug/l)	18.2	>10	6.2	9.38	3.31

[a]Lethal concentrations needed to kill 50% of the test population within 96 hours; 95% confidence intervals in parentheses.

[b]Data from Bridges et al. 2002.

[c]Data from USEPA (1999).

[d]Data from Mayer and Ellersieck (1986).

[e]Data from USEPA (1995).

[f]PCP = pentachlorophenol.

It has been suggested that amphibians are particularly susceptible to environmental contamination because of their obligate aquatic larval periods, limited mobility, ectothermy, or because they favor habitats throughout their life cycle that may be more vulnerable to exposure from direct application, leaching, inundation from flooding events, or atmospheric deposition (Bishop and Petit 1992). However, data for conclusively making this determination for amphibians are more limited than for other taxa; a recent survey of vertebrate toxicological data reported that only 2.7% of studies included amphibians (Sparling et al. 2000). Available data suggest that amphibians may actually be less sensitive to pesticides than the vertebrate species typically used for toxicity testing (Table 12.1; Mayer and Ellersieck 1986; Bridges et al. 2002), although this trend does not necessarily hold for other types of chemical contamination (e.g., metals; Birge et al. 2000; reviewed in Linder and Grillitsch 2000). Birge et al. (2000) compared the sensitivity of amphibians to multiple contaminants with sensitivity of other vertebrates (e.g., fathead minnow, rainbow trout). These authors found that, compared with fish, amphibian species were more sensitive to metals in 67% of cases, and more sensitive to metals and organic chemicals (combined) in 64% of cases. These data suggest that amphibians are frequently, but not always, more sensitive than other vertebrate species to contaminants. Existing data for pesticides are relatively limited, however, and the role that they play in altering amphibian populations and communities is largely unknown and, potentially, of critical importance in light of recent amphibian declines (Barinaga 1990; Blaustein 1994; Corn 1994).

INTRODUCTION

History and Regulation of Pesticides

Insects are a major agricultural nuisance; one of every 70 species is officially recognized as a pest for destruction of food grown for human consumption (Green 1976). Pesticides (defined by the Environmental Protection Agency [EPA] as a substance or mixture of substances intended for preventing, destroying, repelling, or mitigating any life form) are credited with doubling the world's food supply without increasing the acreage farmed. However, all pesticides possess an inherent degree of toxicity for most living organisms (Ecobichon 1996). The presence of a pesticide, even at sublethal concentrations, may have detrimental effects on amphibians, even though they are not the target of pesticide application. Local pesticide use does not always remain confined to the application site, and may be leached, accidentally released, moved atmospherically, or transmitted through the food web. For instance, DDT has been found in human tissue where application has never occurred (Carson 1962; Colburn et al. 1996), and wind currents are known to mobilize sprayed pesticides across great distances (e.g., Bidleman 1999; Thurman and Cromwell 2000). Recently, Davidson et al. (2001) found a correlation between amphibian population declines in California and regional pesticide use, suggesting that amphibians even in seemingly pristine environments may suffer the consequence of regional pesticide use.

It was not until World War II that efficient pesticides, namely organochlorine insecticides, were developed and began to have widespread application (Green 1976; Rand 1995). Many wartime nerve gases were chemical precursors of the synthetic pesticides that soon became widely available to rid areas of agricultural and disease-carrying pests. But within several decades of use, it became clear that organochlorine pesticides like DDT carried a considerable cost. By 1946, the U.S. Fish and Wildlife Service was performing field studies on DDT, because it was applied more than all other pesticides combined and evidence indicated that organochlorine residues were widely dispersed and had longer persistence times than initially expected (Peterle 1991). With the publication of *Silent Spring*, Rachel Carson (1962) articulated the consequences of continued pesticide use to nontarget wildlife and humans and proffered a number of alternatives to broad-scale release of pesticides, many of which are still germane today. By the 1970s and 1980s, restrictions on the use of DDT and other organochlorines permitted sensitive wildlife to recover, but organophosphorus and carbamate insecticides became more prevalent (Peterle 1991). Many newer synthetic pesticides are currently used because they are relatively short-lived and do not bioaccumulate (Cowman and Mazanti 2000). Furthermore, the benefits of most products now on the market are thought by many to outweigh the risks to wildlife. Nevertheless, 40 years after the publication of *Silent Spring*, Carson's statement is still true: "The chemicals are pretested against a few individual species but not against living communities."

Although federal regulations require that all pesticides be tested, there are approximately 19,000 to 20,000 pesticides approved for release (M. Hardy, L. Arrington, EPA, personal communications), and many have been studied on a limited number of species and under few environmental contexts. The first major pesticide law to be signed in the United States was the Federal Insecticide, Fungicide, and Rodenticide Act (FIFRA) originally endorsed in 1942. FIFRA emphasizes consumer protection and product efficacy, and mandates determination of safe levels for humans and nontarget wildlife (Touart 1995; Ecobichon 1996). This legislation is unique in that it licenses toxic substances for intentional environmental release, in contrast to statutes designed to prevent or limit the release of these substances (e.g., Clean Water Act; Touart 1995). FIFRA registration procedures assure that a chemical will not cause "unreasonable adverse effects on the environment" (Public Law 95395, sec. 3 [c][5][D]). These procedures involve basic toxicological tests on a number of model species that can range from laboratory to field studies and consider endpoints like mortality, growth, and development. However, most studies performed for licensing are acute toxicity tests (e.g., LC50s, the lethal concentration needed to kill 50% of the test population) that determine mortality that takes place within 96 hours (Rand et al. 1995). Typically, concentrations necessary to induce direct, acute mortality in amphibians are much higher than expected environmental concentration (based on LC50s in Mayer and Ellersieck 1986; Bridges 1999c; Bridges and Semlitsch 2000, 2001). Therefore, data generated from acute lethality tests may not be applicable for understanding effects of exposures in natural settings. Although criteria for setting water quality standards commonly include data from sublethal exposures, there are many cases in which permissible, though sublethal, concentrations have profound and unexpected effects on organisms that may indirectly lead to mortality (e.g., Bridges 1997, 1999a, 1999b, 1999c). Consequently, examining the effects of sublethal concentrations is ecologically relevant, but extrapolating the consequences of these effects in the field can be difficult. Although large-scale studies can show high variability among treatments and replicates, they have a high degree of realism that is lacking in laboratory studies (Diamond 1986). Use of outdoor cattle tanks for larval amphibians, particularly in ecological studies, has been an effective method to bridge the gap between large-scale natural experiments and laboratory studies by combining elements of both: realistic exposure to physical factors with maximum control of treatments and adequate replication (Rowe and Dunson 1994).

Types of Pesticides and Their Effects on Individuals and Communities

Several classes of new-generation pesticides are employed today. The largest groups can be broadly classified as herbicides or insecticides (see Ecobichon 1996; Cowman and Mazanti 2000). Common insecticides include, but are not limited to, organophosphates, carbamates, and pyrethroids. Organophosphates and carbamates are neurotoxins that function by inhibiting nervous system acetylcholinesterase (AChE), which causes constant firing of nerve impulses. At high concentrations, death can result, but at sublethal concentrations, behavioral and motor impairment occur (Hill and Fleming 1982). Organophosphates can irreversibly inhibit enzymes, so they are more likely to cause persistent effects than reversible AChE inhibitors like carbamates. Furthermore, whereas organophosphates can bioaccumulate in biological tissues, exposure to carbamates is typically acute because the chemicals break down relatively quickly and are rapidly metabolized and eliminated from the body (days to weeks). Pyrethroids are synthetic mimics of natural insecticides derived from plants. They disrupt the sodium channel membranes of nerves, which impairs neurotransmission. Pyrethroids are variably persistent in the environment and can bioaccumulate within organisms. Herbicides have modes of action specific to physiological processes in plants (e.g., photosynthetic processes) and for this reason were initially believed to have minimal effects on animals (Ecobichon 1996). The mechanisms of herbicides are understood in terms of the effects they have on photosynthetic plants, but the biochemical effects on amphibians is not clear. The limited data available indicate a wide variability in sensitivity to herbicides among amphibian species (Berrill et al. 1997). However, the total volume of herbicides applied is greater than that of insecticides (Cowman and Mazanti 2000), which increases the likelihood of herbicide exposure in the field.

Pesticides can influence amphibian communities by direct and/or indirect effects. Direct effects affect an individual's physiology. For instance, an insecticide that inhibits AChE directly affects an organism by binding with the enzyme responsible for breaking down the neurotransmitter acetylcholine. Acetylcholine lingers and the nerve is continuously stimulated, which may instigate twitching, paralysis, or death due to respiratory failure. At sublethal concentrations, an organism's behavior (which is a manifestation of physiology) may be affected by pesticide exposure. If an insecticide impairs movements, individuals may be directly affected and unable to feed, which could increase the chance of starvation or reduce mass at metamorphosis in amphibians. Behavioral changes can also eventuate in death or alter important life history functions (e.g., growth and development) through reduced foraging (Little et al. 1985; Weis and Khan 1990) or increased vulnerability to predators (Farr 1977; Dodson et al. 1995; Bridges 1999c). In tadpoles, sublethal concentrations of contaminants are also known to alter behaviors (Berrill et al. 1993; Jung and Jagoe 1995; Semlitsch et al. 1995; Bridges 1997, 1999b, 1999c), which may increase predation rates, prohibit or delay metamorphosis in a temporary pond before it dries and ultimately reduce juvenile recruitment. Therefore concentrations that appear safe in laboratory studies, from a direct mortality standpoint, may have a different effect in natural environments containing competitors and predators.

A pesticide can have no observable direct effect on an organism, but it may indirectly affect the organism if the pesticide changes the food web. For instance, a herbicide may have no direct effects on an anuran at expected environmental concentrations, but it may directly reduce algal food resources (e.g., Diana et al. 2000). In this scenario, a reduction in the food base could increase an anuran's probability of dying from starvation, which will indirectly affect the population. Because the structure of the food web influences amphibians (Leibold and Wilbur 1992; Werner and McPeek 1994), a chemical's indirect effects may be as important as or more than its direct effects. Certainly, direct and indirect effects can lead to the same outcome, but the mechanism of this effect may materialize through different pathways. However, these effects are not mutually exclusive, and organisms may incur consequences from both direct and indirect effects of a contaminant. Additionally, although direct consequences of pesticide exposure may be obvious from simple study designs, more complex environments may be necessary to discern indirect effects.

Determining cause-and-effect relationships requires experimental manipulation on relevant endpoints. Although a chemical may reduce hatching success, for instance, it is necessary to determine the consequences at the population level if we want to make predictions about population viability. A chemical may reduce hatching success by 50%, but there may be no effect at the population level because predators and competitors naturally decrease the number of individuals that reach metamorphosis; experimental evidence is necessary to determine if such a reduction would have population-level consequences. Measures such as hatching success and survival for short periods of time are common in toxicological studies, and while these endpoints are an important first step, they are not sufficient. To determine population-level effects, we must determine effects at this level, which requires population- and community-level studies along with demographic data from long-term population monitoring of pristine populations as a point of comparison.

Initially, however, there are critical endpoints, which are or may be correlated with fitness (i.e., survival and reproduction) and population viability, that are important for ecotoxicological investigations. Regulation of amphibian communities may occur in the larval stage for amphibians having complex life cycles (Wilbur and Collins 1973; Wilbur 1980), as in most North American amphibians (Chapter 2, this volume), so the duration of the larval period, mass at metamorphosis, and survival to metamorphosis are important measures for determining the effects of pesticides. These larval measures have been correlated with adult survival and reproductive success (Berven and Gill 1983; Smith 1987; Semlitsch et al. 1988; Scott and Fore 1995), so they may also be an indicator for long-term effects of pesticides for species that follow these life history patterns.

For instance, if a pesticide produces smaller individuals at metamorphosis (e.g., Fioramonti et al. 1997; Bridges 2000), adult female amphibians may lay fewer eggs because body size and egg production are positively correlated (e.g., Semlitsch and Gibbons 1990). Reduction in the number of offspring may cause population sizes to decrease through diminished juvenile recruitment. Similarly, individuals that metamorphose at smaller sizes may reach reproductive maturity later than those metamorphosing at larger sizes (Berven and Gill 1983; Smith 1987; Scott 1994), which would increase the chance of those individuals dying before they reproduce, thereby reducing the population growth rate (Stearns 1992). Certainly, all of these links need to be established, but because conservation decisions often must be made before long-term population data are available, traits at metamorphosis may be a useful predictor for effects manifested at the population level.

We must emphasize, furthermore, that pesticide contamination is an additional stressor, not the only stressor in a community. Because populations exist in habitats inevitably influenced by multifarious stresses (e.g., predation, competition, desiccation, disease), determining how these stresses interact will be necessary in understanding the effects on communities and ecosystems. A factor may have an effect that changes in the presence of another environmental or biological factor, or that causes a benign factor to become detrimental. Multiple factors may interact additively (so that the effect of both stressors is the sum of the individual effects), antagonistically (so that the effect of one factor reduces the effect of the other), or synergistically (so that the effect of both factors together is greater than the sum of their individual effects). Demonstrating the interaction of factors, however, will necessitate rigorous experimentation to establish the necessary links (Alford and Richards 1999).

Some studies have assessed the effects on amphibian communities of contaminants with natural and anthropogenic factors. Evaluation of contaminants occurring in mixtures in the field may prove useful for common mixtures (e.g., coal ash; Hopkins et al. 1998, 2000; Rowe et al. 2001) or for site-specific studies (C. Bridges, U.S. Geological Survey, Columbia Environmental Research Center, unpublished data), even if underlying mechanisms are uncertain initially. Abiotic conditions can also influence chemical toxicity and persistence. UV radiation (Zaga et al. 1998; C. Bridges, U.S. Geological Survey, unpublished data), temperature (Boone and Bridges 1999), and pH (Fioramonti et al. 1997) have all been demonstrated to increase the potency of pesticides to amphibians and can alter amphibian community interactions (Warner et al. 1993). Fort et al. (1999a, 1999b) reported finding a number of contaminants in a site in Minnesota where a high incidence of deformities had been reported. When Bridges (unpublished data) exposed tadpoles to a composite sample of some of the compounds present in Minnesota ponds, they found that contaminants from this site were made more toxic in the presence of UV radiation. Contaminants from another site, however, were made less toxic (perhaps broken down) in the presence of UV radiation. This illustrates the importance of incorporating multiple factors into toxicity tests. Biotic factors such as predators (Bridges 1999b; Boone and Semlitsch 2001; Relyea and Mills 2001) and tadpole density or competition (Warner et al. 1991; Boone and Semlitsch 2001) can also influence the role a pesticide plays in a community (see below).

Many factors must be considered when attempting to establish causal links between pesticides and population declines. Even after the regulation of a pesticide, it is still necessary to investigate how it can influence population dynamics at environmentally allowable concentrations. This can be done using a variety of assays, but each one, when used singly, leaves other questions unanswered. For example, examining the direct effects of a pesticide on behavior is useful, but does not address the potential indirect effects the compound may have on the food chain. For this reason, it is essential, although difficult, to conduct many tests with the same pesticide to gain a full understanding of how it can affect amphibian populations.

A HIERARCHICAL APPROACH TO STUDYING THE EFFECTS OF AN INSECTICIDE: A CASE STUDY

We provide an example from our own investigations to demonstrate a toxicological approach that incorporates important ecological and evolutionary aspects. Since 1995, we (and others) have been working with the insecticide carbaryl in the laboratory, in mesocosms, and in seminatural ponds. We have used carbaryl (the active ingredient in Sevin), a short-lived carbamate, as a model insecticide for understanding the effects of field-level exposures on amphibians. One goal of this approach is to help researchers make predictions about the effects of other neurotoxins in the carbamate and organophosphorus families that are routinely released into the environment. Using a single chemical has a number of limitations, just like using a model species. But by focusing on a single pesticide we are able to determine how it affects a number of endpoints: behavior, genetic variation, population dynamics, competitive and predator–prey relationships, and food web structure. The major limitation is that the selected pesticide may be unique from other neurotoxins, although existing data for amphibians and other species suggests that this is not the case (Devillers and Exbrayat 1992). We believe that the benefits outweigh the limitations, especially at this stage when little is known about the effect of any pesticide on amphibian communities.

Laboratory Studies

Laboratory studies are a necessary starting point in understanding how contaminant effects manifested at the community level begin. These studies can be used to assess basic lethal toxicity, as well as sublethal effects on behavior and differences in heritable genetic variation. LC50 data indicate that the concentrations of carbaryl needed to induce mortality in larval amphibians are higher than those found in the environment (Bridges 1999a). For this reason, sublethal levels of carbaryl have a greater chance of affecting amphibians in nature. Concentrations not causing death can alter amphibian behaviors. For example, tadpoles have reduced swimming capacity and activity levels with sublethal exposures to carbaryl (Bridges 1997). Bridges (1997) suggested, therefore, that compared with unexposed tadpoles, exposed individuals impaired by sublethal carbaryl toxicosis would be less able to escape predation, would feed less, and would thus be smaller at metamorphosis. Other studies have shown that carbaryl-exposed tadpoles also exhibit nonadaptive predator avoidance responses (Bridges 1999a), which can alter predator–prey dynamics (Bridges 1999c). If pesticides are short-lived (days), however, behavioral effects may also be short-lived. For instance, if the behavioral impairment renders amphibians more vulnerable to predators for a short period of time, the risk may be reduced once they have recovered. Some short-lived effects, however, could have lasting consequences. If the pesticide reduces feeding behavior for days or a week, the length of the larval period may be increased and size at metamorphosis may be reduced (Bridges 1997). Such responses may increase vulnerability to predators later in the larval period or decrease the probability of overwinter survival for smaller metamorphs. Although laboratory studies suggest that acute exposure to pesticides could have serious population-level consequences, the effects of chronic exposures could be more severe. When tadpoles are chronically exposed to carbaryl at concentrations that are an order of magnitude lower than expected environmental concentrations, there is a dramatic increase in mortality over what is anticipated from LC50s, as well as an unnaturally high deformity rate (Bridges 2000). These and other laboratory studies (e.g., Marian et al. 1983) reveal that pesticide exposure during larval development could have direct effects that outlive the chemical and negatively affect responses beyond the larval stage and metamorphosis.

How pesticides (e.g., carbaryl) may influence the evolution of resistance has also been investigated. Bridges and Semlitsch (2001) found significant differences in responses among half-sibling families within a population of southern leopard frogs (*Rana sphenocephala*), indicating the presence of additive genetic variance (i.e., heritability). Because the response to carbaryl was genetic, selection for resistant individuals could occur. Semlitsch et al. (2000) found that gray treefrog (*Hyla versicolor*) tadpoles from families most resistant to high levels of carbaryl had lower survival under some field conditions (i.e., high density), indicating that resistance may come at the price of reduced competitiveness in natural, clean habitats. Although resistance to pesticides may be beneficial in chronically contaminated environments, these populations may be more sensitive to other stressors (like disease, as suggested by Carey et al. 1999), may be less successful if pesticide application ceases, and may be less genetically diverse (Rapport et al. 1985).

In examining several hierarchical levels (i.e., among ranid frog species, within a single ranid species in multiple populations, among families of a single species in a single population), Bridges and Semlitsch (2000) found significant variability in pesticide tolerance among and within amphibian species, and within populations of a single species. They suggest that testing a single species, or sampling too few egg masses within a population, can limit the ability to draw solid conclusions regarding other species or populations. Such results have broad implications for other pesticides, indicating that we may not always be able to predict sensitivity of a population or species to a chemical because of inherent variation in responses. Using standard test species to determine the toxicity of a compound has the advantage of being readily available and easily tested, but the ability to make inferences is limited (Bridges and Semlitsch 2000). Therefore, use of nonnative amphibian species (e.g., African clawed frog, *Xenopus laevis*) or broadly distributed species (e.g., northern leopard frog, *Rana pipiens*) with little consideration to local chemical contamination, specific environmental problems, or species of conservation concern may not be desirable. Although such studies are initially useful and efficient, targeting ecologically relevant species is the most valuable method for solving conservation problems.

Field Studies: Cattle Tank Ponds and Experimental Wetlands

Because amphibians in natural environments may be affected by contaminants differently than individuals reared in controlled laboratory conditions, it is necessary to determine if effects found in the laboratory ensue in the field. Studies in outdoor cattle tanks demonstrate that short-lived contaminants at expected environmental concentrations can affect mass, time, and survival to metamorphosis, although not always as laboratory studies predicted. For instance, because Bridges (1997) indicated that carbaryl impaired tadpole swimming, we would anticipate reduced survival, mass, and/or longer larval periods as a result of higher predation risks and lower feeding rates. Nevertheless, several field studies have revealed positive effects on mass, time, and survival to metamorphosis (Boone 2000; Boone et al. 2001; Boone and Semlitsch 2002). Boone and Semlitsch (2002) found that the presence of carbaryl increased survival to metamorphosis of Woodhouse's toad (*Bufo woodhousii*). The effect on survival across carbaryl treatments differed with the competitive level (i.e., density), with those in high density ponds having the greatest survival. This effect is attributable to indirect effects in the food web (see below).

Not all effects are positive, however, and the nature of the chemical effect may depend on the organisms' life history characteristics. Some anuran species, typically those with longer larval periods (e.g., southern leopard frog, *Rana sphenocephala;* plains leopard frog, *R. blairi*) appear consistently unaffected by carbaryl exposure (Boone and Semlitsch 2001, 2002). Anuran species with shorter larval periods are more commonly affected (e.g., American toad, *Bufo americanus;* Woodhouse's toad; gray treefrog), although it is not predictable whether the effect will be positive or negative. Carnivorous salamander species may be more predictably, negatively affected, however. The presence of carbaryl at expected environmental concentrations resulted in the near elimination of salamander larvae, even though these concentrations were not directly lethal. Mortality was likely induced indirectly through starvation since the invertebrate food supply was essentially eliminated (Boone and James, in press). Such results indicate that expected environmental concentrations of carbaryl could cause population declines for salamander species.

Ecological studies reveal that pond hydroperiod, competition, and predation are strong regulators of amphibian population abundance (Semlitsch et al. 1996), and because of their importance, these factors may modify the magnitude of any pesticide effect. Factors such as the presence of predators or larval density (i.e., competition) can influence the potency of carbaryl (Boone and Semlitsch 2001, 2002). In one case, more toads (Woodhouse's toad) survived to metamorphosis when exposed to carbaryl in high-density conditions than in low-density or control environments (Boone and Semlitsch 2002). Under favorable environmental conditions (e.g., low density) the presence of a chemical may not affect individuals, but under more stressful conditions (e.g., high density) this can change. Consideration of natural exposure conditions (e.g., multiple exposures, chemical mixtures) is also necessary in assessing pesticide effects on populations in those habitats. Exposure to three pulsed doses of carbaryl 10 days apart enhanced survival and size at metamorphosis under high-density conditions (Boone et al. 2001); these results suggest that carbaryl may directly affect metamorphosis by stimulating stress hormones, as well as by acting indirectly through the food web. Although laboratory studies predicted reduced mass or survival from expected environmental concentrations of carbaryl, field studies often indicate that carbaryl has stimulatory effects on these same responses. These unexpected positive effects, in turn, suggested that carbaryl may be changing the amphibian community indirectly.

Studies designed to distinguish indirect and direct effects of carbaryl indicate that, in the field, the direct effects of carbaryl on metamorphosis were small to nonexistent. Effects on metamorphosis in response to carbaryl-induced changes in the aquatic community (i.e., indirect effects) were much greater. Mills and Semlitsch (2002) observed that spring peeper (*Pseudacris crucifer*) and southern leopard frog tadpoles were larger at metamorphosis when raised in communities previously exposed to carbaryl, and determined that the direct effects from exposure were small relative to the indirect effects on the food web. These positive effects can be linked with increases in algal food resources. Algal blooms are common after carbaryl exposure, because zooplankton (which feed on algae) are very sensitive to carbaryl. Reduction or elimination of zooplankton leads to an increase in algae (tadpole food) and can have a positive effect on anuran size and survival to metamorphosis. Such outcomes emphasize the significance of understanding the effects of a contaminant in more realistic, complex conditions.

Cattle tank ponds are idealized environments with minimized risks of predation or harsh environmental conditions (e.g., pond drying). To determine if effects occur in more natural pond environments where the complexity of biotic and abiotic factors may be so great that it could obscure any chemical effects, Boone (2000) conducted an experiment in 55,000-liter experimental ponds. She showed that even in these large wetlands, which included predators and competitors typically excluded in cattle tank studies, a short-lived pesticide can alter amphibian abundance and mass at metamorphosis for some species. Further, effects in the seminatural ponds were similar to results in cattle tank studies, and illustrate how cattle tanks may be a useful surrogate for testing the effects of contaminants in nature.

Summary from Studies of an Insecticide on Amphibians

By studying the effects of a single contaminant on amphibians in the laboratory, in seminatural ponds, and in the field, we are developing an understanding of how this broad-spectrum insecticide could affect natural larval amphibian communities. This research also helps establish causal links between pesticides and their effects on amphibians, and demonstrates the importance of incorporating genetic variation, biological complexity, and realistic exposures into toxicological studies. Additionally, this research illustrates that even a short-lived pesticide that has relatively modest toxicity can alter the structure of amphibian communities by direct or indirect effects on individual species. Because these results suggest that environmentally relevant levels of contaminants could alter abundance of species, both positively and negatively, we must begin to question whether short-lived pesticides are truly benign to nontarget populations. Populations of amphibians throughout the world, particularly in agricultural and industrial areas, may be routinely exposed to contaminants and other stressors that can alter both biodiversity and population size over time.

Using a model chemical may be very useful when little is known about the small- and large-scale effects of contaminants in the field. From this work, we are able to make predictions about the effects of other contaminants with the same mode of action (i.e., other carbamates and organophosphates). We would anticipate that species may be differentially susceptible to other neurotoxins in the carbamate and organophosphate families and that vulnerability in the field may relate to life history characteristics such as length of the larval period. Most importantly, any pesticide that affects zooplankton or algal resources of an amphibian community may change mass, time, and survival to metamorphosis of amphibians; so, although a contaminant may have no direct biochemical or physiological effect on amphibians, it may have a profound effect on processes within the community.

SOLUTIONS AND CONCLUSIONS

The solutions to many problems are often obvious, though seldom practical. Likely the greatest threat to biodiversity is habitat destruction and alteration (Pechmann and Wilbur 1994; Corn 1994); not destroying and altering habitat could remedy this predicament. Because this solution is either not desirable, not possible, or both, conservation biologists and managers are forced to focus on other issues that are of concern, but that are unlikely to significantly decrease the magnitude of the problem. When Carson (1962) published *Silent Spring*, pesticides were having a devastating effect on wildlife, and one of the outcomes of her book was intensified research into the effects of pesticides on nontarget wildlife and the eventual banning of the most dangerous pesticides (Palumbi 2001b). Preventing the use of potent chemicals has been instrumental in the recovery of affected populations.

Although pesticides may have a large effect on wildlife today, the impact is not as straightforward as it was in the 1950s and 1960s. This is not meant to diminish the problem of pesticides, because (although they have been understudied in amphibians; Sparling et al. 2000) they have been demonstrated to induce mortality (e.g., from mine drainage; Porter and Hakanson 1976), alter food web dynamics (Mills 2002), and disrupt the endocrine systems (reviewed in Hayes 2000). Certainly, research directed at appropriate ecological and evolutionary scales is necessary for both aquatic and terrestrial life stages. Theoretically, widespread use of pesticides could be responsible for amphibian population declines through complex pathways, but presently we do not have evidence that supports such hypotheses. Contaminants could suppress immune systems (as suggested by Carey et al. 1999), which may make amphibians more susceptible to pathogens like the chytrid fungus that has been implicated in a number of declines (Berger et al. 1998; Bosch et al. 2001). It is possible, even likely, that the interaction of contaminants with other anthropogenic stressors may have potent negative effects on amphibian populations. Most effects of pesticide exposure may be sublethal and may elicit effects that are not obvious when encountering amphibians in the field. For instance, even if a pesticide influences species abundance, this sensitivity varies widely within species (Bridges and Semlitsch 2000) and discriminating between natural and pesticide-induced declines would be difficult (Pechmann and Wilbur 1994). If pesticides alter mass at metamorphosis or the duration of the larval period, then distinguishing chemical effects from natural effects of density or predator presence would be even more problematic. Although the effects of pesticides may be difficult to recognize in the field, understanding the causal links between pesticides and amphibians in complex environments will help us to recognize their capacity and make efforts to minimize their impacts.

Although the general assumption is that pesticides are effective in minimizing pest problems, this assumption may not be completely accurate. In 1986, approximately 100 million pounds of insecticides were used and 13% of crops were lost to insects; compare this with 10% losses before insecticide use in the early 1900s or with 10% losses typically experienced by organic farms (Buttel 1993; Edwards 1993; Osteen 1993; Palumbi 2001b). Some have estimated that for every dollar invested in pesticides, there is a $4 return in profit (Pimentel et al. 1993a). Others surmise that the economic benefit of pesticide use may be negated when costs are factored in for extracting pesticides from drinking water, reduced crops from decreased pollination by insects, state and federal regulation and monitoring programs needed to control pollution, and related public illnesses (Edwards 1993; Osteen 1993; Pimentel et al. 1993a).

One reason for relatively high pest-induced loss of crops despite pesticide use is related to the evolution of resistance. It is common for pests to become resistant to pesticides within 3 to 10 years (Palumbi 2001a); there are more than 500 documented cases of insect adaptations to insecticides (reviewed in Gould 1991). For instance, DDT was introduced in 1945, but some insects were resistant to it by 1952 (Georghiou 1986). Resistance is an inevitable consequence of widespread application of pesticides if tolerance is genetically based (McKenzie 1996). Applying a lethal dose of an insecticide will eliminate most insects initially, but if a few individuals have genes that confer resistance, many if not all of their progeny will also be resistant to the pesticide. In such cases, the crops are even more vulnerable to destruction because populations of the pests' ecological enemy (i.e., insect predators) may also have been reduced by pesticide application.

Because a selective force like a pesticide will increase the frequency of existing resistant genotypes, pesticide application becomes an evolutionary arms race between humans and pests (Lewis et al. 1997). Pesticide resistance can be slowed, however, by minimizing the selective force maintaining resistant genotypes within the population. For instance, alternating pesticides with different modes of actions among years is a way to slow adaptation, because the chemical environment is frequently changing (Palumbi 2001b). Other techniques involve reducing the number of times the pesticide is applied, using more potent chemical mixtures, applying different pesticides in various locations (i.e., mosaic application), and rotating crops. These techniques help maintain some genetic variation. It has been demonstrated that when contamination (or another potential deleterious factor) is removed, a population can revert to being dominated by primarily susceptible genotypes within a few generations (Klerks and Levinton 1989), thus ameliorating the effects of pesticide-induced selection. Such techniques are not permanent solutions, however; other tactics can and do evolve. For instance, some pests have developed diapause cycles to accommodate rotation of crops—a natural way farmers can deal with pests—which results in destructive larvae emerging every other year when the food source (i.e., crop) is available (Georghiou 1986; Palumbi 2001b).

Although evidence suggests pesticide use may only be a short-term pest management solution and that pesticides have fewer benefits than their costs to nontarget wildlife would warrant, farmers continue to use pesticides for several reasons. Farmers avoid unnecessary risks with their livelihood, so they use pesticides as an insurance against crop loss (Georghiou 1986) and because the costs of pollution are not borne by them (Pimentel et al. 1993a). Additionally, early agricultural research documented the successes of pesticides and encouraged their use (Buttel 1993), so farmers had evidence that justified pesticide use. Further, as agriculture became more mechanized, farmers invested in specialized machinery that helped reduce labor costs, but reinforced a monoculture planting that makes crops more vulnerable to pests and increases the usefulness of pesticides (Buttel 1993). Since farmers began using pesticides, they have witnessed their efficacy, or apparent efficacy, and many farmers' experience may exclusively include pesticide use as a matter of course. These factors may make farmers understandably unlikely to change, given the inherent risks associated with their profession. Certainly, pesticides may have a role in the production of crops to feed the world's growing population, but many researchers indicate that using pesticides as a last resort, rather than a first choice, may be the optimal way to deal with pests and minimize environmental consequences (Lewis et al. 1997; Palumbi 2001a; Obrycki et al. 2001).

The growing literature on pesticides at environmental concentrations suggests that pesticides can affect amphibian species abundance and the quality of individuals reaching metamorphosis (in terms of size at metamorphosis and the duration of the larval period), and these effects are noteworthy. Chemical effects that manifest themselves as changes in population size, whether or not contaminants contribute to declines, are important considerations if the aspiration of pesticide regulation is to maintain community processes of nontarget species and ecosystem function. There are several ways to reduce widespread application of chemicals, however. Carson (1962) suggested a number of techniques that have been used to some degree, and that are frequently proposed by others as potential ways to reduce pesticide use. These techniques include male sterilization techniques for pests, pheromone traps, biological control with bacterial or viral infections, introduction of pest predators, unsprayed refuges to maintain genetic variation in the pest population, and traditional farming methods like heterogeneous crop planting and crop rotation (Carson 1962; McKenzie 1996; Lewis et al. 1997; Palumbi 2001b). Genetically modified crops have also become available, but they also allow for pest-resistance. "Bt-corn" contains a gene made by the bacterium *Bacillus thuringiensis* that produces a toxin that kills certain caterpillar pests. Originally it was hoped that such techniques would reduce pesticide application rates, but resistance to this toxin has also evolved and there is considerable debate over whether it reduces pesticide usage (Watkinson et al. 2000; Obrycki et al. 2001; Ortman et al. 2001; Palumbi 2001b).

Because environmental concentrations of pesticides can affect amphibian communities (including the plankton and invertebrate communities on which amphibians rely for food), because amphibians breed in habitats that may frequently encounter pesticides (e.g., floodplains), and because pesticides can be transported atmospherically, reduction of pesticides would benefit these and other nontarget populations. There are several things land managers can do (and public citizens can advocate for) that may benefit amphibians. A change in the philosophy of pesticide management may be the first step. Integrated pest management strategies recommend using pesticides as a last resort when a pest becomes a threat to the crop, rather than proactively before a pest is a problem (Hammock and Soderlund 1986; Lewis et al. 1997). Lewis et al. (1997) suggest that the goal should not be to eliminate the pests completely, but to keep the pests in check, which can be done by maintaining some ecological integrity (e.g., maintaining habitats, like field margins, for pest predators). Using pesticides as a last resort would significantly reduce problems associated with pesticides, whereas pesticides would remain potent because pests would not become resistant from repeated exposures. Simple reduction in pesticide use would benefit nontarget species (e.g., amphibians) as well. Pimentel et al. (1993b) indicated that reducing pesticide practices by 50% would not increase crop losses, but would reduce environmental damage; therefore, reducing the amount and frequency of spraying would be beneficial to amphibian communities by reducing environmental concentrations and duration of exposure.

Amphibian declines have stimulated keen interest in determining the link between a number of potential stressors, like chemical contamination, and amphibian populations and communities. Existing research indicates that amphibians can be affected at the individual, population, and community levels by environmental concentrations of contaminants in both negative and apparently positive ways. When a chemical affects community processes by altering abundance in a seemingly positive way, we must ask if this is something to be concerned about, particularly in light of potential reductions in fitness (Semlitsch et al. 2000; McKenzie 1996). The ecological answer to this conundrum may be that a no-effect level is the only acceptable effect on nontarget populations, because both positive and negative effects indicate fundamental alterations that may signify ecosystem-level changes (Rapport et al. 1985). More experimental research is needed to establish cause-and-effect links, particularly research that will determine population-level responses and physiological responses that may affect the population (e.g., endocrine disruption). Examining the effects of multiple stressors is also germane to population declines, and environmental concentrations of pesticides may be a sublethal stress that can make amphibians more susceptible to other stresses, such as habitat alteration or disease. The effects of a pesticide may be very subtle, so it may be impossible to look at a declining population and differentiate chemical effects from natural effects, for instance. Only through experimental research will these links be established and conservation efforts enhanced.

ACKNOWLEDGMENTS

This manuscript was improved by the thoughtful comments of Stacey James, Nathan Mills, Chris Rowe, and Ray Semlitsch.

13

WHAT IS CAUSING DEFORMED AMPHIBIANS?

STANLEY K. SESSIONS

CENTRAL ISSUES

The occurrence of morphological abnormalities in natural populations of amphibians has become a major environmental issue over the last few years. Potential causes include chemical pollution, ultraviolet (UV)-B radiation, predation, and parasites. Some researchers have suggested that extra limbs and other limb abnormalities in frogs are caused by chemical pollutants, especially contaminants that contain or mimic retinoids, a class of biochemicals that can cause birth defects in humans and other organisms. Other researchers have found evidence that many of these abnormalities are caused by a parasitic trematode flatworm that uses amphibians as a second intermediate host in a complex life cycle. It is possible that multiple factors, acting alone or in combination, may be involved in causing different kinds of abnormalities. This chapter includes an analysis of amphibian abnormalities and possible causes from morphogenetic as well as ecological and evolutionary perspectives.

INTRODUCTION

The widespread occurrence of morphological abnormalities in natural populations of amphibians, especially anurans, has recently been perceived as a major environmental issue (Tietge et al. 1996; Kaiser 1997; Ouellet et al. 1997; Helgen et al. 1998). Most observed abnormalities include frogs with missing limbs or parts of limbs, or with one to several partial or complete extra (supernumerary) limbs (Figure 13.1). Similar kinds of abnormalities have been found in the past, but renewed attention

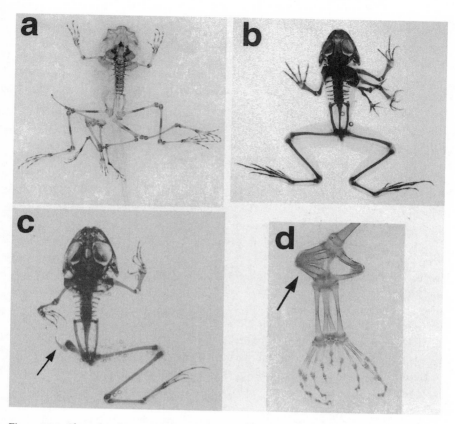

Figure 13.1. Cleared and stained abnormal frog specimens. (a) Pacific treefrog (*Pseudacris regilla*) from northern California showing multiple hind limbs (polymelia). (b) Green frog (*Rana clamitans*) from New York showing duplicated forelimbs. (c) Northern leopard frog (*Rana pipiens*) from Vermont with a cartilagenous spike growing from the stump of a missing hind limb. (d) An abnormal limb showing a mirror-image duplication (PMID; see Table 13.1), and taumelia or "bony triangles" (arrow). (Images courtesy of Brandon Ballengée and S. K. Sessions, Institute of Electronic Arts, Alfred University)

has been focused on them since 1996 when a group of students found some "malformed" frogs in Minnesota and broadcast their findings on the Internet (Helgen et al. 1998). Recent reports of morphological abnormalities in wild-caught amphibians are geographically widespread across the United States and Canada (North American Reporting Center for Amphibian Malformations, NARCAM). There is current concern that these reports reflect a sudden increase in the incidence of such abnormalities in natural populations of amphibians, possibly indicating an environmental problem linked to the general problem of amphibian decline, and even of possible risk to other organisms, including humans (Ouellet et al. 1997).

Leading hypotheses to explain these abnormalities are chemical pollution, especially agents with retinoid activity, UV radiation, parasites, especially trematode cysts, and predation (National Science Foundation workshop, "Mechanisms of Developmental Disruption in Amphibians," San Diego, 1998). It is also possible, of course, that the observed abnormalities are caused by several different factors, acting alone or in combination. The purpose of this chapter is to try to identify the kinds of information needed to test each of these hypotheses and to review the main research results to date.

The terminology used to describe the observed abnormalities has not been completely standardized. There is current disagreement over whether these abnormalities should technically be considered *deformities,* defined as abnormalities resulting from the response of normal tissues to mechanical forces (trauma), or *malformations,* defined as abnormalities resulting from an intrinsic defect in their development (Winter et al. 1988). Although both terms are used by different researchers, neither is very accurate when applied to frogs. For example, a missing limb due to amputation is clearly a deformity, but if that limb forms an incomplete, misshapen outgrowth due to regenerative decline, which is an intrinsic deficiency in postmetamorphic frogs, it also becomes a malformation. In other words, the regulative, regenerative properties of amphibian limbs blur the distinction between deformity and malformation. Thus, in this chapter I will avoid using the terms deformity and malformation and instead simply refer to amphibians with morphological abnormalities.

Even the terminology for specific types of abnormalities has not been standardized. For example, developmental biologists who work on amphibian limbs commonly refer to extra limbs as *supernumerary limbs,* a condition in the medical literature known as *polymelia.* Wisely, several researchers are beginning to pull these disparate terminologies together to facilitate analysis (Meteyer et al. 2000; Johnson et al. 2001). A catalogue of the most commonly observed morphological abnormalities in wild-caught amphibians, using consolidated terminologies, is presented in Table 13.1.

Considerable confusion has also been generated by reports of particular treatments causing deformities or malformations, when in actuality the experimentally induced morphological abnormalities show little or no similarity to those seen in wild-caught amphibians. It is very easy to induce developmental anomalies in laboratory-raised embryos. For example, exposing fertilized eggs to abnormal salt concentrations can induce substantial developmental defects or mortality (Spemann 1967). To identify the causes of morphological abnormalities in natural populations of amphibians, we need to consider all of the following:

- The geographic distribution of reported abnormalities.
- The species of amphibians and their particular biological characteristics.
- The specific kinds and patterns of observed abnormalities, for example extra limbs (polymelia), missing limbs (ectromelia), different kinds of

Table 13.1

Morphological abnormalities observed in field-caught deformed amphibians (modified from Johnson et al. 2001)

Abnormality	Description
Anophthalmy	Absence of one or both eyes.
Apody	Absence of one or more feet.
Brachydactyly	Abnormal shortness of one or more digits.
Cartilaginous spike	A cartilaginous outgrowth from the end of an amputated limb, representing maximal regenerative response in a perimetamorphic frog that has undergone regenerative decline.
Cutaneous fusion	Constriction or fusion of limb long bones by a superficial skin layer; skin webbing.
Ectrodactyly	Complete absence of one or more digits.
Ectromelia	Complete absence of one or more limbs.
Edema	Fluid-filled swelling; either localized or general.
Hemimelia	Partial or complete absence of distal portions of one or more limbs.
Hypomorphic limb[a]	Presence of one or more non-articulating microappendages from the soft tissues of a hindlimb; may contain ossified elements.
Limb hyperextension	Excessive or rigid flexure of a limb joint.
Mandibular dysplasia	Underdevelopment of mandible.
Micromelia	Abnormal smallness of one or more limbs.
Mirror-image duplication	Digit series duplication in the anterior–posterior axis; may be either a posterior mirror-image duplication (PMID) of the digit pattern 5-4-3-2-1-2-3-4-5 or anterior mirror image duplication (AMID) of the pattern 1-2-3-4-5-4-3-2-1. Mirror-image duplications may also occur in the dorsoventral axis, generating a dorsoventral mirror-image duplication (DVMID).
Mirror-image triplication	Digit series triplication in the anterior-posterior axis, usually in the pattern 1-2-3-4-5-4-3-2-1-2-3-4-5.
Polydactyly	Presence of one or more extra digits or parts of digits.
Polymelia	Presence of one or more extra limbs or parts of limbs; supernumerary limbs.
Polypody	Presence of one or more extra feet or parts of feet.
Syndactyly	Partial or complete fusion of one or more digits.
Taumelia	One or more sharp folds in a limb longbone; bone with limb elements at right angles, externally appear truncated; bony triangle.

[a]Includes "femoral projection" (Johnson et al. 2001).

mirror-image limb duplications (AMID, PMID, MIT), bony triangles (taumelia), and cartilaginous spikes (Table 13.1).
- The relative involvement of hind limbs, forelimbs, or other body parts.
- The specificity of the abnormalities to amphibians.
- The natural history of the amphibians and other organisms with which they interact, including parasites and predators.

- The cellular and molecular mechanisms of amphibian development and regeneration, especially of the limbs.
- The presence or absence of putative causal factors in the amphibians' habitat (e.g., pollutants, parasites, levels of UV-B radiation, likely predators).
- Finally, and crucially, a particular hypothesis must be tested in the laboratory, using what is found in the field, and shown to cause *exactly* the same kinds of abnormalities as are seen in the field-caught specimens. A pathogenic microorganism (such as a parasite), at least ideally, should be shown to fit Koch's postulates (Davis et al. 1973): (a) the suspected pathogen is regularly found in the lesions of the disease, (b) the pathogen can be isolated, (c) inoculation of the isolated pathogen causes a similar disease in experimental animals, and (d) the pathogenic organism can be recovered from the lesions in the experimental animals.

CHEMICAL POLLUTION

Several published reports have investigated the possibility that something dissolved in the water and/or sediments at localities that produce abnormal amphibians can cause developmental abnormalities in amphibians. A commonly used procedure in these investigations is called FETAX (frog embryo teratogenesis assay-*Xenopus*), a teratogenic assay using laboratory-raised embryos of the African clawed frog, *Xenopus laevis* (Burkhart et al. 1998; Fort et al. 1999a, 1999b). Although these papers report that the water and/or sediment causes mortality and developmental abnormalities in *Xenopus* embryos, the specific causative agent has not been identified, and the induced abnormalities (e.g., gut miscoiling, craniofacial abnormalities, hypognathia, tail kinking) do not resemble the major kinds of deformities reported from natural populations of amphibians.

A correlation between agricultural habitats and anuran abnormalities was reported by Ouellet et al. (1997). However, the differences in the incidence of abnormalities between agricultural sites and "control sites" was not found to be statistically significant, and no attempt was made to quantify or confirm the existence of pesticides in the water at any site. Bridges (2000) found that treatment with the insecticide carbaryl, alternating with plain well water, induced limb abnormalities in a very small fraction (2.0%) of treated tadpoles of the southern leopard frog (*Rana sphenocephala*). However, this frequency is well within the baseline of 1.0 to 5.0% abnormalities normally expected for amphibian populations (Johnson et al. 2001). Unfortunately, none of the abnormalities were illustrated or described in any detail.

One of the most alarming possible causes of abnormalities in natural populations of amphibians is a chemical contaminant that has retinoid activity. Retinoids are one of the most powerful teratogens known, capable of producing developmental defects in amphibians and other organisms, including humans (Gardiner and Hoppe 1999). It has long been known that retinoic acid, for example, can cause certain kinds of limb abnormalities in amphibians, including the African clawed frog; the common frog (*Rana temporaria*); and the Mexican axolotl (*Ambystoma mexicanum*) (Maden 1983; Thoms and Stocum 1984; Kim and Stocum 1986; Scadding and Maden 1986a, 1986b; Bryant and Gardiner 1992). These retinoic acid–induced abnormalities resemble a subset of the range of abnormalities observed in field-caught abnormal amphibians (Sessions et al. 1999). No other class of chemical pollutant is yet known that could cause a high frequency of supernumerary limbs (polymelia) in amphibians. The mode of action of endogenous as well as synthetic retinoids is well characterized and the effects, both normal and teratogenic, are mediated through activation of members of the nuclear hormone receptor family (RARs and RXRs; Gardiner and Hoppe 1999). The specific effects of retinoids on the morphogenesis of developing and regenerating amphibian limbs have been extensively studied (Maden 1983; Thoms and Stocum 1984; Kim and Stocum 1986; Scadding and Maden 1986a, 1986b) and have been used to construct hypotheses for how retinoids alter the developmental fates of cells in the developing limb (Bryant and Gardiner 1992).

Retinoic acid has different effects on developing and regenerating limbs in amphibians. In developing limbs, retinoic acid usually causes bilateral limb truncations in both forelimbs and hind limbs (Scadding and Maden 1986b). Regenerating limbs show a wider range of effects of exogenous retinoic acid, from inhibition to complete limb duplications. Two main categories of limb duplications are induced by retinoic acid in regenerating amphibian limbs: double posterior mirror-image duplications (PMIDs; Figure 13.2b; Table 13.1) and proximal–distal duplications (PDDs; Figure 13.2a). Retinoic acid can also induce mirror-image duplications in the dorsal–ventral axis. Thus, retinoic acid appears to alter the developmental fates of cells in the developing or regenerating amphibian limb bud in specific, nonrandom ways (Bryant and Gardiner 1992): (1) posteriorization of anterior cells; that is, retinoic acid changes the developmental fates of cells in the anterior, or big toe side, of the limb bud so that they develop into posterior, or pinky toe side, structures; (2) ventralization of dorsal cells; and (3) proximalization of distal cells (Maden 1982; Kim and Stocum 1986; Ludolph et al. 1990). Significantly, retinoids are the only known cause of PDDs, and thus a PDD represents a "signature" abnormality indicating retinoids as the probable cause (Sessions et al. 1999). A recent paper claims that retinoic acid causes another signature abnormality called "bony triangles" (taumelia, Table 13.1; Gardiner and Hoppe 1999). However, recent research has shown that bony triangles (Figure 13.1d) are also produced by surgical limb bud rotation as well as by trematode cyst infestation (Johnson et al. 1999; Hecker and Sessions 2001). Thus, bony triangles are not diagnostic of retinoids.

Retinoic acid activity has been found in pond water, but it is not known whether

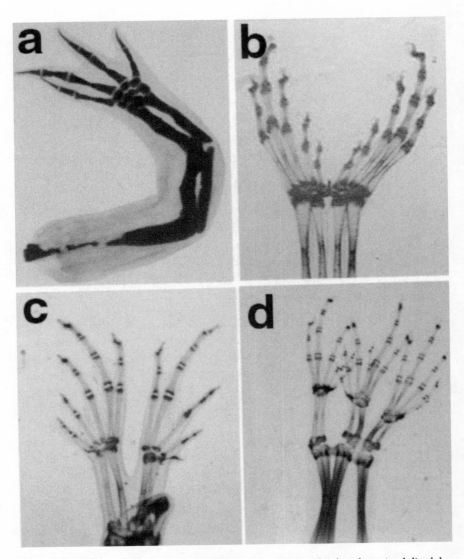

Figure 13.2. Examples of mirror-image duplications. (a) Retinoid-induced proximal-distal duplication (PDD) in the limb of a salamander larva. (b) Double posterior mirror-image duplication (PMID) in a cyst-infected frog. (c) Double anterior mirror-image duplication (AMID) in a cyst-infected frog. (d) Mirror-image triplication in a cyst-infected frog. (Modified from Sessions et al. 1999)

it is at high enough levels to cause any of the observed abnormalities (Gardiner and Hoppe 1999). Neither is it known if the source of the retinoic acid activity is biotic (reflecting natural levels of retinoids in aquatic microorganisms, plants, etc.) or xeno-biotic (reflecting chemical contamination from human activity). One possible candi-date contaminant is methoprene, a synthetic insect growth hormone used for mos-quito control that is known to mimic retinoids in its biochemical activity (Harmon et al. 1995). However, methoprene has not been shown to induce limb abnormalities in amphibians in the laboratory (Ankley et al. 1998; LaClair et al. 1998).

The morphological abnormalities observed in natural populations of amphibians do not appear to be consistent with the known effects of endogenous retinoic acid on developing or regenerating amphibian limbs (Sessions et al. 1999). Field-caught abnormal frogs are characterized by unilateral, asymmetrical limb abnormalities in the hind limbs, and the forelimbs are rarely affected. In anurans, the forelimbs de-velop within the gill chamber where they are exposed to a constant influx of water from the environment. Retinoic acid, therefore, does not provide a very satisfactory explanation for why the vast majority of observed limb abnormalities involve only the hind limbs. One idea is that forelimb abnormalities are more lethal than hind limb abnormalities, but this conjecture is not supported by experiments in the labo-ratory (Maden 1983; Thoms and Stocum 1984; Kim and Stocum 1986; Scadding and Maden 1986a, 1986b). Furthermore, some cleared and stained wild-caught abnormal northern leopard frogs (*Rana pipiens*) with missing limbs exhibit cartilaginous "spikes" extending from the limb stump (Figure 13.1c; Sessions et al. 2001). Anurans normally undergo regenerative decline in which they gradually lose the ability to completely regenerate a limb as metamorphosis is approached (Muneoka et al. 1986; Sessions and Bryant 1988). A cartilaginous spike is a maximal regenerative response in a post-metamorphic frog and is inhibited by exogenous retinoic acid; it indicates that the limb was probably amputated after normal development, and then regenerated in a toxin-free environment.

The one limb abnormality that is truly diagnostic of retinoic acid, proximal–distal duplication (PDD), has never been reported in field-caught abnormal amphibians to my knowledge (Sessions and Ruth 1990; Helgen et al. 1998; Sessions et al. 1999; Ouel-let 2000; Johnson et al. 2001). Field-caught abnormal amphibians show two addi-tional kinds of mirror-image duplications that retinoic acid either does not cause, or very rarely causes, in developing or regenerating amphibian limbs in the laboratory (Sessions et al. 1999): double anterior mirror-image duplications (AMIDs; Figure 13.2c) and mirror-image triplications (MITs; Figure 13.2d). On the other hand, AMIDs and MITs are common in both wild-caught abnormal amphibians and in laboratory-raised amphibians with parasite-induced limb abnormalities, including the Pacific treefrog (*Pseudacris regilla*) and two species of *Rana* (Sessions et al. 1999, 2001; John-son et al. 2001). Few other researchers have described these particular kinds of ab-normalities in their samples of abnormal amphibians, but this appears to be due to different interpretations and lack of a standardized terminology since different kinds of mirror-image duplications can be clearly seen in published illustrations.

Although the evidence for involvement of chemical pollution in causing high frequencies of morphological abnormalities in natural populations of amphibians seems weak at this point, the potential dangers to humans and other organisms argue in favor of continued research. This is particularly true if the pollutant is a retinoid. Groundwater contaminated with retinoids at a high enough concentration to cause limb deformities in amphibians would constitute an environmental disaster of truly enormous proportions.

UV-B RADIATION

Laboratory experiments have shown that UV irradiation inhibits development and regeneration in amphibian limbs by destroying the ability of their cells to proliferate (Holder et al. 1979). Ankley et al. (1998) showed that UV-B irradiation can cause some limb abnormalities and truncation of limb development under conditions of constant exposure of less than ambient UV-B levels. Field experiments show that ambient UV-B levels can cause severe developmental abnormalities and death in early embryos, but the effects of ambient UV-B levels on limb development in the field have not been studied (Blaustein et al. 1997a).

The UV-B hypothesis is consistent with the relative rarity of forelimb compared with hind limb abnormalities in anurans, since the forelimbs develop within the gill chamber where they are protected by three layers of skin. However, the effects of UV irradiation on developing hind limbs in the laboratory are bilateral and in this sense do not resemble limb truncations seen in field-caught abnormal frogs, which are almost always unilateral or asymmetrical. Also, UV-B radiation does not account for the presence of cartilaginous spikes, which have been reported in wild-caught abnormal frogs that are missing limbs (Sessions 1997; Sessions et al. 2001; Figure 13.1c), since UV irradiation also inhibits the outgrowth of cartilaginous spikes.

Because the known deleterious effects of UV-B radiation include inhibition of cell proliferation, it seems possible that UV radiation could interfere with immunological function in amphibians, allowing increased infection rates by pathogens such as parasites. This seems doubtful, however, because the thymus gland, necessary to produce T-cells required for an effective immunological defense against helminthe parasites (e.g., trematodes), does not mature until near metamorphosis in anurans (Nieuwkoop and Faber 1994). This means that tadpoles at early limb bud stages, when the abnormalities are induced, probably have very little immunological defense against these parasites anyway. Furthermore, helminthe parasites usually have very effective coadaptive mechanisms by which they are able to thwart the host's immune system or even use it for their own biological needs (Capron and Capron 1994;

Roitt et al. 1996). More research is required to understand the possible relationship between UV radiation, immunodeficiency, and parasite infection in amphibians.

In summary, there is no compelling evidence that UV-B radiation is playing a major role in the induction of limb abnormalities in natural populations of amphibians. However, the potential dangers of UV-B levels high enough to cause developmental abnormalities in amphibians would seem to justify further research. In particular, we need to measure ambient UV-B levels at sites that have produced abnormal amphibians and determine whether these same levels are sufficient to induce a range of abnormalities in experimental animals similar to those seen in natural populations.

PREDATION

Predation, either inter- or intraspecific, can cause missing appendages identical to those seen in field-caught amphibians (Sessions 1997; Johnson et al. 2001). Enclosure–exclosure experiments in the field and in the laboratory led to the conclusion that missing hind limbs in western toads (*Bufo boreas*) were caused by stickleback fishes, an introduced predator (Johnson et al. 2001; J. Bowerman, Sunriver Nature Center, Oregon, personal communication). I have actually observed stickleback fishes attack and destroy the developing hind limbs of toad tadpoles. The results are missing limb structures that look identical to those of field-caught amphibians with missing appendages (S. Sessions, R. Franssen, and V. Horner, Hartwick College, Oneonta, NY, unpublished). Certain crustaceans and other invertebrate predators, especially leeches, are also known to attack anuran limbs, sometimes causing limb loss or injury (Licht 1974; Formanowicz and Brodie 1982; Duellman and Trueb 1986; Viertel and Veith 1992, cited in Johnson et al. 2001).

Anuran tadpoles undergo regenerative decline as their limbs complete development (Muneoka et al. 1986). Thus the regenerative response to injury or amputation can be irregular, depending on the developmental stage of the tadpole, and can mask the traumatic origin of the abnormality. For this reason, it is probably impossible to determine the cause of missing appendages simply by examining metamorphosed frogs. One must examine tadpoles. American bullfrog (*Rana catesbeiana*) and green frog (*R. clamitans*) tadpoles captured at sites in New York that produced high frequencies of metamorphs with missing appendages showed obvious evidence of recent trauma to their hind limbs, including bloody stumps and protruding limb bones (Sessions 1997). Bullfrog tadpoles raised under crowded conditions in the laboratory were observed to attack each other, causing missing limbs, missing feet, and even missing eyes in the metamorphs, the same range and kinds of abnormalities observed in field-caught tadpoles and newly metamorphosed frogs (Sessions 1997).

Given the available evidence, the predation/cannibalism hypothesis seems at least as likely, and probably more likely as an explanation for missing appendages than either the retinoid or the UV-B hypothesis. It is also consistent with the observation that missing forelimbs are much less frequent than missing hind limbs in field-caught anurans. Additional research is needed to determine if there is a correlation between recent outbreaks of frogs with missing appendages and introduced predators, especially fishes, in amphibian breeding habitats. My own results indicate that in some cases increased abnormalities may indicate high population densities and cannibalistic interactions between tadpoles, at least in bullfrogs (Sessions 1997). Future research should include analyses of developing cohorts of tadpoles over time in addition to examination of adult frog morphology.

PARASITES

The parasite hypothesis was first presented by Sessions and Ruth (1990) to explain the occurrence of limb abnormalities, mainly duplicated limbs, in large samples of Pacific treefrogs and long-toed salamanders (*Ambystoma macrodactylum*) from northern California. The abnormalities were found to be associated with heavy infection by trematode cysts. Sessions and Ruth (1990) hypothesized that the cysts physically disrupted the limb at early stages of development, partitioning the limb bud and causing the abnormalities. This idea was tested by surgically implanting beads, meant to mimic trematode cysts, into the limb buds of laboratory-raised amphibian larvae. This treatment induced supernumerary limbs (Sessions and Ruth 1990). These results indicated that mechanical perturbation of early limb buds, such as that caused by trematode cysts, is sufficient to induce limb duplications and other abnormalities in amphibians. The trematode has subsequently been identified as a species of the genus *Ribeiroia* (Sessions et al. 1999), probably *R. ondatrae* (Pratt and McCauley 1961; Johnson et al. 2001); here I will simply refer to it as *Ribeiroia*. *Ribeiroia* has now been implicated in abnormalities in at least 12 species of amphibians from sites in both the western and eastern United States (Sessions et al. 1999, 2001; Johnson et al. 2001): long-toed salamanders; rough-skinned newts (*Taricha granulosa*); California newts (*T. torosa*); Pacific treefrogs; western toads; Cascades frogs (*Rana cascadae*); American bullfrogs; green frogs; Columbia spotted frogs (*R. luteiventris*); northern leopard frogs; red-legged frogs (*R. aurora*); and wood frogs (*R. sylvatica*). *Ribeiroia*-infected snails are abundant at most of these sites and *Ribeiroia* cysts have been recovered from affected animals (Johnson et al. 2001).

The Life Cycle of *Ribeiroia*

Ribeiroia is a genus of digenetic trematode with a complex life cycle involving a primary host and two intermediate hosts (Figure 13.3). *Ribeiroia* uses aquatic birds and, more rarely, mammals as its primary, or definitive, host and amphibians as its second

intermediate host (Schell 1985). A diagnostic feature of this trematode is a pair of diverticulae just posterior to the muscular pharynx (Figure 13.4; Schell 1985). The
trematode eggs are released from the primary host into the environment, including
ponds, where they hatch into a free-swimming stage called a miracidium that pene-
trates aquatic snails (I have found them mainly in planorbids). Once in a snail, each
miracidium produces numerous embryos of the next larval stage, called a redia.
Each redia, in turn, contains numerous embryos of a third larval stage, which is either another redia or the infectious swimming larval stage called a cercaria. This process results in a kind of embryonic amplification in which hundreds, thousands, or
even hundreds of thousands of cercariae are ultimately produced (Schell 1985). Thus
the snails serve as a kind of incubator for embryonic amplification of the trematodes.

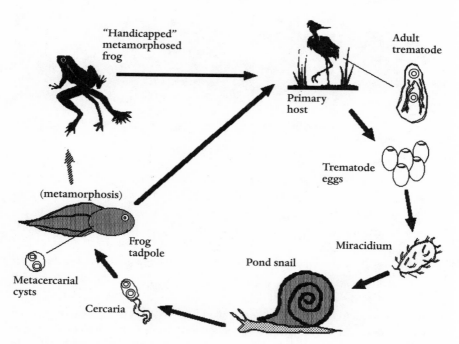

Figure 13.3. Life cycle of *Ribeiroia*. The adult trematode lives in the digestive system of birds,
which thus serve as the primary host. The trematode eggs are released into water where
they hatch to release infectious miracidia. The miracidia then infect aquatic snails. Once in-
side a snail, each miracidium develops into a sporocyst which then commenses "embryonic
amplification" in which each sporocyst produce numerous rediae, each of which in turn produces numerous infectious cercariae. The fully developed cercariae exit the snail and infect
amphibian tadpoles, producing metacercarial cysts in and around the hind limb buds per-
turbing their development and eventually producing disabled metamorphic frogs. Consumption of infected tadpoles or frogs by the primary host completes the trematode's life cycle.
(From Sessions et al. 2001)

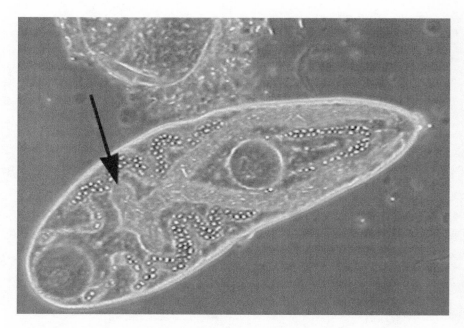

Figure 13.4. Phase contrast photomicrograph of an excysted *Ribeiroia* metacercarial cyst illustrating the esophageal diverticulae diagnostic of this genus (arrow). (From Sessions et al. 2001)

The cercariae next exit the snail in response to particular environmental stimuli such as light and/or temperature and swim vigorously around until they encounter a suitable second intermediate host, in this case an amphibian.

The cercariae form cysts, called metacercariae, on the surface of the tadpoles' skin that penetrate into the tissues over the next few hours (S. K. Sessions, unpublished data). The result is extensive inflammation, swelling, and tissue outgrowths at the sites of cercaria infestation (S. K. Sessions, unpublished data). If a cyst-infected tadpole is eaten by the primary host (a bird or mammal), the metacercariae excyst to form adult trematode worms, thus completing their life cycle. *Ribeiroia*-infected snails and abnormal amphibians have been found in New York as well as in Oregon and California, so this trematode may be very widespread (Sessions et al. 2001). The possibility that *Ribeiroia* is spread by migrating birds needs to be investigated.

Trematodes and Koch's Postulates

The role of trematodes as the cause of morphological abnormalities in amphibians may be much more difficult to disprove than one might assume and requires more than a simple determination of presence or absence of cysts in affected specimens.

Trematodes can attack amphibians at any stage of the amphibians' development, but only attack at early limb bud stages will induce substantial abnormalities, especially in anurans. Thus, the presence of cysts in otherwise normal frogs cannot be used to conclude that the cysts have no effect on limb development. On the other hand, my own research indicates that laboratory-raised *Rana* tadpoles with trematode-induced abnormalities and visually confirmed cysts at early stages can clear themselves of the cysts as they get older, apparently through immunological rejection (Sessions et al. 2001; S. K. Sessions, unpublished data). Therefore the absence of cysts from affected specimens must likewise be interpreted cautiously. In other words, the spatial and temporal relationships between the trematode cysts and the induced abnormalities make it difficult to apply Koch's postulates, at least in a strict sense. The trematode hypothesis is nevertheless testable by determining the presence or absence of infected snails at sites that produce abnormal frogs, and by determining whether the released cercariae can induce deformities in experimental animals that are the same as those observed in wild-caught amphibians.

It has recently been shown that *Ribeiroia* can cause limb abnormalities in laboratory-raised tadpoles in five amphibian species: western toads, Pacific treefrogs, northern leopard frogs, wood frogs, and long-toed salamanders (Johnson et al. 1999, 2001; Sessions et al. 2001; S. K. Sessions, unpublished). When infectious larval stages (cercariae) were used at concentrations determined from observed infection levels in field-caught specimens, the results revealed a dose-response relationship in which increased numbers of infecting cercariae induced more severe abnormalities (Johnson et al. 1999, 2001). The parasite induced all of the limb abnormalities described in Table 13.1, including duplicated limbs, missing limbs, and bony triangles, although the frequency and exact composition of the abnormalities resulting from infection varied among the amphibian species (Johnson et al. 2001).

Ribeiroia provides a satisfactory explanation for the particular "syndrome" of limb abnormalities seen in different species of amphibians. *Ribeiroia* cercariae attach to the surface of the skin and form metacercarial cysts that penetrate the epidermis into deeper tissues, triggering localized tissue growth (S. K. Sessions, unpublished data). The precise effects on limb development probably depend on the number as well as location of the cysts, their size relative to the limb bud, differences in skin characteristics such as the thickness of the epidermis and dermis, the presence of skin toxins and other glandular secretions, and the developmental stage of the tadpole. For example, cutaneous fusions were reported to be the predominant cyst-induced abnormalities in western toads, whereas polymely (supernumerary limbs) was reported to be the most common cyst-induced abnormality in Pacific treefrogs (Sessions and Ruth 1990; Johnson et al. 2001).

Parasite infection may provide an explanation for why forelimb abnormalities are rarely seen in anurans compared with the frequency of hind-limb abnormalities.

First, the cercariae actively target the hind limb region in frog tadpoles (Sessions et al. 1999). Also, in anurans, the forelimbs develop within the gill chamber, protected by three layers of skin, with only two limited points of entry for cercariae: mouth and spiracle. *Ribeiroia* cysts have been found in the mouth and at the base of abnormal forelimbs in several species of frogs, and at the base of the limbs and in the gular fold in salamanders (Sessions et al. 1999, 2001; S. K. Sessions, unpublished). Differences in the location and length of the spiracle may help explain differences in the frequency of front-limb abnormalities in different anuran species, although this possibility has not yet been investigated. Abnormalities are more equally distributed between the front limbs and the hind limbs in salamanders, reflecting the fact that in urodeles, forelimbs and hind limbs both develop exposed to the environment (Sessions and Ruth 1990; Johnson et al. 2001). However, even in salamanders, abnormalities more often involve the hind limbs than the forelimbs, perhaps reflecting the fact that the forelimbs complete most of their development within the egg capsule, whereas the hind limbs undergo their entire development exposed to the external environment (Sessions and Ruth 1990).

Given the available evidence, and especially the fact that most observed limb abnormalities can be experimentally induced, the parasite hypothesis appears to be the most likely explanation for abnormal amphibians with supernumerary limbs (polymelia), and it can also account for at least some cases of missing appendages (Johnson et al. 1999, 2001; Sessions et al. 1999). The presence of bony triangles among the *Ribeiroia*-induced abnormalities might be taken to suggest that the trematodes secrete a retinoid (Gardiner and Hoppe 1999). However, as pointed out previously, bony triangles can also be produced through mechanical perturbation of early limb buds (Hecker and Sessions 2001), so the mechanical effects of *Ribeiroia* cysts appear to be sufficient to explain most of the observed abnormalities.

Trematodes and Limb Pattern Formation

From a developmental perspective, extra limbs are easier to explain than missing limbs. A wide variety of factors could cause a missing limb, depending on whether it is a developmental defect or a traumatic injury (Ouellet 2000). On the other hand, there are only two alternative confirmed causes of high frequencies of duplicated limbs in amphibians: exogenous retinoids and mechanical perturbation. The mechanical effects of trematode cyst infestation have been shown to be sufficient to cause the outgrowth of supernumerary limbs in amphibians (Sessions and Ruth 1990), and this has been recently confirmed by additional work (Hecker and Sessions 2001). It has now been possible to observe the process of *Ribeiroia* cyst infection of tadpoles in the laboratory, including histological analysis of the effects of the cysts on developing amphibian limb buds (Stopper et al. 2002). The cercariae cause extensive damage when they encyst in or around the developing limb bud, triggering extensive localized cellular growth and clearly disrupting the normal limb pattern-forming mechanisms.

Many years of research have shown that pattern formation in developing amphibian limb buds depends on intimate interactions among cells in the embryonic limb field (Gilbert 2000). These early limb cells have information about their positions in the major axes of the limb field (positional values), and if their spatial organization is disturbed, they undergo a characteristic cellular growth response called intercalation (French et al. 1976; Bryant et al. 1981). This phenomenon is the basis of the well-known polar coordinate model of limb pattern formation (French et al. 1976; Bryant et al. 1981).

The polar coordinate model was developed not only to understand the results of grafting experiments but is also a powerful model for conceptualizing normal limb outgrowth even though it has not yet been fully integrated with information from developmental genetics. According to the polar coordinate model, if cells with different positional values are forced to interact, they will undergo intercalation, producing daughter cells (via mitosis) with intermediate positional values and thereby re-establishing pattern continuity at the cellular level. In other words, intercalation fills in gaps between cells with disparate positional information. The astonishing effects of this simple regulatory mechanism on amphibian limb morphology have been noticed for decades (Swett 1926; Harrison 1969). Intercalation is usually manifested at the morphological level by mirror-image duplications, including AMIDs, PMIDs, and MITs (Table 13.1).

Intercalation has been demonstrated in the laboratory with simple grafting experiments in both amphibians and amniotes that result in the outgrowth of symmetrical supernumerary limb structures and other limb abnormalities (Swett 1926; Bryant et al. 1987). For example, simply splitting a limb bud into anterior and posterior halves often leads to mirror-image duplications along the anterior–posterior axis (Swett 1926). Likewise, rotating a limb bud around its anterior–posterior axis can induce the outgrowth of two or more limbs from a single limb bud (Hecker and Sessions 2001). These results support the idea that cyst-induced abnormalities in amphibians result from mechanical disruption of early limb buds followed by intercalation (Sessions and Ruth 1990; Sessions et al. 1999, 2001; Hecker and Sessions 2001).

ECOLOGY AND EVOLUTION

The case for trematode cysts as the proximate cause of limb abnormalities in natural populations of amphibians is very strong. However, it is still important to explain the recent apparent increase in reports of morphological abnormalities in natural populations of amphibians. One possible explanation is that there are simply more people out there looking for abnormal amphibians. Another is that chemical pollution or UV-B radiation is causing immunodeficiency in one or more of the trematode's hosts. Assuming that the increased reports reflect a true increase in occurrence, the answer probably has something to do with the trematode's primary hosts (mostly birds), which spread the pathogen from pond to pond, and snails, since they serve as the all-important first intermediate host in which embryonic amplification of the parasite occurs. Changes in the pond snail population, for example from cultural eutrophication or sudden reduction in habitat, may be expected to have enormous consequences for trematodes as well as the other hosts involved in their life cycle. For example, since each miracidium is amplified in the snail to produce large numbers of free-swimming infectious cercariae, a relatively small increase in the snail population size or, more accurately, the number of infected snails, would result in an enormous increase in the number of cercariae produced. A periodic burst of cercaria production could in turn produce a major epidemic of morphological abnormalities in amphibians. There is not much evidence thus far connecting morphological abnormalities to the general problem of amphibian decline. However, for species or populations of amphibians that are already in decline, a major outbreak of cercariae could be dangerous, since it can badly maim and kill most of a cohort of metamorphosing individuals. The good news is that populations at risk for such an outbreak can be identified simply by examining snails for evidence of trematode larval stages, and the outbreak could probably be prevented by reducing the size of the snail population.

The interaction between amphibians and their trematode parasites is an ancient struggle reflecting millions of years of coevolution. The possibility that the induction of limb abnormalities constitutes a host modification strategy by *Ribeiroia* needs to be investigated (Sessions and Ruth 1990; Johnson et al. 1999, 2001). Trematodes that use amphibians as second intermediate hosts are at a selective advantage only if the infected amphibians are eaten by the primary host, in this case a bird. Targeting the developing limb buds of early tadpoles effectively produces disabled frogs whose primary antipredator defense mechanism, a functional pair of jumping hind limbs, has been destroyed. Thus it is to a trematode's selective advantage to produce cercariae at a time when the chances of producing handicapped frogs is maximal. This interval of time constitutes a critical window of early limb bud development when the bud is capable of undergoing a full intercalary regulatory response. As the hind limbs develop, they gradually lose this ability, undergoing regenerative decline (Muneoka et al. 1986) until, at metamorphosis, they can no longer regenerate a limb at all and they will not develop abnormalities in response to cyst infestation. Another feature of tadpole development underlines just how important this critical window is for the trematode: in the African clawed frog, the thymus gland gradually becomes functional and capable of producing T-lymphocytes as metamorphosis is approached (Nieuwkoop and Faber 1994). Since T-cells are essential for an effective immunological defense specifically against parasitic flatworms, attacking young tadpoles allows the trematode to avoid an initial immunological attack (Roitt et al. 1996).

It is easy to see how a coevolutionary "arms race" becomes established between trematodes and their amphibian hosts. Trematodes that are coadapted with developing tadpoles such that their cercariae are released during the critical window of limb bud and thymus development are at a selective advantage. But this creates a reciprocal selective advantage for frogs that breed either late or early in the season so that their tadpoles develop their limbs in the absence of cercariae, and so forth and so on. This sort of scenario is well-rooted in evolutionary theory as the "red queen hypothesis" (Van Valen 1973), of which host/parasite coevolution is a prime example (Ridley 1996). Evolutionary adaptations in frogs may include modifications of the mature skin to prevent cyst penetration (Ingles 1933) and development of the fore-limbs within the protective gill chamber, as well as diversification among different species of frogs in the timing of their breeding activity. Coevolutionary interactions among trematodes and their hosts could generate long-term cycles lasting many years, and may help explain why abnormal amphibians suddenly appear at particular sites and then disappear.

SUMMARY

Recent research is beginning to generate an understanding of what is causing at least some of the abnormalities in natural populations of amphibians. There is as yet little convincing data that chemical pollution or UV radiation is involved, but the stakes are high enough that continued research seems advisable. On the other hand, evidence is accumulating that missing limbs may be caused by predation or cannibalism, and extra limbs are most likely caused by trematodes. The case for trematodes (i.e., *Ribeiroia*) is particularly good and fulfills at least most of Koch's postulates: *Ribeiroia* cysts are regularly found in amphibians with morphological abnormalities, at least when they are searched for by researchers with experience in identifying them; the infectious cercariae can be isolated from snails and used to infect experimental animals, which then form similar abnormalities; the cysts can then be recovered from the experimental animals. However, Koch's postulates are simplistic when strictly applied to *Ribeiroia* because of the spatial and temporal relationships between the pathogen and the induced abnormalities. *Ribeiroia* has now been implicated in abnormalities in at least 12 species of amphibians in both western and eastern North America. The teratogenic effects of trematode cysts demonstrate how a single causal factor can generate a wide variety of morphological abnormalities in amphibians, depending on the species, the intensity of infection, and the developmental stage at which infection occurred. It is possible that the phenomenon of trematode-induced limb abnormalities in amphibians reflects long-standing coevolutionary dynamics between parasite and hosts. Further research is needed to understand the apparent recent increases in the frequency of trematode-induced abnormalities in amphibian populations.

POTENTIAL SOLUTIONS

It is important to understand whether the abnormalities in natural populations of amphibians are caused by a single factor or several factors, acting alone or in combination. At minimum, to be considered a likely candidate, a putative causal factor must be found at sites where abnormal amphibians have been found and shown to produce the same classes of abnormalities under controlled conditions. At the moment, the only putative causes that come close to fitting these prerequisites are trematode infection and injury due to predation. Of course, none of the results so far preclude the possibility that chemical pollution and/or UV-B radiation, or some other factor, may be involved, alone or in combination with other factors. The trematodes themselves are environmental indicators, since they may be even more sensitive to environmental toxins than amphibians (D. Sutherland, University of Wisconsin, personal communication). Much more research is needed, especially to generate multi-year data on the patterns of abnormalities to facilitate comparisons among sites and species. Development of some kind of diagnostic system, based on the documented teratogenic effects of different causal agents, could be used in the field to facilitate broad-based regional surveys. For parasite-induced abnormalities, future studies are needed to better understand the ecological relationships between these parasites and their hosts, the impact of human activities on these relationships, the implications of parasite-induced abnormalities for the larger issue of amphibian declines, and the precise developmental and cellular mechanisms by which these parasites induce the abnormalities. There is much more work to do.

ACKNOWLEDGMENTS
This chapter benefited from discussions with Geffrey Stopper, Department of Evolution and Ecology, Yale University, and Louise Hecker, Department of Biological Sciences, Binghamton University, as well as from the comments of two anonymous reviewers. Brandon Ballengée of the Institute of Electronic Arts, Alfred University, provided assistance with some of the figures. This work was supported by a grant from the Hartwick College Board of Trustees and from a Rockefeller Foundation grant to the Institute of Electronic Arts at Alfred University.

14

GLOBAL CHANGE
Challenges Facing Amphibians

ANDREW R. BLAUSTEIN, AUDREY C. HATCH, LISA K. BELDEN,
ERIN SCHEESSELE, AND JOSEPH M. KIESECKER

CENTRAL ISSUES

In this chapter we address several key questions concerning the effects of environmental change on amphibian populations. Are amphibian populations affected by global environmental change? What are the major environmental changes affecting amphibian populations? How are amphibian populations affected? What means do we have to remedy the causes of global environmental change? In addressing these questions, we summarize how amphibian populations may be presently affected by global environmental changes, identify some of the main agents contributing to environmental change, and briefly review some of the treaties and problems associated with mitigating the causes contributing to global environmental change.

PERSPECTIVE

In the 1970s, environmental biologists and atmospheric scientists predicted that two significant human-induced environmental changes—global warming and ozone depletion—could potentially affect the biology of a wide array of plants, animals, and microorganisms. Increased emissions of "greenhouse" gases resulting from burning fossil fuels, increased land use, and the burning and destruction of forests were projected to cause a significant rise in global temperatures in the coming decades (discussion in Reaser and Blaustein, in press). Moreover, it was shown that chlorofluorocarbons (CFCs) and other commonly used industrial gases were depleting the earth's protective ozone layer, increasing the amount of cell damaging ultraviolet (UV)-B (280–315 nm) radiation that reaches ground level (Van der Leun et al. 1998). Scientists projected that species might respond to these global changes by altering their behavior, by shifting ranges, and perhaps by experiencing increased mortality and significant sublethal effects. A number of scientists suggested that global warming and ozone depletion would affect entire ecological communities (e.g., Peters and Lovejoy 1992; Cockell and Blaustein 2001; Reaser and Blaustein, in press).

An increasing body of evidence provides a picture of a warming world accompanying other significant climate changes (IPCC 2001). The average global surface temperature has risen by about 0.6°C since 1861 (IPCC 2001). In addition, the 1990s were the warmest decade since 1861 and data for the Northern Hemisphere indicate that the increase in temperature in the twentieth century is probably the largest of any century during the past 1,000 years (IPCC 2001). The global average sea level has risen (about 1 to 2 mm/year in the twentieth century; IPCC 2001) and ocean heat content has increased during the twentieth century (IPCC 2001). Changes have also occurred in other aspects of climate. For example, precipitation patterns have changed over most middle and high latitudes of Northern Hemisphere continents and in the tropics (IPCC 2001). During the twentieth century, cloud cover has changed over middle and high latitudes. A number of extreme events in weather and climate are predicted for the twenty-first century. These include more hot days, higher minimum temperatures, fewer cold days, more intense precipitation events, and increased summer continental drying associated with drought (IPCC 2001).

Some of the predictions concerning global climate changes have been supported by recent studies. For example, global climate changes in temperature and precipitation seem to be influencing the distribution and abundance of butterflies, amphibians, reptiles, and a number of other taxa (e.g., Parmesan 1996; Pounds et al. 1999). Warming trends may have led to the extinction of some populations (Parmesan 1996; Parmesan et al. 1999; Pounds et al. 1999) and may be influencing the breeding patterns of others (Beebee 1995; Forchhammer et al. 1998; Crick and Sparks 1999; Gibbs and Breisch 2001; Post et al. 2001).

Just as climate change may have wide and varied effects on numerous organisms, so might increasing UV-B radiation. At the terrestrial surface, UV-B radiation is extremely important biologically. Critical biomolecules absorb light of higher wavelength (UV-A; 315–400 nm) less efficiently, and stratospheric ozone absorbs most light of lower wavelength (UV-C; 200–280 nm; Cockell and Blaustein 2001). UV-B radiation can cause mutations and cell death (Tevini 1993; Cockell and Blaustein 2001). At the individual level, UV-B radiation can slow growth rates, cause immune dysfunction, and induce sublethal damage (Tevini 1993).

Over evolutionary time, UV radiation has been a ubiquitous stressor on living organisms (Cockell 2001). Natural events such as impact from asteroids and comets, volcanic activity, cosmic events such as supernova explosions, and solar flares can cause large-scale ozone depletion with accompanying increases in UV radiation (Cockell 2001). However, these natural events are transitory and may have significant effects on stratospheric ozone for only a few years.

This is markedly different from human-induced production of CFCs and other chemicals that are continuously depleting stratospheric ozone, inducing long-term increases in UV-B radiation at the surface. Decreases in stratospheric ozone, climate warming, and lake acidification leading to decreases in dissolved organic carbon concentrations (e.g., Schindler et al. 1996) all result in increasing levels of UV-B radiation. Indeed, information from numerous sources indicates that levels of UV-B radiation have risen significantly in modern time (especially since 1979) both in the tropics and in temperate regions (Kerr and McElroy 1993; Herman et al. 1996; Middleton et al. 2001).

UV-B radiation adversely affects a wide variety of organisms (e.g., Tevini 1993; Cockell and Blaustein 2001). For example, recent studies have demonstrated that UV-B radiation affects photosynthesis in plankton, may contribute to coral bleaching, and is lethal to a number of species of invertebrates, fishes, and amphibians (Van der Leun et al. 1998; Cockell and Blaustein 2001). Moreover, UV-B radiation interacts with other stressors to affect a wide array of organisms and entire ecological communities (Tevini 1993; Van der Leun et al. 1998; Cockell and Blaustein 2001).

Living organisms have had less than 100 years to cope with a gradual human-induced rise in UV radiation. Moreover, combined effects of UV-B radiation with pollutants, pesticides, and other agents that have been on earth for a relatively short period of time may be especially damaging to organisms that have not had time to develop mechanisms to survive their effects. Indeed, environmental change and contamination appear to be contributing to the current unprecedented loss in biodiversity (Eldridge 1998).

As part of this overall "biodiversity crisis," amphibian populations have been declining throughout the world (e.g., Alford and Richards 1999; Houlahan et al. 2000). No single cause for amphibian population declines has been identified. However, the diversity of locations where amphibian populations have declined has prompted consideration of global environmental changes. Changes in global temperature, precipitation, and levels of UV radiation may contribute to amphibian population declines. Moreover, contamination from airborne pollutants and other chemicals may act alone or in conjunction with global environmental changes to adversely affect amphibian populations.

SOME AMPHIBIAN POPULATIONS APPEAR TO BE AFFECTED BY CLIMATE CHANGE

Remote Sensing

Several approaches have been used to examine the potential effects of climate change on amphibian populations. One strategy is the use of remote sensing information that incorporates a wide array of tools and databases to examine the relationship between climate and amphibian population declines. Another strategy is to examine amphibian populations directly by observation or experimentation or both.

Alexander and Eischeid (2001) examined the relationship between amphibian declines and climate variations in Colorado, Puerto Rico, Costa Rica, Panama, and Queensland, Australia, using information gathered from airplanes, land stations, satellites, ships, and weather balloons with outputs from a weather forecast model. They showed that although declines occurred when temperature and precipitation anomalies occurred, these anomalies were not beyond the range of normal variability. They concluded that unusual climate measured as regional estimates of temperature and precipitation is unlikely to be a direct cause for amphibian population declines in the regions they examined.

Stallard (2001) measured time series datasets for Puerto Rico that extended into the 1980s. The data included forest cover; annual mean, minimum, and maximum daily temperatures; annual rainfall; rain and stream chemistry; and atmospheric dust transport. He also used satellite imagery and air chemistry samples from a single aircraft flight across the Caribbean. Like the datasets of Alexander and Eischeid (2001), none of Stallard's datasets pointed to changes so extreme that they would directly cause amphibian population declines. Stallard suggested that more experimental research is needed to examine the problem of amphibian population decline.

Breeding Phenology

A more direct approach for assessing whether amphibians have been affected by climate change comes from recent studies of the breeding phenology of amphibians (Table 14.1). Beebee (1995), by plotting the start of breeding activities for six amphibian species in southern England over 16 years, suggested that amphibians in temperate countries may be responding to climate change by breeding earlier. Furthermore, he found that the breeding dates of two species of April–June-breeding anurans were negatively correlated with average minimum temperatures in March and April and maximum temperatures in March. In one early-breeding anuran species, whose average breeding date did not shift from 1978 to 1994, the spawning date was negatively correlated with overall winter maximum temperatures. An analysis of the most abundant newt species showed a strong negative correlation between pond arrival time and average maximum temperature in the month before arrival.

Gibbs and Breisch (2001) showed that over the last century, daily temperatures increased near Ithaca, New York, and several species of anurans have shifted their breeding patterns accordingly (Table 14.1). Thus, in a comparison of calling dates from 1990 to 1999 with calling dates from 1900 to 1912, four species of anurans vocalized 10 to 13 days earlier, two species were unchanged, and no species called later.

Not all amphibians appear to be responding to climate change in the same fashion as those described above (Table 14.1). Reading's (1998) study of the common toad

Table 14.1

Trends in breeding phenologies of temperate amphibians

Species (common name)	Breeding Earlier?	Reference
England		
Bufo bufo (common toad)	No	Reading 1998
B. calamita (natterjack toad)	Yes	Beebee 1995
Rana esculenta (edible frog)	Yes	Beebee 1995
R. temporaria (common frog)	No	Beebee 1995
Triturus helveticus (palmate newt)	Yes	Beebee 1995
T. vulgaris (smooth newt)	Yes	Beebee 1995
T. cristatus (great-crested newt)	Yes	Beebee 1995
North America		
Bufo americanus (American toad)	No	Gibbs and Breisch 2001
B. boreas (western toad)	No	Blaustein et al. 2001
B. fowleri (Fowler's toad)	No	Blaustein et al. 2001
Hyla versicolor (gray treefrog)	Yes	Gibbs and Breisch 2001
Pseudacris crucifer (spring peeper)	No	Blaustein et al. 2001
P. crucifer (spring peeper)	Yes	Gibbs and Breisch 2001
Rana cascadae (Cascades frog)	No	Blaustein et al. 2001
R. catesbeiana (American bullfrog)	Yes	Gibbs and Breisch 2001
R. clamitans (green frog)	No	Gibbs and Breisch 2001
R. sylvatica (wood frog)	Yes	Gibbs and Breisch 2001

(*Bufo bufo*) in England from 1980 to 1998 showed that the main arrival at breeding sites was highly correlated with the mean daily temperatures over the 40 days immediately preceding the main arrival. However, a significant trend toward earlier breeding in recent years compared with previous years was not found.

At one site in Oregon, there was a nonsignificant trend for western toads (*Bufo boreas*) to breed increasingly early and this was associated with increasing temperature (Blaustein et al. 2001b). However, at four other sites, neither western toads nor Cascades frogs (*Rana cascadae*) showed statistically significant positive trends toward earlier breeding. At three of four of these sites, breeding time was associated with warmer temperatures. The southern spring peeper (*Pseudacris crucifer*) in Michigan did not show a statistically significant trend to breeding earlier, but did show a significant positive relationship between breeding time and temperature. Fowler's toads (*Bufo fowleri*) in eastern Canada did not show a trend for breeding earlier nor was there a positive relationship between breeding time and temperature.

The broad pattern emerging from available breeding studies is that some temperate zone amphibian populations show a trend toward breeding earlier, but others do not. The reasons for this variation are not known.

Complex Interrelationships

A recent study in the tropics by Pounds et al. (1999) illustrates the complex interrelationships among global environmental changes and amphibian population declines. They found that changes in water availability associated with changes in large-scale climate processes, such as the El Niño/Southern Oscillation (ENSO), may significantly affect amphibian, reptile, and bird populations in the Monteverde cloud forest of Costa Rica. These authors showed that dry periods associated with global warming are correlated with amphibian and reptile losses and changes in the bird community. In Costa Rica, and potentially in other high-altitude tropical sites, global warming appears to have resulted in a decrease in the amount of mist precipitation received in the forest due to increased altitude of the cloud bank.

Changes in ambient temperature may influence amphibian behaviors, including those related to reproduction. Potentially, changes in ambient temperature on a global scale could disrupt the timing of breeding, periods of hibernation, and the ability to find food (Donnelly and Crump 1998; Blaustein et al. 2001b). One potential consequence of global warming is the increased spread of infectious disease (Cunningham et al. 1996; Epstein 1997). This may occur, for example, if rising temperatures affect the distribution of the vectors of a pathogen, making additional hosts susceptible, or if an environmental agent renders a host's immune system more susceptible. Changes in precipitation, acidification, pollutants, and increased UV-B radiation are some of the stressors that may affect the immune systems of amphibians. Immune-system damage from multiple stressors could make amphibians more susceptible to pathogens whose ranges may change due to global warming (Blaustein et al. 1994b; Kiesecker and Blaustein 1995; Blaustein and Kiesecker 1997). Thus, rising temperatures and changes in precipitation could be stressful and might be associated with disease outbreaks in amphibian populations (Pounds et al. 1999; Kiesecker et al. 2001a).

AMBIENT UV-B RADIATION IS HARMFUL TO AMPHIBIANS

Spectral measurements made at Toronto, Canada, from 1989 to 1993 indicate a 35% increase in UV-B radiation per year in winter and a 7% increase in summer (Kerr and McElroy 1993). These increases were caused by a downward trend in the thickness of the ozone layer that was measured at Toronto during the same period. Moreover, it was suggested that increased UV-B levels in late spring may have a disproportionately larger effect on some species if the increase occurs at critical phases of their development (Kerr and McElroy 1993). This supports the results of studies showing the adverse effects of UV-B radiation in spring-conducted field experiments on developing amphibian embryos (discussed below).

Middleton et al. (2001) assessed trends in solar UV-B radiation above more than 20 sites in Central and South America using data derived from the Total Ozone Mapping Spectrometer satellite. These authors showed that the annually averaged UV-B dose, as well as the maximum values, has been increasing in both regions since 1979. The UV index was consistently higher for Central America, where many amphibian declines have been documented (Lips 1998; Pounds et al. 1999). Middleton et al. (2001) conclude that further investigation of the role of UV-B radiation in amphibian declines is warranted.

As discussed in detail by Middleton et al. (2001), data gathered from remote sensing has many limitations. For example, few long-term datasets on amphibian populations are available to provide a baseline for remote sensing data (Blaustein et al. 1994b). Moreover, the resolution of the satellite-generated data is not accurate enough to approximate ground-level interpretations (Middleton et al. 2001). However, their study is consistent with mounting experimental evidence that UV-B radiation is harmful to amphibians and that increasing UV-B levels may be contributing to amphibian population declines (Blaustein et al. 1998, 2001a).

Investigators at various sites around the world have shown that ambient UV-B radiation decreases the hatching success of some amphibian species at natural oviposition sites in the field (reviewed in Blaustein et al. 1998, 2001a). These investigators typically placed fertilized eggs in enclosures with filters that removed UV-B radiation or allowed UV-B to penetrate (control filters) (Blaustein et al. 1998). In some studies, enclosures with no filters were used as an additional control. Researchers compared the hatching success of eggs under each regime.

These studies have demonstrated that the embryos of some species are more resistant to UV-B radiation than others (reviewed in Blaustein et al. 1998). For example, in Oregon, the hatching success of Cascades frogs, western toads, long-toed (*Ambystoma macrodactylum*) and northwestern (*A. gracile*) salamanders was lower when eggs were exposed to ambient UV-B radiation than when they were shielded (Blaustein et al. 1998). However, the hatching success of Oregon (*Rana pretiosa*) and Columbia (*R. luteiventris*) spotted frogs, red-legged frogs (*R. aurora*), and Pacific treefrogs (*Pseudacris regilla*) was not significantly different between the UV-shielded and UV-exposed treatments (Blaustein et al. 1998). In California, the hatching success of Pacific treefrogs was not affected by ambient levels of UV-B radiation, but hatching success was lower in California treefrogs (*Pseudacris cadaverina*) and California newts (*Taricha torosa*) exposed to UV-B (Anzalone et al. 1998). The hatching success of common toads in Spain was lower in exposed eggs than in shielded eggs, but there was no effect on the hatching success of the natterjack toad (*B. calamita*; Lizana and Pedraza 1998).

Just as there are different responses in how various amphibian species tolerate chemical pollutants, acidification, and diseases, there are differences in how species cope with UV-B radiation. For some species, in field experiments, hatching success is lower when eggs are exposed to UV-B radiation than with shielded controls. In other species, hatching success is not affected by UV-B exposure (e.g., Starnes et al. 2000; Häkkinen et al. 2001). This is not a contradiction; rather, these studies illustrate clear interspecific differences in tolerance to UV-B radiation at early life stages. In fact, within the same study, conducted at the same time and on the same site, it has been shown that the eggs of some species were sensitive to UV-B, whereas the eggs of other species were resistant (e.g., Blaustein et al. 1994a; Anzalone et al. 1998; Lizana and Pedraza 1998).

Importantly, although hatching rates of some species may appear unaffected by ambient UV-B radiation in field experiments, an increasing number of studies illustrate a variety of sublethal effects due to UV exposure (Table 14.2). For example, when exposed to UV-B radiation, amphibians may change their behavior (Nagl and Hofer 1997; Blaustein et al. 2000; Kats et al. 2000), growth and development may be slowed (e.g., Belden et al. 2000; Pahkala et al. 2000, 2001; Smith et al. 2000), or a number of developmental and physiological malformations may form (e.g., Worrest and Kimeldorf 1976; Hays et al. 1996; Blaustein et al. 1997a; Fite et al. 1998; Table 14.2). Sublethal effects may become evident even in species whose embryos appear to be resistant in field experiments. Moreover, numerous field and laboratory experiments have shown that UV-B radiation interacts synergistically with a variety of chemicals, low pH levels, and certain pathogens (Kiesecker and Blaustein 1995; Long et al. 1995; Blaustein et al. 2001a).

An experimental field study in Oregon by Kiesecker et al. (2001a) illustrates the complex interrelationships among environmental change, UV radiation, and am-

Table 14.2

Examples of sublethal effects of ultraviolet (UV)-B exposure on amphibians

Effect	Species (Life Stage)[a]	Reference
Reduced hatchling size	*Rana temporaria* (E)	Pahkala et al. 2000
Reduced larval growth	*Ambystoma macrodactylum* (L); *Xenopus laevis* (L)	Bruggeman et al. 1998; Belden et al. 2000
Reduced larval growth after embryonic UV-B exposure	*Rana blairi* (L); *R. temporaria* (L)	Smith et al. 2000; Pahkala et al. 2001
Eye damage	*Rana cascadae* (A)	Fite et al. 1998
Altered activity or behavior	*Bufo boreas* (J); *Hyla versicolor* (L); *Rana cascadae* (L); *Taricha granulosa* (A); *Triturus alpestris* (L)	Nagl and Hofer 1997; Zaga et al. 1998; Blaustein et al. 2000; Kats et al. 2000
Skin darkening	*Hyla arborea* (L); *H. versicolor* (E, L); *Xenopus laevis* (E, L)	Zaga et al. 1998; Langhelle et al. 1999
Developmental abnormalities	*Ambystoma macrodactylum* (E); *Bufo boreas* (L); *Hyla regilla* (L, J); *Rana cascadae* (L, J)	Worrest and Kimeldorf 1976; Hays et al. 1996; Blaustein et al. 1997c

[a] Life stage: E = embryo; L = larva; J = juvenile; A = adult.

phibian population declines, paralleling the tropical study by Pounds et al. (1999). Kiesecker et al. (2001a) linked El Niño/Southern Oscillation events with decreased winter precipitation in the Oregon Cascade Range. They suggested that less winter snow pack resulted in lower water levels when western toads breed in early spring. Toad embryos developing in shallower water are exposed to higher levels of UV-B, which results in increased mortality from the pathogenic oomycete, *Saprolegnia ferax*. Disease may also have been the proximate cause for losses in Costa Rica, although that has not been established (Pounds et al. 1999).

Merilä et al. (2000) present an interesting scenario combining climate change, UV radiation, and amphibian breeding. These authors suggest that if amphibians are breeding earlier in northern ecosystems, as suggested by Beebee (1995) and Gibbs and Breisch (2001), then their annual life cycle will not only start earlier relative to the calendar date but also with regard to maximum UV-B exposure. UV-B exposure would be less than if amphibians bred later in the spring. Thus, they suggest that global warming—which may induce amphibians to breed earlier—may counteract the effects of increasing UV-B levels generated by a thinning ozone layer.

Some species of amphibians may be more resistant to UV-B radiation than others because they evolved efficient mechanisms to counteract its harmful effects. Thus, there are behavioral, physiological, anatomical, and molecular mechanisms to cope with UV-B radiation (discussed in Blaustein et al. 2001a). For example, embryos of some amphibian species may be more resistant to UV-B radiation because they can repair UV-induced DNA damage more efficiently than can other species (Blaustein et al. 1994a, 2001a; Van de Mortel et al. 1998). One important repair process, enzymatic photoreactivation, uses one enzyme, CPD-photolyase to remove the most frequent UV-induced lesion in DNA, cyclobutane pyrimidine dimers (CPDs; Blaustein et al. 2001a). CPD-photolyase appears to be the first level of defense against CPDs for many organisms exposed to sunlight (Blaustein et al. 2001a). Because photoreactivation is probably the most important repair mechanism in amphibians, a parsimonious explanation is that those species with the highest photolyase activities are the most resistant to UV damage. Indeed, the amount of CPD-photolyase in eggs is positively correlated with survival of embryos in field experiments (Blaustein et al. 2001a). For example, eggs of the most resistant species in field experiments (e.g., Pacific treefrogs; red-legged frogs; Oregon and Columbia spotted frogs; Peron's treefrog, *Litoria peronii;* Keferstein's treefrog, *L. dentata*) have higher CPD-photolyase activity than eggs of more susceptible species (e.g., California treefrog, Cascades frog, western toad, and long-toed and northwestern salamanders) (Blaustein et al. 1998, 2001a; Van de Mortel et al. 1998; Table 14.3).

Even if eggs are laid in the open at high altitudes (where under certain conditions UV levels may be high) and have long developmental periods in which they are subjected to prolonged UV-B exposure, they may not be adversely affected by UV-B radiation if they have efficient DNA repair mechanisms. Conversely, species with low photolyase levels may be quite sensitive to UV-B radiation even if they live at very low

Table 14.3

Hatching success and photolyase activity levels of North American amphibian species whose eggs were exposed to ambient levels of ultraviolet (UV)-B radiation

Species	Photolase Activity[a]	Hatching Success	Reference
Ambystoma gracile	1.0	Reduced	Blaustein et al. 1994a, 1995
A. macrodactylum	0.8	Reduced	Blaustein et al. 1994a, 1997a
Bufo boreas	1.3	Reduced	Blaustein et al. 1994a
Hyla cadaverina	3.5	Reduced	Anzalone et al. 1998; Blaustein et al. 2001
H. regilla	7.5	No effect	Blaustein et al. 1994a; Ovaska et al. 1997; Anzalone et al. 1998
Rana aurora	6.1	No effect	Blaustein et al. 1996; Ovaska et al. 1997
R. cascadae	2.4	Reduced	Blaustein et al. 1994a
R. luteiventris	6.8	No effect	Blaustein et al. 1999
R. pretiosa	6.6	No effect	Blaustein et al. 1999

Note: Methods used to calculate photolyase activity are given in Blaustein et al. 1994c.

[a]Specific activity of photolyase in 10^{11} cyclobutane pyrimidine dimers per hour per gram.

altitudes (Blaustein et al. 1998). Moreover, within a species, individuals from one population may differ from members of another population in their sensitivity to UV-B radiation. This may be due to differences in their ability to repair DNA damage or to differences in individual egg-laying behavior. Thus, interspecific differences in DNA repair is a parsimonious explanation for the resistance of some species to UV-B radiation and the susceptibility of others.

AIRBORNE CONTAMINANTS AFFECT AMPHIBIANS

In addition to global environmental changes, numerous agents, including airborne pollutants, may be toxic to amphibians by themselves or may interact with warming trends and UV radiation in a synergistic fashion. Thus, as worldwide agricultural demands rise, pesticide use will increase significantly (Tilman et al. 2001). Pesticides have the potential for atmospheric transport (Davidson et al. 2001) and deposition where they may be available for uptake by biota, especially by amphibians through their permeable skin, may alter nutrient dynamics, or increase water clarity, allowing greater penetration of UV radiation (Wright and Schindler 1995). Contaminants transported atmospherically are potentially harmful to amphibians (discussed in more detail in Chapter 12, this volume) and they may interact with UV-B radiation, other contaminants, and environmental changes (Blaustein et al. 1997b, 2001a). For example, acid deposition from the atmosphere to aquatic systems has been linked to both lethal and sublethal effects on developing amphibians, particularly those that breed in temporary ponds (e.g., Dunson and Wyman 1992; Kiesecker 1996). How-ever, the effects of other atmospheric contaminants on amphibians have not been well documented.

Pounds and Crump (1994) suggested that atmospheric scavenging of contami-nants by clouds might concentrate the contaminants and release them in remote areas such as Monteverde, Costa Rica, where many populations of amphibians have declined. This effect may be particularly important under unusually hot, dry condi-tions (Pounds and Crump 1994; Pounds et al. 1999). In California, atmospheric dep-osition of organophosphate pesticides from the highly agricultural Central Valley may be contributing to declines in frog populations (Aston and Seiber 1997; Sparling et al. 2001). Pesticides may adhere to foliage where they may threaten native species (Aston and Seiber 1997). Activity of the enzyme cholinesterase in Pacific treefrogs was impaired in areas where populations of ranid frogs were declining (Sparling et al. 2001). Cholinesterase impairment might be linked to the presence of organo-phosphate pesticides (Sparling et al. 2001). Using geographic information system analysis, Davidson et al. (2001) concluded that pesticides carried upwind from the Central Valley of California may be contributing to declines in red-legged frogs in California.

POTENTIAL SOLUTIONS

Obviously, global warming, ozone depletion, and airborne contaminants cross in-ternational boundaries, generating significant political problems in implementing and enforcing laws for mitigation (Starke 2001). One of the most successful treaties dealing with an international environmental problem is the Montreal Protocol, which resulted from increasing concern over the effects of ozone depletion. The pro-tocol was developed to reduce and eventually eliminate certain anthropogenic ozone-destroying substances and was signed by a number of nations on 16 September 1987 in Montreal, Quebec. The 175-member protocol, which consisted of a plan that would dramatically cut CFC production, was recognized as the first worldwide effort to solve a massive environmental problem. The protocol has been strengthened sev-eral times since 1987. It calls for phasing out about 95 ozone-depleting chemicals, in-cluding CFCs. Industrial countries were required to stop CFC production by 1996. Developing countries must stop production by 2010. Most but not all countries have met their deadlines for phasing out CFC production. By 1997, global CFC produc-tion was down 85% from 1986 levels (French and Mastny 2001). Despite this agree-ment, worsening environmental news about CFCs and ozone depletion in the 1990s led certain nations to adopt stricter measures to limit CFC production.

Several industrial companies have developed CFC substitutes. Although CFCs, and several other chemicals that contribute to ozone depletion have been phased out in the United States and several other countries, existing stockpiles of these chemicals can be used until the deadline. Unfortunately, CFCs are very stable and estimates suggest that those in use today will continue to deplete stratospheric ozone for 50 to 150 years. Atmospheric scientists believe that the Antarctic ozone hole will reappear each year until about 2050. However, because of the Montreal Protocol and other measurements to limit ozone-depleting substances, there is some optimism about ozone depletion being curtailed.

On the other hand, treaties to limit the production of gases that contribute to global warming and those directed toward limiting the use of toxic substances have been less successful. Thus, the Kyoto Protocol, which the United States does not presently support, requires that industrial countries reduce emissions of carbon dioxide by 6 to 8% by 2008 to 2012 to help stabilize atmospheric gases that contribute to global warming. The Rotterdam Convention on the Prior Informed Consent Procedure for Certain Hazardous Chemicals and Pesticides in International Trade (PIC Convention) is not yet in force (Starke 2001). On 23 May 2001, 127 nations adopted the Stockholm Convention on Persistent Organic Pollutants (POPS). The treaty initially targeted 12 chemicals for immediate banning. The convention is open for signing until 24 May 2002 (United Nations Environment Programme 2001).

SUMMARY

Amphibians, like many other organisms, have survived numerous environmental changes over millions of years and have persisted. Yet, in the last 100 years or so, amphibians have endured unprecedented changes in their environment, including a gradual warming of the planet, increased levels of UV radiation, and the presence of new chemicals (e.g., pollutants, pesticides) in their environment. Recent observational and experimental evidence strongly suggests that many amphibian populations are suffering significant damage due to these global environmental insults. Moreover, taken together, studies such as those by Pounds et al. (1999) and Kiesecker et al. (2001a) strongly suggest that complex global processes that affect local populations contribute to amphibian declines. Because it is difficult to regulate global environmental damage, it remains questionable as to how populations of amphibians as well as those of other organisms will cope with future global environmental insults.

ACKNOWLEDGMENTS

Financial support was provided by the National Science Foundation (DEB-942333 and IBN-9904012) and by the Katherine Bisbee Fund of the Oregon Community Foundation. We also thank David Aaronson, Max Bercouicz, Frankie Monaldi, and Jimmy O'Donnell for their help.

15

HUMAN EXPLOITATION OF AMPHIBIANS
Direct and Indirect Impacts

JOHN B. JENSEN AND CARLOS D. CAMP

CENTRAL ISSUES

Humans have exploited wildlife since the beginning of measured time, using them as sources of food, clothing, weapons, and tools as well as in the practice of religion and medicine. The effects of these uses have varied with the degree of exploitation and resilience of the utilized species, with the most severe effect being extinction (e.g., the passenger pigeon). When compared to other vertebrate classes (e.g., reptiles, Gibbons et al. 2000), amphibians are not generally thought of as being a heavily exploited group. Regardless of the relative degree of impact from human use, conservation of amphibians worldwide requires knowledge of and attention to issues relating to their exploitation.

Throughout the world, amphibians are collected or raised for a variety of uses, including, but not limited to, food, pets, medicine, research and education, fish bait, and leather. We present examples of the various human uses of amphibians, emphasizing those uses and amphibian groups of greatest concern. We also provide information on the direct and indirect impacts this exploitation has had on amphibians and their environment, as well as provide suggestions for overcoming some of the related obstacles both amphibians and conservationists face. Many of the reported conditions and trends, such as the status of local populations and species, leading exporters/importers, and amphibian species most involved in a particular trade, are subject to change due to changing environmental, economic, and societal dynamics.

DIRECT IMPACTS

Amphibians as Food

Although certain large salamanders (e.g., Andrias in China and Japan) have been used locally as food (Fitzgerald 1989), frog legs are the primary form of amphibians used for human ingestion. There remains a large market for frog legs in the European Union (EU), Canada, and the United States. Frog legs are so popular in France that they are regularly served in school cafeterias (Patel 1993). In the 1990s, the countries of the European Community (now the EU) imported more than 6,000 metric tons of frog legs each year, with more than 80% going to Belgium, Luxembourg, and France (Hardouin 1995). Secondary markets occur in Asia, with six million *Hoplobatrachus rugulosus* (aptly named the Chinese edible frog) shipped from Thailand to Hong Kong in one year (Lau et al. 1997).

Historically, frog legs were locally collected and served as seasonal delicacies. Virtually any medium- to large-sized ranid has served as a potential source, with the edible frog (*Rana esculenta*), pool frog (*R. lessonae*), marsh frog (*R. ridibunda*), and agile frog (*R. dalmatina*) being the most popular in Europe. The resulting decline and subsequent protection of native European frogs have combined with the modern technology of packaging frozen foods to shift the source of legs to Asia. By 1981, India was the major supplier of frogs (e.g., *Euphlyctis hexadactylus* and *Hoplobatrachus tigerinus*) to the West for culinary purposes, exporting more than 4,000 tons in that year alone (Abdulali 1985). Concern for the inhumane killing of frogs and for the loss of natural controls of pestiferous insects, however, led India to ban the export of frogs in 1987. These concerns contributed to the listing of *Euphlyctis hexadactylus* and *Hoplobatrachus tigerinus* by the Convention on International Trade in Endangered Species of Wild Fauna and Flora (CITES). (Supported by more than 150 signatory countries, CITES provides varying degrees of protection to certain species of wild plants and animals, depending on their biological status and the impact of their international trade.) Similar concerns have been expressed for Indonesia, which has replaced India as the primary exporter of frog legs. In 1990, the European Community imported nearly 5,000 tons of frog legs from Indonesia, primarily *Limnonectes blythii, L. cancrivorus, L. limnocharis,* and *L. macrodon.* At 20 to 50 individual frogs per kilogram, that translates into more than 100 million frogs per year (Patel 1993; Veith et al. 2000).

Before World War II, there was an active frogging industry in many regions of the United States, including Florida (American bullfrog, *Rana catesbeiana,* and pig frog, *R. grylio;* Enge 1993), Iowa (northern leopard frog, *R. pipiens;* Lannoo et al. 1994), and California (red-legged frog, *R. aurora;* Jennings and Hayes 1985). Culinary exploitation led to the decline of local populations, including the species-wide decline of the red-legged frog in California, eventually rendering commercial frogging economically infeasible. Although sport frogging still occurs, American restaurants, like their European counterparts, now procure their frog legs largely from Asia.

Most frog legs come from wild-caught frogs. In countries where collection and trade are banned, poaching continues to be a problem. Estimates place the annual illegal export from India in the tens of millions of frogs (Oza 1990). Unsustainable collection has had severe impacts on local populations of frogs. For example, large frogs have been extirpated from wetlands near villages in many parts of Java and Sumatra, where local farmers supplement their income by selling frogs to exporters (Veith et al. 2000).

Amphibians as Pets

Amphibians have long been popular as pets. Many species are easy to maintain because they require very little space and food requirements are easy to satisfy. Many children growing up outside of urbanized areas have kept frogs, toads, and/or salamanders as pets, typically after catching them in nearby wetlands or forests. However, amphibians are not just for the younger generations anymore, and most are now purchased rather than caught by the pet owner.

Hobbyists are becoming increasingly interested in unique and, especially, brightly colored amphibians, often paying high prices for some species. This increased demand has created a significant market for amphibians in the pet trade, negatively affecting natural populations in some instances. For example, aided by changing economics and relaxation of border controls, trade in amphibians has become one of the most profitable businesses in the former U.S.S.R., placing Russia among the top world exporters of herptiles for terraria (Kuzmin 1996). Overcollection to support this trade has been implicated in the decline of several rare salamanders, including the Semirechensk salamander (*Ranodon sibiricus*), spotted salamander (*Salamandra salamandra*), and the banded newt (*Triturus vittatus*, Kuzmin 1996). Protected and rare amphibian species are not uncommon in the trade elsewhere. The Chinese giant salamander (*Andrias davidianus*), a protected species in China and listed on CITES Appendix I (species on Appendix 1 are threatened with extinction and cannot be legally traded internationally for commercial purposes), is regularly found in food and pet markets in southeastern Asia (Lau et al. 1997).

The poison-dart frogs (*Dendrobates* and *Phyllobates*) of Central and South America and Malagasy poison frogs (*Mantella*) of Madagascar are among the most sought-after pet amphibians worldwide. Most are brightly colored with interesting patterns, display elaborate courtships, and oviposit terrestrially (Zimmermann and Zimmermann 1994). *Dendrobates azureus*, perhaps the most desired dendrobatid in the pet trade, often sells for more than US $100 per individual. Between 1987 and 1993, nearly 16,000 dendrobatid frogs were reported in international trade, more than 80% of which were wild-caught. Most dendrobatid species are considered common within their native habitats. One museum biologist collected 7,600 *Dendrobates histrionicus* from a single population over a 4-year period without any obvious effects (Bringsøe 1992). Regardless, the habitats in which many of these species occur are rapidly being destroyed (Colwell 1994), and the added stress of collection may become a contributing threat to the future viability of their respective populations.

All species of *Dendrobates* and *Phyllobates* were listed on CITES Appendix II (species on Appendix II are those that may become threatened if their trade is not controlled; commercial trade of these species requires an export or re-export permit from the country of origin or re-export, respectively) in 1987, which subsequently increased the trade in then-unregulated *Mantella* spp., especially the Malagasy golden frog, *Mantella aurantiaca*. With a very restricted natural range (~3,000 km²) that is threatened by rapidly increasing habitat destruction, the exploitation of this species for the pet trade may be a very significant threat (Zimmermann and Zimmermann 1994; Raxworthy and Nussbaum 2000). All *Mantella* spp. have since been added to CITES Appendix II, yet trade in wild-caught Malagasy golden frogs is increasing (UNEP World Conservation Monitoring Center 1998), with the United States responsible for 75% (>12,500 animals) of the imports. Other *Mantella* species, especially *Mantella cowani* and *Mantella viridis,* are also highly vulnerable to overcollection, with collectors reporting drastic reductions in the average daily harvest from previous years. Most *Mantella* spp. and dendrobatids are imported by Germany and the Netherlands; however, Japan and the United States are becoming increasingly involved in this particular trade (Gorzula 1996; CITES 2000).

Florida, long known as a center in the international pet trade, is one of few states in the United States that has monitored the impact of commerce on its native herpetofauna. From 1990 to 1992, 1,050 salamanders and 41,500 anurans were reported as being collected in Florida and sold in the pet trade. Some, such as southern leopard frogs (*Rana sphenocephala*) and southern toads (*Bufo terrestris*), were purchased as food for captive snakes. Destinations for these amphibians included most of the states and territories of the United States, as well as 16 other countries. States with high human-population densities, such as New York, California, and New Jersey, led the demand for Florida amphibians, and Germany was the largest foreign customer (Enge 1993). This trade is thought to be of minor importance, ranking ninth of 10 identified principal threats to South Florida herpetofauna (Wilson and Porras 1983). It may be a more significant threat in other areas, such as Louisiana, which has reported an annual harvest of at least 3 to 5 million herptiles, including 54,000 hylid treefrogs (Reptile and Amphibian Task Force 1992).

Amphibians in Education and Research

Amphibians, particularly frogs, have a historical connection with classroom education in Western countries. Many people have had their first, and sometimes only, exposure to amphibians through dissecting frogs in high school biology. Curricula in introductory biology, particularly at the secondary level, have traditionally included the study of the organs of the human body, a study often mandated by state-generated standards (e.g., Quality Core Curriculum in Georgia, U.S.A.). Relevant laboratory exercises have typically included animal dissection. The low cost and ready availability of grass frogs (*Rana pipiens* complex) and bullfrogs have made frog dissection a staple of many high school and introductory college curricula. A survey of Georgia high schools (Table 15.1) indicates that most use grass frogs for dissection.

The mudpuppy (*Necturus maculosus*) has been considered to represent a "primitive tetrapod," and as such has been a subject for dissection in college laboratories focusing on vertebrate anatomy and evolution. The past importance of such courses to curricula organized around organismal themes (e.g., zoology) led to the dissection of large numbers of mudpuppies. In addition, amphibians (*Rana* or *Necturus*) have traditionally been used for classroom investigations of physiological phenomena, including neural, muscular, and renal function. Ranid and ambystomatid eggs have been common subjects of embryological studies.

Demand for amphibians for dissection and experimentation has been met by companies specializing in scientific products. All of the companies in a survey of 14 catalogs (Table 15.2) sell grass and/or bullfrogs for dissection, and most offer mudpuppies.

Table 15.1

Amphibians most commonly used for educational purposes in surveyed institutions in Georgia, U.S.A., in 2001

Species	Secondary Schools[a]			Colleges and Universities[b]		
	N	%	n/year	N	%	n/year
Rana pipiens complex	7	64	53	7	44	20
Rana catesbeiana	0	—	—	3	19	1
Hyla cinerea	0	—	—	1	6	<1
Rana egg masses	0	—	—	1	6	2
Necturus maculosus	1	9	1	8	50	3

Notes: Numbers are rounded to the nearest integer. N = number of schools using a species; % = percentage of sampled schools using a species; n/year = mean number of specimens used per year by all schools answering the respective surveys.

[a]Public school systems participating in the survey: Dodge County, Douglas County, Franklin County, Gwinnett County, Jackson County, Winder-Barrow.

[b]Colleges and universities participating in the survey: Armstrong State University, Berry College, Covenant College, Columbus State University, Emmanuel College, Georgia Institute of Technology, Georgia Southwestern College, Middle Georgia College, North Georgia College, Oglethorpe University, Piedmont College, Savannah State University, University of Georgia, Valdosta State University, Wesleyan College, West Georgia University.

We requested information from companies on the number of amphibians sold but were told that those data are confidential. Many companies also sell live specimens for observation and/or experimentation, although concerns have been expressed over the quality of the health of these specimens for research purposes (Gibbs et al. 1971). One company (Charles D. Sullivan, Tennessee) raises amphibians on its own farm. Most others, however, deal in wild-caught amphibians. Five companies (Finn, Frey, Nasco, Sargent-Welch, and Ward) publish statements claiming that their grass frogs are collected in a sustainable fashion. A large number of grass frogs (*Rana for-*

Table 15.2

Amphibian species provided (live and/or preserved) by U.S. biological suppliers[a] for educational purposes

Common Name (Scientific Name)	Number of Suppliers Offering the Species
True frogs (*Rana* spp.)	14
Grass frogs (*R. pipiens* complex)	14
American bullfrog (*R. catesbeiana*)	13
Eurasian common frog (*R. temporaria*)	1
Ranid eggs/larvae	10
Treefrogs (*Hyla* spp.)	3
Cope's gray treefrog (*H. chrysoscelis*)	1
Barking treefrog (*H. gratiosa*)	1
Green treefrog (*H. cinerea*)	1
Hylid eggs/larvae	1
Toads (*Bufo* spp.)	5
Cane toad (*B. marinus*)	4
American toad (*B. americanus*)	2
Fowler's toad (*B. fowleri*)	1
Oak toad (*B. quercicus*)	1
Toad eggs/larvae	2
African clawed frog (*Xenopus laevis*)	6
Eastern newt (*Notophthalmus viridescens*)	11
Mudpuppy (*Necturus maculosus*)	11
Mole salamanders (*Ambystoma* spp.)	9
Tiger salamander (*A. tigrinum*)	8
Spotted salamander (*A. maculatum*)	3
Mexican axolotl (*A. mexicanum*)	2
Ambystomatid eggs/larvae	4
Amphiumas (*Amphiuma tridactylum* or *A. means*)	5
Sirens (*Siren* sp.)	1

[a]Surveyed suppliers: American 3B Scientific, Berkshire Biological Supply, Blue Spruce Biological Supply, Carolina Biological Supply, Charles D. Sullivan, Connecticut Valley Biological Supply, Delta Biologicals, Flinn Scientific, Frey Scientific, Nasco Biologicals, Nebraska Scientific, Sargent-Welch, Southern Scientific, Ward Scientific.

reri) are collected from irrigation canals in agricultural areas of Mexico, although many are also collected in the northern United States. According to state-agency records, one collector reported taking more than 450 kg of northern leopard frogs from Wisconsin during the last 6 months of 2000.

Although amphibians, particularly grass frogs, are still used for educational purposes in many schools (Table 15.1), their use in dissection is declining. Ethical concerns over the use of animals have grown in recent years, and legal decisions in U.S. courts have forced schools in some states to offer nondissection alternatives to conscientious objectors. These concerns have grown concomitantly with the availability of computer-based dissection-simulation programs and a spreading technophilia among public educators. Together these factors have encouraged the movement away from traditional dissection and toward computer-based programs. This trend, however, has been slowed by cost considerations and traditional teacher preferences (Smith 1994).

A decline in the use of *Necturus* in colleges has paralleled the reorganization of college curricula, especially at the university level. Curricula for academic majors are becoming increasingly based on conceptual (e.g., evolutionary biology) rather than organismal (e.g., zoology) themes. In addition, studies of broad patterns of evolution are becoming reliant on genetic patterns rather than traditional morphological ones. As a result, many programs no longer require courses in comparative vertebrate anatomy, and the subsequent demand for *Necturus* is relatively small (Table 15.1).

Amphibians remain popular subjects for scientific studies of morphology, physiology, behavior, ecology, evolution, and systematics. Although amphibians are occasionally procured from supply houses, many of them are collected from wild populations. In studies dealing with characteristics of specific populations (e.g., studies of geographic variation), there may be no alternative. However, the need for statistically valid sample sizes may drive researchers or museum curators toward overcollection, which, in turn, may have the unintended consequence of threatening the population(s) in question. Although some believe that it may be underrated as a factor in local population declines (Hairston and Wiley 1993), the impact of scientific collecting on amphibian populations is unknown. The greatest threat would seem to be large collections from small or isolated populations (e.g., 177 specimens of a now extinct population of southern dusky salamanders, *Desmognathus auriculatus;* Dodd 1998) or involving species with relatively small ranges (e.g., 356 individuals of Tellico salamanders, *Plethodon aureolus,* from the type locality; Highton 1983). Conversely, several species, including certain *Desmognathus* spp. in the Appalachian Mountains, occur so densely that systematic attempts to remove them from study plots have succeeded only with great difficulty or not at all (Hairston 1986; Petranka and Murray 2001). The appearance of high density may itself invite overcollection, however, especially at times when a significant portion of the population is vulnerable (e.g., during breeding congregations).

Amphibians in Medicine

Humans have recognized the chemical properties of amphibians for thousands of years. Indigenous peoples of South America used extracts from the skins of the endemic brightly colored frogs, giving rise to such common names as poison dart frogs (Dendrobates). Amphibian products continue to be widely used in traditional medicine in many parts of the world and are used to treat such varied ailments as warts and heart disease (Anderson 1993).

The use of plants and animals in healing in Western cultures historically has been associated with the "black art" of divination (Shakespeare's "eye of newt and toe of frog . . ." in Act 4 of *Macbeth*) and, as such, they are regarded as evil. This attitude traveled to Africa during the reign of European colonial powers, which sought to replace the beliefs of indigenous peoples with Christianity, resulting in a decline in traditional medical practice there during the nineteenth century. There has been a recent revival of the use of traditional medicine, however, in conjunction with the recognition of the importance of native cultures (Marshall 1999). Amphibians have continued to be included in the traditional pharmacopoeia of many Asian cultures. Parts of certain amphibians, like the parts of other animals (e.g., gall bladders of bears), are believed to have medicinal and/or aphrodisiacal properties. The dried oviducts of *Rana chensinensis* and skins of bufonids, for example, are sold in China by traditional medicine companies, in drug stores, and in open markets (Yinfeng et al. 1997).

The use of amphibians in western medicine is much more recent. Since the 1940s, frogs from a variety of families have been successfully used to test for human pregnancy (Hansen 1960); the African clawed frog, *Xenopus laevis*, is commonly used. In addition, the integuments of amphibians produce a diversity of biologically active compounds (Erspamer 1994), which have only recently come under scrutiny for their pharmacological potential. Researchers have identified peptides from the skins of *Xenopus laevis* and *Litoria caerulea* that show promise as antibiotics, and alkaloids from other species (e.g., *Epipedobates*) demonstrate analgesic properties. The skins of plethodontid salamanders harbor resident microbial floras; some member bacteria produce compounds that exhibit antibacterial and antifungal activity (Austin 2000).

The effect of the medical use of amphibians on endemic populations is not known. The main sources of amphibians used in Chinese traditional medicine are from the wild. The use of amphibians in Western medicine is so new that it has probably had little effect on natural populations. However, should current research lead to the successful production of widely marketed compounds, the impact could be large.

Amphibians as Bait

One needs only to visit a tackle or fishing store to understand the connection between sport fishing and amphibians. Many types of lures are colored and shaped to resemble frogs, and a variety of soft-plastic artificial baits are designed to mimic salamanders. However, despite the large numbers of amphibian-mimicking lures, live frogs and salamanders are relatively uncommon as commercial baits. Meronek et al. (1997) conducted surveys of the bait industry in the north-central region of the United States and found that amphibians were of minor importance and value when compared to fishes, earthworms, grubs, leeches, mayflies, and crickets. In certain regions of the country, however, the bait trade in amphibians is noteworthy and a potential conservation concern.

Most state wildlife agencies do not require permits specific to amphibian bait-collection or sale and only a few require a fishing license. Data on the number of animals collected and sold are, therefore, scanty, making evaluation of the trade's impact difficult.

Although sirens, amphiumas, and other amphibians turn up occasionally in the bait trade, ranid frogs, salamanders of the genus *Desmognathus*, and eastern tiger salamanders (*Ambystoma t. tigrinum*) are the groups most often involved. Bait trade involving amphibians may not be limited to the United States, but we are unaware of published information pertaining to this in other countries.

Although "farms" exist as commercial sources of ranid frogs, most if not all of these frogs are destined for biological supply houses and research institutions rather than bait shops (Gibbs et al. 1971). Meronek et al. (1997) revealed that 100% of the frogs sold in the north-central United States were harvested from the wild. Most frogs destined for the bait trade are hand-captured in and around wetlands. Large hibernating aggregations are often targeted, frogs being sometimes taken from under the ice. Most of the bait trade involving frogs occurs in the midwestern and north-central United States, where some states have established harvest seasons, size restrictions, and bag limits (Levell 1997). During 1998 and 1999, an estimated 250,000 frogs were reported taken from the wild in Minnesota (license-sales report to the Minnesota Department of Natural Resources), but these data include frogs taken for purposes other than for bait. Exploitation of frogs specifically for bait is thought to be of minor conservation concern, and any noted declines are more frequently attributed to habitat loss and invasive species.

Salamanders of the genus *Desmognathus* are commonly sold and used for bait in portions of the southeastern United States, particularly in Appalachian regions. They are used primarily for catching various species of centrarchid and temperate bass. Bait salamanders in this part of the country are colloquially known as "spring lizards," presumably because of their preference for spring-fed aquatic habitats and their gross resemblance to lizards. Spring lizards are less regulated than frogs; licenses or permits, bag limits, seasons, and size limits are not established in most states in which they are traded. Jensen and Waters (1999) interviewed the owners and inventoried the bait boxes of shops in northern Georgia that sold spring lizards. One bait-shop owner reported purchasing approximately 1,400 spring lizards per year from collectors. The salamanders were then sold to customers for US $4 to $6 a dozen. This trade is seasonal, and only a small proportion of bait shops in the region sell spring lizards. Approximately 95% of the 1,026 salamanders inventoried in the study were either seal salamanders (*Desmognathus monticola*) or black-bellied salamanders (*D. quadramaculatus*), but this is likely a result of what species are available at the collection sites rather than selective harvesting. Five other species, including three additional *Desmognathus* spp., made up the remaining salamanders encountered, none of which are considered rare or protected species in Georgia. *Desmognathus* spp. are abundant in the areas where the spring lizard trade is prominent. One study conducted in western North Carolina estimated the density of a local *Desmognathus* population to be 14,366 individuals per hectare (Petranka and Murray 2001). Although heavily collected local populations may experience short-term declines, the overall abundance of *Desmognathus* spp. and the limited extent of their trade would suggest that this group is not likely to be significantly affected by current levels of collection as bait.

Like spring lizards, "waterdogs" found in the bait trade are not what their name would suggest. The term waterdog correctly refers to salamanders of the genus *Necturus*; but those typically marketed as such for bait are actually the gilled, larval stage of the eastern tiger salamander. Waterdogs are primarily used to catch various species of centrarchid bass, mostly in the southwestern United States. They are obtained by seining from three primary sources: (1) natural populations from local wetlands; (2) natural populations from wetlands in distant states and then imported; and (3) introduced populations established as brood stock in local wetlands (Collins et al. 1988). Introduced populations of waterdogs in the southwestern United States are rarely composed of local subspecies, creating concern because of the negative impacts of alien introductions on endemic ecosystems.

Because the waterdog trade is not well regulated in most states where it occurs, few data are available on the numbers involved and their effect on natural populations. One dated study revealed that 2,440,000 waterdogs were sold as bait in the Lower Colorado River basin in one year (1968), and this total well exceeded the volume of bait-fish sales (Espinoza et al. 1970). A bait dealer recently interviewed by personnel with the California Game and Fish Commission indicated that he annually sells approximately 120,000 waterdogs, representing 15% of his total sales. Tiger salamanders remain quite common in most of the states from which they are harvested. Biologists in those states where the species is of conservation concern implicate nonnative fish introductions, wetland loss, deforestation, and possibly acid rain as more significant threats (Petranka 1998; Lannoo and Phillips, in press).

Amphibians in the Leather Trade

Although not typically thought of as sources of leather, frogs have recently begun to be used for fashion purposes. The species involved are usually large with thick hides and include Asian (*Limnonectes macrodon, Bufo melanostictus,* and *Kaloula pulchra*) and

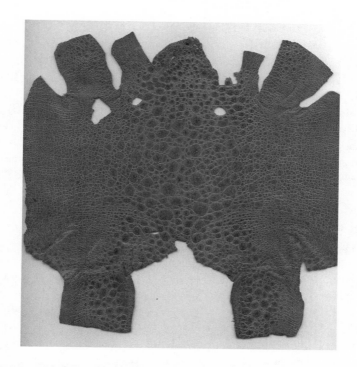

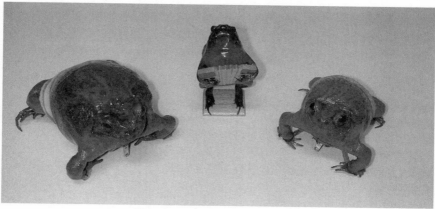

Figure 15.1. Cane toad (*Bufo marinus*) hide (a) prepared for use in various curios (b). (Photo by Barry Baker, U.S. Fish and Wildlife Service)

North American (American bullfrog) species (Fitzgerald 1989). A cottage industry has arisen in Australia that deals in novelty items made from the hides of the cane toad (*Bufo marinus*) (Figure 15.1). The cane toad is an exotic species that has caused severe ecological problems in Australia, from feeding on small wildlife to poisoning predators. Because of its effects on native species, including indigenous amphibians, the destruction of this species for its leather, at least in Australia, is probably helpful to amphibian conservation. It could have negative impacts, however, if this species were to be purposefully introduced into other countries to farm it for its leather. The potential impacts on other species involved in the leather trade are largely unknown, but are probably insignificant relative to those caused by their exploitation for other purposes.

INDIRECT IMPACTS

Removing amphibians from the wild to support various human needs and uses can obviously have direct impacts on the "donor" populations. Some of the more insidious, and perhaps wider reaching results of this trade are those in which other forms of wildlife, including other amphibians, are indirectly affected. Amphibians are both predators of prey and prey of predators. In the simplest sense, reductions of amphibian populations can result in an overabundance of those species' prey and leave their predators with a more limited food supply. For example, the decline of frogs in both India and Indonesia has been blamed for exploding insect populations and, subsequently, an increased necessity for insecticides (Barfield 1986; Fitzgerald 1989). In some areas, amphibians likely constitute most of the vertebrate biomass (Burton and Likens 1975; Petranka and Murray 2001), and predators that specialize on amphibians would certainly be affected by their reductions.

Perhaps the most troubling indirect impact of amphibian trade is the establishment of amphibian populations outside of their natural ranges. Intentional establishment is often pursued to provide new sources of food, bait, or other products in an effort to further commerce. Releases of unwanted pet, laboratory, or leftover bait amphibians, as well as escapees from commercial farms, have led to many unintentionally established populations. Exotic populations of amphibians have consequently caused great stress to native wildlife in many regions of the world (see Chapter 9, this volume). American bullfrogs, for example, have become established in Europe as a consequence of the trade of their tadpoles as pets, and they have been intentionally introduced to many areas of the world as a reliable food source (Stumpel 1992; Hardouin 1995). Cane toads have been introduced into several countries, including Australia and the United States. Many of these introductions have negatively affected certain native wildlife species that now have to contend with a new predator or a new competitor, or both (Collins et al. 1988; Lannoo et al. 1994). In addition, invasive species represent a significant threat to endemic species through the spread of exotic diseases (Chapter 9, this volume).

Another significant concern pertinent to introduced amphibians involves the genetic disruption they may cause through contamination of the gene pools of locally adapted ecotypes, intergradation with native conspecifics, or even hybridization with similar species. The latter is cause for concern with the California tiger salamander (*Ambystoma californiense*). Although the greatest threat to this federally endangered species is loss of habitat, hybridization with the eastern tiger salamander, which was introduced to support the waterdog bait trade, compounds the vulnerability of this highly restricted taxon (U.S. Fish and Wildlife Service 2000). In response to this issue, the state of California recently enacted controversial legislation prohibiting the sale and use of waterdogs as bait.

Certain techniques used for collecting commercially valuable amphibians add yet another concern. Bait-salamander collectors in the southeastern United States employ at least two different environmentally damaging practices to increase their catch. Small stream channels are occasionally diverted to expose streambeds and allow easier capture of salamanders sheltered under rocks. Similar to cyanide used to force tropical reef fishes out from crevices and cavities (Schrope 2000), liquid bleach poured into streams is used to drive salamanders (spring lizards) from under rocks (Jensen and Waters 1999). Clearly, these destructive collecting techniques are capable of having significant negative effects on the viability of associated aquatic flora and fauna, including declining species such as the hellbender (*Cryptobranchus alleganiensis*).

POTENTIAL SOLUTIONS

In a market economy, when demand outstrips supply, the resulting imbalance is correctable by either lowering demand or increasing supply. There is both precedent and opportunity for the first option. Modern concerns for the humane treatment of animals were effectively used in a campaign ("Lasst den Fröschen ihre Schenkel!" or "Let the frogs keep their legs!") to significantly cut the consumption of frog legs in Germany (Oza 1990). Similar campaigns expressing ecological and ethical concerns in regions where amphibians are heavily consumed might further reduce the demand for dead amphibians. Because of the long association of frog legs and French cuisine, obvious target areas would be regions of French historical culture in western Europe, Canada, and the United States. Other likely target areas are countries that use amphibians for traditional medicine (e.g., China) or as laboratory-dissection animals (the United States and other countries). An effective campaign needs to seek to educate (1) government officials, whose understanding of the need for wild frogs (e.g., for insect control) could translate into tighter restrictions on trade; (2) venders, both at the wholesale and retail levels; and (3) the consumers themselves. The opportunity for reducing demand for laboratory frogs is great because dissection is already in decline. Computer-simulated dissections are as effective as actual dissection in teaching the fundamentals of anatomy (Strauss and Kinzie 1994) and offer viable options to traditional dissection. The decline in dissection needs to be accelerated by focusing on changing the attitudes of teachers and procuring adequate funding for computer-based programs—and educating teachers in their use. This could be accomplished effectively during teacher training as part of science methods courses, which are required curricula in teacher education.

Cultural roots run deep, however, and educational campaigns may not be able to eliminate the demand for amphibians. The other option is to increase supply by captive-rearing species in high demand as pets or by farming food species agriculturally, thereby taking pressure off the wild populations. The increased availability of captive-reared tomato frogs (*Dyscophus antongilii*), for example, has apparently satiated the commercial demand for this CITES Appendix I-listed species (Fitzgerald 1989). Attempts at commercial raniculture for food have been less successful, because of problems associated with the control of bacterial disease and the need to provide live, moving prey. In addition, special techniques and facilities are required for managing each life-cycle stage, from hatching eggs to the maintaining brood stock (Lutz and Avery 1999). Even so, the potential for growth in this industry is large, particularly in tropical countries where suitable climatic conditions are coupled with the need for opportunities for economic development (Hardouin 1995). The bullfrog is currently farmed as "minilivestock" in the United States and has been imported into Brazil, Java, and the Philippines for this purpose (Hardouin 1995). Frog-farming operations are not without potentially negative side effects for wild amphibians, however. Unless only native species are farmed, there is the potential for introducing exotic species with all of their attendant difficulties (see Chapter 9, this volume). In addition, cultured frogs are a potential source of disease for their wild counterparts.

A continuing problem for trade officials attempting to enforce national and international law in the frog legs trade is the difficulty in correctly identifying species from frozen legs. With a number of countries allowing both the legal export of some species and farming of others, correct identification is essential to effective law enforcement. Although biochemical techniques (e.g., tests for allozymes) have been tried experimentally, a quick and inexpensive test is needed (Veith et al. 2000).

Governments should more effectively monitor the effects of potential overcollecting of amphibians in their respective principalities. Above a certain threshold number of animals, collectors should be licensed and required to report numbers taken, as is done for certain game species. Studies of population dynamics are still needed for many species so that agencies can determine sustainable collection numbers. However, regulations intended to set these sustainable levels should not wait on this biological information if, in the interim, the use may prove to be unsustainable. Sustainable-use policies should err on the side of caution and be amended later if necessary. Furthermore, government agencies should be more considerate of the importance of amphibians, enact necessary regulations and laws, and enforce them equally to those relating to other wildlife.

Companies seeking to exploit amphibians for pharmacological purposes should do so in a sustainable manner. In addition, should any companies reap large profits from marketing amphibian-generated compounds, those companies should consider "giving something back" and donate part of their proceeds for amphibian conservation.

Care should be taken within the scientific community to avoid overcollecting populations. Morphological studies should seek first to use museum specimens when feasible. With the development of biochemical techniques for studying variation and evolution, efforts to use regenerating body parts (e.g., tail tips of salamanders) in lieu of killing animals should be made. A system of banks that store tissues, similar to how museums store specimens, would eliminate the need for collecting specimens over and over from the same localities for new studies. Some museums (e.g., National Museum of Natural History, Smithsonian Institution) already have limited holdings of such material. In addition, journals that publish studies of wild-caught amphibians should require evidence from the authors that large collections from local populations do not irreparably harm those populations. There is precedent in behavioral journals, which routinely require authors to provide evidence that subject animals were treated according to ethical standards (e.g., author's instructions for journals such as *Animal Behaviour*).

To prevent the problems caused by the introduction of alien species, those who acquire living amphibians for pets or educational/research purposes should avoid releasing them into the wild. Educating the animal-using public on this issue is critical. To this end, Partners in Amphibian and Reptile Conservation (PARC) has developed a brochure outlining the dangers posed by invasive species. The intent is for supply houses and pet stores to include the brochure with every order of living amphibians. The brochure, *Please . . . Don't turn it loose!*, is available through the Arizona Game and Fish Department, Phoenix, AZ, and www.parcplace.org.

ACKNOWLEDGMENTS
We would like to thank the following people for providing information relative to this chapter: David Bechler, Kurt Buhlmann, Bruce Bury, Jan Caldwell, Chellu Chetty, Rod Christian, Jim Collins, Cris Cook, Steve Corn, F. Corotto, Mark Davis, Kay Dejno, Harold Dundee, Sharon Epperson, Dennis Ferraro, Tony Gamble, Tom Gehl, Christine Geist, Chris Hall, Robert Hay, Susan Healey, Robert Herrington, Kathy Hill, Craig Hoover, Sheila Hughes, Christopher Jones, Richard King, David Leonard, Sue Lieberman, Chuck Loeffler, Mitchell Lockhart, Chis McAllister, Chris McGrath, Grace McLaughlin, C Miller, Mark Mills, Paul Moler, John Moriarty, William Nelson, Jennifer Nolan, Marc Pline, Jamie Reaser, Kenneth Relyea, B. Rhoades, Bryan Rogers, Tara Seay, Brad Shaffer, Carol Smith, Cheryl Sniker, Kristina Sorensen, Mike Sredl, G. Stanton, Dirk Stevenson, Leigh Touchton, Art Tyson, Jerry Wenger, and J. Yearwood.

16

SOCIETAL VALUES AND ATTITUDES

Their History and Sociological Influences
on Amphibian Conservation Problems

J. WHITFIELD GIBBONS

CENTRAL ISSUES

For more than a decade, the loss of biodiversity (Gore 1992; Wilson 1992), especially in the context of species richness or of selected species, has been a prevalent issue of concern among environmentalists and today is the impetus for most applied ecological research. Reports on biodiversity losses have focused on declines in specific taxonomic groups, including mollusks (Hallac and Marsden 2001), spiders (Horton et al. 2001), and reptiles (Gibbons et al. 2000), as well as on environmental principles or processes, such as river ecology (Ward and Tockner 2001), forest management (Noss 2001), or the ecology of small isolated wetlands (Semlitsch 2000b). Hence the loss of biodiversity has become a central and overriding theme of conservation biology.

Amphibians, especially anurans, have been among the most thoroughly documented taxonomic groups to exhibit declines on a global scale during the latter part of the twentieth century (Vitt et al. 1990; Wake 1991; Houlahan et al. 2000). Accepting the premise that amphibians are in trouble environmentally, I examine some of the public's cultural and environmental attitudes on the issue and recommend changes that might ameliorate the situation. A tentative assumption is that changing negative or indifferent societal values and attitudes about amphibians into positive ones will best be achieved through prescribed educational efforts. Some of the strategies I recommend and positions I have taken can be viewed as testable hypotheses whose confirmation would be useful in developing conservation education programs.

THE STATUS OF AMPHIBIANS IN HUMAN SOCIETY

From a conservation perspective, the status of a taxonomic group can be viewed in two ways. One definition of status is the level of prestige, appreciation, or value placed on the group by society that directly enhances public awareness and appreciation. A second measure of status is the biological and environmental condition of a species in the taxonomic group. A basic assumption is that programs or projects that familiarize the public with amphibians and their habitats will raise public awareness and hence the status of amphibians. Because public support of conservation efforts is a vital ingredient for assuring long-term solutions, a secondary assumption is that public awareness will lead indirectly to greater environmental protection for species and habitats (Hypothesis 1).

Attitudes of the General Public toward Amphibians

Although some people have either strongly negative or strongly positive attitudes about one or more amphibian species, most people are unaware of or indifferent to the plight of amphibians in general. Apathy is always a major obstacle that must be overcome to bring about societal change, including a greater conservation commitment toward wildlife.

To address the issue of how to engender public support for amphibian conservation efforts, we must examine the reasons that amphibians are beleaguered and maligned in certain situations and are viewed favorably in others. Amphibians generally are not directly competitive with humans for resources, are not venomous, and ordinarily are not harmful to people or human resources, and thus are seldom viewed as a negative biological feature of a region. Features of amphibians that might taint some people's attitudes include superstitions about anurans causing warts, a vague association between toads, wizardry, and witchery (e.g., the witches in *Macbeth*), and the image of being slimy and repulsive. However, negative public attitudes about amphibians (when they do exist) could be a consequence of being psychologically grouped with reptiles (Hypothesis 2). Thus, some unfounded anxieties and phobias commonly associated with snakes (Wilson 1993; Gibbons and Dorcas 2002) may unwittingly be transferred to frogs, toads, and salamanders. This association is often reinforced by herpetological field guides that include both reptiles and amphibians. Thus, in some situations, lack of public awareness of a distinction between one group of animals for which some people have an irrational loathing and another group with which they are equally uninformed results in negative attitudes toward both groups.

Wildlife conservation attitudes vary considerably among the general public, scientists, politicians, and land managers, but a consensus toward proactive amphibian conservation appears to be closer at hand than in the past. Throughout the twentieth century, until as little as a decade ago, the general public's attitude toward amphibians was indifference (e.g., the merit badge booklet of the Boy Scouts of America that dealt with both amphibians and reptiles was titled "Reptile Study" until 1993 when the name was changed to "Reptile and Amphibian Study") and insensitivity (e.g., one of the original Beavis and Butthead TV cartoons revolved around killing toads).

Today, projects and initiatives undertaken by many organizations, including public and private schools, are focused on amphibian conservation in a positive manner. For example, amphibian species have been selected as the representative animals at more than a dozen habitats in the Student Partners in Amphibian and Reptile Conservation (SPARC) cross-curriculum Internet project "Herps of the Southeast" (available online at www.parcplace.org/education/sparc/index.htm). Although untested experimentally, positive associations created among school-age children and amphibians presumably lead to positive attitudes toward amphibians in these same children in adulthood. In 1999, students at an elementary school in South Carolina proposed the spotted salamander (*Ambystoma maculatum;* Figure 16.1) as the official state amphibian. Subsequent approval by the South Carolina legislature brought a level of endorsement for this taxonomic group that would be difficult to achieve otherwise.

Figure 16.1. Spotted salamander (*Ambystoma maculatum*). (Photo by David Scott, Savannah River Ecology Laboratory)

Environmental Status of Amphibians and Approaches to Conservation

Little more need be said here regarding documentation and confirmation of declining numbers of populations of amphibians on a global scale, as extensive evidence has been provided for more than a decade that a problem exists (Vitt et al. 1990; Wake 1991; Rabb 1999; Houlahan et al. 2000). The six primary categories known or suspected to be responsible for amphibian declines, as established by Partners in Amphibian and Reptile Conservation (PARC; Gibbons and Stangel 1999), are habitat loss and degradation, environmental pollution, introduced invasive species, disease and parasitism, unsustainable use, and global climate change. Single and cumulative effects among the categories, as well as interactions among them, are generally accepted as causes of amphibian losses. Although in some instances the cause was unknown and remains unexplained, most current amphibian declines are a consequence of human activities. In most instances, a human-caused problem requires a human-based solution.

The scientific community, government agencies, politicians, and both public and private land managers have all been influential in shaping amphibian conservation programs, although wide-scale, formal efforts extend back less than half a century. The Endangered Species Preservation Act of 1966, followed by the powerful Endangered Species Act of 1973, was the first U.S. legislation to focus on protecting particular species of amphibians. Nonetheless, despite the numerous accounts of amphibians in distress, of approximately 200 indigenous species in the United States, only 27 were on the 2001 list in any capacity (including proposed for listing and candidate for listing) and only 18 are currently protected by the Endangered Species Act (Table 1.1). Formal recognition as endangered or threatened presumably depends as much or more on the political process as on the actual biological status of a species (Hypothesis 3). Even using the most liberal approach of considering proposed, candidate, and threatened and endangered species, fewer than one amphibian species per year has been catalogued in any category since the passage of the Endangered Species Act by the U.S Congress in 1973 (Table 1.1).

Attitudes of scientists toward conservation issues in general and amphibian issues in particular have changed notably during the last quarter of the twentieth century. Even through the 1960s and 1970s, most professional academic herpetologists thought that scientists could collect data that might be applicable to current environmental issues, but "pure" science was not to be sullied by "applied" research directed toward solving environmental problems. Likewise, most herpetologists and other scientists of that era seldom took opinion positions on environmental issues, even about situations that clearly were detrimental to the specialty taxonomic group of the researcher. Instead, a researcher might present "facts" that were then open for interpretation. Today, many researchers in herpetological ecology will readily declare that, based on scientific findings of their own or others, they strongly support or contest one conservation stand or another. Thus, directed efforts to collect data that address controversial environmental issues are common. The collective strength of such efforts is seen in the vigor and effectiveness of responses to amphibian declines that have resulted because professional scientists throughout North America and the world have taken adamant stands on behalf of amphibian conservation. Publication of Lannoo's (2003) book with updated species accounts and geographic ranges of all North American amphibians will greatly facilitate assessments of the status of particular species by both researchers and land managers.

Political attitudes toward amphibian conservation have, understandably, tracked those of the general public and within a region cannot usually be separated from those of their constituencies. Each listing of a species under the Endangered Species Act has involved some level of local public and political support. Before the late 1960s, amphibians received limited attention from the political arena. In the 1990s, the efforts of several herpetologists to familiarize the Secretary of the Interior, Bruce Babbitt, and his staff with the problem led to budgetary support for amphibian research and conservation efforts in some federal agencies, including the U.S. Geological Survey (USGS) and the U.S. Fish and Wildlife Service.

In the late 1990s and early 2000s, the efforts of Republican Congressman Jack Kingston of Georgia, a member of the House Interior Appropriations Subcommittee, to direct funding to USGS amphibian conservation programs was highly effective. During a talk to herpetologists at USGS headquarters in 2001, Kingston noted that one of his colleagues in the House of Representatives had asked, "What is an amphibian?" Explaining that U.S. amphibians include toads, frogs, and salamanders had been relatively simple for Congressman Kingston compared to answering his colleague's next question: "Why do you care about saving them?" To answer that sort of environmental question in a manner that satisfies the pragmatic nature of some people is not always easy. But Kingston supplied the simple, practical, and acceptable answer that amphibians represent a major part of our natural heritage and are indicators of environmental health. His answer was based on an assumption that most people accept the ecological maxim that if these animals are in trouble, we are in trouble. A testable hypothesis is that most of the general public accedes to the view that amphibians are sentinels of our environmental health, and that if amphibians are declining and ultimately disappearing, we need to make amends (Hypothesis 4).

In referencing the USGS Amphibian Research and Monitoring Initiative (ARMI) that he helped to launch, Kingston said, "This is a model of twenty-first-century science at its best. The work of experts is weighed in partnership and cooperation among USGS, the U.S. Department of the Interior, and other organizations, universities and with the states." The U.S. Congress will forever be bombarded with such major issues as social security, budget surpluses or deficits, and military might, so it is important that some members of Congress recognize that the plight of amphibians could signal deeper environmental problems and that they are willing to put amphibian declines on the congressional agenda. Having advocates for amphibians in Congress could be vital for developing certain conservation initiatives.

The attitudes of land managers toward amphibian conservation have followed a general trend in wildlife attitudes that began during the latter third of the twentieth century. One perception is that the traditions and conventions of wildlife and fisheries management have reached a turning point (Muth et al. 1998). The more enlightened conservation advocates recognize and accept that the role of all plants and animals must be considered as ecosystem components. Thus, traditional wildlife goals, with an emphasis on production and management of game species and their habitats for human use, have gradually evolved into conservation objectives that now include nongame species and consider the importance of biodiversity and landscape-level ecology. This shift in management focus is reflected in the inclusion of amphibians in a new textbook on wildlife management in southern forest communities (Dickson 2001).

Of course, a challenge to many conservation movements will continue to be: Why should people care? Such a question will understandably be asked more often about a lesser-known vertebrate group like amphibians than about birds or mammals. Should herpetologists respond with the assertion that millions of people do care? If enough people were asked, would it be true that for every person who is indifferent about what happens to frogs, toads, or salamanders, an order of magnitude more could be found who are concerned? Perhaps more people need to be asked (Hypothesis 2).

Amphibians in Human Culture

A premise among many conservationists is that everyone should be involved in making the world a better place environmentally, or at least that everyone has a responsibility not to exacerbate problems that already exist. Yet conservation actions are often only as effective as the appeal of a region, habitat, or group of organisms. For example, supportive conservation attitudes among the general public prevail toward profound and mysterious tropical ecosystems or toward fascinating megamammals such as pandas, big cats, and elephants. A campaign to protect biodiversity in the world's temperate zones or to save the noctuid moths of North America would undoubtedly rally much less support.

Thus, part of the mix that shapes society's views on and strategies for conservation is the impact that a particular group of organisms has on human culture. For example, the extent to which a group of organisms is used in art, literature, music, and religion is one measure of a taxonomic group's cultural status within society (Table 16.1). From a commercial standpoint, the extent of use in entertainment and advertising can be used as a gauge of public attitudes and may indicate public awareness and appreciation of and favorable attitudes toward a taxonomic group (see Hypothesis 5). Many of the references to amphibians listed in Table 16.1 are positive, a few are negative, and others can be viewed as neutral. Most references are of anurans with a few salamanders and virtually no caecilians. The list is not exhaustive and is intended only to provide an example of the extent and diversity to which amphibians (primarily frogs) have become incorporated into certain aspects of human culture. The list is also not comparative with other taxonomic groups, which is an exercise that might prove instructive about how much of human psyche is dominated by particular organisms.

In another look at how taxonomic groups pervade art, I made an informal survey of the plant and animal species depicted in various cultures and time periods represented in antiques stores in Charleston, South Carolina. Of the wild animals used on furniture, plates, brass door knockers, and other items, frogs were among the most common organisms (in addition to bears, beetles, foxes, lions, monkeys, owls, parrots, storks, and turtles). Interestingly, salamanders are seldom used in painting, sculpture, or other forms of art, and caecilians are virtually absent. Anurans are also displayed on the postage stamps of dozens of countries (available online at http://members .nbci.com/quioui/frogs/frogs.html). The dominance of frogs in this regard com-

Table 16.1

Some amphibians represented in human (primarily Western) culture

Art Form	Title, Author or Source
Literature, music	*The Frogs*, Aristophanes
	The Frog King, The Brothers Grimm
	The Celebrated Jumping Frog of Calaveras County, Mark Twain
	Mr. Toad of Toad Hollow (*The Wind in the Willows*), Kenneth Grahame
	A Frog He Would A-Wooing Go, Randolph Caldecott
	The Tale of Mr. Jeremy Fisher, Beatrix Potter
	War with the Newts, Karel Capek
	Jeremiah was a Bullfrog, Three Dog Night
	Toad, Mary Oliver
	The Death of a Toad, Richard Wilbur
	Toads Are Nice People, Ronn Altig
Advertising, entertainment	Budweiser Bullfrogs
	Peace Frogs
	Kermit the Frog
	Game of Leap Frog
	Videogame of Frogger
Decorations, jewelry	Frog dish towels
	Salamander and frog earrings, pins, pendants
	Frog-shaped soap, vases, candleholders
	Frog-call clock
	Stuffed toy frog Ty in the Beanie Babies Collection

pared to salamanders and caecilians is presumably an indication of the unawareness or disinterest of most people about the latter two, a situation that can best be addressed through education efforts directed toward the general public (Hypothesis 1).

In the various cultural arenas, amphibians fare better than most kinds of animals, which suggests that frogs especially—and to a lesser degree toads and salamanders—are among the animal groups in the forefront of western bioculture (Table 16.1). Hence, favored with a greater appeal to the public than most animals, amphibians should be featured in promotion of conservation programs.

CHALLENGES TO CHANGING PUBLIC ATTITUDES AND DEVELOPING AMPHIBIAN CONSERVATION PROGRAMS

Developing any wildlife conservation program can be a difficult task because acquiescence is needed among disparate groups, including the general public, government agencies, and land managers. Amphibian conservation faces the added challenge that education of the public about the dependence of each species on certain habitats and about the species themselves is essential for gaining public support.

Most members of the general public, regardless of level of education, age, or profession, have some level of appreciation for intact, healthy natural habitats or at least accept that such habitats have value for the native wildlife. Furthermore, public awareness and appreciation of visible wildlife, such as charismatic megafauna and colorful birds, is widespread, due in part to the admirable programs of conservation groups, organizations, and individuals. Even small, neotropical migrant birds have gained attention through programs such as Partners in Flight, and sea turtles have benefited from several highly successful programs that evolved from the early efforts of Archie Carr. A common denominator of successful conservation efforts on behalf of a taxonomic group is that they focus on familiarizing the public with representative species and making connections between the fate of those species and human actions (Hypothesis 1).

Amphibians as Hidden Biodiversity

Most people are herpetologically ignorant or misinformed, although today's glut of wildlife specials on television and in magazines has presumably brought a greater awareness of some species than was true a generation ago. Nonetheless, irrational fear of some animals, especially snakes but occasionally even frogs, exist. A basic goal for educating the public about amphibians is to develop an appreciation and sense of ownership by familiarizing people with the animals. In developing an effective conservation program for amphibians, amphibian biologists must educate the public under the principle that people must know and appreciate their native wildlife before they can be motivated to protect it. The concept of "hidden biodiversity" is particularly relevant to amphibians, the challenge being to get the public to appreciate species so secretive that they may go unseen by most people living in an area.

Although the general public encompasses all levels of education, the relationship between formal education and familiarity with amphibians appears to be tenuous or possibly nonexistent. In 2001, I surveyed two classes of honors biology students at the University of Georgia. The state of Georgia is home to 51 species of salamanders, more than any other state. The students were exposed to three species of live reptiles and amphibians during each class: the canebrake rattlesnake (*Crotalus horridus*), American alligator (*Alligator mississippiensis*), and marbled salamander (*Ambystoma opacum*). The students were asked about their previous experiences with each of the three species. That none had ever seen a venomous snake in the wild was no surprise; even hikers, bird watchers, and hunters might go years without seeing a rattlesnake. Seeing an alligator that is truly wild is not likely to be in the realm of experience of most high school or college students either, especially for those who live outside of the alligator's range, as do most members of the class. But of the 42 students who planned to major in biology, only 2 had ever held or seen a live salamander up close. If the experience of these future biologists is indicative of nature backgrounds in other parts of the country, the findings do not bode well for field biology and conservation efforts. A careful testing of the level of knowledge about native amphibians among college students nationwide could be a revealing, albeit a potentially disquieting, study.

All field herpetologists know that amphibians can be present but virtually unknown to people living in a region for various reasons, including camouflage, fossorial behavior, nocturnal activity, seasonality, or because they are truly rare. To the average person in the southeastern United States, marbled salamanders that remain beneath leaf litter or logs most of the year and are active above ground in abundance primarily on rainy nights in autumn are as rare as Tennessee cave salamanders (*Gyrinophilus palleucus*). Neither species would normally be encountered by a typical Southerner, and as more people in the region become suburbanized and urbanized, the likelihood of someone becoming familiar with native regional amphibians continues to decrease. Thus, because most people are unaware of the presence of most amphibian species indigenous to their area, educational programs that emphasize the concept of hidden biodiversity and familiarize the public, including the "educated public," with local amphibians is a key step in gaining public support for amphibian conservation programs.

Educating the Public about Threats to Amphibians and Their Habitats

For the public to become supportive of conservation efforts for amphibians, active educational programs to increase familiarity with local and regional species and the environmental risks that they face will be essential (Hypothesis 1).

Although most people are unfamiliar with the appearance or habits of amphibian species native to their region, people who see live specimens for the first time are usually fascinated, especially with species that are colorful (e.g., tiger salamander), or large (e.g., *Amphiuma*), or have entertaining behavior (e.g., the climbing antics of a barking treefrog, *Hyla gratiosa*). Salamanders are particularly useful for making a point that someone could live in an area for many years without knowing that a particular species exists. Showing an audience a double handful of spotted salamanders (Figure 16.1) during the late winter breeding period can bring responses of appreciation, wonder, and astonishment. Knowing that an attractive and appealing species is a natural neighbor can invoke a sense of protectiveness, ownership, and environmental responsibility in the public that cannot be acquired through legislation.

From a conservation perspective, the combination of awareness and appreciation can also have a positive extension of making people aware of and curious about whether they have been missing other fascinating aspects of native biodiversity in the region. If people were more aware of the spectacular beauty, environmental importance, and unusual behavior of seldom-seen amphibians that live around them, they would be more supportive of efforts to protect them.

An extension of the hidden biodiversity message that can be readily delivered to a public informed of the presence, appearance, and habits of regional species is that to preserve populations of a species, their natural habitats must also be preserved. A point that comes naturally and need not be forced is that if development or other environmental degradation destroys the habitat of a species, the species will soon be extirpated from the region. Once the connection has been made between appealing, interesting animals and their required habitats, many people become solid advocates of amphibian conservation programs that focus on habitat loss. People familiar with their native species usually come to view them as natural treasures, and attitudes generally shift from neutral or mildly negative to positive. Such attitudes are necessary for public support of amphibian conservation.

Teaching people to respect amphibians and their habitats should be a consistent theme in public education efforts related to amphibian conservation. Familiarizing people with amphibians, their habitats, and their environmental requirements leads not only to admiration and respect for the group but to an overall conservation ethic.

RESPONSIBILITIES FOR STEWARDSHIP AND CONSERVATION OF AMPHIBIANS

The responsibilities for amphibian conservation reside with everyone, although the ways that individuals and organizations can contribute effectively differ considerably. Recognition and awareness that diverse capabilities must be applied to conservation problems is key to developing long-term amphibian conservation programs.

Responsibilities of the Academic Community

The responsibilities of conservation biologists, including herpetologists, in universities vary depending on their status and job classification. Whether an individual's role within the academic community involves research, teaching, or service, one obligation remains consistent—all must communicate. Some individuals are most effective through scientific publication, others through teaching undergraduates and graduate students, and still others as volunteers in scientific societies or in communication with the public, politicians, government agencies, and the news media. But anyone who serves the cause of higher education directly or indirectly does so by communicating effectively in some manner to audiences that range from local to international.

To be properly responsible, each individual must be supportive of efforts to communicate to the general public about environmental stewardship, about maintaining natural biodiversity, and about developing an appreciation for the natural world. Amphibians would be included within the general effort and are especially suitable for presentations using live animals.

In addition to taking advantage of opportunities to promote amphibian conservation through direct contact with public audiences, writing of popular books or magazine articles can also be effective (e.g., Crump 2000; *International Wildlife; Natural History*) and research ecologists studying amphibians can contribute directly to policy/management-related publications (e.g., *National Wetlands Newsletter, Wildlife Society Bulletin, Biological Conservation*).

Responsibilities of State and Federal Governments

No country can develop effective conservation programs without at least passive and preferably active support from the controlling government. Several federal agencies within the U.S. government, as well as many state agencies, have taken active roles in amphibian conservation. Their contributions include the creation of highly informative Websites, fact sheets, brochures, and hands-on educational or training programs. For example, the USGS developed the North American Amphibian Monitoring Program (NAAMP) in which volunteer observers use calling surveys to monitor frog populations. With NAAMP, the USGS Website (http://www.mp2-pwrc.usgs.gov/naamp/) provides links to other national and international amphibian programs and information on an extensive amphibian database managed by the Patuxent Wildlife Research Center.

One measure of federal proactivity on behalf of amphibians is shown in the many federal organizations active in PARC, including U.S. Geological Survey, U.S. Fish and Wildlife Service, National Park Service, U.S. Forest Service, Environmental Protection Agency, Department of Transportation, Department of Energy, Department of the Army, and several others. Their contributions have greatly aided amphibian conservation efforts throughout the country. The U.S. Forest Service took a major step toward conservation of both amphibians and reptiles in 2000 with the initiation of a national effort to develop habitat guidelines for amphibians that could be used by both public and private land managers. The program has been particularly effective in identifying concerns related to amphibian habitat within the context of forest management and in bringing a broad array of public, academic, and private industry groups together to reach consensus. Likewise, the wildlife departments of at least 35 states are actively involved in the amphibian conservation efforts of PARC and have been responsible for many research projects and public education efforts.

Some state and federal agencies have taken a positive step by hiring staff trained in herpetology rather than in conventional wildlife management that focuses on game species. The importance of nongame wildlife programs in research and management is becoming widely recognized and the inclusion of amphibians in wildlife management books (e.g., Dickson 2001) and journals will benefit amphibian conservation efforts.

Responsibilities of the General Public

Educators generally assume that the audience is receiving the message being delivered. However, the public has no obligation to listen to and accept messages about amphibian conservation, so the burden lies on herpetologists and conservation biologists to deliver a captivating message. Some conservation groups have arisen in recent years that focus on amphibians. Among the most effective is the Declining Amphibian Populations Task Force (DAPTF; http://www.open.ac.uk/daptf/index.htm), established in 1991 by the Species Survival Commission of the World Conservation Union (IUCN). The DAPTF mission is "to determine the nature, extent and causes of declines of amphibians throughout the world, and to promote means by which declines can be halted or reversed." The DAPTF newsletter, *Froglog*, provides current updates on research, political, and other activities related to the decline of amphibians.

The essence of effective communication to the public regarding conservation efforts is apparent in the PARC mission statement: "To conserve amphibians, reptiles and their habitats as integral parts of our ecosystem and culture through proactive and coordinated public/private partnerships." PARC differs in several ways from other conservation groups, particularly in diversity of participation, which may be crucial to the success of future amphibian conservation efforts. PARC is the most diverse group of individuals and organizations ever to work together to address problems confronting amphibians. Among the participants at the PARC organizational meeting in June 1999 were 170 organizations, including museums, nature centers, state wildlife departments, universities, federal agencies, conservation societies, research laboratories, the forest products industry, the pet trade, and environmental consultants and contractors. Such diversity is essential to long-term consensus-building conservation programs.

On the other hand, this diversity can also bring problems. Government agencies, conservation groups, and private industry all have different agendas and may be unaccustomed to working together. However, an effective amphibian conservation program must have input from all members. A diverse mix of people and organizations can identify problems confronting amphibians and can also implement solutions and provide the support needed to assure effective conservation. Widespread, long-term amphibian conservation will be achieved only when individuals and organizations with differences of opinion are willing to hear all sides. Total agreement on the best solutions will not be reached, but consensus can be achieved, and the resulting program will be as strong as the diversity of its participants.

TESTABLE HYPOTHESES RELATED TO PUBLIC AWARENESS AND APPRECIATION OF AMPHIBIANS

Although certain public education programs are presumed to be the most likely to be successful in the development of amphibian conservation efforts, the actual effectiveness of such approaches is equivocal. The following testable hypotheses are examples of expectations and assumptions that herpetologists and environmental educators often hold about public attitudes toward amphibians. Although not typical of biological hypotheses that are usually tested by field or laboratory experiments or systematic observations, these hypotheses could be verified or refuted with properly planned surveys or polls of human subjects. Determining the authenticity or invalidity of each assumption should help guide the most effective approaches for engendering public support of amphibian conservation.

> Working hypothesis 1: Environmental education programs and projects that familiarize the public with amphibians and their habitats will raise public awareness, enhance public support of conservation efforts, and lead to greater environmental protection for amphibians and their habitats.
> Working hypothesis 2: Most people have either indifferent or positive attitudes toward amphibians. When negative attitudes exist, they are based minimally on negative feelings toward amphibians themselves (e.g., the belief that toads cause warts), but are primarily caused by the psychological grouping of amphibians with reptiles.
> Working hypothesis 3: Because fewer than one amphibian species per year has been catalogued in any category of the Endangered Species Act

since its passage in 1973, formal recognition of the need to protect a species depends more on the political process than on the actual biological and environmental status of the species.

Working hypothesis 4: Conservation biologists often use a taxonomic group as an indicator or sentinel of environmental health to create public support for its protection. The environmental welfare of that group becomes equated with the welfare of humans. Informing members of the general public that amphibians can serve as indicators of some forms of environmental degradation and that amphibian declines are occurring on a widespread basis will lead to strong public support of amphibian conservation efforts.

Working hypothesis 5: The extent to which a group of organisms is used in art, literature, music, and religion is a measure of that group's cultural status within society and indicates the level of public awareness and attitudes toward the group.

CONCLUSIONS

Amphibian conservation should be approached with the attitude that public support is necessary and that most people, once familiar with the animals and educated about the problems they face, will support local, regional, national, or global conservation efforts. Educating the public about amphibians and their habitat requirements should be viewed as the single most important step toward assuring that amphibians can persist in natural systems in today's world. However, the most effective approaches and most critical factors to consider in implementing educational programs remain untested. Verifying or refuting several testable hypotheses related to public attitudes, education, and perceptions about amphibians will help clarify the most meaningful directions that herpetological conservationists should take.

ACKNOWLEDGMENTS

I thank Tracey Tuberville and Michelle Boone for reading the manuscript and providing constructive comments. Steve Bennett, Kurt Buhlmann, and David Scott provided comments on particular sections. I appreciate the suggestions of Erin Clark, Judy Greene, Chris Winne, Karen Kinkead, and Tony Mills on the use of amphibians in human culture. Manuscript preparation was supported by Contract DE-AC09-76SROO819 between the University of Georgia's Savannah River Ecology Laboratory and the U.S. Department of Energy and with Financial Assistance Award DE-FC09-96SR18546 from the U.S. Department of Energy to the University of Georgia Research Foundation. This chapter supports the national program of Partners in Amphibian and Reptile Conservation (PARC) to promote education about reptiles and amphibians.

17

MANAGING ECOSYSTEMS FOR AMPHIBIAN CONSERVATION

ARAM J. K. CALHOUN AND MALCOLM L. HUNTER JR.

CENTRAL ISSUES

Does a riparian buffer strip designed to protect water quality from logging impacts also adequately protect the habitat of stream-dwelling amphibians? How do you design a reserve to sustain a metapopulation of amphibians? To what extent are agricultural fields a barrier to the movement of amphibians to and from breeding ponds? There are scores of interesting and important questions about the interface between land-use practices and amphibian ecology and conservation. Indeed, if you insert the names of some particular species (recognizing the pitfalls of making generalizations for amphibians en masse), there are thousands of such questions. In this chapter, we attempt to answer a few of the overarching questions.

To bring some harmony to the cacophony of potential questions, we have organized this chapter around three basic types of ecosystems, defined in terms of how people use them (Hunter and Calhoun 1996). The first, and least common, are natural ecosystems that have been little altered by humans and are typically protected in reserves. Here the habitat requirements of amphibians and other native biota will be paramount among management goals. The second are seminatural or modified ecosystems that are manipulated by people to produce commodities such as lumber, livestock, and fish, but still retain much of their native biota. Here amphibian habitat needs must be balanced against human-centered activities. The third are the cultivated and built ecosystems that we create in our farms and cities. Few amphibians will find suitable habitat here, but proper management is still important to the integrity of the overall landscape.

With these ecosystem types in mind we can articulate three central questions:

1. How can the habitat needs of amphibians shape broad-based ecosystem protection efforts such as wetland protection and reserve design? (protection scenario.)

2. How can the maintenance of amphibian habitat be integrated with the management of ecosystems for producing commodities such as timber and fish? (integration scenario.)

3. How can we minimize the impacts of very intensive land-use (e.g., agriculture and suburban development) on amphibian habitat? (impact minimization scenario.)

PROTECTION SCENARIO

The most direct method of conserving amphibians is protection, through either regulation or creation of reserves.

Regulation

Currently, amphibians usually receive direct regulatory protection only if they are listed as endangered species, and even then the species, and not necessarily their habitat, is protected. Amphibians may benefit from existing regulations for rivers, lakes, and wetlands, but often these regulations focus on water quality or management of game species. For example, in the United States, wetlands are regulated through the Clean Water Act; there is no federal law specifically for wetlands. Wetlands receiving the most protection tend to be large, herbaceous wetlands important to game species. This pattern is evident in both local situations (where marshes and ponds of tens of hectares are the focus) and international arenas (e.g., the Ramsar Convention's Wetlands of International Importance are usually critical habitat for migratory birds, especially waterfowl).

To enhance conservation of amphibians and the full spectrum of wetland biota, wetland regulations should:

1. Regulate wetlands as landscape features rather than as isolated entities. This may require regulating adjacent terrestrial ecosystems beyond the traditional water-quality buffers and addressing issues of aquatic–terrestrial habitat connectivity (see Chapter 2, this volume).

2. Regulate wetlands regardless of size and vegetation structure. Small wooded wetlands are critical landscape features for many amphibian species (Gibbs 1993; Snodgrass et al. 2000; Chapter 2, this volume).

3. Track cumulative losses of wetlands within watersheds and adjust permitting and mitigation strategies based on these trends. Currently, per-

mits for filling or dredging wetlands are not based on either the past history of permitting for a given wetland or wetland loss in a given watershed. Therefore, at the landscape scale, the loss of small wetlands is not tracked. Identifying wetland classes and sizes regularly lost will help managers identify habitats or species at risk and establish wetland management priorities (Bedford 1996, 1999; Gwin et al. 1999; Tiner et al. 1999).

4. Revisit and perhaps tighten agricultural and timber exemptions to wetland regulations.

5. Develop and enforce best management practices (guidelines for ecologically sensitive forestry) for wildlife (expanding on the water quality models; Schuler and Briggs 2000).

6. Develop wetland assessment models that assess wetland functions as habitat for metapopulations. For example, current models assign low value to wooded and small, isolated wetlands and higher values to hydrological functions (flood control, filtering human pollutants) and to large, herbaceous wetlands (Bartoldus 1999). For example, models could evaluate wetland density, interwetland distance, and percentage of undisturbed habitat within 1 km of breeding pools.

Changing the way we regulate wetlands will require breaking a universal tradition of perceiving wetlands as wastelands unless they provide humans with food (fish, waterfowl, and other game species) or hydrological functions that are economically beneficial (flood desynchronization and abatement, waste-water treatment). This tradition is slowly being transformed by advances in ecology and conservation education, but the pace needs to be increased. Amphibian conservation strategies should include modifying regulatory tools to reflect these advances in science and changes in societal values.

Reserves and Other Public Lands

Only about 5% of the earth's terrestrial surface area has been set aside in reserves where the primary goal is the protection of nature, and this figure is not increasing very rapidly (Ryan 1992). Global initiatives, such as the Convention on Wetlands signed in Ramsar, Iran, in 1971, provide the framework for wide-scale amphibian conservation. This intergovernmental treaty, with more than 130 countries participating and overseeing more than 87 million hectares of wetland reserve, provides the framework for national action and international cooperation for the wise use of wetlands and their resources. The Convention provides outreach services for wetland managers, such as consultations for specific geographic regions and species, including amphibians and reptiles (available online at www.ramsar.org).

The European Union's (EU) Habitat Directive on nature conservation, Natura

2000, is another initiative that provides opportunities for incorporating amphibian conservation concerns in reserve selection and/or management in all EU member states (Jongman 1995).

Despite the small percentage of lands in reserve, these places are exceedingly important to many species and it is important to ask how the habitat requirements of amphibians can inform the selection, design, and management of ecological reserves. While addressing this question, we must recognize that the needs of amphibians are, more often than not, subsumed under larger considerations faced by reserve managers. For example, the initial selection of a potential reserve is often driven by the goal of protecting a whole set of ecosystems on the assumption that habitat for all of the taxa constituting these ecosystems will be protected (Hunter 1990). The particular needs of any one species are usually considered only if the species merits special attention (e.g., it is endangered or has unusual ecological, social, or economic value). Occasionally amphibians will be one of the special species that drive reserve selection (e.g., the Houston toad, *Bufo houstonensis,* Texas), but these are the exception.

Turning to reserve design—primarily deciding where to place the boundaries of a reserve—the key drivers are usually major natural boundaries like shorelines, watersheds, and the borders of ecosystems, and anthropogenic boundaries like property lines, roads, and utility corridors. In the best-case scenario, a reserve system would encompass a range of elevational, geological, and hydrological gradients and thus be more likely to capture the diversity of amphibian fauna in a given region (Hunter et al. 1988). For example, in the U.S. Pacific Northwest, Wilkins and Peterson (2000) found that habitat selection of headwater amphibian species was strongly influenced by landform characteristics, including basin lithology. Unfortunately, reserve design is not always primarily driven by ecological principles; often reserves encompass lands that are least arable or habitable by humans. Inevitably, these designs will not adequately conserve amphibian populations.

Reserve designers also commonly address the issue of encompassing enough habitat to support viable populations of certain species and assuring that there is some form of ecological connectivity that will allow these species to move among different reserves. These focal taxa are usually wide-ranging species that require large areas, such as the migratory ungulates of the African savannas or large carnivores, not nonvagile species like amphibians. However, it is now widely understood that not all amphibian species have a metapopulation structure because of their ties to patchy breeding habitat and that this necessitates addressing their conservation at a landscape scale (Semlitsch 2000a; Marsh and Trenham 2001). This means that reserves designed to protect amphibians with a metapopulation structure must incorporate habitat for breeding, foraging, and seasonal dormancy, all in a configuration that allows movement among habitat types and among subpopulations. These movements are critical to maintaining genetic diversity, both within and among populations that have been shown to merit conservation concern (Kimberling et al. 1996; Bridges and Semlitsch 2001). In large reserves ($\geqslant$10,000 ha) designed to protect entire landscapes and their wide-ranging mammals and birds, these needs of amphibians will probably be met almost inevitably. In more modest-sized reserves, we should not make that assumption, and amphibian habitat needs could become a major design factor. The feasibility of addressing amphibian conservation concerns at the reserve level is demonstrated in the Ambohitantely Reserve in Madagascar where Vallan (2000) investigated the size distribution of forest patches, vegetation structure, and array of wetlands necessary to support amphibian populations.

The interface between amphibian conservation and reserves is most likely to come to the fore after the reserve has been created and must be managed. In theory, reserve management is quite easy; you just "guard the gate and let nature take its course." In practice, it can be extremely challenging. Common issues for reserve managers include controlling human visitors and exotics, as well as invasive native species released from limiting factors (see Chapters 9 and 15, this volume). Managing natural phenomena such as overabundant native species, fires, and floods is probably more difficult because it leads reserve managers into philosophical controversies surrounding the question of what is natural. Managing beaver as wetland engineers rather than as pests may contribute to expanding amphibian habitat, for example, depending on one's assessment of "natural."

Special opportunities for reserve management arise when reserves or other public lands encompass degraded natural systems. In these cases, specific proactive management may promote amphibian conservation, including restoration of breeding and terrestrial habitats and the connections between them. In particular, removing nonnative fish populations could recreate amphibian habitat in many reserves where these fish have eradicated native amphibians. Eradication of trout in a lake in a protected area of California's Sierra Nevada range has resulted in an increase in the population of mountain yellow-legged frogs (*Rana muscosa;* Knapp and Matthews 2000). Carp (*Cyprinus carpio*) control, coupled with other habitat restoration measures, have resulted in the recovery of amphibians species in a marsh system owned by the Royal Botanical Gardens near Hamilton, Ontario (Royal Botanical Gardens 1998).

INTEGRATION SCENARIO

It is sobering to think that the most dramatic examples of amphibian declines in the past two decades have occurred in reserves or relatively pristine areas (e.g., the golden toad, *Bufo periglens,* in Costa Rica, the corroboree frog, *Pseudophryne corroboree,* in Australia, and the western toad, *Bufo boreas,* in the U.S. Rocky Mountains). Clearly, reserves can only partially address the conservation needs of amphibians when human activities create stresses that transcend boundaries. Consequently, managing ecosystems for amphibian conservation requires addressing activities in human-dominated landscapes outside of the reserves.

Much of the earth's surface could be described as seminatural; it is covered by lands and waters that are free of major human enterprises such as cities and croplands, but it is too extensively used to warrant the adjective "natural." Forests managed for timber, grasslands managed for livestock forage, and aquatic ecosystems used for fisheries are three major examples. Historically, we can identify four phases in our use of these ecosystems, starting with an early period when human impact was curbed by small populations and limited technology. With the industrial revolution and burgeoning populations came a second phase of rampant overexploitation. In the third phase, we learn how to sustainably use the commodity in demand. In phase four, we hope to have learned how to balance our commodity use with other values provided by an ecosystem, such as biodiversity and recreational opportunities. Looking around the world, we can readily find examples of all four phases, but among terrestrial ecosystems of industrialized nations, the sustainable-use phase tends to dominate. With care and intelligence we can move into the fourth phase, but it is not an easy undertaking.

In this section we will discuss how to make this shift with an eye on integrating amphibian conservation with managing ecosystems for three commodities: timber, livestock forage, and fish.

Timber and Forest Ecosystems

Although most people do not associate forests with amphibians, amphibians are the most abundant vertebrate group in many forest ecosystems (Burton and Likens 1975; Hairston 1987; Welsh and Droege 2001). As such, they may be key players in forest ecosystem dynamics (Wyman 1998). It is easy for forest managers to overlook this group because amphibians spend most days hidden from view under leaf litter or logs, or in subterranean burrows—a habit that belies their importance to forest ecosystems. Consider two facts: most amphibians spend all or part of their lives in forests and most forests are used for timber production. It is apparent that there is enormous scope for exploring the interface between timber management and amphibian conservation. Indeed, this topic has spawned a fair amount of research that we will summarize here based on a review article by deMaynadier and Hunter (1995) and more recent literature.

The clearest message that emerges from the existing literature on the effects of timber management on amphibians is that clearcuts have a strong negative impact on the abundance of many amphibian species, especially salamanders (e.g., Means et al. 1996; Mitchell et al. 1997). Research on the effect of alternative harvesting methods (such as group selection cuts) on amphibians is limited but suggests that these too may have negative consequences for amphibians commensurate with their alteration of key microsite variables, including soil moisture and temperature, availability of coarse woody debris, and litter depth and composition (Pough et al. 1987; Harpole and Haas 1999). To date, research has addressed short-term effects on population densities, although any effects on reproduction might not be manifested for several years in the population densities of long-lived species. It is also unclear how long it takes for the amphibian community to recover from the effects of harvesting through immigration or reproduction; estimates range from 30 to 60 years (Pough et al. 1987; Bonin 1991; Petranka et al. 1993; Ash 1997). Further complicating the management picture, amphibian species differ in dispersal and colonization abilities, risk of local extinction, and sensitivity to habitat fragmentation and disturbance (Marsh and Trenham 2001). For example, some authorities speculate that if an amphibian species is negatively affected by even slight canopy disturbances, then clearcutting may be the harvesting method of choice because a smaller area is affected for the same amount of timber (fewer roads, single entry; Harpole and Haas 1999).

Some general management guidelines will facilitate conservation of amphibians, regardless of species, in forests managed for timber production:

1. Forest managers should severely limit their use of clearcuts, with the possible exception of certain forest types (e.g., boreal forests) in which clearcutting can be designed as a rough approximation of the large-scale, fairly frequent disturbances that characterize these forests (Hunter 1993).

2. Mature forest stands should be conserved in the landscape because they have the greatest potential for maintaining the richness and abundance of native amphibian populations. They are more likely than disturbed forests to have cool, moist forest floors with ample coarse woody debris for amphibian cover, as well as foraging and breeding microhabitats (Mitchell et al. 1997).

3. Species generally associated with older forests may persist in young stands and should be specifically managed to maintain key microsite features such as ample leaf litter and coarse woody debris of various size and decay classes (Pough et al. 1987; deMaynadier and Hunter 1995).

4. Plantations may be detrimental to amphibian species and should be balanced with other types of management. Existing literature suggests that coarse woody debris, nonacidic soils, shrub abundance, and leaf litter are important variables in predicting amphibian diversity in some areas and may be limiting factors in conifer plantations (deMaynadier and Hunter 1995; Hartley 2002). The decline of the flatwoods salamander (*Ambystoma cingulatum*), now rare and being considered for official listing as an endangered species, is an example of a decline driven by conversion of natural forest structure (long-leaf pine [*Pinus palustris*]–

wire grass savannah) to bedded plantations of slash pine (*Pinus elliottii;* Means et al. 1996).

5. The long-term survival of amphibians in aquatic breeding sites requires management of terrestrial habitats to maintain connectivity between breeding sites and nonbreeding habitats, and also as nonbreeding habitat. Juvenile and adult pond-breeding amphibians may travel hundreds of meters from breeding pools (Mitchell et al. 1997; Semlitsch 1998; Chapter 2, this volume); in fact, they may travel farther to nonbreeding terrestrial habitats than they do to other wetlands (Marsh and Trenham 2001).

6. Forest managers should avoid operating in wetlands with saturated soils, standing water, or discrete pools. Rutting or compaction in saturated soils can destroy soil structure. Operating in woodland pools can alter the pool's water-holding capacity and chemistry and disturb eggs or larvae buried in the organic layer. Harvesting operations in the pool, even during the winter, can disturb woody vegetation that may serve as egg attachment sites or provide shading. Excess slash and treetops in the pool basin can hinder amphibian movement and alter water chemistry (Calhoun and deMaynadier 2002). Buffers should be maintained around these wetlands sufficient to maintain water quality and to support nutrient cycling (i.e., buffer for sediment and erosion control, litter input, and shading).

7. Riparian zones should be left intact to support stream-dwelling amphibians, including riparian areas of headwater streams (Brinson 1993; Dupuis and Steventon 1999).

8. Following best management practices for sediment and erosion control, road construction, and adhering to existing riparian buffer zone regulations are a step in the right direction, but additional measures will increase the likelihood of conserving amphibians (see Chapter 3, this volume).

A tool for codifying the guidelines addressed above may be the development of best management practices (i.e., guidelines for ecologically sensitive forestry) specific to amphibians or other wildlife. Most best management practices address water quality issues associated with road building and control of sediment from harvesting operations (Ellefson et al. 2001).

These general guidelines are just that—general. More research is needed on species-specific responses to different forest management practices and differential responses within species across their geographic range. Ecologically sensitive management should benefit all flora and fauna, except in instances where rare species require specific management practices.

Livestock Forage and Grassland and Shrubland Ecosystems

The aridity of most natural grasslands and shrublands often concentrates amphibian fauna around rivers, streams, or ponds. Herpetofauna in these areas may be more diverse than in adjacent ecosystems (Godreau et al. 1999; Raxworthy and Attuquayefio 2000). Unfortunately, livestock often gravitate toward these areas too because of the availability of water and superior forage. Consequently, riparian zone management is likely to be the key to maintaining amphibian populations in these ecosystems.

In Europe, biodiversity in riparian grasslands has declined owing to such practices as river channelization and embankment, agricultural intensification, and floodplain drainage and fertilization (Godreau et al. 1999); these practices are also common in other parts of the world (Dugan 1993). Riparian management in an agricultural context is discussed below under the "Impact Minimization Scenario."

In rare cases, grazing may be used as a management tool to halt or slow succession when natural controls (such as wild herbivores, natural fire regimes) have been extirpated or suppressed. The recovery program for Britain's endangered natterjack toad (*Bufo calamita*), which is dependent on coastal sand dunes, salt marshes, and inland heaths for foraging and hibernation, is a good example (Denton et al. 1997). Historically, populations of toads were maintained in early successional dunes (maintained by wind) and heaths (maintained by rabbits and other wild herbivores). Populations increased as a result of low-density grazing of sheep and cattle during the nineteenth century. With the decline in grazing, the introduction of aggressive exotic shrub and tree species, and the degradation or destruction of ephemeral breeding pools came a dramatic decline in the natterjack toad. The current recovery program includes restoring early successional systems through low-density grazing, creating or restoring breeding pools, and reintroducing toads to historical breeding grounds. This example illustrates an extreme case of a landscape managed for recovery of a species that may historically have been maintained at higher population levels through anthropogenic activities that mimicked successional processes. Livestock have also been used to manage wildlife in grasslands in the western United States (Kie and Loft 1990).

The perennial challenge to land managers is deciding what the desirable condition of a given ecosystem is and which species should be managed in that ecosystem.

Fish and Aquatic Ecosystems

The simple fact that fish need water for their habitat and so do most species of amphibians (at least during breeding) creates some important points of convergence and divergence between the interests of fisheries managers and amphibian conservationists. The good news is that any efforts to maintain the quality and quantity of water in aquatic ecosystems (e.g., constructing sewage treatment facilities and restoring natural hydrological regimes) are likely to benefit both amphibians and fish. On the other hand, large populations of fish mean large populations of potential predators from the perspective of many amphibians (Chapter 9, this volume). Although fish predation on amphibians may not be detrimental to amphibian populations when it involves naturally occurring fish populations (Townsend 1996; Gillespie 2001; Knapp et al. 2001), far too often, ambitious fisheries managers have moved fish to waterbodies where they do not belong. Sometimes these are exotics from another region; sometimes they are local species that have been moved to places they could not colonize naturally (e.g., a pond isolated by a waterfall). Perhaps the most egregious examples involve trout, introduced worldwide to innumerable lakes and rivers for sport fishing. They have compromised populations of riverine frogs in southeastern Australia (Gillespie 2001), pond-breeding amphibians in Ontario, Canada (Hecnar and M'Closkey 1997b), amphibians in high-elevation lakes in Spain (Brana et al. 1996), and anurans in the western United States (Knapp and Mathews 2000). Trout may even be indirectly responsible for the disappearance of amphibians from trout-free waters owing to isolation of frog populations and restriction of populations to marginal habitats (Knapp and Mathews 2000). Fisheries managers also face the problem of pathogens introduced to amphibians from exotic fish (sport fish or aquarium fish; Laurane et al. 1996; Kiesecker et al. 2001c).

The bottom line is that the integration of fisheries management and amphibian conservation will often require fisheries managers to cease moving fish to new waterbodies and to consider eliminating some existing fish populations. For an in-depth discussion of management of invasive species in aquatic ecosystems, see Chapter 9, this volume.

IMPACT MINIMIZATION SCENARIO

Can amphibians persist in human-created landscapes such as agricultural lands and suburban developments? Can we manage these landscapes for amphibian conservation without creating biological sinks? We would offer a guarded "Yes" to both questions. We may not be able to maintain populations of the most sensitive species, yet some species will persist in the short term, and potentially in the long term. We also recognize at least two indirect benefits of managing such landscapes with an eye toward a "kinder, gentler" environment for amphibians:

- Environmental conditions that support amphibians are beneficial for humans; amphibians may suffer detrimental effects of environmental degradation sooner than humans and serve as our "canary in the mine." Almost all species benefit from reduced use of agrochemicals and suburban chemicals, reduced sedimentation of waterbodies, and preservation of wetlands and natural corridors or greenways.

• Conserving amphibians in suburban settings helps maintain the already tenuous connection between suburban/urban dwellers and the natural world, which includes amphibians. Raising our young without frogs seems like a recipe for environmental apathy further feeding the growing alienation of the public from nature. It is extremely difficult to educate the public if they have had no first-hand experience with the ecosystems or species we are trying to conserve, particularly if our focus is an inconspicuous, slimy species (Chapter 16, this volume). Connections such as these can be turned into support for conservation initiatives.

Minimizing Effects on Agricultural Lands

Agricultural lands dominate landscapes in many regions of the world, and they are changing rapidly. Family farms with a mosaic of pastureland, farm ponds, woodlots, and cropland are being replaced by intensive agriculture, especially in Europe and North America (Joly et al. 2001). With intensive agriculture comes degradation of water quality (49% of total nonpoint source pollution in the United States is attributed to agriculture; Schuler and Briggs 2000) and loss of riparian corridors (more than 80% of the riparian corridor area of North America and Europe has disappeared in the last 200 years; Naiman et al. 1993). This bleak picture is being brightened by recent policy initiatives and planning strategies that reflect a changed perception of sustainable agriculture. The goal has shifted from just maintaining a crop to managing cropping systems that are ecologically sustainable. For example, agricultural policies in Switzerland provide financial incentives to encourage farmers to maintain biological diversity (e.g., organic farming, grassland cultivation, and integrated production; Hehl-Lange 2001). In the United States, the government no longer subsidizes farmers who destroy wetlands associated with their agricultural lands (Food Security Act [Farm Bill] as amended by PL 101-624). The Common Agricultural Policy of the European Union and the Ministry of Agriculture in the Czech Republic support managing landscapes for multiple uses. For example, they encourage maintenance of traditional settlements in the landscape, intensification in highly productive lands, and creation of ecological networks in less desirable agricultural land. Ultimate goals include an overall reduction in agricultural acreage and use of chemicals, and establishment of a network of ecological areas (Jongman 1995). There is a tremendous opportunity here for conservation biologists to provide guidance in further developing these planning strategies, including consideration of amphibian habitat requirements.

Farms that maintain combined cropland, forests, and pasture (as opposed to intensive cropping) can support some amphibians. The potential for ranches and dairy farms to support herpetofauna—and to improve management practices for those species that are even less resilient—has been documented (Meshaka 1997; Jones et al. 2000). For example, management of pesticide and fire regimes, grazing intensity, and ditch maintenance (time and frequency of dredging, water quality, nutrient regimes in adjacent fields) can maximize natural amphibian diversity (Twisk et al. 2000).

Most of the literature on amphibian conservation in agricultural landscapes focuses on maintaining riparian zones. A key question is: Are the buffer widths and structure recommended for maintaining stream water quality (Karr 1991; Twery and Hornbeck 2001) or for supporting bird communities (Spackman and Hughes 1995) sufficient to maintain populations of stream-dwelling or pond-breeding amphibians? Riparian zone management presents the recurring challenge that landscapes and their attendant processes will vary depending on the setting and the species in question. Riparian zones may function as travel corridors or they may satisfy some or all the life-history needs of some species (see Chapter 3, this volume). In the first scenario, riparian zones act as connections between habitat patches, thus supporting metapopulation dynamics (dispersal, colonization, gene flow). Bridges and Semlitsch (2001) suggest that populations may be more likely to adapt to environmental stressors, including agricultural pesticides, if genetic variability is maintained by providing connectivity. In the second scenario, riparian areas serve as amphibian habitat. Maisonneuve and Rioux (2001) tested the hypothesis that populations of crop pest species (insects, birds, mammals) were reduced in grassy riparian zones. They found that the proportion and abundance of mammalian pest species diminished with complexity of vegetation structure, whereas the abundance of herpetofauna species increased; herpetofaunal diversity was highest in shrubby strips. To maintain amphibian diversity, riparian zone management must focus on vegetation structure and the presence of key habitat elements (ephemeral pools or upland forest) rather than standardized widths. Furthermore, knowledge of the natural-history requirements of target species should guide riparian-zone design (Burbink et al. 1998).

Some sophisticated approaches to managing agricultural landscapes with ecological sensitivity are emerging and at least two of them use amphibians as model taxa. In northeastern Germany, a decision-support system for optimizing farm income under defined restrictions for nature conservation has been developed (Meyer-Aurich et al. 1998). The model is based on the temporal overlap between periods of amphibian migration and periods of disturbing activities (e.g., application of pesticides and fertilizers) associated with different crops. In a watershed of Lake Lauerz, Switzerland, landscape visualization and geographic information system modeling tools were used to predetermine landscape elements critical for conserving various taxa. The common toad (*Bufo bufo*) was used to represent five species of endangered amphibian (Hehl-Lange 2001).

Minimizing Effects in Suburban Developments

Suburban development presents an even greater challenge to amphibian conservation because often the matrix is impermeable surfaces (e.g., asphalt, concrete), and habitat patches are isolated and intersected by roads. The effects of roads and urbanization on amphibian dispersal and abundance (Gibbs 1998a; Lehtinen et al. 1999) and the correlation between isolation effects or urbanization and genetic divergence (Reh and Seitz 1990; Hitchings and Beebee 1997; Gibbs 1998b; Skelly et al. 1999) are well known. Amphibian conservation strategies in suburbia should include an inventory of resources (both habitat availability and species). The next step is to prioritize areas of potential conservation value; for example, areas with some intact terrestrial and wetland ecosystems and opportunities for restoring adjacent ecosystems. In some cases, "hands-on" management of populations may be necessary and desirable. For example, translocating individuals may be more practical, and successful, than establishing connectivity (Marsh and Trenham 2001). Maintaining amphibians in human-developed landscapes will require proactive management, especially conserving wetlands, maintaining connectivity among habitat patches, and integrating these areas into the urban planning process. Principles for conserving amphibians in suburban landscapes will mirror those already discussed for forestry or agriculture (for example, maintaining connections among breeding and nonbreeding habitats, conserving wetlands, and managing lands adjacent to wetlands). Some additional issues in suburban contexts include:

- Maintaining hydrology of existing wetlands.
- Extirpating exotic species.
- Controlling subsidized predators such as raccoons (*Procyon lotor*), skunks (*Mephitis mephitis*), and feral cats (domestic cats as well) that may prey on amphibians.
- Reducing salt and pesticide applications (homeowners, public lands, road maintenance) near sensitive areas, especially wetlands and open waterbodies.
- Educating the public. For example, manicured lake shores devoid of pond weeds and park-like forests are not beneficial to wildlife (Tilton 1995).
- Using planning tools and guidelines already available. For example, many guidelines or best management practices are available for maintaining water quality and more are becoming available that address managing habitat for various taxa in developing landscapes (Meyer-Aurich et al. 1998; Braune and Wood 1999).

CONCLUSION

The key challenges for people who wish to manage ecosystems for amphibian conservation include balancing human needs with those of amphibians (and other taxa), and communicating to the public that maintaining biodiversity is directly related to the long-term well-being of humans. In some cases, managing to benefit amphibians will not result in monetary loss or other sacrifices and these decisions will meet with little resistance; however, in other cases, real sacrifices will have to be made. For example, reserves and other protected ecosystems still tend to be on the least productive or least accessible lands rather than in highly productive areas (e.g., with fertile soils and benign microclimates). To meet these challenges, conservationists must capitalize on the good will of an educated public raised with first-hand knowledge of amphibians, wetlands, and the beauty of undeveloped landscapes.

ACKNOWLEDGMENTS

We thank Ray Semlitsch and two anonymous reviewers for their useful input. Support was, in part, provided by the USDA National Research Initiative Competitive Grants Program and Maine Audubon Society. This is Maine Agricultural and Forest Experiment Station Paper No. 2581.

18

A FOUNDATION FOR CONSERVATION
AND MANAGEMENT OF AMPHIBIANS

RAYMOND D. SEMLITSCH AND BETSIE B. ROTHERMEL

CENTRAL ISSUES

At present, there is no unifying framework for efforts to conserve amphibians. Because amphibians are vulnerable to environmental stressors and because many possess a biphasic life cycle, they face unique challenges in a changing world. Those management and recovery strategies currently applied are typically based on experience with other taxa, often drawn from general knowledge of both amphibians and reptiles, and are not necessarily tested or biologically based. Further, we lack adequate data to evaluate management and recovery practices. There also may be conflicts between current management practices for game species such as waterfowl and those needed for amphibians. Amphibians are not given the same priority, nor are they assigned the same value, as other nongame species, despite their importance as prey and in overall ecosystem functioning. We need a general framework for amphibian conservation efforts that incorporates social, political, and economic realities but is biologically based. Finally, it is clear that we cannot take a preservationist's perspective and simply protect all land from human use. Rather, we must develop new ways to balance land use with the ecological requirements of amphibians.

INTRODUCTION

Before investing heavily in strategies to conserve amphibians, conservation organizations may be justified in asking whether amphibian-specific initiatives are truly needed or if amphibian conservation is secured by existing conservation practices and models. We believe the answer lies between these two extremes. Certain features of amphibian life history and population structure are different enough from rep-

242

tiles, mammals, and other taxa that they warrant special consideration and often require separate conservation actions. There is already some momentum in this direction with increasing public awareness of amphibian declines, greater attention to nongame conservation, and movement away from single-species management toward a more holistic, ecosystem-based and landscape-level approach. In this chapter, we discuss the biological features of amphibians that dictate changes in existing management practices, the ecological processes that are essential to maintaining amphibian populations, and critical elements for effective conservation.

BIOLOGICAL BASIS FOR CONSERVATION STRATEGIES

One of the key features of all amphibians, and one that distinguishes them from other vertebrates, is their strong dependence on moisture to maintain hydration and for reproduction. Most other vertebrates have thick skin that protects them from water loss (i.e., reptiles, birds, mammals) or they are fully aquatic (i.e., fish). For terrestrial amphibians with direct development, such as plethodontid salamanders, this requirement usually is satisfied by using cool and moist habitats, and by restricting surface activity to cool seasons or wet, rainy nights. Terrestrial breeders often deposit eggs in caves, in rotten logs, or deep underground, where eggs and young are well protected from harsh, drying conditions. Most other amphibians require both aquatic and terrestrial habitats for completion of their life cycle. Amphibians with complex life cycles usually migrate to and from wetlands to breed. Most temperate species fit this pattern, having eggs and larvae that develop in pools, ponds, or streams. In other species, however, adults are completely terrestrial and only the larvae develop in the water (e.g., tadpoles of some tropical species drop into pools or streams after hatching or are carried to water by the parent). Obligate use of aquatic and terrestrial habitats likely exposes amphibians to a greater variety of anthropogenic stressors than is experienced by most birds or mammals. In addition, such requirements restrict the range of habitats that can be used and times when activity can occur, as well as dictate the level of habitat alteration or disturbance that can be tolerated.

Amphibians possess a variety of reproductive modes (Duellman and Trueb 1994) encompassing direct and indirect development, viviparous and ovoviviparous reproduction, internal and external fertilization, parental care or not, and large versus small clutch sizes. The range of approaches to reproduction in amphibians exceeds that found in other groups of vertebrates, and hence dictates a broader range of management considerations. Certain traits especially constrain the ability of some species to tolerate anthropogenic stresses or to recover from low population sizes. For example, the lack of parental care in most species makes eggs and young highly susceptible to predation and habitat alteration. Small plethodontid salamanders with direct development have maternal care but often reproduce at irregular intervals (i.e., not annually) and have small clutch sizes (usually <10 ova; see Table 1 in Herbeck and Semlitsch 2000), making rapid population growth difficult and recovery slow relative to many ranid frogs that can produce thousands of ova each year (e.g., 50,000 for American bullfrogs). Even species that produce large numbers of eggs usually have low average annual recruitment due to high larval mortality (>95%) and irregular bouts of reproduction.

The limited migration and orientation ability of amphibians in terrestrial habitats is another feature that differs from other vertebrates. Amphibians are small and relatively nonvagile compared with mammals and birds. Studies documenting interpopulation dispersal in pond-breeding amphibians indicate that adults exhibit low dispersal rates and a high degree of fidelity to the site where they first reproduce (Oldham 1966; Breden 1987; Berven and Grudzien 1990; Sinsch and Seidel 1995). Most populations are likely concentrated within 200 to 300 m of breeding ponds (e.g., Semlitsch 1998), although groups of these local populations may be linked by occasional dispersal, forming larger metapopulations (e.g., Gill 1978). Amphibians cannot migrate long distances due to physiological constraints. The physiological demands of ectothermy and hydration restrict activity to seasons of the year that are neither too hot nor too cold, and to times of the day (i.e., night-time) when risk of desiccation is minimal. Such restricted activity limits their access to different habitats and their ability to escape threats such as habitat destruction and chemical contamination. In addition, amphibians are relatively limited in their perceptual ability (i.e., ability to search out and detect potential habitat from a distance).

Whereas mammals, birds, and reptiles are capable of true navigation, amphibians generally are restricted to simple compass orientation and piloting mechanisms (Sinsch 1990). Newts of the genus *Notophthalmus* are an apparent exception, having demonstrated true navigational ability using the earth's magnetic field (Phillips et al. 1995), raising the possibility that other amphibians may also have this ability. The question of reduced navigational ability is important because it may strongly influence habitat choice and the success of dispersal to new sites. For example, frogs cannot efficiently search for new habitats because they lack the ability to detect distant ponds in an unfamiliar landscape. Because adults rarely switch breeding sites (e.g., Gill 1978; Breden 1987; Berven and Grudzien 1990), in most species, new sites are likely found by chance and colonized by wandering juveniles. It is important that these and other unique features of amphibians be incorporated into conservation or management plans.

ECOLOGICAL PROCESSES TO CONSIDER IN MANAGEMENT

Restoration of early successional vegetation by low-level grazing was a key step in conserving populations of the natterjack toad (*Bufo calamita;* Denton et al. 1997). Natural and anthropogenic processes, including succession, hydrology, stochastic events (e.g., fire, floods, and drought), habitat fragmentation, spread of disease, and spread of nonnative species, affect the availability and stability of amphibian habitats and therefore the persistence of amphibian populations. It is also important to understand the effects of a given process on population dynamics, which processes are most important for a particular region or taxonomic group, the interactions among processes, and the effects of humans on natural processes. Although we know these processes are important, it is often difficult to determine the historical frequency and extent of natural disturbances, and whether that regime is now compatible with current land-use practices.

Natural Processes

For aquatic species using either wetlands or streams, hydrology is a primary determinant of habitat availability, breeding phenology, and reproductive success. For example, the timing of breeding migrations and courtship is usually highly synchronized with the filling of ephemeral wetlands (Semlitsch et al. 1993). This filling of ephemeral wetlands usually coincides with winter snow melt, spring rains, or tropical rainy seasons. Drying is also a natural process in wetlands that occurs during the warmest season, usually mid-to-late summer. Amphibians are well adapted to these cycles, thus the maintenance of natural seasonal hydrological cycles in a region is critical to successful reproduction and recruitment of young into the adult population (Semlitsch et al. 1996). Ditching, draining, groundwater withdrawal for irrigation, and other human activities that disrupt the filling process or shorten the hydroperiod of breeding sites can have severe negative effects on reproductive success and the maintenance of populations. In river systems, natural hydrological processes such as groundwater and over-bank flow connect river and riparian habitats and provide habitat complexity through hydraulic erosion and deposition (Galat et al. 1998; Bodie 2001). Wetlands that result from these processes vary in hydroperiod from permanent to ephemeral depending on their distance from and connection to the river. Maintaining this variety of riparian wetlands helps to maintain species diversity.

Successional change occurs in both aquatic and terrestrial environments as vegetation grows and the plant community proceeds through a series of stages to mature forest or other "climax" communities. Amphibians favor different stages as the vegetation in these habitats changes. Some species require mature, closed-canopy forests that provide a cool, moist microclimate and coarse woody debris for cover (e.g., plethodontid and ambystomatid salamanders). Other species require early successional stages of aquatic and terrestrial habitats dominated by grasses and open habitat with ponds exposed to full sunlight (e.g., natterjack toad; spadefoots, *Scaphiopus*). Vegetational succession strongly influences the species composition of amphibian communities (Skelly et al. 1999) and, if allowed to proceed, increases the probability of extinction of early successional species (e.g., Denton et al. 1997). The establishment of trees in wetland basins increases water transpiration and reduces light for primary production by closing the canopy. Large regions of the northeastern United States may be experiencing species declines due to the succession of former agricultural lands to mature hardwood forests (i.e., perhaps more representative of presettlement times), especially the closing of canopy over breeding ponds (Skelly et al. 1999).

The persistence of amphibians sometimes depends on changes in the habitat brought about by other native species. Burrowing animals, such as tortoises and small mammals, provide underground refuges for some amphibians (e.g., gopher frog, *Rana capito*) inhabiting hot, xeric environments. The American bison (*Bison bison*) and the American alligator (*Alligator mississippiensis*) are responsible for creating and maintaining aquatic habitats (i.e., wallows and gator holes) in some regions. These habitats may serve as important breeding sites and refuges for amphibians during periods of drought (Gerlanc 1999). Few native species have had such a strong influence on amphibian habitat as the beaver (*Castor canadensis;* e.g., Metts et al. 2001). Beavers regularly build dams and remove trees along streams, thereby creating wetland habitats in various stages of succession. Thus, they are an important biotic factor to consider in historical patterns of species abundance and distribution, and also in current conservation efforts. Although historically widespread over North America, their numbers were reduced dramatically and they were eliminated in parts of their range due to trapping for their fur. Only in the last 40 to 50 years have their numbers recovered to the point of being common in the landscape. Beaver-created wetlands are especially important to amphibians that require lentic aquatic habitats in areas not rich in other forms of isolated wetlands (e.g., montane or nonglaciated regions). Beaver ponds and vernal pools are temporary over geological time, so new breeding sites become available as beavers abandon old sites. Their importance for amphibians is illustrated by the development of a "beaver pond" metapopulation model for red-spotted newts (*Notophthalmus viridescens*) that relates observed dispersal rates and recolonization dynamics of newts to beaver pond succession and loss (Gill 1978).

Disturbance and Stochastic Events

Certain processes that are not seasonal but occur at irregular or unpredictable intervals also affect the persistence of amphibian populations, especially by creating new habitats across the landscape. Events such as droughts, floods, and landslides are each capable of reversing succession or creating new wetlands. Also, landslides, wind-throw, fire, and even tree pest or pathogen outbreaks are important disturbances affecting habitat structure and quality for fully terrestrial species like plethodontids. Blowdowns can create small, ephemeral pools that are used as oviposition sites by treefrogs, for example. Global climate change will affect the frequency, extent, and severity of many of these disturbances, with largely unpredictable consequences for amphibians (Donnelly and Crump 1998).

Severe flooding strongly affects hydrological processes in wetlands and also provides a powerful periodic regime of habitat fluctuation. The primary effects of severe floods of importance to amphibians are erosion or "scouring," which creates new wetlands, filling or sedimentation of old wetlands, and the reversal of vegetational succession. Amphibians are well adapted to these severe natural fluctuations, which occur at a low frequency relative to most human disturbances. In addition, such flooding helps create a diversity of habitats in the floodplain, including early successional aquatic habitats created by the removal of canopy trees.

Droughts also sometimes reverse vegetational succession by allowing wetlands to dry, thereby increasing the probability of wildfires. Fires eliminate the accumulated organic matter and woody plants and trees from the wetland basin. During extended droughts, even the most permanent wetlands may dry, eliminating fish predators and exposing deep sediments to oxidation processes that release nutrients. Many amphibians are adapted to skipping reproduction, instead remaining underground in the terrestrial habitat and emerging to reproduce whenever the drought ends and aquatic habitats refill.

Landslides may be an important process for creating new pools and small ponds in montane regions. Such pools are frequently colonized and used by newts (*Triturus alpestris*) in the Alps of Switzerland (R. Semlitsch, personal observation). Landslides are common in this and other areas with steep slopes, heavy precipitation, and thin soils.

Anthropogenic Processes

Since the time that humans began altering the landscape in many regions, our activities have modified natural processes and created new conditions that affect amphibian habitats and populations. Habitat fragmentation, hydrological manipulation, and introductions of nonnative species now occur so frequently and affect so many ecosystems that these processes must receive consideration. Further, these anthropogenic processes can mimic natural processes or interact with natural processes to drive the population dynamics of amphibians.

The conversion of once-continuous natural habitats to smaller patches can create landscapes that are no longer capable of sustaining amphibian populations. Landscape-level studies have shown that amphibian occurrence and species richness decline as habitat area decreases and habitat patches become increasingly isolated due to fragmentation (e.g., Laan and Verboom 1990; Gibbs 1998a; Koloszvary and Swihart 1999). Populations of pond-breeding species are centered on discrete sites such as vernal pools, bogs, fens, limestone sinks, and other ephemeral wetlands. If we consider these ponds as habitat patches, then loss of wetlands reduces the total number of ponds where amphibians can reproduce. Reducing the number of wetlands also reduces the total number of individual amphibians available to found new populations or reestablish extirpated populations. Further, a reduction in pond density across the landscape changes the spatial configuration of remaining ponds. Reduced pond density increases the distance between neighboring ponds, thereby decreasing the probability of recolonization for species that exist as metapopulations (Brown and Kodric-Brown 1977; Gibbs 1993; Semlitsch and Bodie 1998). Occasional dispersal is the critical factor that maintains ecological connectivity among subpopulations in a metapopulation (Hanski and Gilpin 1991a; Sjogren 1991), some of which might face permanent extinction in the absence of immigrants from nearby source populations (Pulliam 1988). A species' sensitivity to habitat fragmentation is a function not only of degree of site fidelity and dispersal ability, but of the degree to which the matrix habitat (e.g., agricultural, urban) between remaining habitats acts as a barrier to movement (i.e., landscape resistance; Ricketts 2001; Rothermel and Semlitsch 2002). In addition, the edge between two habitat types may be relatively impermeable to individuals of some species if they exhibit behavioral avoidance at habitat boundaries (Stamps et al. 1987; Haddad 1999).

In moderately fragmented landscapes, large tracts of habitat remain and the most important effect of fragmentation may simply be the loss of habitat rather than isolation. Gibbs (1998b) found that terrestrial eastern red-backed salamanders (*Plethodon cinereus*), for example, persisted even in highly fragmented landscapes. This could be because the fragmentation was not severe enough to disrupt metapopulation dynamics, which (if they occur) are likely operating at smaller spatial and longer temporal scales for plethodontids than for pond-breeding amphibians. Alternatively, the severity of edge effects could prove to be the most important factor limiting populations of terrestrial-breeding amphibians in fragmented landscapes. If habitat quality within small patches were severely degraded due to edge effects, then small patches would act as sinks regardless of the rate of influx of individuals dispersing from other patches.

In floodplain habitats, the human modification of river hydrology also exacerbates the problem of fragmentation. Most large rivers have been modified for hydropower, commercial navigation, and agriculture through the creation of reservoirs, navigation channels and locks, and levees (U.S. Army Corps of Engineers 2000), and natural hydrological cycles are usually severely disrupted (Galat et al. 1998). Upland forested habitats (i.e., nonflooded macrotopographic features) in the floodplain are essential for feeding and overwintering of amphibians. Disruption of connectivity among habitat fragments and interactions with adjacent habitats (aquatic and terrestrial) are key to understanding the impacts of human activities on life history events such as oviposition, hatching, and metamorphosis (e.g., Lind et al. 1996).

Last, the factors influencing the spread and effect of nonnative species and infectious diseases must be considered important factors in management plans (Chapters 9, 10, and 11, this volume). Invasive species must either be regulated, such as by preventing the introduction of invasives (Chapters 9 and 15, this volume), or, potentially, be controlled by restoring natural ecological processes. For example, allowing the natural drying of wetlands may purge aquatic habitats of invasive species (e.g.,

American bullfrog, *Rana catesbeiana*) that cannot tolerate fluctuating conditions or pond drying as well as ranids native to the western United States. Conversely, the spread of invasive species may be facilitated by certain practices such as roadbuilding. The cane toad (*Bufo marinus*) used roadways as it dispersed rapidly across Australia (Alford and Richards 1999). Invasion by nonnative species is a factor that has been frequently cited in listings of declining amphibian species in the western United States (e.g., California red-legged frog, *Rana aurora draytonii*). Further, regulations to control the spread of disease in amphibian populations are probably necessary (Chapters 10 and 11, this volume). Two important pathways for the spread of disease that should be targeted for regulation are the release of infected pets and the stocking of infected fish into breeding habitats of amphibians.

ESSENTIAL MANAGEMENT ELEMENTS

If our conservation goal is to maintain or enhance present levels of amphibian diversity, then we must incorporate several critical elements into current management plans. Amphibians, along with some birds, turtles, snakes, and insects, depend on the management of both terrestrial and aquatic ecosystems as well as critical natural processes. This necessitates managing at the landscape level for the quality and quantity of aquatic and terrestrial habitat to maintain viable populations and communities of amphibians. An important implication of amphibians' biological features and the ecological processes we have just discussed is that environmental stochasticity might play a much larger role than demographic stochasticity in determining the persistence of amphibian populations. Much of the work in conservation biology has been directed toward other taxa (birds, mammals) and has been based on the "small population paradigm" (Caughley 1994) that addresses the negative consequences of small population sizes such as inbreeding and extinction due to stochastic demographic factors. Such concerns may be of much less importance to amphibians, most of which have very high reproductive potential and high local densities. Factors like drought may have an effect long before a population becomes small enough for inbreeding to be a potential problem (but see Hitchings and Beebee 1997). Conservation of amphibians, therefore, may need to borrow not only from approaches aimed at other vertebrates but also from those for invertebrates (e.g., Murphy et al. 1990), because the latter tend to emphasize the environmental factors that influence population persistence.

Management of Wetlands

At the local population level, management of aquatic habitats should minimize effects (direct or indirect) on growth and survival of larvae. An obvious remedy is to restrict chemical use, especially near pools, ditches, streams, and ponds. Consider the variety of harmful chemicals used along roadways, including herbicides and growth retardants to control weeds and woody vegetation, salt to eliminate ice, and chemicals to suppress dust on unpaved roads. In agricultural areas, consider the use and application of various pesticides and fertilizers (see Chapter 12, this volume). Sedimentation in aquatic habitats from permanent roads, temporary logging roads, and utility rights-of-way should be minimized to prevent harmful effects on eggs, embryos, and gilled larvae. Livestock use of riparian areas also contributes to increased sedimentation and degradation of water quality.

Management plans also should eliminate avenues of fish colonization, such as drainage ditches that connect fish-inhabited areas (streams or rivers) with amphibian breeding ponds. Restoring the hydrology of temporary wetlands will ensure that natural drying processes can work effectively to eliminate fish if they do invade. Elimination of other invasive species, such as exotic fish or bullfrog larvae, where they are not native may be accomplished by manipulated drying to promote successful metamorphosis of native species. In more permanent ponds or lakes, elimination of stocking practices, manual fish removal, and as a last resort, the use of chemicals such as rotenone may be needed to eliminate fish.

In regions where wetlands are routinely destroyed during development, compensatory wetland mitigation has become a widespread practice. For example, there are now approved wetland mitigation banks in 42 states in the United States (Environmental Law Institute 2001). The value of mitigated wetlands for amphibians depends on a variety of factors and in many cases could be enhanced if specific measures were taken to ensure colonization and habitat quality. For example, the amphibian species richness of restored wetlands is affected by distance to other existing wetlands that are sources of potential colonists (Lehtinen and Galatowitsch 2001). Alternatively, establishment of amphibian populations in newly created or restored wetlands can be accomplished by translocating eggs or larvae (e.g., Denton et al. 1997), but this is largely untested (Semlitsch 2002). Indeed, translocation may be required if existing breeding sites are going to be destroyed, if natural colonization is unlikely due to isolation, or if existing populations are small and limited geographically (Marsh and Trenham 2001; Pechmann et al. 2001). Of course, such efforts are futile if the new breeding sites are of poor quality (Semlitsch 2002), as often occurs with mitigated wetland sites. In most cases, mitigated wetlands have stable hydroperiods that do not replicate the hydrological variability of naturally occurring wetlands (National Research Council 2001). Further, mitigated wetlands often are not restored "in kind" or "one-for-one," but rather are constructed as one large wetland to offset the loss of many small wetlands. This "banking" practice lowers the density of wetlands and alters their spatial distribution across the landscape, thereby disrupting metapopulation dynamics of amphibians (e.g., Semlitsch and Bodie 1998). Thus, the potential utility of wetland mitigation projects for amphibians must be evaluated based on species' ecological requirements, including both local population success and metapopulation structure. With these caveats in mind, establishing new ponds has great potential for offsetting the increased rates of local extinctions brought about by anthropogenic stressors and habitat destruction.

Management of Terrestrial Habitats

Maintaining natural terrestrial habitats peripheral to wetlands is essential. Depending on the current state of those habitats in a particular management area or reserve system, plans should always try to maintain existing habitat along with any important natural processes of the region (e.g., hydrology, fire). To maintain the complete amphibian community in any region, it is essential to manage for a diversity of successional stages of both aquatic and terrestrial habitats at a frequency that mimics historical levels. Often the simplest approach is to preserve the natural processes that create early successional stages. In regions where fire is the natural process that reverses succession, however, safety and economic issues must be balanced with allowing wildfires to burn unchecked. In these regions, active management by controlled burns during the natural season of wildfires, light grazing by livestock, or periodic mowing may produce the desired outcome (e.g., Denton et al. 1997). However, too-frequent burning or burning during periods of terrestrial breeding migration (such as during the cool, wet, winter months in the southeastern United States), could have negative consequences for amphibians (Vogl 1973; Russell et al. 1999).

In reserve areas that have "total protection," plans should eliminate land-use practices that historically degraded terrestrial habitat surrounding breeding sites, such as intensive timber harvest, agriculture (including the periodic planting of food plots for game species or mowing), construction of buildings or utility lines, and site preparation (e.g., roads, herbicide use). Such practices will likely reduce the adult breeding population in the terrestrial environment surrounding ponds or along streams. Recent studies show that most amphibians must have access to specific feeding and overwintering habitats in terrestrial environments, often some distance from breeding sites (e.g., Madison 1997; Lamoureux and Madison 1999). Maintaining the maximum amount of terrestrial habitat will fully protect aquatic and core habitats of target species like salamanders (recommended 164 m from the edge of wetlands; Semlitsch 1998), and will provide buffers from edge effects (50 m; Murcia 1995) from surrounding land-use (Figure 18.1).

In lands where activities such as timber harvest, recreational use, and nongame management must be balanced, buffer zones should be maintained around wetlands or along streams to prevent sedimentation, and soil compaction and removal of coarse woody debris should be minimized (deMaynadier and Hunter 1995). Plans should maintain "buffer zones" of natural vegetation around ponds and along streams (Figure 18.1) that can be adjusted for stream width, slope, and site use (Rudolph and Dickson 1990; McComb et al. 1993; deMaynadier and Hunter 1995) to increase the

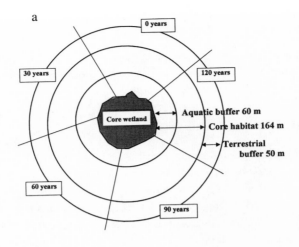

Figure 18.1. Proposed zones of protection and timber harvest scheme for isolated wetlands (a) and streams (b). Both core habitat and aquatic buffer requirements are met within the 164-m zone (Semlitsch and Jensen 2001). An additional 50-m buffer is recommended to protect core habitat from edge effects. Stands for timber harvest are indicated by lines drawn perpendicular to the protection zones. An example of potential harvest times are given (years to harvest) for each quadrant, but times should be modified according to local and regional forestry practices.

probability of species persistence. Creative management plans that distribute the disturbance in space or time around wetlands and streams, such as rotational harvesting of timber that leaves refuges for sources of colonists, will be most effective in maintaining local populations (Figure 18.1). Selectively cutting the whole area is not an ideal solution because it does not leave undisturbed refuges. Such a scheme of rotating land use that maintains undisturbed refuges could also be applied to grasslands and prairies subjected to burning or mowing practices.

Minimizing roads or motorized vehicle traffic near breeding sites will reduce the number of road-kills of breeding adults (Fahrig et al. 1995; Lamoureux and Madison 1999) and also reduce the loss of juveniles during the postmetamorphic dispersal period. Planners should redirect new roads away from wetlands and consider the use of culverts or tunnels under existing roads to channel amphibian movements at known concentration points near breeding ponds. Several tunnel projects in the United States and Europe suggest that such practices may be useful if migration paths across roads are clearly identified and tunnels do not become predation sinks (van Leeuwen 1982; Langton 1989).

Integrated Management of Aquatic and Terrestrial Habitats

The practices described above help to ensure local connectivity by protecting the critical habitats needed by a single population or an individual amphibian throughout its lifetime. Connectivity among populations, that is, landscape connectivity, must also be maintained to allow for dispersal and recolonization of habitats that experience occasional extinction events. As habitat becomes increasingly fragmented, local populations become more isolated and the amount and spatial arrangement of remaining suitable habitat become important. Sometimes a landscape-level analysis of the patterns of diversity and occurrence reveals unexpected effects of habitat alteration that have important conservation implications. For instance, a 10-year study of anuran communities in forest fragments in Amazonian Brazil found, as expected, that species richness was positively related to forest fragment size (Tocher et al. 1997). An unexpected finding was that species richness increased in forest fragments of all sizes due to invasion of small fragments by species characteristic of the surrounding pasture lands. Likewise, a study of amphibian occurrence along a gradient of increasing urbanization and forest fragmentation revealed that the species generally assumed to have the best dispersal ability, the red-spotted newt (*Notophthalmus v. viridescens*), was actually the one most sensitive to fragmentation (Gibbs 1998b). A landscape-level perspective is also needed in situations where suspected threats to amphibian populations originate from distant sources, as in the case of airborne pollutants (e.g., Sparling et al. 2001).

Some may find it incongruous to think of conservation for small-bodied, relatively nonvagile organisms in a landscape context. If one defines a landscape as a mosaic of patches of different habitat types, then landscapes for amphibians encompass a smaller spatial scale than for larger, more mobile organisms. Amphibians perceive "patchiness" and use their environment in a finer-grained way than most birds and mammals. From a management perspective, however, a landscape is usually defined according to the scale at which humans perceive patchiness, and thus on the order of several kilometers (Forman and Godron 1986). Even if we do not adjust our management efforts to the small scales important to individual amphibians, the success of conservation efforts depends on understanding the spatial and temporal scales at which the processes affecting amphibian population dynamics are operating. For example, assessing population trends for a species with a long life span would require a much longer dataset than for a species with a short life span. A patch of remnant forest that supports only a small number of breeding territories of a particular songbird species might support several local populations of amphibians. Thus, decisions made by a manager of a single park or conservation area could affect the fate of whole populations of amphibians. In any particular case, the factors most influencing population trends for amphibians may be operating at scales either much larger (e.g., climate change) or much smaller (e.g., characteristics of the forest floor community) than the ones we readily perceive or understand.

Issues of scale also intervene in any discussion of the design and efficacy of habitat corridors that have been proposed as a way of maintaining landscape connectivity for a variety of taxa. A habitat corridor connecting different resources used by a large vertebrate (i.e., the landscape mosaic scale; Noss 1991) might be too long for an individual amphibian to traverse in its lifetime. Such corridors might provide connectivity among populations over the long term, however, if they contain breeding sites, allowing movement of amphibians over multiple generations. Fencerow-scale corridors (Noss 1991), such as a narrow strip of trees bordering an agricultural field, are used by small mammals, but it is unclear whether similar corridors connecting breeding sites with upland habitats would be used by migrating amphibians. Radio-tracking studies of salamanders show that many species take straight-line paths during migration (e.g., Madison 1997; Joly et al. 2001). As far as we know, amphibians rely on simple orientation mechanisms rather than a cognitive map for finding their way among known points in the landscape (Sinsch 1990; Joly et al. 2001). These characteristics make it unlikely they would find and preferentially use narrow strips of natural vegetation like fencerows left in the landscape. The value of natural vegetation corridors among wetlands remains controversial (Saunders and Hobbs 1991) and depends on whether animals recognize and select corridors during movement and whether they achieve higher rates of movement and survival within the corridors than within the matrix habitat (Rosenberg et al. 1998). Some biologists advocate their consideration in management plans (e.g., Gibbs 1998; Semlitsch 2000a), but there is clearly a need for more information on movement behavior by adult amphibians during regular migrations and by juveniles and adults during longer-distance dispersal movements. Even in the absence of vegetation corridors, the restoration of small wetlands to serve as "stepping stones" could likely increase the probability of rescue and species persistence because of the important effect of distance on dispersal success (e.g., Gibbs 1993; Semlitsch and Bodie 1998; Skelly et al. 1999).

Species–area relationships have been important considerations in conservation planning for other taxa. Some studies have found positive relationships between wetland area and measures of amphibian abundance, probability of occupancy, or species richness, but others have not. The different results may be a function of differences in landscape characteristics among regions, the species studied, and sampling techniques used. The lack of consistent correlations between patch area and abundance or species richness perhaps is not surprising given the specialized habitat needs of many amphibians. Yet, one consistent finding is the negative correlation with fish presence, which in turn is positively associated with wetland size and permanence. For species with complex life cycles, the failure to find a positive relationship between habitat area and species diversity is likely a consequence of not including terrestrial habitat in measurements of patch size. The need for adjacent breeding and non-breeding habitat is an example of the kind of landscape complementation (Dunning et al. 1992) that must be considered when examining relationships between landscape structure and amphibian distribution (Pope et al. 2000). For these and other reasons, Marsh and Trenham (2001) suggested that the "ponds-as-patches" approach to characterizing amphibian metapopulation dynamics may be inadequate. The potential role of edge effects must also be considered. Some species tend to be less abundant near forest edges (deMaynadier and Hunter 1998; Gibbs 1998a), but more research is needed to determine whether plethodontid salamanders or other sensitive amphibians require areas of core forest, as do so-called interior species of migratory songbirds. At present, it is unclear whether very small patches can support populations of forest-associated species, or whether negative edge effects, especially abiotic changes such as increased temperature and decreased moisture (Murcia 1995), render small patches unsuitable.

Finally, it is also important to consider how a plan for amphibian management may conflict with plans for other wildlife species, that is, the possible tradeoff in management efforts and outcomes. As management plans become more inclusive of non-game species, the complexity of efforts will increase and pose new problems to solve. For example, wetland management practices that "draw down" marshes (thereby lowering the water table of ephemeral pools) to enhance waterfowl production may decrease the probability of metamorphosis of amphibian species, especially species with long larval periods. Likewise, flooding marshes (thereby raising the water table of ephemeral pools) for waterfowl may facilitate the colonization of ephemeral pools by fish. Although no data are available on the effects of traditional management practices for game species, such as draw downs, burning, and mowing, on nongame species like amphibians, managers should be aware of potential conflicts. It is important to be explicit about one's management targets, which can be a particular species, one taxonomic group, or overall biodiversity. Management strategies that promote clearing forest patches and creating more edge habitats for game species like rabbits, quail, and deer are detrimental to some nongame species (Faaborg 1980; Yahner 1988). Unfortunately, the "edge is good" paradigm still lingers and, in our view, needs to be purged once and for all. Blanket recommendations regarding management for "wildlife" should be interpreted with caution because management practices that benefit one species are very often neutral or harmful to others. A good example illustrating this point is management for game fish such as trout, bass, and bluegill, which are efficient predators of amphibian larvae. Plans should restrict stocking to only some lakes and ponds, perhaps based on their quality for amphibian habitat or accessibility by fisherman. The common practice of making every temporary pond more permanent for fish should also be discontinued.

POTENTIAL SOLUTIONS AND STRATEGIES FOR EFFECTIVE AMPHIBIAN CONSERVATION

Although amphibians are not unique in experiencing declines on a global scale, the information presented in this book makes it clear that they are worthy of focused attention and specific conservation efforts. Clearly, steps must be taken to identify and mitigate the causes of decline of amphibians in areas that are already set aside as nature reserves. Such areas, at least in theory, are protected from outright habitat destruction, yet their ability to maintain amphibian populations over the long-term is in jeopardy unless certain management practices (e.g., fish stocking) are changed and negative external influences identified and ameliorated. In addition, some amphibian species and important habitats currently receive little or no protection under existing policies and reserve systems. For example, very small (<4.0 ha) wetlands and non-navigable, isolated wetlands are not federally protected in the United States, yet these are the most critical breeding sites for many species (e.g., Semlitsch and Bodie 1998).

One way to ensure that amphibians receive consideration and become a higher priority in programs targeting nongame wildlife, in general, is to increase the level of knowledge on the part of biologists and others who implement such programs and who routinely interact with the public. The degree of ignorance and antipathy exhibited toward amphibians and reptiles can hardly be overstated and remains one of the major barriers to conservation efforts (see Chapter 16, this volume). Engaging private landowners in wildlife conservation is now recognized as essential for the protection of biodiversity. The Missouri Department of Conservation, for example, recently established a Private Lands Services Division that provides information and technical assistance to landowners regarding options for improving wildlife habitat. With funding and other support generated at the regional level through programs like these, much could be done to accomplish amphibian conservation goals. By restoring wetlands or altering certain management practices, individual landowners can have a significant, positive impact on local amphibian populations, and they may gain great personal satisfaction by doing so. However, because amphibians are poorly understood and have not been the focus of traditional wildlife management efforts, it is unlikely that most landowners are currently motivated to protect them or are aware of how their actions may affect them. In Europe and increasingly in the United States, garden ponds or water gardens are popular additions to home landscapes. Such artificial ponds have the potential to offer breeding habitat for native amphibians, but landowners must be encouraged to allow their natural colonization, rather than stocking them with nonnative species or translocated individuals. The latter practices are potentially harmful because of the potential for introduction of diseases and establishment of nonnative species. The bottom line is that amphibians need more ambassadors—that is, herpetologists and conservationists making a concerted effort to correct misperceptions regarding "herps" (Chapter 16, this volume), advising landowners of the ways in which amphibian habitats can be protected and restored, and informing them of the potential tradeoffs between traditional management practices and amphibian conservation (e.g., stocking ponds with predatory fish, mowing and clearing natural vegetation around wetlands).

In the tropics, where amphibian diversity is highest, tapping into existing programs is not an option because there are simply too few programs and resources in place currently to meet the daunting conservation challenges (Young et al. 2001; Chapters 5 and 6, this volume). Whereas amphibians receive legal protection in many developed regions, there is need for greater legal protection of amphibians in developing countries. In the United States and other countries where laws protecting wildlife, endangered species, and wetlands are already in place, advocacy efforts must be focused on strengthening the laws and defending them against legal challenges. A U.S. Supreme Court decision in January 2001 eliminated the need for a federal permit to fill "nonnavigable, isolated, intrastate" wetlands (Environmental Law Institute 2001), thus many amphibian breeding sites currently have no legal protection in most states. On the legal front, it is also necessary to advocate for better laws and regulations concerning specific harmful practices (e.g., harvesting for bait trade, overharvesting and exporting for food; Chapter 15, this volume). At a local level, biologists and conservation organizations can influence land-use decisions for the benefit of amphibians. As an example, we can provide input regarding amphibian habitat needs during the development of wetland and stream buffer ordinances by counties and municipalities.

At regional or continental scales, a two-pronged strategy is needed. The first part of the strategy is to ensure that the needs of amphibians are considered in coarse-filter conservation planning efforts, such as GAP analysis, identification of biodiversity hotspots, and design of reserve networks. The goal here is not to divert resources from efforts that may be directed toward other taxonomic groups, but rather to increase overall support by making a stronger case for amphibian conservation and by enhancing their level of protection under existing or planned large-scale conserva-tion strategies. Opportunities may exist, for example, to influence the design of re-gional reserve networks for "umbrella" species, such as grizzly bears in the western United States and panthers in Florida. If amphibian conservation were to become an explicit consideration in the planning and management of such linked reserve sys-tems, then it might be possible to incorporate or enhance habitat (i.e., through cre-ation of small wetlands) for amphibians in what are essentially movement corridors for other species. Large-scale reserve networks designed with multiple criteria in mind, rather than the needs of just one species, will result in protection for a wider array of species, including amphibians (Noss et al. 1996). The distribution of am-phibians, indeed all vertebrates, is considered along with vegetation in state-by-state GAP analyses in the United States. However, limited distributional information and the lack of clear associations between amphibian species and vegetation types (ver-sus wetlands or other landscape features) present a challenge for modeling predicted species distributions (Scott et al. 1993; N. Gerlanc, Kansas State University, personal communication).

Because some species will inevitably fall through the cracks of any coarse-filter approach, the second part of a strategy is to use our knowledge of local amphibian diversity and threats to supplement these larger-scale efforts. For example, specific habitats important to amphibians, such as caves, seeps, and headwater streams, might not receive high priority under the types of approaches just mentioned (e.g., Prather and Briggler 2001). In highly developed regions, where reserve establishment is severely constrained because of intensive human use, the focus must be on ways to balance land-use with amphibian conservation (Chapter 17, this volume). Biological reserves are essential in the tropics where amphibian diversity is highest but our knowledge of the distribution and status of amphibians is limited. The crisis unfold-ing in the tropics warrants an analysis of geographic patterns of amphibian diversity relative to existing broad-based conservation schemes (e.g., biodiversity hotspots; Myers et al. 2000) and protected areas. In addition, we need much greater investment in research to understand the causes of amphibian declines at tropical high-elevation sites that lack obvious signs of human disturbance (Young et al. 2001).

Strength in numbers dictates that those concerned with amphibian conservation join together to advocate for solutions and to ensure a voice in critical decision-making processes. National and international organizations, such as PARC and DAPTF, play a significant role by focusing attention on emerging issues, bringing together people with expertise in different fields, exchanging new information, and promoting effec-tive strategies as they are developed and tested. Again, this is especially critical in places like Latin America where extinctions are eroding global amphibian diversity the most, yet scientists lack the infrastructure and funding to do the necessary research and monitoring.

Where more research is needed, it should be designed to answer pressing questions and to take approaches that have the best chance of identifying cause-and-effect relationships between stressors and population declines, or between specific management actions and population responses. Greater strides could be made by choosing treatments representative of actual land-use practices, conducting research at spatial and temporal scales that are most relevant to a particular problem, and incorporating interactions among multiple factors. Many of the current hypotheses regarding declines in North America and elsewhere amount to "causes looking for an effect." In other words, negative effects of various factors have been documented at the individual level, but links have yet to be made to population dynamics. There is no reason we cannot conduct large-scale field experiments to test the effects of management practices or the efficacy of buffers, corridors, wetland mitigation, and other strategies for amphibians.

We hope our chapter and the others in this book provide a greater understanding of the problems amphibians face, as well as potential solutions. Although there is always a need for more research, the basic biological principles we have outlined and the contents of this book provide convincing evidence that we know enough to take common-sense actions: protect and enhance both aquatic and terrestrial habitats, cease harmful management practices, and promote amphibian conservation to the public. To accomplish this goal, a convincing case must be made as to why individuals and the larger society should invest in conserving amphibians. Experience from conservation efforts for other wildlife tells us that it is that simple—and that difficult.

ACKNOWLEDGMENTS

We thank Russ Bodie, Nathan Mills, and Michelle Boone for thoughtful comments and suggestions on the manuscript. RDS also thanks John David for release time from teaching to work on this project. Preparation of the manuscript was partially supported by grants from U.S. Environmental Protection Agency (827095-01), U.S. National Science Foundation (DEB 99 03761), and U.S. Geological Survey (01CRAG0007).

LITERATURE CITED

Abdulali, H. 1985. On the export of frog legs from India. Journal of the Bombay Natural History Society 82:347–375.

Adams, M. J. 1999. Correlated factors in amphibian decline: Exotic species and habitat change in western Washington. Journal of Wildlife Management 63:1162–1171.

Adams M. J., and R. B. Bury. 2002. The endemic headwater stream amphibians of the American Northwest: Associations with environmental gradients in a large forested preserve. Global Ecology and Biodiversity 11:169–178.

ALASV (Arbeitsgruppe unter Leitung der Abteilung Strassenbau des Verkehrsministeriums). 1994. Amphibienschutz. Leitfaden für Schutzmassnahmen an Strassen. Schrifttenreihe der Strassenbauverwaltung Baden Württemberg, Heft 4, Germany.

Albertini, G., and B. Lanza. 1987. *Rana catesbeiana* Shaw, in Italy. Alytes 6:117–129.

Alexander, M. A., and J. K. Eischeid. 2001. Climate variability in regions of amphibian declines. Conservation Biology 15:930–942.

Alexandratos, N. 1999. World food and agriculture: Outlook for the medium and longer term. Proceedings of the National Academy of Sciences (USA) 96:5908–5914.

Alford, R. A., P. M. Dixon and J. H. K. Pechmann. 2001. Global amphibian population declines. Nature 414:449–500.

Alford, R. A., and R. N. Harris. 1988. Effects of larval growth history on anuran metamorphosis. American Naturalist 131:91–106.

Alford, R. A., and S. J. Richards. 1997. Lack of evidence for epidemic disease as an agent in the catastrophic decline of Australian rain forest frogs. Conservation Biology 11:1026–1029.

Alford, R. A., and S. J. Richards. 1999. Global amphibian declines: A problem in applied ecology. Annual Review of Ecology and Systematics 30:133–165.

AmphibiaWeb: Information on amphibian biology and conservation. [Web application]. 2002. Berkeley, CA. Available online at: http://amphibiaweb.org/.

Anderson, I. 1993. Keep taking the frog skin. New Scientist 140:10.

Anderson, P. D., and S. D'Apollonia. 1978. Aquatic animals. Pp. 187–221 *in* G. C. Butler, editor. Principles of Ecotoxicology. Wiley, Toronto, Canada.

Anderson, R. M., and R. M. May. 1986. The invasion, persistence, and spread of infectious diseases within animal and plant communities. Philosophical Transactions of the Royal Society of London B Biological Sciences 354:533–570.

Ankley, G. T., J. E. Tietge, D. L. DeFoe, K. M. Hjensen, G. W. Holcombe, E. J. Durhan, and A. Diamond. 1998. Effects of ultraviolet light and methoprene on survival and development of *Rana pipiens*. Environmental Toxicology and Chemistry 17:2530–2542.

Anthony, C. D. 1993. Recognition of conspecific odors by *Plethodon caddoensis* and *P. ouachitae*. Copeia 1993:1028–1033.

Anzalone, C. R., L. B. Kats, and M. S. Gordon 1998. Effects of solar UV-B radiation on embryonic development in *Hyla cadaverina*, *Hyla regilla* and *Taricha torosa*. Conservation Biolology 12:646–653.

Arita, H. T., F. Figueroa, A. Frisch, P. Rodríguez, and K. Santos del Prado. 1997. Geographical range size and the conservation of Mexican mammals. Conservation Biology 11: 92–100.

Ash, A. 1988. Disappearance of salamanders from clearcut plots. Journal of the Elisha Mitchell Scientific Society 104:116–122.

Ash, A. N. 1997. Disappearance and return of Plethodontid salamanders to clearcut plots in the southern Blue Ridge Mountains. Conservation Biology 11:983–989.

Ash, A. N., and R. C. Bruce. 1994. Impacts of timber harvesting on salamanders. Conservation Biology 8:300–301.

Aston, L. S., and J. N. Seiber. 1997. Fate of summertime airborne organophosphate pesticide residues in the Sierra Nevada Mountains. Journal of Environmental Quality 26: 1483–1492.

Aubry, K. B., and P. A. Hall. 1991. Terrestrial amphibian communities in the southern Washington Cascade Range. Pp. 326–338 *in* L. F. Ruggiero, K. B. Aubry, A. B. Carey, and M. H. Huff, technical coordinators. Wildlife and Vegetation of Unmanaged Douglas-Fir Forests. USDA Forest Service, General Technical Report PNW-285.

Aubry, K. B., C. M. Senger, and R. L. Crawford. 1987. Discovery of Larch Mountain salamanders (*Plethodon larselli*) in the central Cascade Range of Washington. Biological Conservation 42:147–152.

Austin, R. M., Jr. 2000. Cutaneous microbial flora and antibiosis in *Plethodon ventralis*. Pp. 451–462 *in* R. C. Bruce, R. G. Jaeger, and L. D. Houck, editors. The Biology of Plethodontid Salamanders. Plenum Publishers, New York, NY.

Azevedos-Ramos, C., W. E. Magnusson, and P. Bayliss. 1999. Predation as the key factor structuring tadpole assemblages in a savanna area in central Amazonia. Copeia 1999: 22–33.

Bahls, P. F. 1992. The status of fish populations and management of high mountain lakes in the western United States. Northwest Science 66:183–193.

Barfield, B. 1986. Indonesia's frog legs. Journal of Environmental Health 48:324.

Barinaga, M. 1990. Where have all the froggies gone? Science 247:1033–1034.

Bartoldus, C. C. 1999. A Comprehensive Review of Wetland Assessment Procedures: A Guide for Wetland Practitioners. Environmental Concern, Inc., St. Michaels, MD.

Barzetti, V. 1993. Parks and Progress. IUCN-The World Conservation Union, Washington, DC.

Bedford, B. 1996. The need to define hydrologic equivalence at the landscape scale for freshwater wetland mitigation. Ecological Applications 6:57–68.

Bedford, B. 1999. Cumulative effects on wetland landscapes: Links to wetland restoration in the United States and Southern Canada. Wetlands 19:775–788.

Beebee, T. J. C. 1995. Amphibian breeding and climate. Nature 374:219–220.

Beebee, T. J. C. 1996. Ecology and Conservation of Amphibians. Chapman & Hall, London, UK.

Belden, L. K., E. L. Wildy, and A. R. Blaustein. 2000. Growth, survival, and behaviour of larval long-toed salamanders (*Ambystoma macrodactylum*) exposed to ambient levels of UV-B radiation. Journal of Zoology (London) 251:473–479.

Berger, L., R. Speare, P. Daszak, D. E. Green, A. A. Cunningham, C. L. Goggin, R. Slocombe, M. Ragan, A. D. Hyatt, K. R. McDonald, H. B. Hines, K. R. Lips, G. Marantelli, and H. Parkes. 1998. Chytridiomycosis causes amphibian mortality associated with population declines in the rain forests of Australia and Central America. Proceedings of the National Academy of Sciences (USA) 95:9031–9036.

Berger, L., R. Speare, and A. D. Hyatt. 2000a. Chytrid fungi and amphibian declines: Overview, implications and future directions. Pp. 21–31 *in* A. Campbell, editor. Declines and Disappearances of Australian Frogs. Environment Australia, Canberra, Australia.

Berger, L., R. Speare, and A. Kent. 2000b. Diagnosis of chytridiomycosis in amphibians by histologic examination. Zoos' Print Journal 15:184–190.

Berkes, F., J. Colding, and C. Folke. 2000. Rediscovery of traditional ecological knowledge as adaptive management. Ecological Applications 10:1251–1262.

Berrill, M., S. Bertram, and B. Pauli. 1997. Effects of pesticides on amphibian embryos and larvae. Herpetological Conservation 1:233–245.

Berrill, M., S. Bertram, A. Wilson, S. Louis, D. Brigham, and C. Stromberg. 1993. Lethal and sublethal impacts of pyrethroid insecticides on amphibian embryos and tadpoles. Environmental Toxicology and Chemistry 12:535–539.

Berven, K. A. 1987. The heritable basis of variation in larval developmental patterns within populations of the wood frog (*Rana sylvatica*). Evolution 41:1088–1097.

Berven, K. A. 1990. Factors affecting population flucuations in larval and adult stages of the wood frog (*Rana sylvatica*). Ecology 71:1599–1608.

Berven, K. A., and D. E. Gill. 1983. Interpreting geographic variation in life-history traits. American Zoologist 23:85–97.

Berven, K. A., and T. A. Grudzien. 1990. Dispersal in the wood frog (*Rana sylvatica*): Implications for genetic population structure. Evolution 44:2047–2056.

Bidleman, T. F. 1999. Atmospheric transport and air-surface exchange of pesticides. Water, Air, and Soil Pollution 115:115–166.

Birge, W. J., A. G. Westerman, and J. A. Spromberg. 2000. Comparative toxicology and risk assessment of amphibians. Pp. 727–791 *in* D. W. Sparling, G. Linder, and C. A. Bishop, editors. Ecotoxicology of Amphibians and Reptiles. SETAC Press, Pensacola, FL.

Bishop, C. A., and K. E. Pettit. 1992. Declines in Canadian Amphibian Populations: Designing a National Monitoring Strategy. Canadian Wildlife Service, Ottawa, Ontario. Occasional Paper 76.

Bishop, S. C. 1943. Handbook of Salamanders. Comstock Publication Co., Ithaca, NY.

Blaustein, A. R. 1994. Chicken little or Nero's fiddle? A perspective on declining amphibian populations. Herpetologica 50:85–97.

Blaustein, A. R., L. K. Belden, A. C. Hatch, L. B. Kats, P. D. Hoffman, J. B. Hays, A. Marco, D. P. Chivers, and J. M. Kiesecker. 2001a. Ultraviolet radiation and amphibians. Pp. 63–79 *in* C. S. Cockell, and A. R. Blaustein, editors. Ecosystems, Evolution and Ultraviolet Radiation. Springer, New York, NY.

Blaustein, A. R., L. K. Belden, D. H. Olson, D.L. Green, T. L. Root, and J. M. Kiesecker. 2001b. Amphibian breeding and climate change. Conservation Biology 15:1804–1809.

Blaustein, A. R., D. P. Chivers, L. B. Kats, and J. M. Kiesecker. 2000. Effects of ultraviolet radiation on locomotion and orientation in roughskin newts (*Taricha granulosa*). Ethology 108:227–234.

Blaustein, A. R., B. Edmond, J. M. Kiesecker, J. J. Beatty, and D. G. Hokit. 1995. Ambient ultraviolet radiation causes mortality in salamander eggs. Ecological Applications 5: 740–743.

Blaustein, A. R., J. B. Hays, P. D. Hoffman, D. P. Chivers, J. M. Kiesecker, W. P. Leonard, A. Marco, D. H. Olson, J. K. Reaser, and R. G. Anthony. 1999. DNA repair and resistance to UV-B radiation in western spotted frogs. Ecological Applications 9:1100–1105.

Blaustein, A. R., P. D. Hoffman, D. G. Hokit, J. M. Kiesecker, S. C. Walls, and J. B. Hays. 1994a. UV repair and resistance to solar UV-B in amphibian eggs: A link to populations? Proceedings of the National Academy of Sciences (USA) 91:1791–1795.

Blaustein, A. R., P. D. Hoffman, J. M. Kiesecker, and J. B. Hays. 1996. DNA repair activity and resistance to solar UV-B radiation in eggs of the red-legged frog. Conservation Biology 10:1398–1402.

Blaustein, A. R., D. G. Hokit, R. K. O'Hara, and R. A. Holt. 1994b. Pathogenic fungus contributes to amphibian losses in the Pacific Northwest. Biological Conservation 67: 251–254.

Blaustein, A. R., and J. M. Kiesecker. 1997. The significance of ultraviolet-B radiation to amphibian population declines. Reviews In Toxicology 1:309–327.

Blaustein, A. R., J. M. Kiesecker, D. P. Chivers, and R. G. Anthony. 1997a. Ambient UV-B radiation causes deformities in amphibian embryos. Proceedings of the National Academy of Sciences (USA) 94:13735–13737.

Blaustein, A. R., J. M. Kiesecker, D. P. Chivers, D. G. Hokit, A. Marco, L. K. Belden, and A. Hatch. 1998. Effects of ultraviolet radiation on amphibians: Field experiments. American Zoologist 38:799–812.

Blaustein, A. R., J. M. Kiesecker, P. D. Hoffman, and J. B. Hays. 1997b. The significance of ultraviolet-B radiation to amphibian population declines. Reviews in Toxicology 1: 147–165.

Blaustein, A. R., and D. B. Wake. 1990. Declining amphibian populations: a global phenomenon? Trends in Ecology and Evolution 5:203–204.

Blaustein, A. R., and D. B. Wake. 1995. The puzzle of declining amphibian populations. Scientific American 272:56–61.

Blaustein, A. R., D. B. Wake, and W. P. Sousa. 1994c. Amphibian declines: Judging stability, persistence, and susceptibility of populations to local and global extinctions. Conservation Biology 8:60–71.

Bodie, J. R. 2001. Stream and riparian management for freshwater turtles. Journal of Environmental Management 62:443–455.

Bollinger, T. K., J. Mao, D. Schock, R. M. Brigham, and V. Gregory. 1999. Pathology, isolation, and preliminary molecular characterization of a novel iridovirus from tiger salamanders in Saskatchewan. Journal of Wildlife Diseases 35:413–429.

Bonin, J. 1991. Effect of forest age on woodland amphibians and the habitat and status of stream salamanders in southwestern Quebec. M.S. Thesis. Department of Renewable Resources, McGill University, Montreal, Canada.

Boone, M. D. 2000. Effects of an insecticide on amphibian communities. Dissertation. University of Missouri, Columbia, MO.

Boone, M. D., and C. M. Bridges. 1999. The effect of temperature on the potency of carbaryl for tadpoles of the green frog, *Rana clamitans*. Environmental Toxicology and Chemistry 18:1482–1484.

Boone, M. D., C. M. Bridges, and B. B. Rothermel. 2001. Effects of multiple exposures to carbaryl on growth and development on larval green frogs (*Rana clamitans*). Oecologia 129:518–524.

Boone, M. D., and S. M. James. In Press. Interactions of an insecticide and herbicide in amphibian community mesocosms. Ecological Applications.

Boone, M. D., and R. D. Semlitsch. 2001. Interactions of an insecticide with larval density and predation in experimental amphibian communities. Conservation Biology 15: 228–238.

Boone, M. D., and R. D. Semlitsch. 2002. Interactions of an insecticide with competition and pond drying in amphibian communities. Ecological Applications 12:43–52.

Bosch, J., I. Martinez-Solano, and M. Garcia-Paris. 2001. Evidence of a chytrid fungus infection involved in the decline of the common midwife toad (*Alytes obstetricans*) in protected areas of central Spain. Biological Conservation 97:331–337.

Bradford, D. F. 1989. Allopatric distribution of native frogs and introduced fishes in high Sierra Nevada lakes of California: Implication of the negative effect of fish introductions. Copeia 1989:775–778.

Bradford, D. F. 1991. Mass mortality and extinction in a high-elevation population of *Rana muscosa*. Journal of Herpetology 25:174–177.

Bradford, D. F., S. D. Cooper, T. M. Jenkens, Jr., K. Kratz, O. Sarnelle, and A. D. Brown. 1998. Influences of natural acidity and introduced fish on faunal assemblages in California alpine lakes. Canadian Journal of Fisheries and Aquatic Sciences 55:2478–2491.

Bradford, D. F., F. Tabatabai, and D. M. Graber. 1993. Isolation of remaining populations of the native frog, *Rana muscosa*, by introduced fishes in Sequoia and Kings Canyon National Parks, California. Conservation Biology 7:882–888.

Bradley, G. A., P. C. Rosen, M. J. Sredl, T. R. Jones, and J. E. Longcore. 2002. Chytridiomycosis in three species of native Arizona frogs (*Rana yavapaiensis, Rana chiricauhuensis,* and *Hyla arenicolor*). Journal of Wildlife Diseases 38:206–212.

Bragg, A. N. 1960. Population fluctuation in the amphibian fauna of Cleveland County, Oklahoma during the past twenty-five years. Southwest Naturalist 5:165–169.

Brana, F., L. Frechilla, and G. Orizaola. 1996. Effect of introduced fish on amphibian assemblages in mountain lakes in northern Spain. Herpetological Journal 6:145–148.

Branch, W. R., editor. 1988. South African Red Data Book: Reptiles and Amphibians. South African Scientific Programmes Report No. 151, Pretoria, South Africa.

Braune, M. J., and A. Wood. 1999. Best management practices applied to urban runoff quantity and quality control. Water Science Technology 39:117–121.

Bray, R., and T. Gent, editors. 1997. Opportunities for Amphibians and Reptiles in the Designed Landscape. Peterborough, UK. English Nature Science Series No. 30.

Breden, F. 1987. The effect of post-metamorphic dispersal on the population genetic structure of Fowler's toad, *Bufo woodhousei fowleri*. Copeia 1987:386–395.

Bridges, C. M. 1997. Tadpole swimming performance and activity affected by acute exposure to sublethal levels of carbaryl. Environmental Toxicology and Chemistry 16:1935–1939.

Bridges, C. M. 1999a. Effects of a pesticide on tadpole activity and predator avoidance behavior. Journal of Herpetology 33:303–306.

Bridges, C. M. 1999b. Predator-prey interactions between two amphibian species: Effects of insecticide exposure. Aquatic Ecology 33:205–211.

Bridges, C. M. 1999c. The Effects of a Chemical Stressor on Amphibian Larvae: Individual, Population and Species Level Responses. Dissertation. University of Missouri, Columbia, MO.

Bridges, C. M. 2000. Long-term effects of pesticide exposure at various life stages of the southern leopard frog (*Rana sphenocephala*). Archives of Environmental Contamination and Toxicology 39:91–96.

Bridges, C. M., F. J. Dwyer, D. K. Hardest, and D. W. Whites. 2002. Comparative contaminant toxicity: Are amphibian larvae more sensitive than fish? Bulletin of Environmental Contamination and Toxicology 69:562–569.

Bridges, C. M., and R. D. Semlitsch. 2000. Variation in pesticide tolerance of tadpoles among and within species of ranidae and patterns of amphibian decline. Conservation Biology 14:1490–1499.

Bridges, C. M., and R. D. Semlitsch. 2001. Genetic variation in insecticide tolerance in a population of southern leopard frogs (*Rana sphenocephala*): Implications for amphibian conservation. Copeia 2001:7–13.

Bringsøe, H. 1992. The adoption of the poison-arrow frogs of the genera *Dendrobates* and *Phyllobates* in Appendix II of CITES. Herpetological Review 23:16–17.

Brinson, M. 1993. Changes in the functioning of wetlands along environmental gradients. Wetlands 13:65–74.

Bronmark, C., and P. Edenhamn. 1994. Does the presence of fish affect the distribution of tree frogs (*Hyla arborea*)? Conservation Biology 8:841–845.

Brooks, R. T. 1999. Residual effects of thinning and high white-tailed deer densities on northern redback salamanders in southern New England oak forests. Journal of Wildlife Management 63:1172–1180.

Brooks, T. M., S. L. Pimm, V. Kapos, and C. Ravilious. 1999. Threat from deforestation to montane and lowland birds and mammals in insular south-east Asia. Journal of Animal Ecology 68:1061–1078.

Brown, J. H., and A. Kodric-Brown. 1977. Turnover rates in insular biogeography: Effect of immigration on extinction. Ecology 58:445–449.

Brown, L. R. 2001. Paving the planet: Cars and crops competing for land. Earth Policy Institute. Available online at: http://www.worldwatch.org/chairman/issue/010214.html.

Bruce, R. C. 1995. The use of temporary removal sampling in a study of population dynamics of the salamander *Desmognathus monticola*. Australian Journal of Ecology 20:403–412.

Bruce, R. C., R. G. Jaeger, and L. D. Houck, editors. 2000. The Biology of Plethodontid Salamanders. Kluwer Academic/Plenum Publishers, New York, NY.

Bruggeman, D. J., J. A. Bantle, and C. Goad. 1998. Linking teratogenesis, growth, and DNA photodamage to artificial ultraviolet-B radiation in *Xenopus laevis* larvae. Environmental Toxicology and Chemistry 17:2114–2121.

Bryant, S. V., V. French, and P. J. Bryant. 1981. Distal regeneration and symmetry. Science 212:993–1002.

Bryant, S. V., and D. M. Gardiner. 1992. Retinoic acid, local cell-cell interactions and pattern formation in vertebrate limbs. Developmental Biology 152:1–25.

Bryant, S. V., D. M. Gardiner, and K. Muneoka. 1987. Limb development and regeneration. American Zoologist 27:675–696.

Buhlmann, K. A., C. A. Pague, J. C. Mitchell, and R. B. Glasgow. 1988. Forestry operations and terrestrial salamanders: Techniques in a study of the Cow Knob salamander, *Plethodon punctatus*. Pp. 38–44 *in* R. C. Szaro, K. E. Severson, and D. R. Patton, editors. Management of Amphibians, Reptiles, and Mammals in North America. USDA Forest Service, Rocky Mountain Forest and Range Experimental Station, Fort Collins, CO, General Technical Report RM-166.

Bulger, A. J., B. J. Cosby, and J. R. Webb. 2000. Current, reconstructed past, and projected future status of brook trout (*Salvelinus fontinalis*) streams in Virginia. Canadian Journal of Fisheries and Aquatic Sciences 57:1515–1523.

Burbink, F. T., C. A. Phillips, and E. J. Heske. 1998. A riparian zone in southern Illinois as a potential dispersal corridor for reptiles and amphibians. Biological Conservation 86:107–115.

Burkhart, J. G., J. C. Helgen, D. J. Fort, K. Gallagher, D. Bowers, T. L. Propst, M. Gernes, J. Magner, M. D. Shelby, and G. Lucier. 1998. Induction of mortality and malformation in *Xenopus laevis* embryos by water sources associated with field frog abnormalities. Environmental Health Perspectives 106:841–848.

Burton, T. M., and G. E. Likens. 1975. Salamander populations and biomass in the Hubbard Brook Experimental Forest, New Hampshire. Copeia 1975:541–546.

Bury, R. B. 1999. A historical perspective and critique of the declining amphibian crisis. Wildlife Society Bulletin 27:1064–1068.

Bury, R. B., and P. S. Corn. 1988a. Douglas-fir forests in the Oregon and Washington Cascades: Abundance of terrestrial herpetofauna related to stand age and moisture. Pp. 11–22 *in* R. C. Szaro, K. E. Severson, and D. R. Patton, editors. Management of Amphibians, Reptiles, and Mammals in North America. USDA Forest Service, Rocky Mountain Forest and Range Experimental Station, Fort Collins, CO, General Technical Report RM-166.

Bury, R. B., and P. S. Corn. 1988b. Responses of aquatic and streamside amphibians to timber harvest: A review. Pp. 165–181 *in* K. J. Raedeke, editor. Streamside Management: Riparian Wildlife and Forestry Interactions. University of Washington Institute of Forest Resources, Seattle, WA. Contribution 59.

Bury, R. B., P. S. Corn, K. B. Aubry, F. F. Gilbert, and L. L. C. Jones. 1991. Aquatic amphibian communities in Oregon and Washington. Pp. 353–362 *in* L. F. Ruggiero, K. B. Aubry, A. B. Carey, and M. H. Huff, technical coordinators. Wildlife and Vegetation of Unmanaged Douglas-Fir Forests. USDA Forest Service, General Technical Report PNW-285.

Bury, R. B., C. K. Dodd, Jr., and G. M. Fellers. 1980. Conservation of the amphibia of the United States: A review. U.S. Department of the Interior, U.S. Fish and Wildlife Service, Washington, DC, Resource Publication 134:1–34.

Bury, R. B., and R. A. Lunkenbach. 1976. Introduced amphibians and reptiles in California. Biological Conservation 10:1–14.

Buttel, F. H. 1993. Socioeconomic impacts and social implications of reducing pesticide and agricultural chemical use in the United States. Pp. 153–181 *in* D. Pimentel, and H. Lehman, editors. The Pesticide Question: Environment, Economics, and Ethics. Chapman & Hall, New York, NY.

Calhoun, A. J. K., and P. M. deMaynadier. 2002. Forest habitat management guidelines for vernal pool wildlife in Maine. Maine Department of Inland Fisheries and Wildlife, Augusta, ME.

Camp, C. D. 1986. Distribution and habitat of the southern red-back salamander, *Plethodon serratus* Grobman (Amphibia: Plethodontidae), in Georgia. Georgia Journal of Science 44:136–146.

Camp, C. D. 1999. Intraspecific aggressive behavior in southeastern small species of *Plethodon:* Inferences for the evolution of aggression in terrestrial salamanders. Herpetologica 55:248–254.

Camp, C. D., and T. P. Lee. 1996. Intraspecific spacing and interaction within a population of *Desmognathus quadramaculatus*. Copeia 1996:78–84.

Campbell, A., editor. 1999. Declines and Disappearances of Australian Frogs. Environment Australia, Canberra, Australia. 234 p.

Campbell, J. A. 1998. Amphibians and Reptiles of Northern Guatemala, the Yucatán, and Belize. University of Oklahoma Press, Norman, OK.

Campbell, J. A. 1999. Distribution patterns of amphibians in Middle America. Pp. 111–210 *in* W. E. Duellman, editor. Patterns of Distribution of Amphibians: A Global Perspective. Johns Hopkins University Press, Baltimore, MD.

Capron, M., and A. Capron. 1994. Immunoglobulin E and effector cells in schistosomiasis. Science 264:1876–1877.

Carey, C. 1993. Hypothesis concerning the causes of the disappearance of Boreal Toads from the mountains of Colorado. Conservation Biology 7:355–362.

Carey, C. 2000. Infectious disease and worldwide declines of amphibian populations, with comments on emerging diseases in coral reef organisms and in humans. Environmental Health Perspectives 108:143–150.

Carey, C., D. F. Bradford, J. Brunner, J. P. Collins, E. W. Davidson, J. E. Longcore, M. Ouellet, A. P. Pessier, and D. Schock. 2002a. Biotic factors in the decline of amphibian populations. *In* G. Linder, D. W. Sparling, and S. Krest, editors. Multiple Stressors and Declining Amphibian Populations: Evaluating Cause and Effect. Society of Environmental Chemistry and Toxicology, Pensacola, FL.

Carey, C., N. Cohen, and L. Rollins-Smith. 1999. Amphibian declines: An immunological perspective. Developmental and Comparative Immunology 23:459–472.

Carey, C., P. S. Corn, M. S. Jones, L. J. Livo, E. Muths, and C. W. Loeffler. 2002b. Environmental and life history factors that limit recovery in Southern Rocky Mountain populations of boreal toads (*Bufo boreas*). *In* M. Lanoo, editor. Status and Conservation of North American Amphibians. University of California Press, Berkeley, CA.

Carey, C., W. R. Heyer, J. Wilkinson, R. A. Alford, J. W. Arntzen, T. Halliday, L. Hungerford, K. R. Lips, E. M. Middleton, S. A. Orchard, and A. S. Rand. 2001. Amphibian declines and environmental change: Use of remote-sensing data to identify environmental correlates. Conservation Biology 15:903–913.

Carr, L. W., and L. Fahrig. 2001. Effect of road traffic on two amphibian species of differing vagility. Conservation Biology 15:1071–1078.

Carson, R. 1962. Silent Spring. Riverside Press, Cambridge, MA.

Castillo, L. E., E. de la Cruz, and C. Ruepert. 1997. Ecotoxicology and pesticides in tropical aquatic ecosystems of Central America. Environmental Toxicology and Chemistry 16: 41–51.

Caughley, G. 1994. Directions in conservation biology. Journal of Animal Ecology 63: 215–244.

Chinchar, V. G. 2002. Ranaviruses (Family Iridoviridae): Emerging cold-blooded killers. Archives of Virology 147:447–470.

Chinchar, V. G., J. Wang, G. Murti, C. Carey, and L. Rollins-Smith. 2001. Inactivation of frog virus 3 and channel catfish virus by esculentin-2P and ranatuerin-2P, two antimicrobial peptides isolated from frog skin. Virology 288:351–357.

Chivers, D. P., and R. J. F. Smith. 1998. Chemical alarm signaling in aquatic predator prey systems: a review and prospectus. Ecoscience 5:338–352.

CITES (Convention on International Trade in Endangered Species of Wild Fauna and Flora). 2000. Draft proposal for the amendment of Appendix II of CITES. Proposal 11.46. Available online at: http://www.cites.org/CITES/eng/cop/11/propose/46.pdf.

Clark, H. F., J. C. Brennan, R. F. Zeigel, and D. T. Karzon. 1968. Isolation and characterization of viruses from the kidneys of *Rana pipiens* with renal adenocarcinoma before and after passage in the red eft (*Triturus viridescens*). Journal of Virology 2:629–640.

Clark, H. F., C. Gray, F. Fabian, R. Zeigel and D. T. Karzon. 1969. Comparative studies of amphibian cytoplasmic virus strains isolated from the leopard frog, bullfrog, and newt. Pp. 310–326 *in* M. Mizell, editor. Biology of Amphibian Tumors, Springer-Verlag, New York, NY.

Coblentz, B. E. 1990. Exotic organisms: A dilemma for conservation biology. Conservation Biology 4:261–265.

Cockell, C. S. 2001. A photobiological history of earth. Pp. 1–35 *in* C. S. Cockell, and A. R. Blaustein, editors. Ecosystems, Evolution and Ultraviolet Radiation. Springer, New York, NY.

Cockell, C. S., and A. R. Blaustein, editors. 2001. Ecosystems, Evolution and Ultraviolet Radiation. Springer, New York, NY.

Colburn, T., D. Dumanoski, and J. P. Myers. 1996. Our Stolen Future. Dutton, New York, NY. 306 p.

Collins, J. P. 1981. Distribution, habitats and life history variation in the Tiger Salamander, *Ambystoma tigrinum*, in East-central and Southeast Arizona. Copeia 1981:666–675.

Collins, J. P., and J. E. Cheek. 1983. Effect of food and density on development of typical and cannibalistic salamander larvae in *Ambystoma tigrinum nebulosum*. American Zoologist 23:77–84.

Collins, J. P., T. R. Jones, and H. J. Berna. 1988. Conserving genetically distinctive populations: the case of the Huachuca tiger salamander (*Ambystoma tigrinum stebbinsi* Lowe). Pp. 45–53 *in* R. C. Szaro, K. C. Severson, and D. R. Patton, editors. Management of Amphibians, Reptiles, and Small Mammals in North America. USDA Forest Service, Rocky Mountain Forest and Range Experiment Station, Fort Collins, CO, General Technical Report RM-166.

Collins, J. P., K. E. Zerba, and M. J. Sredl. 1993. Shaping intraspecific variation: Development, ecology and the evolution of morphology and life history variation in tiger salamanders. Genetica 89:167–183.

Colwell, G. J. 1994. In response to Bringsøe on the inclusion of *Dendrobates* and *Phyllobates* in Appendix II of CITES. Herpetological Review 25:10.

Conlon, J. M., and J. B. Kim. 2000. A protease inhibitor of the Kinitz family from skin secretions of the tomato frog, *Dyscophs guineti* (Microhylidae). Biochemical and Biophysical Research Communications 279:961–964.

Connell, J. H. 1978. Diversity in tropical rain forests and coral reefs. Science 199:1302–1310.

Connell, J. H., and W. P. Sousa. 1983. On the evidence needed to judge ecological stability or persistence. American Naturalist 121:789–824.

Corn, P. S. 1994. What we know and don't know about amphibian declines in the west. Pp. 59–67 *in* W. W. Covington, and L. F. Debano, editors. Sustainable Ecological Systems: Implementing an Ecological Approach to Land Management. UDSA Forest Service, General Technical Report RM-247.

Corn, P. S. 2000. Amphibian declines: Review of some current hypotheses. Pp. 663–696 *in* D. W. Sparling, C. A. Bishop, and G. Linder, editors. Ecotoxicology of Amphibians and Reptiles. Society of Environmental Toxicology and Chemistry, Pensacola, FL.

Corn, P. S., and R. B. Bury. 1989. Logging in western Oregon: Responses of headwater habitats and stream amphibians. Forest Ecology and Management 29:39–57.

Corn, P. S., and R. B. Bury. 1991. Terrestrial amphibian communities in the Oregon Coast Range. Pp. 304–317 *in* L. F. Ruggiero, K. B. Aubry, A. B. Carey, and M. H. Huff, technical coordinators. Wildlife and Vegetation of Unmanaged Douglas-Fir Forests. USDA Forest Service, General Technical Report PNW-285.

Corse, W. A., and D. A. Metter. 1980. Economics, adult feeding and larval growth of *Rana catesbeiana* on a fish hatchery. Journal of Herpetology 14:231–238.

Cowardin, L. M., V. Carter, F. C. Golet, and E. T. LaRoe. 1979. Classification of wetlands and deepwater habitats of the United States. U.S. Department of Interior, U.S. Fish and Wildlife Service, Washington, DC. FWS/OBS-79/31.

Cowman, D. F., and L. E. Mazanti. 2000. Ecotoxicology of "new generation" pesticides to amphibians. Pp. 233–268 *in* D. W. Sparling, G. Linder, and C. A. Bishop, editors. Ecotoxicology of Amphibians and Reptiles. Society of Environmental Toxicology and Chemistry, Pensacola, FL.

Crick, H. Q. P., and T. H. Sparks. 1999. Climate change related to egg laying trends. Nature 399:423–424.

Crossland, M. R. 1997. Impact of eggs, hatchlings and tadpoles of the introduced toad *Bufo marinus* (Anura: Bufonidae) on native aquatic fauna in northern Queensland, Australia. Ph.D. Thesis. James Cook University of North Queensland, Australia.

Crossland, M. R. 1998. A comparison of cane toad and native tadpoles as predators of native anuran eggs, hatchlings and larvae. Wildlife Research 25:373–381.

Crossland, M. R., and R. A. Alford. 1998. Evaluation of the toxicity of eggs hatchlings and tadpoles of the introduced toad *Bufo marinus* (Anura: Bufonidae) on native Australian aquatic predators. Australian Journal of Ecology 23:129–137.

Crossland, M. R., and C. Azevedo-Ramos. 1999. Effects of *Bufo* (Anura: Bufonidae) toxins on tadpoles from native and exotic *Bufo* habitats. Herpetologica 55:192–199.

Crother, B. I. (Chair, Committee on Standard English and Scientific Names). 2000. Scientific and Standard English Names of Amphibians and Reptiles of North America North of Mexico, with Comments Regarding Confidence of Scientific Understanding. Society for the Study of Amphibians and Reptiles, St. Louis, MO. Herpetological Circular 29. 82 p.

Crump, M. L. 1974. Reproductive strategies in a tropical anuran community. Miscellaneous Publications of the Museum of Natural History, University of Kansas 61:1–68.

Crump, M. L. 2000. In Search of the Golden Frog. University of Chicago Press, Chicago, IL.

Crump, M. L., F. R. Hensley, and K. L. Clark. 1992. Apparent decline of the golden toad: underground or extinct? Copeia 1992:413–420.

Cunningham, A. A. 1996. Disease risks of wildlife translocations. Conservation Biology 10:349–353.

Cunningham, A. A., T. E. S. Langton, P. M. Bennet, S. E. S. Drury, R. E. Gough, and J. K. Kirkwood. 1993. Unusual mortality associated with poxvirus-like particles in frogs (*Rana temporaria*). Veterinary Record 133:141–142.

Cunningham, A. A., T. E. S. Langton, P. M. Bennett, J. F. Lewin, S. E. N. Drury, R. E. Gough, and S. K. MacGregor. 1995. Investigations into unusual mortalities of the common frog (*Rana temporaria*) in Britain. Pp. 19–27 *in* P. Zwart, and G. Matz, editors. Fifth International Colloquium on the Pathology of Reptiles and Amphibians, Netherlands.

Cunningham, A. A., T. E. S. Langton, P. M. Bennett, J. F. Lewin, S. E. N. Drury, R. E. Gough, and S. K. MacGregor. 1996. Pathological and microbiological findings from incidents of unusual mortality of the common frog (*Rana temporaria*). Philosophical Transactions of the Royal Society London B 351:1539–1557.

Czechura, G. V., and G. J. Ingram. 1990. *Taudactylus diurnus* and the case of the disappearing frogs. Memoirs of the Queensland Museum 29:361–365.

Dahl, T. E. 2000. Status and trends of wetlands in the conterminous United States 1986 to 1997. U.S. Fish and Wildlife Service, Washington, DC.

Das, I. 2001. Threatened herpetofauna of India. Pp. 63–70 *in* C. N. B. Bambaradeniya, and

V. N. Samaraselera, editors. An Overview of the Threatened Fauna of South Asia. IUCN Sri Lanka and Asia Biodiversity Programme, Colombo, Sri Lanka.

Daszak, P., L. Berger, A. A. Cunningham, A. D. Hyatt, D. E. Green, and R. Speare. 1999. Emerging infectious diseases and amphibian population declines. Emerging Infectious Diseases 5:735–748.

Daszak, P., A. A. Cunningham, and A. D. Hyatt. 2000. Emerging infectious diseases of wildlife-threats to biodiversity and human health. Science 287:443–449.

Davidson, C., H. B. Shaffer, and M. R. Jennings. 2001. Declines of the California red-legged frog: Climate, UV-B, habitat, and pesticides hypotheses. Ecological Applications 11: 464–479.

Davidson, C., H. B. Shaffer, and M. R. Jennings. In Press. Spatial tests of the pesticide drift, habitat destruction, UV-B and climate change hypotheses for California amphibian declines. Conservation Biology.

Davis, B. D., R. Dulbecco, H. N. Eisen, H. S. Ginsberg, and W. B. Wood, Jr. 1973. Microbiology. 2nd edition. Harper and Row, New York, NY. 1561 p.

de Vlaming, V. L., and R. B. Bury. 1970. Thermal selection in tadpoles of the tailed-frog, *Ascaphus truei*. Journal of Herpetology 4:179–189.

DeGraaf, R. M., and M. Yamaski. 1992. A non-destructive technique to monitor the relative abundance of terrestrial salamanders. Wildlife Society Bulletin 20:260–265.

Delis, P. R., H. R. Mushinsky, and E. D. McCoy. 1996. Decline of some west-central Florida anuran populations in response to habitat degradation. Biodiversity and Conservation 5:1579–1595.

deMaynadier, P. G., and M. L. Hunter, Jr. 1995. The relationship between forest management and amphibian ecology: A review of the North American literature. Environmental Reviews 3:230–261.

deMaynadier, P. G., and M. L. Hunter, Jr. 1998. Effects of silvicultural edges on the distribution and abundance of amphibians in Maine. Conservation Biology 12:340–352.

deMaynadier, P. G., and M. L. Hunter, Jr. 1999. Forest canopy closure and juvenile emigration by pool-breeding amphibians in Maine. Journal of Wildlife Management 63:441–450.

deMaynadier, P. G., and M. L. Hunter, Jr. 2000. Road effects on amphibian movements in a forested landscape. Natural Areas Journal 20:56–65.

Denton, J. S., S. P. Hitchings, T. J. C. Beebee, and A. Gent. 1997. A recovery program for the natterjack toad (*Bufo calamita*) in Britain. Conservation Biology 11:1329–1353.

Devillers, J., and J. M. Exbrayat. 1992. Ecotoxicity of chemicals to amphibians. Gordon and Breach Science Publishers, Pjiladelphia, PA. 351 p.

Diamond, J. 1986. Overview: laboratory experiments, field experiments, and natural experiments. Pp. 3–22 in T. J. Case, and J. Diamond, editors. Community Ecology. Harper and Row, Publishers, New York, NY.

Diamond, J. M. 1996. A-bombs against amphibians. Nature 383:386–387.

Diana, S. G., W. J. Resetarits, D. J. Schaeffer, K. B. Beckmen, and V. R. Beasley. 2000. Effects of atrazine on amphibian growth and survival in artificial aquatic communities. Environmental Toxicology and Chemistry 19:2961–2967.

Diaz, H. F., and N. E. Graham. 1996. Recent changes in tropical freezing heights and the role of sea surface temperature. Nature 383:152–155.

Díaz, J. A. 1999. Amphibians in Michoacán, Mexico. FROGLOG 31:1.

Dickson, J. G., editor. 2001. Wildlife of the Southern Forests. Habitat and Management. Hancock House Publishers, Blaine, WA.

Diller, L. V., and R. L. Wallace. 1996. Distribution and habitat of *Rhyacotriton variegatus* in managed, young growth forests in north coastal California. Journal of Herpetology 30:184–191.

Dixon, P. M. A. R. Olsen, B. M. Kahn. 1998. Measuring trends in ecological resources. Ecological Applications 8:225–227.

Dobson, A. P., and R. M. May. 1986. Disease and conservation. Pp. 345–365 *in* M. E. Soulé, editor. Conservation Biology: The Science of Scarcity and Diversity. Sinauer Associates, Sunderland, MA.

Dodd, C. K., Jr. 1989. Status of the Red Hills salamander is reassessed. Endangered Species Technical Bulletin 14:10–11.

Dodd, C. K., Jr. 1991. The status of the Red Hills salamander *Phaeognathus hubrichti*, Alabama, USA, 1976–1988. Biological Conservation 55:57–75.

Dodd, C. K., Jr. 1992. Biological diversity of a temporary pond herpetofauna in north Florida sandhills. Biodiversity and Conservation 1:125–142.

Dodd, C. K., Jr. 1993. Cost of living in an unpredictable environment: The ecology of striped newts *Notophthalmus perstriatus* during a prolonged drought. Copeia 1993:605–614.

Dodd, C. K., Jr. 1995. The ecology of a sandhills population of the eastern narrow mouthed toad, *Gastrophryne carolinensis*, during a drought. Bulletin of the Florida Museum of Natural History 38:11–41.

Dodd, C. K., Jr. 1997. Imperiled amphibians: a historical perspective. Pp. 165–200 *in* G. W. Benz, and D. E. Collins, editors. Aquatic Fauna in Peril: The Southeastern Perspective. Southeast Aquatic Research Institute, Lenz Design and Communications, Decatur, GA. Special Publication 1.

Dodd, C. K., Jr. 1998. *Desmognathus auriculatus* at Devil's Millhopper State Geological Site, Alachua County, Florida. Florida Scientist 6:38–45.

Dodd, C. K., Jr., and B. S. Cade. 1998. Movement patterns and the conservation of amphibians breeding in small, temporary wetlands. Conservation Biology 12:331–339.

Dodson, S. I., T. Hanzato, and P. R. Gorski. 1995. Behavioral responses of *Daphnia pulex* exposed to carbaryl and *Chaoborus kairomone*. Environmental Toxicology and Chemistry 14:43–50.

Donnelly, M. A., and M. L. Crump. 1998. Potential effects of climate change on two neotropical amphibian assemblages. Climatic Change 39:541–561.

Drake, D. C., and R. J. Naiman. 2000. An evaluation of restoration efforts in fishless lakes stocked with exotic trout. Conservation Biology 14:1807–1820.

Driscoll, C. T., G. B. Lawrence, A. J. Bulger, T. J. Butler, C. S. Cronan, C. Eagar, K. F. Lambert, G. E. Likens, J. L. Stoddard, and K. C. Weathers. 2001. Acidic deposition in the Northeastern United States: Sources, inputs, ecosystem effects, and management strategies. BioScience 51:180–198.

Driscoll, D. A. 1998. Genetic structure, metapopulation processes and evolution influence the conservation strategies for two endangered frog species. Biological Conservation 83:43–54.

Drost, C. A., and G. M. Fellers. 1996. Collapse of regional frog fauna in the Yosemite area of the California Sierra Nevada. Conservation Biology 10:414–425.

Drury, S. E. N., R. E. Gough, and A. A. Cunningham. 1995. Isolation of an iridovirus-like agent from common frogs (*Rana temporaria*). Veterinary Record 137:72–73.

Du Pasquier, L., J. Schwager, and M. F. Flajnik. 1989. The immune system of *Xenopus*. Annual Review of Immunology 7:251–275.

Duellman, W. E. 1978. The biology of an equatorial herpetofauna in Amazonian Ecuador.

Miscellaneous Publications of the Museum of Natural History University of Kansas. 65:1–352.

Duellman, W. E. 1979. The herpetofauna of the Andes: Patterns of distribution, origin, differentiation, and present communities. Pp. 371–460 *in* W. E. Duellman, editor. The South American Herpetofauna: Its Origin, Evolution, and Dispersal. Monographs of the Museum of Natural History University of Kansas 7:1–485.

Duellman, W. E. 1995. Temporal fluctuations in abundances of anuran amphibians in a seasonal Amazonian rainforest. Journal of Herpetology 29:13–21.

Duellman, W. E. 1999a. Distribution patterns of amphibians in South America. Pp. 255–328 *in* W. E. Duellman, editor. Patterns of Distribution of Amphibians: A Global Perspective. Johns Hopkins University Press, Baltimore, MD.

Duellman, W. E. 1999b. Global distribution of amphibians: Patterns, conservation, and future challenges. Pp. 1–30 in W. E. Duellman, editor. Patterns of Distribution of Amphibians: A Global Perspective. Johns Hopkins University Press, Baltimore, MD.

Duellman, W. E. 2001. Hylid Frogs of Middle America. Volumes 1 and 2. Society for the Study of Amphibians and Reptiles, St. Louis, MO.

Duellman, W. E., and L. Trueb. 1986. Biology of Amphibians. McGraw-Hill, Inc. New York, NY. 670 p.

Duellman, W. E., and L. Trueb. 1994. Biology of Amphibians. Johns Hopkins University Press, Baltimore, MD.

Duellman, W. E., and S. S. Sweet. 1999. Distributional patterns of amphibians in the Nearctic region of North America. Pp. 31–109 *in* W. E. Duellman, editor. Patterns of Distribution of Amphibians: A Global Perspective. Johns Hopkins University Press, Baltimore, MD.

Dugan, P., editor. 1993. Wetlands in danger: A world conservation atlas. Oxford University Press, New York, NY.

Dunning, J. B., B. J. Danielson, and H. R. Pulliam. 1992. Ecological processes that affect populations in complex landscapes. Oikos 65:169–175.

Dunson, W. A., and R. L. Wyman, editors. 1992. Amphibian declines and habitat acidification. Journal of Herpetology 26:349–433.

Dunson, W. A., R. L. Wyman, and E. S. Corbett. 1992. A symposium on amphibian declines and habitat acidification. Journal of Herpetology 26:349–352.

Dupuis, L. A., J. N. M. Smith, and F. Bunnell. 1995. Relation of terrestrial-breeding amphibian abundance to tree-stand age. Conservation Biology 9:645–653.

Dupuis, L. A., and D. Steventon. 1999. Riparian management and the tailed frog in northern coastal forests. Forest Ecology and Management 124:35–43.

Easteal, S., E. K. Van Beurden, R. B. Floyd, and M. D. Sabath. 1985. Continuing geographical spread of *Bufo marinus* in Australia: Range expansion between 1974 and 1980. Journal of Herpetology 19:185–188.

Ebert, D. 1999. The evolution and expression of parasite virulence. Pp. 161–172 *in* S. C. Stearns, editor. Evolution in Health and Disease. Oxford University Press, New York, NY.

Ecobichon, D. J. 1996. Toxic effects of pesticides. Pp. 643–689 *in* C. D. Klaassen, editor. Casarett and Doull's Toxicology: The Basic Science of Poisons. 5th edition. McGraw-Hill Companies, New York, NY.

Edwards, C. A. 1993. The impact of pesticides on the environment. Pp. 13–46 *in* D. Pimentel, and H. Lehman, editors. The Pesticide Question: Environment, Economics, and Ethics. Chapman & Hall, New York, NY.

Ehrlich, D. 1979. Predation by bullfrog tadpoles (*Rana catesbeiana*) on eggs and newly hatched larvae of the plains leopard frog (*Rana blairi*). Bulletin of the Maryland Herpetological Society 15:25–26.

Eklund, T. J., W. H. McDowell, and C. M. Pringle. 1997. Seasonal variation of tropical precipitation chemistry: La Selva, Costa Rica. Atmospheric Environment 31:3903–3910.

Eldridge, N. 1998. Life in the Balance: Humanity and the Biodiversity Crisis. Princeton University Press, Princeton, NJ.

Ellefson, P. V., M. A. Kilgore, and M. J. Phillips. 2001. Monitoring compliance with BMPs: The experience of state forestry agencies. Journal of Forestry 99:11–17.

Enge, K. M. 1993. Herptile use and trade in Florida. Final Performance Report, Bureau of Nongame Wildlife, Florida Game and Fresh Water Fish Commission, Quincy, FL.

Environmental Law Institute. 2001. Wetland banking mitigation study, preliminary findings. September 25, 2001. Available online at: www.eli.org/wmb/tools.htm.

Epstein, P. R. 1997. Climate, ecology, and human health. Consequences 3:3–19.

Erspamer, V. 1994. Bioactive secretions of the amphibian integument. Pp. 178–350 in H. Heatwole, editor. Amphibian Biology. Volume 1. The Integument. Surrey Beatty and Sons, Chipping Norton, New South Wales, Australia.

Eshleman, K. N., R. P. Morgan II, J. R. Webb, F. A. Deviney, and J. N. Galloway. 1998. Temporal patterns of nitrogen leakage from mid-Appalachian watersheds: Role of insect defoliation. Water Resources Research 34:2005–2016.

Espinoza, F. A., J. E. Deacon, and A. Simmons. 1970. An Economic and Biostatistical Analysis of the Bait Fish Industry in the Lower Colorado River. Special Publication of the University of Nevada, Las Vegas, NV.

Evans, M., C. Yaber, and J.-M. Hero. 1996. Factors influencing choice of breeding site by *Bufo marinus* in its natural habitat. Copeia 1996:904–912.

Faaborg, J. 1980. Potential uses and abuses of diversity concepts in wildlife management. Transactions of the Missouri Academy of Sciences 14:41–49.

Fahrig, L. 1997. Relative effects of habitat loss and fragmentation on population extinction. Journal of Wildlife Management 61:603–610.

Fahrig, L., and G. Merriam. 1994. Conservation of fragmented populations. Conservation Biology 8:50–59.

Fahrig, L., J. H. Pedlar, S. E. Pope, P. D. Taylor, and J. F. Wegner. 1995. Effect of road traffic on amphibian density. Biological Conservation 73:177–182.

Fairchild, J. F., T. W. LaPoint, J. L. Zajicek, M. K. Nelso, F. J. Dwyer, and P. A. Lovely. 1992. Population-, community- and ecosystem-level responses of aquatic mesocosms to pulsed doses of a pyrethroid insecticide. Environmental Toxicology and Chemistry 11:115–129.

FAO (Food and Agriculture Organization). 2001. State of the World's Forests 2001. Part II. Key Issues in the Forest Sector Today. The Status of Forests: The Global Forest Resources Assessment 2000. United Nations, Rome, Italy. Available online at: http://www.fao.org/docrep/003/y0900e/y0900e00.htm.

Farr, J. A. 1977. Impairment of antipredator behavior in *Palaemonetes pugio* by exposure to sublethal doses of parathion. Transactions of the American Fisheries Society 106:287–290.

Feder, M. E. 1978. Environmental variability and thermal acclimation in neotropical and temperate zone salamanders. Physiological Zoology 51:7–16.

Feinsinger, P. 2001. Designing Field Studies for Biodiversity Conservation. Island Press, Washington, DC.

Fellers, G. M., and C. A. Drost 1993 Disappearance of the Cascades frog *Rana cascadae*, at the southern end of its range. Biological Conservation 65:177–181.

Fellers, G. M., D. E. Green, and J. E. Longcore. 2001. Oral chytridiomycosis in mountain yellow-legged frogs (*Rana muscosa*). Copeia 2001:945–953.

Fioramonti, E., R. D. Semlitsch, H. Reyer, and K. Fent. 1997. Effects of triphenyltin and pH on the growth and development of *Rana lessonae* and *Rana esculenta* tadpoles. Environmental Toxicology and Chemistry 16:1940–1947.

Fisher, R. N., and H. B. Shaffer. 1996. The decline of amphibians in California's great central valley. Conservation Biology 10:1387–1397.

Fite, K.V., A. R. Blaustein, L. Bengston, and H. E. Hewitt. 1998. Evidence of retinal light damage in *Rana cascadae*: A declining amphibian species. Copeia 1998:906–914.

Fitzgerald, S. 1989. International wildlife trade: Whose business is it? World Wildlife Fund, Baltimore, MD.

Forchhammer, M. C., E. Post, and N. C. Stenseth. 1998. Breeding phenology and climate. Nature 391:29–30.

Ford, W. M., B. R. Chapman, M. A. Menzel, and R. H. Odum. 2002. Stand age and habitat influences on salamanders in Appalachian cove hardwood forests. Forest Ecology and Management 155:131–141.

Forman, R. T. T., and L. E. Alexander, 1998. Roads and their major ecological effects. Annual Review of Ecology and Systematics 29:207–231.

Forman, R. T. T., D. S. Friedman, D. Fitzhenry, J. D. Martin, A. S. Chen, and L. E. Alexander. 1995. Ecological effects of roads: Toward three summary indices and an overview for North America. Pp. 40–54 *in* K. Canters, editor. Habitat Fragmentation and Infrastructure. Proceedings of the International Conference on Habitat Fragmentation, Infrastructure and the Role of Ecological Engineering, Maastricht and The Hague, Netherlands.

Forman, R. T. T., and M. Godron. 1986. Landscape Ecology. Wiley, New York, NY.

Formanowicz, D. R., Jr., and E. D. Brodie, Jr. 1982. Relative palatabilities of members of a larval amphibian community. Copeia 1982:91–97.

Fort, D. J., T. L. Propst, E. L. Stover, J. C. Helgen, R. B. Levey, K. Gallagher, and J. G. Burkhart. 1999a. Effects of pond water, sediment, and sediment extracts from Minnesota and Vermont, USA, on early development and metamorphosis of *Xenopus*. Environmental Toxicology and Chemistry 18:2316–2324.

Fort, D. J., R. L. Rogers, H. F. Copley, L. A. Bruning, E. L. Stover, J. C. Helgen, and J. G. Burkhart. 1999b. Progress toward identifying causes of maldevelopment induced in *Xenopus* by pond water and sediment extracts from Minnesota, USA. Environmental Toxicology and Chemistry 18:2316–2324.

Frank, W. C., and W. W. Dunlap. 1999. Colonization of high-elevation lakes by long-toed salamanders (*Ambystoma macrodactylum*) after the extinction of local trout populations. Canadian Journal of Zoology 77:1759–1767.

Fraser, D. F. 1976. Coexistence of salamanders in the genus *Plethodon*: A variation of the Santa Rosalia theme. Ecology 57:238–251.

Freda, J., and W. A. Dunson. 1985. Field and laboratory studies of ion balance and growth rates of ranid tadpoles chronically exposed to low pH. Copeia 1985:415–423.

Freeland, W. J., and K. C. Martin. 1985. The rate of range expansion by *Bufo marinus* in northern Australia, 1980–84. Australian Wildlife Research 12:555–559.

French, H., and L. Mastny. 2001. Controlling international environmental crime. Pp. 166–188 *in* L. Starke, editor. State of the World 2001. W.W. Norton and Company, New York, NY.

French, V., P. J. Bryant, and S. V. Bryant. 1976. Pattern regulation in epimorphic fields. Science 193:969–981.

Frisbie, M. P., and R. L. Wyman. 1991. The effects of soil pH on sodium balance in the red-backed salamander, *Plethodon cinereus* and three other terrestrial salamanders. Physiological Zoology 64:1050–1068.

Frisbie, M. P., and R. L. Wyman. 1992. The effects of soil chemistry on sodium balance in the red-backed salamander: A comparison of two forests types. Journal of Herpetology 26:434–442.

Frisbie, M. P., and R. L. Wyman. 1995. A field simulation of the effect of acidic rain on ion balance in a woodland salamander. Archives of Environmental Contamination and Toxicology 28:327–333.

Frost, D., editor. 1985 Amphibian Species of the World. Association of Systematics Collections, Allen Press, Lawrence, KS.

Galat, D. L., L. H. Fredrickson, D. D. Humburg, K. J. Bataille, J. R. Bodie, J. Dohrenwend, G. T. Gelwicks, J. E. Havel, D. L. Helmers, J. B. Hooker, J. R. Jones, M. F. Knowlton, J. Kubisiak, J. Mazourek, A. C. McColpin, R. B. Renken, and R. D. Semlitsch. 1998. Flooding to restore connectivity of regulated, large-river wetlands: Natural and controlled flooding as complementary processes along the lower Missouri River. BioScience 48: 721–733.

Gamrandt, S. C., and L. B. Kats. 1996. Effect of introduced crayfish and mosquitofish on California newts. Conservation Biology 10:1155–1162.

Gamrandt, S. C., L. B. Kats, and C. B. Anzalone. 1997. Aggression by non-native crayfish deters breeding in California newts. Conservation Biology 11:793–796.

Gandon, S., Y. Capowiez, Y. Dubois, Y. Michalakis, and I. Olivieri. 1996. Local adaptation and gene-for-gene coevolution in a metapopulation model. Proceedings of the Royal Society of London, Series B 263:1003–1009.

Gandon, S., and P. A. Van Zandt. 1998. Local adaptation and host-parasite interactions. Trends in Ecology and Evolution 13:214–216.

Gardiner, D. M., and D. M. Hoppe. 1999. Environmentally induced limb abnormalities in mink frogs (*Rana septentrionalis*). Journal of Experimental Zoology 284:207–216.

Gates, J. E., C. H. Hocutt, J. R. Stauffer, Jr., and G. J. Taylor. 1985. The distribution and status of *Cryptobranchus alleganiensis* in Maryland. Herpetological Review 16:17–18.

Gent, T., and R. Bray, editors. 1994. Conservation and management of great crested newts. Proceedings of a symposium held on 11 January 1994 at Kew Gardens, Richmond, Surrey. English Nature Series No. 20, Peterborough, UK.

Georghiou, G. P. 1986. The magnitude of the resistance problem. Pp. 11–44 *in* National Research Council, compiler. Pesticide Resistance: Strategies and Tactics for Management. National Academy Press, Washington, DC.

Gerlanc, N. M. 1999. Effects of breeding pool permanence on developmental rate of western chorus frogs, *Pseudacris triseriata,* in tallgrass prairie. M.S. Thesis. Kansas State University, Manhattan, KS.

Gibbons, J. W., and D. H. Bennett. 1974. Determination of anuran terrestrial activity patterns by a drift fence method. Copeia 1974:236–243.

Gibbons, J. W., and M. E. Dorcas. Defensive behavior of cottonmouths (*Agkistrodon piscivorus*) towards humans. Copeia 2002:195–198.

Gibbons, J. W., D. E. Scott, T. R. Ryan, K. A. Buhlmann, T. D. Tuberville, B. S. Metts, J. L. Greene, T. Mills, Y. Leiden, S. Poppy, and C. T. Winne. 2000. The global decline of reptiles, déjà vu amphibians. Bioscience 50:653–666.

Gibbons, J. W., and R. D. Semlitsch. 1981. Terrestrial drift fences with pitfall traps: An effective technique for quantitative sampling of animal populations. Brimleyana 7:1–16.

Gibbons, J. W., and P. W. Stangel, coordinators. 1999. Conserving amphibians and reptiles in the new millenium. Proceedings of the Partners in Amphibian and Reptile Conservation (PARC) Conference. June, 1999. Aiken, SC. Savannah River Ecology Laboratory Herp Outreach Publication #2.

Gibbs, E. L., G. W. Nace, and M. B. Emmons. 1971. The live frog is almost dead. Bioscience 21:1027–1034.

Gibbs, J. P. 1993. Importance of small wetlands for the persistence of local populations of wetland-associated animals. Wetlands 13:25–31.

Gibbs, J. P. 1998a. Amphibian movements in response to forest edges, roads, and streambeds in southern New England. Journal of Wildlife Management 62:584–589.

Gibbs, J. P. 1998b. Distribution of woodland amphibians along a forest fragmentation gradient. Landscape Ecology 13:263–268.

Gibbs, J. P. 1998c. Genetic structure of redback salamander *Plethodon cinereus* populations in continuous and fragmented forests. Biological Conservation 86:77–81.

Gibbs, J. P. 2000. Wetland loss and biodiversity conservation. Conservation Biology 14:314–317.

Gibbs, J. P., and A. R. Breisch. 2001. Climate warming and calling phenology of frogs near Ithaca, New York, 1900–1999. Conservation Biology 15:1175–1178.

Gilbert, F. F., and R. Allwine. 1991. Terrestrial amphibian communities in the Oregon Cascade Range. Pp. 318–324 *in* L. F. Ruggiero, K. B. Aubry, A. B. Carey, and M. H. Huff, technical coordinators. Wildlife and Vegetation of Unmanaged Douglas-Fir Forests. USDA Forest Service, General Technical Report PNW-285.

Gilbert, S. F. 2000. Developmental Biology. 6th edition. Sinauer, Sunderland, MA.

Gill, D. E. 1978. The metapopulation ecology of the red-spotted newt, *Notophthalmus viridescens* (Rafinesque). Ecological Monographs 48:145–166.

Gillespie, G. R. 2001. The role of introduced trout in the decline of the spotted tree frog (*Litoria spenceri*) in south-eastern Australia. Biological Conservation 100:187–198.

Gillespie, G. R. and J.-M. Hero. 1999. Potential impacts of introduced fish and fish translocations on Australian amphibians. Pp.131–144 *in* A. Campbell, editor. Declines and Disappearances of Australian Frogs. Environment Australia, Canberra, Australia.

Goater, C. P., R. D. Semlitsch, and M. V. Bernasconi. 1993. Effects of body size and parasite infection on the locomotory performance of juvenile toads, *Bufo bufo*. Oikos 66:129–136.

Godreau, V., G. Bornette, B. Frochot, C. Amoros, E. Castella, B. Oertli, F. Chambaud, D. Oberti, and E. Craney. 1999. Biodiversity in the floodplain of Saone: A global approach. Biodiversity and Conservation 8:839–864.

Good, D. A., and D. B. Wake. 1992. Geographic variation and speciation in the torrent salamanders of the genus *Rhyacotriton* (Caudata: Rhyacotritonidae). University of California Publications in Zoology 126:1–91.

Goodsell, J. A., and L. B. Kats. 1999. Effect of introduced mosquitofish on Pacific treefrogs and the role of alternative prey. Conservation Biology 13:921–924.

Gore, A. 1992. Earth in the Balance. Houghton Mifflin, Boston, MA.

Gore, J. A. 1983. The distribution of desmognathine larvae (Amphibia: Plethodontidae) in coal surface impacted streams of the Cumberland Plateau, USA. Journal of Freshwater Ecology 2:13–83.

Gorzula, S. 1996. The trade in dentrobatid frogs from 1987 to 1993. Herpetological Review 27:116–123.

Gould, F. 1991. The evolutionary potential of crop pests. American Scientist 79:496–507.

Granoff, A. 1969. Viruses of Amphibia. Pp. 107–137 *in* Volume 50, Current Topics in Microbiology and Immunology. Springer-Verlag, New York, NY.

Granoff, A., P. E. Came, and D. C. Breeze. 1966. Viruses and renal carcinoma of *Rana pipiens* I. The isolation and properties of virus from normal and tumor tissue. Virology 29: 133–148.

Granoff, A., P. E. Came, and K. A. Rafferty. 1965. The isolation and properties of viruses from *Rana pipiens*: Their possible relationship to the renal adenocarcinoma of the leopard frog. Annals of the New York Academy of Sciences 126:237–255.

Grant, P. R., and B. R. Grant. 1996. Finch communities in a climatically fluctuating environment. Pp. 343–390 in M. L. Cody, and J. A. Smallwood, editors. Long-term Studies of Vertebrate Communities. Academic Press, San Diego, CA.

Green, D. E., and C. K. Sherman. 2001. Diagnostic histological findings in Yosemite toads (*Bufo canorus*) from a die-off in the 1970s. Journal of Herpetology 35:92–103.

Green, M. B. 1976. Pesticides—Boon or Bane? Westview Press. Boulder, CO.

Grialou, J. A., S. D. West, and R. N. Wilkins. 2000. The effects of forest clearcut harvesting and thinning on terrestrial salamanders. Journal of Wildlife Management 64(1):105–113.

Grinnell, J., and T. I. Storer. 1924. Animal Life in the Yosemite. University of California Press, Berkeley, CA.

Grover, M. C. 1998. Influence of cover and moisture on abundances of the terrestrial salamanders *Plethodon cinereus* and *Plethodon glutinosus*. Journal of Herpetology 32:489–497.

Grover, M. C. 2000. Determinants of salamander distributions along moisture gradients. Copeia 2000:156–168.

Groves, C. R., E. F. Cassirer, D. L. Genter, and J. D. Reichel. 1996. Coeur d'Alene salamander (*Plethodon idahoensis*). Elemental Stewardship Abstract. Natural Areas Journal 6:238–247.

Gwin, S. E., M. E. Kentula, and P. W. Shaffer. 1999. Evaluating the effects of wetland regulation through hydrogeomorphic classification and landscape profiles. Wetlands 19: 447–489.

Haddad, N. M. 1999. Corridor use predicted from behaviors at habitat boundaries. American Naturalist 153:215–227.

Hairston, N. G. 1980. Evolution under interspecific competition: Field experiments on terrestrial salamanders. Evolution 34:409–420.

Hairston, N. G. 1986. Species packing in *Desmognathus* salamanders: Experimental demonstration of predation and competition. American Naturalist 127:266–291.

Hairston, N. G. 1987. Community ecology and salamander guilds. Cambridge University Press, Cambridge, UK.

Hairston, N. G., and R. H. Wiley. 1993. No decline in salamander (Amphibia: Caudata) populations: A twenty-year study in the southern Appalachians. Brimleyana 18:59–64.

Häkkinen, J., S. Pasanen, and J. V. K. Kukkonen. 2001. The effects of solar UV-B radiation on embryonic mortality and development in three boreal anurans (*Rana temporaria, Rana arvalis,* and *Bufo bufo*). Chemosphere 44:441–446.

Hall, J. D., M. L. Murphy, and R. S. Aho. 1978. An improved design for assessing impacts of watershed practices on small streams. Internationale Vereinigung für Theoretische und Angewandte Limnologie. Verhandlungen 20:1359–1365.

Hallac, D. E., and J. E. Marsden. 2001. Comparison of conservation strategies for unionids threatened by zebra mussels (*Dreissena polymorpha*): Periodic cleaning vs quarantine and translocation. Journal of the North American Benthological Society 20:200–210.

Halliday, T. 1998. A declining amphibian conundrum. Nature 394:418–419.

Hammock, B. D., and D. M. Soderlund. 1986. Chemical strategies for resistance management. Pp. 111–129 *in* National Research Council, compiler. Pesticide Resistance: Strategies and Tactics for Management. National Academy Press, Washington, DC.

Hanken, J. 1999. Why are there so many new amphibian species when amphibians are declining? Trends in Ecology and Evolution 14:7–8.

Hansen, K. L. 1960. The use of male southern toads and southern leopard frogs for pregnancy diagnosis. Herpetologica 16:33–38.

Hanski, I. 1990. Density dependence, regulation and variability in animal populations. Philosophical Transactions of the Royal Society of London B 330:141–150.

Hanski, I., and M. E. Gilpin. 1991a. Metapopulation dynamics: Brief history and conceptual domain. Biological Journal of the Linnean Society 42:3–16.

Hanski, I., and M. E. Gilpin. 1991b. Metapopulation Dynamics. Academic Press, London, UK.

Hanski, I., and D. Simberloff. 1997. The metapopulation approach, its history, conceptual domain, and application to conservation. Pp. 5–26 in I. A. Hanski, and M. E. Gilpin, editors. Metapopulation Biology: Ecology, Genetics, and Evolution. Academic Press, San Diego, CA.

Harding, J. S., E. F. Benfield, P. V. Bolstad, G. S. Helfman, and E. B. D. Jones III. 1998. Stream biodiversity: The ghost of land use past. Proceedings of the National Academy of Sciences (USA) 95:14843–14847.

Hardouin, J. 1995. Minilivestock: From gathering to controlled production. Biodiversity and Conservation 4:220–232.

Harmon, M. A., M. F. Boehm, R. A. Heyman, and D. J. Mangelsdorf. 1995. Activation of mammalian retinoid X receptors by the insect growth regulator methoprene. Proceedings of the National Academy of Sciences (USA) 92:6157–6160.

Harpole, D. N., and C. A. Haas. 1999. Effects of seven silvicultural treatments on terrestrial salamanders. Forest Ecology and Management 114:349–356.

Harrison, R. G. 1969. Organization and Development of the Embryo. Yale University Press, New Haven, CT.

Harte, J., and E. Hoffman. 1989. Possible effects of acidic deposition on a Rocky-Mountain population of the tiger salamander *Ambystoma tigrinum*. Conservation Biology 3:149–158.

Hartley, M. J. 2002. Rationale and methods for conserving biodiversity in plantation forests. Forest Ecology and Management 155:81–95.

Hayes, J. P., and R. J. Steidl. 1997. Statistical power analysis and amphibian population trends. Conservation Biology 11:273–275.

Hayes, M. P., and M. R. Jennings. 1986. Decline of ranid frog species in Western North America: Are bullfrogs (*Rana catesbeiana*) responsible? Journal of Herpetology 20:490–509.

Hayes, T. B. 2000. Endocrine disruption in amphibians. Pp. 573–593 in D. W. Sparling, G. Linder, and C. A. Bishop, editors. Ecotoxicology of Amphibians and Reptiles. Society of Environmental Toxicology and Chemistry, Pensacola, FL.

Hayes, T. B., A. Collins, M. Lee, M. Mendoza, N. Noriega, A. A. Stuart, and A. Vonk. 2002. Hermaphroditic, demasculinized frogs after exposure to the herbicide atrazine at low ecologically relevant doses. Proceedings of the National Academy of Sciences (USA) 99:5476–5480.

Hays, J. B., A. R. Blaustein, J. M. Kiesecker, P. D. Hoffman, I. Pandelova, C. Coyle, and T. Richardson. 1996. Developmental responses of amphibians to solar and artificial UV-B sources: A comparative study. Photochemistry and Photobiology 64:449–456.

He, J. G., L. Lu, M. Deng, H. H. He, S. P. Weng, X. H. Wang, S. Y. Zhou, Q. X. Long, X. Z. Wang, and S. M. Chan. 2002. Sequence analysis of the complete genome of an iridovirus isolated from the tiger frog. Virology 292:185–197.

Heard, R. M., W. E. Sharpe, R. F. Carline, and W. G. Kimmel. 1997. Episodic acidification and changes in fish diversity in Pennsylvania headwater streams. Transactions of the American Fisheries Society 126:977–984.

Heatwole, H. 1962. Environmental factors influencing local distribution and activity of the salamander, *Plethodon cinereus*. Ecology 43:460–472.

Hecker, L., and S. K. Sessions. 2001. Developmental analysis of limb abnormalities in amphibians. Bios 72:9–13.

Hecnar, S. J., and R. T. M'Closkey. 1996. Regional dynamics and the status of amphibians. Ecology 77:2091–2097.

Hecnar, S. J., and R. T. M'Closkey. 1997a. Patterns of nestedness and species association in a pond-dwelling amphibian fauna. Oikos 80:371–381.

Hecnar, S. J., and R. T. M'Closkey. 1997b. The effects of predatory fish on amphibian species richness and distribution. Biological Conservation 79:123–131.

Hedges, S. B. 1993. Global amphibian declines: A perspective from the Caribbean. Biodiversity and Conservation 2:290–303.

Hedges, S. B. 1999. Distribution patterns of amphibians in the West Indies. Pp. 211–254 *in* W. E. Duellman, editor. Patterns of Distribution of Amphibians: A Global Perspective. Johns Hopkins University Press, Baltimore, MD.

Hehl-Lange, S. 2001. Structural elements of the visual landscape and their ecological functions. Landscape and Urban Planning 54:105–113.

Helgen, J., R. G. Mckinnell, and M. C. Gernes. 1998. Investigation of malformed northern leopard frogs in Minnesota. Pp. 288–297 *in* M. J. Lanoo, editor. Status and Conservation of Midwestern Amphibians. University of Iowa Press, Ames, IA.

Henneman, M. L., and J. Memmott. 2001. Infiltration of a Hawaiian community by introduced biological control agents. Science 293:1314–1316.

Herbeck, L. A., and R. D. Semlitsch. 2000. Life history and ecology of the southern redback salamander, *Plethodon serratus*, in Missouri. Journal of Herpetology 34:341–347.

Herlihy, A. T., P. R. Kaufmann, M. R. Church, P. J. Wigington, Jr., J. R. Webb, and M. J. Sale. 1993. The effects of acidic deposition on streams in the Appalachian Mountain and Piedmont region of the Mid-Atlantic United States. Water Resources Research 29:2687–2703.

Herman, J. R., P. K. Bhartia, J. Ziemke, Z. Ahmad, and D. Larko. 1996. UV-B increases (1979–1992) from decreases in total ozone. Geophysical Research Letters 23:2117–2120.

Hero, J.-M. 2001. Assessing the conservation status of Australian frogs. FROGLOG 48:6.

Hero, J.-M., C. Gascon, and W. E. Magnusson. 1998. Direct and indirect effects of predation on tadpole community structure in the Amazon rainforest. Australian Journal of Ecology 23:474–482.

Hero, J.-M., W. E. Magnusson, F. Duarte da Rocha, and C. Catterall. 2001. Survival strategies influence prey distributions and community diversity. Biotropica 33:131–141.

Herreid, C. F., and S. Kinney. 1966. Survival of Alaskan woodfrog (*Rana sylvatica*) larvae. Ecology 47:1039–1041.

Hess, G. R. 1996. Disease in metapopulation models: implications for conservation. Ecology 77:1617–1632.

Hews, D. K. 1995. Overall predator feeding rates and relative susceptibility of large and small tadpoles to fish predation depend on microhabitat: A laboratory study. Journal of Herpetology 29:142–145.

Heyer, W. R., M. A. Donnelly, R. W. McDiarmid, L.-A. C. Hayek, and M. S. Foster. 1994. Measuring and Monitoring Biological Diversity: Standard Methods for Amphibians. Smithsonian Institution Press, Washington, DC.

Heyer, W. R., R. W. McDiarmid, and D. L. Weigmann. 1975. Tadpoles, predation, and pond habitats in the tropics. Biotropica 7:100–111.

Heyer, W. R., A. S. Rand, C. A. Goncalvez de Cruz, and O. L. Peixoto. 1988. Decimations, extinctions, and colonizations of frog populations in southeast Brazil and their evolutionary implications. Biotropica 20:230–235.

Highton, R. 1983. A new species of woodland salamander of the *Plethodon glutinosus* group from the southern Appalachian Mountains. Brimleyana 9:1–20.

Highton, R. 1995. Speciation in eastern North American salamanders of the genus *Plethodon*. Annual Review of Ecology and Systematics 26:579–600.

Highton, R. 1999. Geographic protein variation and speciation in the salamanders of the *Plethodon cinereus* group with the description of two new species. Herpetologica 55:43–90.

Highton, R., G. C. Maha, and L. R. Maxson. 1989. Biochemical evolution in the slimy salamanders of the *Plethodon glutinosis* complex in eastern United States. University of Illinois Biological Monograph 57:1–153.

Highton, R., and T. Savage. 1961. Functions of the brooding behavior in the female red-backed salamander, *Plethodon cinereus*. Copeia 1961:95–98.

Hill, E. F., and W. J. Fleming. 1982. Anticholinesterase poisoning of birds: Field monitoring and diagnosis of acute poisoning. Environmental Toxicology and Chemistry 1:27–38.

Hillis, D. M., D. A. Chamberlain, T. P. Wilcox, and P. T. Chippindale. 2001. A new species of subterranean blind salamander (Plethodontidae: Hemidactyliini: Eurycea: Typhlomolge) from Austin, Texas, and a systematic revision of central Texas paedomorphic salamanders. Herpetologica 57(3):266–280.

Hilton-Taylor, C., compiler. 2000. 2000 IUCN Red List of Threatened Species. IUCN, Gland, Switzerland and Cambridge, UK. xviii + 61 p.

Hitchings, S. P., and T. J. Beebee. 1997. Genetic substructuring as a result of barriers to gene flow in urban *Rana temporaria* (common frog) populations: Implications for biodiversity conservation. Heredity 79:117–127.

Hofer, U., L.-F. Bersier, and D. Borcard. 1999. Spatial organization of a herpetofauna on an elevational gradient revealed by null model tests. Ecology 80:976–988.

Holbrook, S. J., and R. J. Schmitt. 1996. On the structure and dynamics of temperate reef fish assemblages. Pp. 19–48 *in* M. L. Cody, and J. A. Smallwood, editors. Long-term Studies of Vertebrate Communities. Academic Press, San Diego, CA.

Holder, N., S. V. Bryant, and P. W. Tank. 1979. Interactions between irradiated and unirradiated tissues during supernumerary limb formation in the newt. Journal of Experimental Zoology 208:303–310.

Holland, C. C., J. Honea, S. E. Gwin, and M. E. Kentula. 1995. Wetland degradation and loss in the rapidly urbanizing area of Portland, Oregon. Wetlands 15:336–345.

Hopkins, W. A., J. Congdon, and J. K. Ray. 2000. Incidence and impact of axial malformations in larval bullfrogs (*Rana catesbeiana*) developing in sites polluted by a coal-burning power plant. Environmental Toxicology and Chemistry 19:862–868.

Hopkins, W. A., M. T. Mendonca, C. L. Rowe, and J. D. Congdon. 1998. Elevated trace element concentrations in southern toads, *Bufo terrestris*, exposed to coal combustion waste. Archives of Environmental Contamination and Toxicology 35:325–329.

Hornung, M., and B. Reynolds. 1995. The effects of natural and anthropogenic environmental changes on ecosystem processes at the catchment scale. Trends in Evolution and Ecology 10:443–449.

Horton, D. R., E. R. Miliczky, D. A. Broers, R. R. Lewis, and C. O. Calkins. 2001. Numbers, diversity, and phenology of spiders (Araneae) overwintering in cardboard bands placed in pear and apple orchards of central Washington. Annals of the Entomological Society of America 94:405–414.

Houck, L. D. 1977. Life history pattern and reproductive biology of Neotropical salamanders. Pp. 43–71 in D. H. Taylor, and S. I. Gutman, editors. The Reproductive Biology of Amphibians. Plenum Press, New York, NY.

Houlahan, J. E., C. S. Findlay, B. R. Schmidt, A. H. Meyer, and S. L. Kuzmin. 2000. Quantitative evidence for global amphibian population declines. Nature 404:752–755.

Houston, D. R. 1994. Major new tree disease epidemics: Beech bark disease. Annual Review of Phytopathology 32:75–87.

Huheey, J. E., and R. A. Brandon. 1973. Rock-face populations of the mountain salamander, Desmognathus ochrophaeus, in North Carolina. Ecological Monographs 43:59–77.

Hulbert, S. H., J. Zedler, and D. Fairbanks. 1972. Ecosystem alteration by mosquitofish (Gambusia affinis) predation. Science 172:639–641.

Hunter, M. L., Jr. 1990. Coping with ignorance: The coarse-filter strategy for maintaining biological diversity. Pp. 266–281 in K. Kohm, editor. Balancing on the Brink of Extinction. Island Press, Washington, DC.

Hunter, M. L., Jr. 1993. Natural disturbance regimes as spatial models for managing boreal forests. Biological Conservation 65:115–120.

Hunter, M. L., Jr., editor. 1999. Maintaining biodiversity in forest ecosystems. Cambridge University Press, Cambridge, UK.

Hunter, M. L., Jr., and A. Calhoun. 1996. A triad approach to land-use allocation. Pp. 477–491 in R. Szaro, and D. Johnston, editors. Biodiversity in Managed Landscapes. Oxford University Press, New York, NY. 778 p.

Hunter, M. L., Jr., G. Jacobson, and T. Webb. 1988. Paleoecology and the coarse-filter approach to maintaining biological diversity. Conservation Biology 2:375–385.

Hyatt, A. D., A. R. Gould, Z. Zupanovic, A. A. Cunningham, S. Hengstberger, R. J. Whittington, J. Kattenbelt, and B. E. H. Coupar. 2000. Comparative studies of piscine and amphibian iridoviruses. Archives of Virology 145:301–331.

Hyatt, A. D., H. Parkes, and Z. Zupanovic. 1998. Identification, characterization and assessment of Venezuelan viruses for potential use as biological control agents against the cane toad (Bufo marinus) in Australia. Australian Animal Health Laboratory, CSIRO, Geelong, Victoria, Australia.

Ibáñez, R. 1999. Report from Panama. FROGLOG 33:1.

Inger, R. F. 1999. Distribution of amphibians in Southern Asia and adjacent islands. Chapter 8. Pp. 445–482 in W. E. Duellman, editor. Patterns of Distribution of Amphibians: A Global Perspective. John Hopkins University Press, Baltimore, MD.

Inger, R. F., and R. B. Stuebing. 1992. The montane amphibian fauna of northwestern Borneo. Malayan Nature Journal 46:41–51.

Ingles, L. G. 1933. Studies on the structure and life-history of Zeugorchis syntomentera Sumwalt, a trematode from the snake Thamnophis ordinoides from California. University of California Publications in Zoology 39:163–177.

IPCC (Intergovernmental Panel on Climate Change). 2001. Climate Change 2001: The Scientific Basis. Contribution of Working Group I to the Third Assessment Report of the Intergovernmental Panel on Climate Change. J. T. Houghton, Y. Ding, D. J. Griggs, M. Noguer, P. J. van der Linden, X. Dai, K. Maskell, and C. A. Johnson, editors. Cambridge, Cambridge, UK.

Jaeger, R. G. 1970. Potential extinction through competition between two species of terrestrial salamanders. Evolution 24:632–642.

Jaeger, R. G. 1971. Moisture as a factor influencing the distributions of two species of terrestrial salamanders. Oecologia (Berlin) 6:191–207.

Jaeger, R. G. 1972. Food as a limited resource in competition between two species of terrestrial salamanders. Ecology 53:535–546.

Jaeger, R. G. 1980a. Density-dependent and density-independent causes of extinction of a salamander population. Evolution 34:617–621.

Jaeger, R. G. 1980b. Microhabitats of a terrestrial forest salamander. Copeia 1980:265–268.

Jaeger, R. G., and C. R. Gabor. 1993. Intraspecific chemical communication by a territorial salamander via the postcloacal gland. Copeia 1993:1171–1174.

James, T. Y., D. Porter, C. A. Leander, R. Vilgalys, and J. E. Longcore. 2000. Molecular phylogenetics of the Chytridiomycota supports the utility of ultrastructural data in chytrid systematics. Canadian Journal of Botany 78:336–350.

Jancovich, J. K., E. W. Davidson, J. F. Morado, J. L. Bertram, and J. P. Collins. 1997. Isolation of a lethal virus from the endangered tiger salamander *Ambystoma tigrinum stebbinsi*. Diseases of Aquatic Organisms 31:161–167.

Jancovich, J. K., E. W. Davidson, A. Seiler, B. L. Jacobs, and J. P. Collins. 2001. Transmission of the *Ambystoma tigrinum* virus to alternate hosts. Diseases of Aquatic Organisms 46:159–163.

Janzen, D. H. 1994. Priorities in tropical biology. Trends in Ecology and Evolution 9: 365–368.

Jennings, M. R., and M. P. Hayes. 1985. Pre-1900 overharvest of California red-legged frogs (*Rana aurora draytonii*): The inducement for bullfrog (*Rana catesbeiana*) introduction. Herpetologica 41:94–103.

Jensen, J. B., and C. Waters. 1999. The "spring lizard" bait industry in the state of Georgia, USA. Herpetological Review 30:20–21.

Jockusch, E. L., K. P. Yanev, and D. B. Wake. 2001. Molecular phylogenetic analysis of slender salamanders, genus *Batrachoseps* (Amphibia: Plethodontidae) from central coastal California with descriptions of four new species. Herpetological Monographs 15:54–99.

Joglar, R. L., and P. A. Burrowes. 1996. Declining amphibian populations in Puerto Rico. Pp. 371–380 *in* R. Powell, and R. W. Henderson, editors. Contributions to West Indian Herpetology. A Tribute to Albert Schwartz. Society for the Study of Amphibians and Reptiles, Ithaca, NY.

Johnson, P. T. J., K. B. Lunde, R. W. Haight, J. Bowerman, and A. R. Blaustein. 2001. *Ribeiroia ondatrae* (Trematoda: Digenea) infection induces severe limb abnormalities in western toads (*Bufo boreas*). Canadian Journal of Zoology 79:370–379.

Johnson, P. T. J., K. B. Lunde, E. G. Ritchie, and A. E. Launer. 1999. The effect of trematode infection on amphibian limb development and survivorship. Science 284:802–804.

Johnson, P. T. J., K. B. Lunde, E. G. Ritchie, J. K. Reaser, and A. E. Launder. 2000. Morphological abnormality patterns in a California amphibian community. Herpetologica 57:336–352.

Johnson, P. T. J., K. B. Lunde, E. M. Thurman, E. G. Ritchie, S. N. Wray, D. R. Sutherland, J. M. Kapfer, T. J. Frest, J. Bowerman, and A. R. Blaustein. 2002. Parasite (*Ribeiroia ondatrae*) infection linked to amphibian malformations in the western United States. Ecological Monographs 72:151–168.

Johnson, S. A. In Press. Conservation and life history of the striped newt (*Notophthalmus perstriatus*): The importance of habitat connectivity. *In* W. E. Meshaka, Jr., and K. J. Babbitt, editors. Status and Conservation of Florida Amphibians and Reptiles. Krieger Publishing, Malabar, FL.

Joly, P., C. Miaud, A. Lehmann, and O. Grolet. 2001. Habitat matrix effects on pond occupancy in newts. Conservation Biology 15:239–248.

Jones, B., S. F. Fox, D. M. Leslie, Jr., D. M. Engle, and R. L. Lochmiller. 2000. Herpetofaunal responses to brush management with herbicide and fire. Journal of Range Management 53:154–158.

Jones, T. R., J. P. Collins, T. D. Kocher, and J. B. Mitton. 1988. Systematic status and distribution of *Ambystoma tigrinum stebbinsi* Lowe. Copeia 1988:621–635.

Jongman, R. H. G. 1995. Nature conservation planning in Europe: Developing ecological networks. Landscape and Urban Planning 32:169–183.

Jung, R. E., and C. H. Jagoe. 1995. Effects of low pH and aluminum on body size, swimming performance, and susceptibility to predation of green tree frog (*Hyla cinerea*) tadpoles. Canadian Journal of Zoology 73:2171–2183.

Kaiser, J. 1997. Abnormal frogs leap into spotlight at health workshop. Science 278: 2051–2052.

Kanachanakhan, S. 1998. An ulcerative disease of the cultured tiger frog, *Rana tigrina*, in Thailand: Virological examination. Aquatic Animal Health Research Institute Newsletter 7:1–2.

Karr, J. R. 1991. Biological integrity: a long-neglected aspect of water resource management. Ecological Applications 4:768–785.

Kats, L. B., J. M. Kiesecker, D. P. Chivers, and A. R. Blaustein. 2000. Effects of UV-B on antipredator behavior in three species of amphibians. Ethology 106:921–932.

Kats, L. B., and L. M. Dill. 1998. The scent of death: Chemosensory assessment of predation risk by prey animals. Ecoscience 5:361–394.

Kats, L. B., W. J. Petranka, and A. Sih. 1988. Antipredator defenses and the persistence of amphibian larvae with fishes. Ecology 69:1865–1870.

Kentula, M. E., J. C. Sifneos, J. W. Good, M. Rylko, and K. Kunz. 1992. Trends and patterns in section 404 permitting requiring compensatory mitigation in Oregon and Washington, USA. Environmental Management 16:109–119.

Kerr, J. B., and C. T. McElroy. 1993. Evidence for large upward trends of ultraviolet-B radiation linked to ozone depletion. Science 262:1032–1034.

Kie, J. G., and E. R. Loft. 1990. Using livestock to manage wildlife habitat: Some examples from California annual grassland and wet meadow communities. USDA Forest Service, General Technical Note RM 194:7–24.

Kiesecker, J. M. 1996. pH induced growth reduction and its effects on predator-prey interactions between *Ambystoma tigrinum* and *Pseudacris triseriata*. Ecological Applications 6:1325–1331.

Kiesecker, J. M., and A. R. Blaustein. 1995. Synergism between UV-B radiation and a pathogen magnifies amphibian embryo mortality in nature. Proceedings of the National Academy of Sciences (USA) 92:11049–11052.

Kiesecker, J. M., and A. R. Blaustein. 1997a. Egg laying behavior influences pathogenic infection of amphibian embryos. Conservation Biology 11:214–220.

Kiesecker, J. M., and A. R. Blaustein. 1997b. Population differences in responses of red-legged frogs (*Rana aurora*) to introduced bullfrogs (*Rana catesbeiana*). Ecology 78:1752–1760.

Kiesecker, J. M., and A. R. Blaustein. 1998. Effects of introduced bullfrogs and smallmouth bass on the microhabitat use, growth and survival of native red-legged frogs. Conservation Biology 12:776–787.

Kiesecker, J. M., and A. R. Blaustein. 1999. Pathogen reverses competition between larval amphibians. Ecology 80:2442–2448.

Kiesecker, J. M., A. R. Blaustein, and L. K. Belden. 2001a. Complex causes of amphibian population declines. Nature 410:681–684.

Kiesecker, J. M., A. R. Blaustein, and C. L. Miller. 2001b. Potential mechanisms underlying the displacement of native red-legged frogs by introduced bullfrogs. Ecology 82: 1964–1970.

Kiesecker, J. M., A. R. Blaustein, and C. L. Miller. 2001c. Transfer of a pathogen from fish to amphibians. Conservation Biology 15:1064–1070.

Kiesecker, J. M., D. P. Chivers, and A. R. Blaustein. 1996. The use of chemical cues in predator recognition by western toad (*Bufo boreas*) tadpoles. Animal Behaviour 52:1237–1245.

Kim, W. S., and D. L. Stocum. 1986. Retinoid acid modifies positional memory in the anteroposterior axis of regenerating axolotl limbs. Developmental Biology 114:170–179.

Kimberling, D. N., A. R. Ferreira, S. M. Shuster, and P. Keim. 1996. RAPD marker estimation of genetic structure among isolated northern leopard frog populations in the southwestern USA. Molecular Ecology 5:521–529.

Kirby, A. 1 February 2002. Frog mortality, Virus—UK. ProMED-mail. Available online at: http://www.promedmail.org. Archive Number 20020201.3458.

Klerks, P. L., and J. S. Levinton. 1989. Rapid evolution of metal resistance in a benthic oligocheate inhabiting a metal-polluted site. Biological Bulletin 176:135–141.

Knapp, R. A., and K. R. Mathews. 1998. Eradication of nonnative fish by gill netting from a small mountain lake in California. Restoration Ecology 6:207–213.

Knapp, R. A., and K. R. Mathews. 2000. Non-native fish introductions and the decline of the mountain yellow-legged frog from within protected areas. Conservation Biology 14: 428–438.

Knapp, R. A., K. R. Mathews, and O. Sarnelle. 2001. Resistance and resilience of alpine lake fauna to fish introductions. Ecological Monographs 71:401–421.

Knutson, M. G., J. R. Sauer, D. A. Olsen, M. J. Mossman, L. M. Hemesath, and M. J. Lannoo. 1999. Effects of landscape composition and wetland fragmentation of frog and toad abundance and species richness in Iowa and Wisconsin, U.S.A. Conservation Biology 13: 1437–1446.

Kolar, C. S., and D. M. Lodge. 2000. Freshwater nonindigenous species: Interactions with other global changes. Pp. 3–30 *in* H. A. Mooney, and R. J. Hobbs, editors. Invasive Species in a Changing World. Island Press, Washington, DC.

Koloszvary, M. B., and R. K. Swihart. 1999. Habitat fragmentation and the distribution of amphibians: Patch and landscape correlates in farmland. Canadian Journal of Zoology 77:1288–1299.

Komak, S., and M. R. Crossland. 2000. An assessment of the introduced mosquitofish (*Gambusia affinis holbrooki*) as a predator of eggs, hatchlings and tadpoles of native and non-native anurans. Wildlife Research 27:185–189.

Kottelat, M., and T. Whitten. 1996. Freshwater biodiversity in Asia, with special reference to fish. World Bank Technical Paper 343. 59 p.

Kramer, P., N. Reichenbach, M. Hayslett, and P. Sattler. 1993. Population dynamics and conservation of the Peaks of Otter salamander *Plethodon hubrichti*. Journal of Herpetology 27:431–435.

Kucken D. J., J. S. Davis, J. W. Petranka, and C. K. Smith. 1994. Anakeesta stream acidification and metal contamination: Effects on a salamander community. Journal of Environmental Quality 23:1311–1317.

Kupferberg, S. J. 1996. Hydrologic and geomorphic factors affecting conservation of a river-breeding frog (*Rana boylii*). Ecological Applications 6:1332–1344.

Kupferberg, S. J. 1997. Bullfrog (*Rana catesbeiana*) invasion of a California river: The role of larval competition. Ecology 78:1736–1751.

Kuzmin, S. L. 1996. Threatened amphibians in the former Soviet Union: The current situation and the main threats. Oryx 30:24–30.

Kuzmin, S., and C. K. Dodd, Jr., editors. 1995. Amphibian Populations in the Commonwealth of Independent States: Current Status and Declines. Pensoft Publishers, Sofia, Bulgaria.

La Marca, E., and S. Lotters. 1997. Monitoring of declines in Venezuelan *Atelopus* (Amphibia: Anura: Bufonidae). Pp. 207–213 *in* W. Bohme, W. Bischoff, and T. Ziegler, editors. Herpetologia Bonnensis. Museum Alexander Koenig, Bonn, Germany.

La Marca, E., and H. P. Reinthaler. 1991. Population changes in *Atelopus* species of the Cordillera de Mérida, Venezuela. Herpetological Review 22:125–128.

Laan, R., and B. Verboom. 1990. Effects of pool size and isolation of amphibian communities. Biological Conservation 54:251–262.

LaClair, J. J., J. A. Bantle, and J. Dumont. 1998. Photoproducts and metabolites of a common insect growth regulator produce developmental abnormalities in Xenopus. Environmental Science and Technology 32:1453–1461.

Lamoureux, V. S., and D. M. Madison. 1999. Overwintering habitats of radio-implanted green frogs, *Rana clamitans*. Journal of Herpetology 33:430–435.

Lang, C., and R. G. Jaeger. 2000. Defense of territories by male-female pairs in the red-backed salamander (*Plethodon cinereus*). Copeia 2000:169–177.

Langhelle, A., M. J. Lindell, and P. Nyström. 1999. Effects of ultraviolet radiation on amphibian embryonic and larval development. Journal of Herpetology 33:449–456.

Langton, T. E. S. 1989. Amphibians and Roads. Proceedings of the Toad Tunnel Conference, Rendsburg, Federal Republic of Germany. ACO Polymer Products Ltd., Shefford, UK.

Lannoo, M. J., editor. 2003. Status and Conservation of U.S. Amphibians. Volumes 1 and 2. University of California Press, Berkeley, CA.

Lannoo, M. J., K. Lang, T. Waltz, and G. S. Phillips. 1994. An altered amphibian assemblage: Dickinson County, Iowa, 70 years after Frank Blanchard's survey. American Midland Naturalist 131:311–319.

Lannoo, M. J., and C. A. Phillips. In Press. *Ambystoma tigrinum*. *In* M. J. Lannoo, editor. Status and Conservation of U.S. Amphibians. Volume 2. Species Accounts. University of California Press, Berkeley, CA.

Lau, M. W., G. Ades, N. Goodyer, and F. Zou. 1997. Wildlife trade in southern China including Hong Kong and Macao. Technical Report No. 27 *in* J. MacKinnon, and W. Sung, editors. Conserving China's Biodiversity. China's Environmental Press, Beijing, China. Available online at: http://monkey.ioz.ac.cn/bwg-cciced/english/bwg-cciced/tech-27.htm.

Laurance, W. F. 2001. Future shock: Forecasting a grim fate for the Earth. Trends in Ecology and Evolution 16:531–533.

Laurance, W. F., K. R. McDonald, and R. Speare. 1996. Epidemic disease and the catastrophic decline of Australian rain forest frogs. Conservation Biology 10:406–413.

Laurance, W. F., K. R. McDonald, and R. Speare. 1997. In defense of the epidemic disease hypothesis. Conservation Biology 11:1030–1034.

Lawler, S. P. 1989. Behavioural responses to predators and predation risk in four species of larval anurans. Animal Behavior 38:1039–1047.

Lawler, S. P., D. Dritz, T. Strange, and M. Holyoak. 1999. Effects of introduced mosquitofish and bullfrogs on the threatened California red-legged frog. Conservation Biology 13:613–622.

Lawton, R. O., U. S. Nair, R. A. Pielke, Sr., and R. M. Welch. 2001. Climatic impact of tropical lowland deforestation on nearby montane cloud forests. Science 294:584–597.

Lehtinen, R. M., and S. M. Galatowitsch. 2001. Colonization of restored wetlands by amphibians in Minnesota. American Midland Naturalist 145:388–396.

Lehtinen, R. M., S. M. Galatowitsch, and J. R. Tester. 1999. Consequences of habitat loss and fragmentation for wetland amphibian assemblages. Wetlands 19:1–12.

Leibold, M. A., and H. M. Wilbur. 1992. Interactions between food-web structure and nutrients on pond organisms. Nature 360:341–343.

Lemckert, F. 1999. Impacts of selective logging on frogs in a forested area of northern New South Wales. Biological Conservation 89:321–328.

Levell, J. P. 1997. A Field Guide to Reptiles and the Law. Serpent's Tale, Lanesboro, MN.

Levin, S. A., and R. T. Paine 1974. Disturbance, patch formation and community structure. Proceedings of the National Academy of Sciences (USA) 71:2744–2747.

Lewis, W. J., J. C. van Lenteren, S. C. Phatak, and J. H. Tumlinson III. 1997. A total system approach to sustainable pest management. Proceedings of the National Academy of Sciences (USA) 94:12243–12248.

Licht, L. E. 1974. Survival of embryos, tadpoles, and adults of the frogs *Rana aurora aurora* and *Rana pretiosa pretiosa* sympatric in southwestern British Columbia. Canadian Journal of Zoology 52:613–627.

Lind, A. J., H. H. Welsh, Jr., and R. A. Wilson. 1996. The effects of a dam on breeding habitat and egg survival of the foothill yellow-legged frog (*Rana boylii*) in northwestern California. Herpetological Review 27:62–67.

Linder, G., C. A. Bishop, and D. A. Sparling, editors. In Press. Global decline of amphibian populations: an integrated analysis of multiple stressor effects. Society of Environmental Toxicology and Chemistry, Pensacola, FL.

Linder, G., and B. Grillitsch. 2000. Ecotoxicology of metals. Pp. 325–459 *in* D. W. Sparling, G. Linder, and C. A. Bishop, editors. Ecotoxicology of Amphibians and Reptiles. Society of Environmental Toxicology and Chemistry, Pensacola, FL.

Lips, K. R. 1998. Decline of a tropical montane amphibian fauna. Conservation Biology 12:106–117.

Lips, K. R. 1999. Mass mortality and population declines of anurans at an upland site in western Panama. Conservation Biology 13:117–125.

Lips, K. R., and M. A. Donnelly. 2002. What the tropics can tell us about declining amphibian populations: Current patterns and future prospects. Pp. 388–406 *in* M. J. Lannoo, editor. North American Amphibians: Status and Conservation. University of California Press, Berkeley, CA.

Lips, K. R., J. K. Reaser, B. E. Young, and R. Ibáñez. 2001. Amphibian Monitoring in Latin America: A Protocol Manual. Monitoreo de Anfibios en América Latina: Manual de Protocolos. Herpetological Circular 30:1–116.

Little, E. E., B. A. Flerov, and N. N. Ruzhinskaya. 1985. Behavioral approaches in aquatic toxicity investigations: A review. Pp. 72–98 *in* P. M. Mehrle, Jr., R. H. Gray, and R. L. Kendall, editors. Toxic Substances in the Aquatic Environment: An International Aspect. American Fisheries Society, Water Quality Section, Bethesda, MD.

Lively, C. M. 1999. Migration, virulence and the geographic mosaic of adaptation by parasites. American Naturalist 153:S34–S47.

Lizana, M., and E. M. Pedraza.1998. Different mortality of toad embryos (*Bufo bufo* and *Bufo calamita*) caused by UV-B radiation in high mountain areas of the Spanish Central System. Conservation Biology 12:703–707.

Lodge, D. M., C. A. Taylor, D. M. Holdrich, and J. Skurdal. 2000. Nonindigenous crayfishes threaten North American freshwater biodiversity: lessons from Europe. Fisheries 25: 7–19.

Long, L. E., L. S. Saylor, and M. E. Soulé. 1995. A pH/UV-B synergism in amphibians. Conservation Biology 9:1301–1303.

Longcore, J. E., A. P. Pessier, and D. K. Nichols. 1999. *Batrachochytrium dendrobatidis* gen. et sp. nov., a chytrid pathogenic to amphibians. Mycologia 91:219–227.

Lovett, G. M., A. W. Thompson, J. B. Anderson, and J. J. Bowser 1999. Elevational patterns of sulfur deposition at a site in the Catskill Mountains, New York. Atmospheric Environment 33:617–624.

Ludolph, D. C., J. A. Cameron, and D. L. Stocum. 1990. The effect of retinoic acid on positional memory in the dorsoventral axis of regenerating axolotl limbs. Developmental Biology 140:41–52.

Lutz, C. G., and J. L. Avery. 1989. Bullfrog Culture. Southern Regional Aquaculture Center, Stoneville, MS. Publication No. 436.

Lynch, M. 1996. A quantitative-genetic perspective on conservation issues. Pp. 471–501 *in* J. C. Avise, and J. L. Hamrick, editors. Conservation Genetics. Chapman & Hall, New York, NY.

Mac, M. J., P. A. Opler, C. E. Puckett Haecker, and P. D. Doran, editors. 1998. Status and Trends of the Nation's Biological Resources. Volumes 1 and 2. U.S. Geological Survey, Reston, VI.

MacArthur, R. H., and E. O. Wilson. 1967. The Theory of Island Biogeography. Princeton University Press, Princeton, NJ.

MacCracken, M., E. Barron, D. Easterling, B. Felzer, and T. Karl. 2001. Scenarios for climate variability and change. Pp. 13–71 *in* National Assessment Synthesis Team, editors. Climate Change Impacts on the United States: The Potential Consequences of Climate Variability and Change. Cambridge University Press, Cambridge, UK.

Maden, M. 1982. Vitamin A and pattern formation in the regenerating limb. Nature 295:672–675.

Maden, M. 1983. The effect of vitamin A on the regenerating axolotl limb. Journal of Embryology and Experimental Morphology 77:273–295.

Madison, D. M. 1997. The emigration of radio-implanted spotted salamanders, *Ambystoma maculatum*. Journal of Herpetology 31:542–552.

Maglia, A. M. 1996. Ontogeny and feeding ecology of the red-backed salamander, *Plethodon cinereus*. Copeia 1996:576–586.

Magnusson, W. E. 2001. Catchments as basic units of management in conservation biology courses. Conservation Biology 15:1464–1465.

Mahony, M. 1996. The decline of the green and golden bell frog *Litoria aurea* viewed in the context of declines and disappearances of other Australian frogs. Australian Zoologist 30:237–247.

Maisonneuve, C., and S. Rioux. 2001. Importance of riparian habitats for small mammals and herpetofaunal communities in agricultural landscapes of southern Quebec. 2001. Agriculture, Ecosystems and Environment 83:165–175.

Mao, J., D. E. Green, G. Fellers, and V. G. Chinchar. 1999. Molecular characterization of iridoviruses isolated from sympatric amphibians and fish. Virus Research 63:45–52.

Marian, M. P., V. Arul, and T. J. Pandian. 1983. Acute and chronic effects of carbaryl on survival, growth and metamorphosis in the bullfrog *(Rana tigrina)*. Archives of Environmental Contamination and Toxicology 12:271–275.

Marsh, D. M., and P. C. Trenham. 2001. Metapopulation dynamics and amphibian conservation. Conservation Biology 15:40–49.

Marshall, N. 1999. Search for a cure in Africa gets increasingly difficult. TRAFFIC Dispatches, January 1999, TRAFFIC International, Cambridge, UK. Available online at: http://www. traffic.org/dispatches/archives/january99/.

Martof, B. S., W. M. Palmer, J. R. Bailey, and J. R. Harrison III. 1980. Amphibians and Reptiles of the Carolinas and Virginia. University of North Carolina Press, Chapel Hill, NC.

Marvin, G. A. 1998. Interspecific aggression and spatial relationships in the salamanders *Plethodon kentucki* and *Plethodon glutinosis*: Evidence of interspecific interference competition. Canadian Journal of Zoology 76:94–103.

Mathis, A., and E. Britzke. 1999. The roles of body size and experience in agonistic displays of the Ozark zigzag salamander, *Plethodon angusticlavius*. Herpetologica 55:344–352.

Matthews, K. R., and K. L. Pope. 1999. A telemetric study of the movement patterns and habitat use of *Rana muscosa*, the mountain yellow-legged frog, in a high-elevation basin in Kings Canyon National Park, California. Journal of Herpetology 33:615–624.

Mayer, F. L., and M. R. Ellersieck. 1986. Manual of acute toxicity: Interpretation and data base for 410 chemicals and 66 species of freshwater animals. U.S. Fisheries and Wildlife Service, Resource Publication No. 160.

McAlpine, D. F. 1997. Helminth communities in bullfrogs (*Rana catesbeiana*), green frogs (*Rana clamitans*), and leopard frogs (*Rana pipiens*) from New Brunswick, Canada. Canadian Journal of Zoology 75:1883–1890.

McCallum, H., and A. Dobson. 1995. Detecting disease and parasite threats to endangered species and ecosystems. Trends in Ecology and Evolution 10:190–194.

McComb, W. C., K. McGarigal, and R. G. Anthony. 1993. Small mammal and amphibian abundance in streamside and upslope habitats of mature Douglas-fir stands, western Oregon. Northwest Science 67:7–15.

McDonald, K. R. 1990. *Rheobatrachus* Liem and *Taudactylus* Straughan & Lee (Anura: Leptodactylidae) in Eungella National Park, Queensland: Distribution and Decline. Transactions of the Royal Society of South Australia 114:187–194.

McDonald, K. R. 1992. Distribution patterns and conservation status of north Queensland rainforest frogs. Conservation Technical Report 1. Queensland Department of Environment and Heritage, Brisbane, Australia.

McIntosh, A. R., and C. R. Townsend. 1996. Interactions between fish grazing invertebrates and algae in a New Zealand stream: A trophic cascade mediated by fish behaviour? Oecologica 108:174–181.

McKenzie, J. A. 1996. Ecological and evolutionary aspects of insecticide resistance. Academic Press, California, Austin, TX. 185 pp.

McKinney, M. L., and J. L. Lockwood. 1999. Biotic homogenization: A few winners replacing many losers in the next mass extinction. Trends in Ecology and Evolution 14:450–453.

Means, D. B., J. G. Palis, and M. Baggett. 1996. Effects of slash pine silviculture on a Florida population of the flatwoods salamander *Ambystoma cingulatum*. Conservation Biology 10:426–437.

Means, R. C., and R. Franz. In Press. Amphibians and reptiles of altered wetlands on municipal well fields in peninsular Florida. *In* W. E. Meshaka, Jr., and K. J. Babbitt, editors. Status and Conservation of Florida Amphibians and Reptiles. University Press of Florida, Gainesville, FL.

Meffe, G. K., and C. R. Carroll. 1997. Principles of Conservation Biology. 2nd edition. Sinauer Associates, Inc., Sunderland, MA.

Merilä, J., M. Pahkala, and U. Johanson. 2000. Increased ultraviolet-B radiation, climate change and latitudinal adaptation-a frog perspective. Annales Zoologici Fennici 37:129–134.

Meronek, T. G., F. A. Copes, and D. W. Coble. 1997. A survey of the bait industry in the north-central region of the United States. North American Journal of Fisheries Management 17:703–711.

Meshaka, W. E., Jr. 1997. The herpetofauna of Buck Island Ranch: An altered wetland in south-central Florida. Florida Scientist 60:1–7.

Messere, M., and P. K. Ducey. 1998. Forest floor distribution of northern redback salamanders, *Plethodon cinereus,* in relation to canopy gaps: First year following selective logging. Forest Ecology and Management 107:319–324.

Meteyer, C. U., I. K. Loeffler, J. F. Fallon, K. A. Converse, E. Green, J. C. Helgen, S. Kersten, R. Levy, L. Eaton-Poole, and J. G. Burkhart. 2000. Hindlimb abnormalities in free-living northern leopard frogs (*Rana pipiens*) from Main, Minnesota, and Vermont suggest multiple etiologies. Teratology 62:151–171.

Metts, B. S., J. D. Lanham, and K. R. Russell. 2001. Evaluation of herpetofaunal communities on upland streams and beaver-impounded streams in the Upper Piedmont of South Carolina. American Midland Naturalist 145:54–65.

Meyer, A. H., B. R. Schmidt, and K. Grossenbacher. 1998. Analysis of three amphibian populations with quarter-century long time-series. Proceedings of the Royal Society of London B 265:523–528.

Meyer-Aurich, A., P. Zander, A. Werner, and R. Roth. 1998. Developing agricultural land-use strategies appropriate to nature conservation goal and environmental protection. Landscape and Urban Planning 41:119–127.

Middleton, E. M., J. R. Herman, E. A. Celarier, J. W. Wilkinson, C. Carey, and R. J. Rusin. 2001. Evaluating ultraviolet radiation exposure with satellite data at sites of amphibian declines in Central and South America. Conservation Biology 15:914–929.

Mills, N. E. 2002. Direct and indirect effects of an insecticide on *Rana sphenocephala* tadpoles. Ph.D. thesis, University of Missouri, Columbia, MO.

Mills, N. M., and R. D. Semlitsch. 2002. Direct and indirect effects of an insecticide on two amphibian species. Ecological Applications. In review.

Minckley, W. L., and J. E. Deacon, editors. 1991. Battle against Extinction: Native Fish Management in the American West. University of Arizona Press, Tucson, AZ.

Mitchell, J. C., S. C. Rinehart, J. F. Pagels, K. A. Buhlmann, and C. A. Pague. 1997. Factors influencing amphibian and small mammal assemblages in central Appalachian forests. Forest Ecology and Management 96:65–76.

MoF and MELP (Ministry of Forests and Ministry of Environment, Lands and Parks). 1995. Riparian Management Area Guidebook. Victoria, British Columbia, Canada. Forest Practices Code of British Columbia Guidebook.

Mittermeier, R. A., N. Myers, J. G. Thompsen, G. A. B. da Fonesca, and S. Olivieri. 1998. Biodiversity hotspots and major wilderness areas: Approaches to setting conservation priorities. Conservation Biology 12:516–520.

Moler, P. E., and R. Franz. 1987. Wildlife values of small, isolated wetlands in the Southeastern coastal plain. Pp. 234–241 *in* R. R. Odum, K. A. Riddleberger, and J. C. Ozier, editors. Proceedings of the 3rd Southeastern Nongame and Endangered Wildlife Symposium. Georgia Department of Natural Resources, Atlanta, GA.

Mooney, H. A. 1999. Global invasive species program (GISP). Pp. 407–418 *in* O. T. Sandlund, P. J. Schei, and A. Viken, editors. Invasive Species and Biodiversity Management. Kluwer Academic Publisher, Dorrecht, Netherlands.

Mooney, H. A., and R. J. Hobbs, editors. 2000. Invasive Species in a Changing World. Island Press, Washington, DC.

Moore, A. L., C. E. Williams, T. H. Martin, and W. J. Moriarity. 2001. Influence of season, geomorphic surface and cover item on capture, size and weight of *Desmognathus ochrophaeus* and *Plethodon cinereus* in Allegheny Plateau riparian forests. American Midland Naturalist 145:39–45.

Morin, P. J. 1981. Predatory salamanders reverse the outcome of competition among three species of anuran tadpoles. Science 212:1284–1286.

Morin, P. J. 1983. Predation, competition, and the composition of larval anuran guilds. Ecological Monograph 53:119–138.

Moyle, P. B. 1973. Effects of introduced bullfrogs, *Rana catesbeiana*, on the native frogs of the San Joaquin Valley, California. Copeia 1973:18–22.

Muneoka, K., G. Holler-Dinsmore, and S. V. Bryant. 1986. Intrinsic control of regenerative loss in *Xenopus laevis* limbs. Journal of Experimental Zoology 240:47–54.

Mungomery, R. W. 1935. The giant American toad (*Bufo marinus*). Cane Growers Quarterly Bulletin 3:21–27.

Murcia, C. 1995. Edge effects in fragmented forests: Implications for conservation. Trends in Ecology and Evolution 10:58–62.

Murphy, D. D., K. E. Freas, and S. B. Weiss. 1990. An environment-metapopulation approach to population viability analysis for a threatened vertebrate. Conservation Biology 4:41–51.

Muth, R. M., D. A. Hamilton, J. F. Organ, D. J. Witter, M. E. Mather, and J. J. Daigle. 1998. The future of wildlife and fisheries policy and management: Assessing attitudes and values of wildlife and fisheries professionals. Transactions of the 63rd North American Wildlife and Natural Resource Conference 63:604–627.

Muths, E., P. S. Corn, A. P. Pessier, and D. E. Green. In Press. Evidence for disease-related amphibian decline in Colorado. Biological Conservation.

Myers, N., R. A. Mittermeier, C. G. Mittermeier, G. A. B. da Fonesca, and J. Kent. 2000. Biodiversity hotspots for conservation priorities. Nature 403:853–858.

Nagel, J. W. 1977. Life history of the red-backed salamander *Plethodon cinereus*, in northeastern Tennessee. Herpetologica 33:13–18.

Nagl, A. M., and R. Hofer. 1997. Effects of ultraviolet radiation on early larval stages of the Alpine newt, *Triturus alpestris*, under natural and laboratory conditions. Oecologia 110:514–519.

Naiman, R. J., H. Decamps, and M. Pollock. 1993. The role of riparian corridors in maintaining regional biodiversity. Ecological Applications 3:209–212.

Naiman, R. J., J. J. Magnuson, D. M. McNight, and J. A. Stanford, editors. 1995. The Freshwater Imperative: A Research Agenda. Island Press, Washington, DC.

NARCAM (North American Reporting Center for Amphibian Malformations). 2000. Northern Prairie Wildlife Research Center Home Page. Jamestown, ND. Available online at: http://www.npwrc.usgs.gov/narcam/.

National Research Council. 2001. Compensating for Wetland Losses under the Clean Water Act. National Academy Press, Washington, DC.

Newman, R. A. 1988a. Adaptive plasticity in development of *Scaphiopus couchii* tadpoles in desert ponds. Evolution 42:774–783.

Newman, R. A. 1988b. Genetic variation for larval anuran (*Scaphiopus couchii*) development time in an uncertain environment. Evolution 42:763–773.

Newman, R. A. 1989. Developmental plasticity of *Scaphiopus couchii* tadpoles in an unpredictable environment. Ecology 70:1775–1787.

Nichols, D. K., E. W. Lamirande, A. P. Pessier, and J. E. Longcore. 2001. Experimental transmission of cutaneous chytridiomycosis in dendrobatid frogs. Journal of Wildlife Diseases
37:1–11.

Nichols, D. K., A. J. Smith, and C. H. Gardiner. 1996. Dermatitis of anurans caused by fungal-
like protists. Proceedings of the American Association of Zoo Veterinarians 220–221.

Nicolas, P., and A. Mor. 1995. Peptides as weapons against microorganisms in the chemical
defense system of vertebrates. Annual Review of Microbiology 49:277–304.

Nielson, M., K. Lohman, and J. Sullivan. 2001. Phylogeography of the tailed frog (Ascaphus
truei): Implications for the biogeography of the Pacific Northwest. Evolution 55:147–160.

Nieuwkoop, P. D., and J. Faber. 1994. Normal Table of Xenopus laevis (Daudin). Garland Publishing, Inc., New York, NY, and London, UK. 252 p.

Noss, R. F. 1991. Landscape connectivity: Different functions at different scales. Pp. 27–39 in
W. E. Hudson, editor. Landscape Linkages and Biodiversity: Defenders of Wildlife. Island
Press, Washington, DC.

Noss, R. F. 2001. Beyond Kyoto: Forest management in a time of rapid climate change. Conservation Biology 15:578–590.

Noss, R. F., H. B. Quigley, M. G. Hornocker, T. Merrill, and P. C. Paquet. 1996. Conservation
biology and carnivore conservation in the Rocky Mountains. Conservation Biology
10:949–963.

Nussbaum, R. A., E. D. Brodie, Jr., and R. M. Storm. 1983. Amphibians and Reptiles of the
Pacific Northwest. University of Idaho Press, Moscow, ID.

Nussbaum, R. A., and C. K. Tait. 1977. Aspects of the life history and ecology of the
Olympic salamander, Rhyacotriton olympicus (Gaige). American Midland Naturalist 98:
176–199.

Nystrum, P., O. Svensson, B. Lardner, C. Bronmark, and W. Graneli. 2001. The influence of
multiple introduced predators on a littoral pond community. Ecology 82:1023–1039.

O'Shea, P., and R. Speare. 1990. Salmonellas from the cane toad, Bufo marinus. Australian
Veterinary Journal 67:310.

Obrycki, J. J., J. E. Losey, O. R. Taylor, and L. C. H. Jesse. 2001. Transgenic insecticidal corn:
Beyond insecticidal toxicity to ecological complexity. BioScience 51:353–361.

Oldham, R. S. 1966. Spring movement in the American toad, Bufo americanus. Canadian Journal of Zoology 44:63–100.

Oldham, R. S. 1999. Amphibians and agriculture: Double jeopardy. Pp. 105–124 in
M. Whitfield, J. Matthews, and C. Reynolds, editors. Aquatic Life Cycle Strategies: Sur-
vival in a Variable Environment. Marine Biological Association of the United Kingdom,
Plymouth, UK.

Ortman, E. E., B. D. Barry, L. L. Buschman, D. D. Calvin, J. Carpenter, G. P. Dively,
J. E. Foster, B. W. Fuller, R. L. Hellmich, R. A. Higgins, T. E. Hunt, G. P. Munkvold,
K. R. Ostlie, M. E. Rice, R. T. Roush, M. K. Sears, A. M. Shelton, B. D. Siegfried,
P. E. Sloderbeck, K. L. Steffey, F. T. Turpin, and J. L. Wedberg. 2001. Transgenic insecti-
cidal corn: The agronomic and ecological rationale for its use. BioScience 51:900–903.

Osteen, C. 1993. Pesticide use trends and issues in the United States. Pp. 309–336 in
D. Pimentel, and H. Lehman, editors. The Pesticide Question: Environment, Economics,
and Ethics. Chapman & Hall, New York, NY.

Otto, R. G. 1973. Temperature tolerance of the mosquitofish. Journal of Fish Biology 5:
575–585.

Otto, S. P., and Y. Michalakis. 1998. The evolution of recombination in changing environments. Trends in Ecology and Evolution 13:145–151.

Ouellet, M. 2000. Amphibian abnormalities: Current state of knowledge. Pp. 617–661 *in* D. W. Sparling, G. Linder, and C. A. Bishop, editors. Ecotoxicology of Amphibians and Reptiles. Society of Environmental Toxicology and Chemistry (SETAC), Pensacola, FL.

Ouellet, M., J. Bonin, J. Rodrigue, J.-L. DesGranges, and S. Lair. 1997. Hind limb abnormalities (ectromelia, ectrodactyly) in free-living anurans from agricultural habitats. Journal of Wildlife Deseases 33:95–104.

Ovaska, K. 1997. Vulnerability of amphibians in Canada to global warming and increased solar ultraviolet radiation. Pp. 206–225 *in* D. M. Green, editor. Amphibians in Decline: Canadian Studies of a Global Problem. Herpetological Conservation 1, Society for the Study of Amphibians and Reptiles, St. Louis, MO.

Ovaska, K., T. M. Davis, and I. M. Flamarique. 1997. Hatching success and larval survival of the frogs *Hyla regilla* and *Rana aurora* under ambient and artificially enhanced solar ultraviolet radiation. Canadian Journal of Zoology 75:1081–1088.

Oza, G. M. 1990. Ecological effects of the frog's legs trade. The Environmentalist 10:39–42.

Pahkala, M., A. Laurila, and J. Merilä. 2000. Ambient ultraviolet-B radiation reduces hatchling size in the common frog *Rana temporaria*. Ecography 23:531–538.

Pahkala, M., A. Laurila, and J. Merilä. 2001. Carry-over effects of ultraviolet-B radiation on larval fitness in *Rana temporaria*. Proceedings of the Royal Society of London B 268: 1699–1706.

Palumbi, S. R. 2001a. Humans as the world's greatest evolutionary force. Science 293: 1786–1790.

Palumbi, S. R. 2001b. The Evolution Explosion. W. W. Norton and Company, New York, NY. 277 p.

Parker, B. R., F. M. Wilhelm and D. W. Schlindler. 1996. Recovery of the *Hesperodiaptomus arcticus* populations from diapausing eggs following elimination by stocked salmonids. Canadian Journal of Zoology 74:1292–1297.

Parmesan, C. 1996. Climate and species' range. Nature 383:765–766.

Parmesan, C., N. Ryrholm, C. Stefanescu, J. K. Hill, C. D. Thomas, H. Descimon, B. Huntley, L. Kaila, J. Kullberg, T. Tammaru, W. J. Tennent, J. A. Thomas, and M. Warren. 1999. Poleward shifts in geographical ranges of butterfly species associated with regional warming. Nature 399:579–583.

Patel, T. 1993. French may eat Indonesia out of frogs. New Scientist 138:7.

Pauley, T. K. 1978. Moisture as a factor regulating habitat partitioning between two sympatric *Plethodon* (Amphibia, Urodela, Plethodontidae) species. Journal of Herpetology 12:491–493.

Pearman, P. B. 1997. Correlates of amphibian diversity in an altered landscape of Amazonian Ecuador. Conservation Biology 11:1211–1225.

Pechmann, J. H. K. 1994. Population regulation in complex life cycles: Aquatic and terrestrial density-dependence in pond-breeding amphibians. Ph.D. Dissertation. Duke University, Durham, NC.

Pechmann, J. H. K., R. A. Estes, D. E. Scott, and J. W. Gibbons. 2001. Amphibian colonization and use of ponds created for trial mitigation of wetland loss. Wetlands 21:93–111.

Pechmann, J. H. K., D. E. Scott, J. W. Gibbons, and R. D. Semlitsch. 1989. Influence of wetland hydroperiod on diversity and abundance of metamorphosing juvenile amphibians. Wetlands Ecology and Management 1:3–11.

Pechmann, J. H. K., D. E. Scott, R. D. Semlitsch, J. P. Caldwell, L. J. Vitt, and J. W. Gibbons. 1991. Declining amphibian populations: the problem of separating human impacts from natural fluctuations. Science 253:892–895.

Pechmann, J. H. K., and D. B. Wake. 1997. Declines and disappearances of amphibian populations. Pp. 135–137 in G. K. Meffe, C. R. Carroll, editors. Principles of Conservation Biology. 2nd edition. Sinauer Associates, Sunderland, MA.

Pechmann, J. H. K., and H. M. Wilbur. 1994. Putting declining amphibian populations in perspective: Natural fluctuations and human impacts. Herpetologica 50:65–84.

Percsy, C. 1995. Les Batraciens sur nos Routes. Ministère de la Région Wallonne, Service de la Conservation de la Nature et des Espaces Verts. Wallonne, Belgium. Brochure technique No. 1.

Pessier, A. P., D. K. Nichols, J. E. Longcore, and M. S. Fuller. 1999. Cutaneous chytridiomycosis in poison dart frogs (Dendrobates spp.) and White's tree frogs (Litoria caerulea). Journal of Veterinary Diagnostic Investigation 11:194–199.

Peterle, T. J. 1991. Wildlife Toxicology. Van Nostrand Reinhold, New York, NY.

Peters, R. L. 1991. Consequences of global warming for biological diversity. Pp. 99–118 in R.L. Wyman, editor. Global Climate Change and Life on Earth. Routledge, Chapman & Hall, New York, NY.

Peters, R. L., and T. E. Lovejoy, editors. 1992. Global warming and biological diversity. Yale University Press, New Haven, CT.

Pethiyagoda, R., and K. Manamendra-Arachchi. 1998. Evaluating Sri Lanka's amphibian diversity. Occasional Papers of the Wildlife Heritage Trust. 2:1–12.

Petranka, J. W. 1983. Fish predation: A factor affecting the spatial distribution of a stream-breeding salamander. Copeia 1983:624–628.

Petranka, J. W. 1989. Density-dependent growth and survival of larval Ambystoma: Evidence from whole-pond manipulations. Ecology 70:1752–1767.

Petranka, J. W. 1993. Effects of timber harvesting on southern Appalachian salamanders. Conservation Biology 7:363–370.

Petranka, J. W. 1994. Response to impact of timber harvesting on salamanders. Conservation Biology 8:302–304.

Petranka, J. W. 1998. Salamanders of the United States and Canada. Smithsonian Press, Washington, DC. 587 p.

Petranka, J. W., M. P. Brannon, M. E. Hopey, and C. K. Smith. 1994. Effects of timber harvesting on low elevation populations of southern Appalachian salamanders. Forest Ecology and Management 67:135–147.

Petranka, J. W., M. E. Eldrige, and K. E. Haley. 1993. Effects of timber harvesting on southern Appalachian salamanders. Conservation Biology 7:363–370.

Petranka, J. W., and S. S. Murray. 2001. Effectiveness of removal sampling for determining salamander density and biomass: a case study in an Appalachian streamside community. Journal of Herpetology 35:36–44.

Petranka, J. W., and A. Sih. 1986. Environmental instability, competition, and density dependent growth and survivorship of a stream-dwelling salamander. Ecology 67:729–736.

Pfennig, D. W. 1990. The adaptive significance of an environmentally-cued developmental switch in an anuran tadpole. Oecologia 85:101–107.

Pfennig, D. W., M. L. G. Loeb, and J. P. Collins. 1991. Pathogens as a factor limiting the spread of cannibalism in tiger salamanders. Oecologia 88:161–166.

Phillips, J. B., K. Adler, and S. C. Borland. 1995. True navigation by an amphibian. Animal Behaviour 50:855–858.

Pilliod, D. S., and C. R. Peterson. 2000. Evaluating effects of fish stocking on amphibian populations in wilderness lakes. USDA Forest Service Proceedings RMRS-P-15-Vol. 5.

Pimentel, D., H. Acquay, M. Biltonen, P. Rice, M. Silva, J. Nelson, V. Lipner, S. Giordano,

A. Horowitz, and M. D'Amore. 1993a. The impact of pesticides on the environment. Pp. 47–84 in D. Pimentel, and H. Lehman, editors. The Pesticide Question: Environment, Economics, and Ethics. Chapman & Hall, New York, NY.

Pimentel, D., L. McLaughlin, A. Zepp, B. Lakitan, T. Kraus, P. Kleinman, F. Vancini, W. J. Roach, E. Graap, W. S. Keeton, and G. Selig. 1993b. Environmental and economic impacts of reducing U.S. agricultural pesticide use. Pp. 223–280 in D. Pimentel, and H. Lehman, editors. The Pesticide Question: Environment, Economics, and Ethics, Chapman & Hall, New York, NY.

Pimm, S. L. 1991. The Balance of Nature?: Ecological Issues in the Conservation of Species and Communities. University of Chicago Press, Chicago, IL.

Pimm, S. L., M. Ayres, A. Balmford, G. Branch, K. Brandon, T. Brooks, R. Bustamante, R. Costanza, R. Cowling, L. M. Curran, A. Dobson, S. Farber, G. A. B. de Fonesca, C. Gascon, R. Kitching, J. McNeely, T. Lovejoy, R. A. Mittermeier, N. Myers, J. A. Patz, B. Raffle, D. Rapport, P. Raven, C. Roberts, J. P. Rodriguez, A. B. Rylands, C. Tucker, C. Safina, C. Samper, M. L. J. Stiassny, J. Supriatna, D. H. Wall, and D. Willcove. 2001. Can we defy nature's end? Science 293:2207–2208.

Pimm, S. L., and A. Redfearn. 1988. The variability of population densities. Nature 334: 613–614.

Poole, R. W. 1972. An autoregressive model of population density change in an experimental population of Daphnia magna. Oecologia 10:205–221.

Pope, S. E., L. Fahrig, and H. G. Merriam. 2000. Landscape complementation and meta-population effects on leopard frog populations. Ecology 8:2498–2508.

Porter, K. R., and D. E. Hakanson. 1976. Toxicity of mine drainage to embryonic and larval boreal toads (Bufonidae: Bufo boreas). Copeia 1976:327–331.

Post, E., M. C. Forchhammer, N. C. Stenseth, and T. V. Callaghan. 2001. The timing of life history events in a changing climate. Proceedings of the Royal Society of London Series B-Biological Sciences 268:15–23.

Potter, F. E., Jr., and S. S. Sweet. 1981. Generic boundaries in Texas cave salamanders, and a redescription of Typhlomolge robusta (Amphibia: Plethodontidae). Copeia 1981:64–75.

Pough, F. H., and S. Kamel. 1984. Post-metamorphic change in activity metabolism of anurans in relation to life history. Oecologia 65:138–144.

Pough, F. H., E. M. Smith, D. H. Rhodes, and A. Collazo. 1987. The abundance of salamanders in forest stands with different histories of disturbance. Forest Ecology and Management 20:1–9.

Pounds, J. A. 2001. Climate and amphibian declines. Nature 410:639–640.

Pounds, J. A., and M. L. Crump. 1994. Amphibian declines and climate disturbance: the case of the golden toad and the harlequin frog. Conservation Biology 8:72–85.

Pounds, J. A., M. P. Fogden, and J. H. Campbell. 1999. Biological response to climate change on a tropical mountain. Nature 398:611–615.

Pounds, J. A., M. P. L. Fogden, J. M. Savage, and G. C. Gorman. 1997. Tests of null models for amphibian declines on a tropical mountain. Conservation Biology 11:1307–1322.

Poynton, J. C. 1999. Distribution of Amphibians in Sub-Saharan Africa, Madagascar, and Seychelles. Chapter 9. Pp. 483–539 in W. E. Duellman, editor. Patterns of Distribution of Amphibians: A Global Perspective. John Hopkins University Press, Baltimore, MD.

Prather, J. W., and J. T. Briggler. 2001. Use of small caves by anurans during a drought period in the Arkansas Ozarks. Journal of Herpetology 35:675–678.

Pratt, I., and J. E. McCauley. 1961. Trematodes of the Pacific Northwest. Oregon State University Press, Corvallis, OR. 118 p.

Pulliam, H. R. 1988. Sources, sinks, and population regulation. American Naturalist 132:652–661.

Puth, L. A., and K. A. Wilson. 2001. Boundaries and corridors as a continuum of ecological flow control: lessons from rivers and streams. Conservation Biology 15:21–30.

Rabb, G. B. 1999. The amphibian crisis. Pp. 23–30 *in*, T. L. Roth et al., editors. Seventh World Conference on Breeding Endangered Species, Cincinnati, OH, 22–26 May 1999.

Rabinowitz, D., S. Cairns, and T. Dillon. 1986. Seven forms of rarity and their frequency in the flora of the British Isles. Pp. 182–204 *in* M. Soulé, editor. Conservation Biology: The Science of Scarcity and Diversity. Sinauer, Sunderland, MA.

Rahbek, C. 1995. The elevational gradient of species richness: A uniform pattern? Ecography 18:200–205.

Rand, G. M. 1995. Fundamentals of Aquatic Toxicology: Effects, Environmental Fate, and Risk Assessment. 2nd edition. Taylor and Francis, Bristol, PA.

Rand, G. M., P. G. Wells, and L. S. McCarty. 1995. Introduction to aquatic toxicology. Pp. 3–70 *in* G. M. Rand, editor. Fundamentals of Aquatic Toxicology: Effects, Environmental Fate, and Risk Assessment. Taylor and Francis, Bristol, PA.

Rapport, D. J., H. A. Regier, and T. C. Hutchinson. 1985. Ecosystem behavior under stress. American Naturalist 125:617–640.

Raverty, S., and T. Reynolds. 2001. Cutaneous chytridiomycosis in dwarf aquatic frogs (*Hymenochirus boettgeri*) originating from southeast Asia and in a western toad (*Bufo boreas*) from northeastern British Columbia. Canadian Veterinary Journal 42:385–386.

Raxworthy, C. J., and D. K. Attuquayefio. 2000. Herpetofaunal communities at Muni Lagoon in Ghana. Biodiversity and Conservation 9:501–510.

Raxworthy, C. J., and R. A. Nussbaum. 2000. Extinction and extinction vulnerability of amphibians and reptiles in Madagascar. Amphibian and Reptile Conservation 2:15–23.

Reading, C. J. 1998. The effect of winter temperatures on the timing of breeding activity in the common toad *Bufo bufo*. Oecologia 117:469–475.

Reaser, J. K., and A. R. Blaustein. In Press. Repercussions of global change in aquatic systems. *In* M. Lanoo, editor. Status and Conservation of North American Amphibians. University of California Press, Berkeley, CA.

Reed, K. D., G. R. Ruth, J. A. Meyer, and S. K. Shukla. 2000. *Chlamydia pneumoniae* infection in a breeding colony of African clawed frogs (*Xenopus tropicalis*). Emerging Infectious Diseases 6:196–199.

Reh, W., and A. Seitz. 1990. The influence of land use on the genetic structure of populations of the common frog *Rana temporaria*. Biological Conservation 54:239–249.

Relyea, R. A., and N. Mills. 2001. Predator-induced stress makes the pesticide carbaryl more deadly to gray treefrog tadpoles (*Hyla versicolor*). Proceedings of the National Academy of Sciences (USA) 98:2491–2496.

Reptile and Amphibian Task Force. 1992. Report of the Louisiana Reptile and Amphibian Task Force to the Joint Natural Resources Committee. Louisiana Department of Wildlife and Fisheries, Habitat Conservation Division, Baton Rouge, LA.

Resetarits, W. J., Jr. 1997. Differences in an ensemble of streamside salamanders (Plethodontidae) above and below a barrier to brook trout. Amphibia-Reptilia 18:15–26.

Resetarits, W. J., Jr. 1991. Ecological interactions among predators in experimental stream communities. Ecology 72:1782–1793.

Richards, R. H., and A. D. Pickering. 1978. Frequency and distribution patterns of *Saprolegnia* infection in wild and hatchery-reared brown trout *Salmo trutta* and char *Salvelinus alpinus*. Journal of Fish Diseases 1:69–82.

Richards, S. J., K. R. McDonald, and R. A. Alford. 1994. Declines in populations in Australia's endemic tropical rainforest frogs. Pacific Conservation Biology 1:66–77.

Richter, B. D., D. P. Braun, M. A. Mendelson, and L. L. Master. 1997. Threats to imperiled freshwater fauna. Conservation Biology 11:1081–1093.

Richter, K. O., and A. L. Azous. 1995. Amphibian occurrence and wetland characteristics in the Puget Sound basin. Wetlands 15:305–312.

Ricketts, T. H. 2001. The matrix matters: Effective isolation in fragmented landscapes. American Naturalist 158:87–99.

Ridley, M. 1996. Evolution. 2nd edition. Blackwell Science, Cambridge, MA.

Roitt, I., J. Brostoff, and D. Male. 1996. Immunology. 4th edition. Times Mirror International Publishers, Baltimore, MD.

Rollins-Smith, L., C. Carey, J. E. Longcore, J. K. Doersam, A. Boutte, J. E. Bruzgul, and J. M. Conlon. 2002a. Activity of antimicrobial peptides from ranid frogs against *Batrachochytrium dendrobatidis,* the chytrid fungus associated with global amphibian declines. Developmental and Comparative Immunology 26:471–479.

Rollins-Smith, L., J. E. Longcore, S. K. Taylor, J. C. Shamblin, J. M. Krepp, and C. Carey. 2002b. Frog skin peptides: A defense against pathogens associated with global amphibian declines. Developmental and Comparative Immunology 26:63–72.

Ron, S. R., and A. Merino. 2000. Amphibian declines in Ecuador: An overview and first report of chytridiomycosis from South America. FROGLOG 42:2–3.

Rosenberg, D. K., B. R. Noon, J. W. Megahan, and E. C. Meslow. 1998. Compensatory behavior of *Ensatina eschscholtzii* in biological corridors: A field experiment. Canadian Journal of Zoology 76:117–133.

Rothermel, B. B., and R. D. Semlitsch. 2002. An experimental investigation of landscape resistance of forest versus old-field habitats to emigrating juvenile amphibians. Conservation Biology 16:1324–1332.

Rowe, C. L., and W. A. Dunson. 1994. The value of simulated pond communities in mesocosms for studies of amphibian ecology and ecotoxicology. Journal of Herpetology 28:346–356.

Rowe, C. L., and J. Freda. 2000. Effects of acidification on amphibians at multiple levels of organization. Pp. 545–571 *in* D. W. Sparling, C. A. Bishop, and G. Linder, editors. Ecotoxicology of Amphibians and Reptiles. Society of Environmental Toxicology and Chemistry, Pensacola, FL.

Rowe, C. L., W. A. Hopkins, and V. R. Coffman. 2001. Failed recruitment of southern toads (*Bufo terrestris*) in a trace element-contaminated breeding habitat: Direct and indirect effects that may lead to a local population sink. Archives of Environmental Contamination and Toxicology 40:399–405.

Royal Botanical Gardens. 1998. The Cootes Paradise Fishway: Carp Control Techniques, Royal Botanical Gardens, Hamilton, Ontario, Canada.

Rudolph, D. C., and J. G. Dickson. 1990. Streamside zone width and amphibian and reptile abundance. Southwestern Naturalist 35:472–476.

Russell, K. R., D. H. Van Lear, and D. C. J. Guynn. 1999. Prescribed fire effects on herpetofauna: Review and management implications. Wildlife Society Bulletin 27:374–384.

Ryan, J. C. 1992. Conserving biological diversity. Pp. 9–26 *in* L. Brown, editor. State of the World 1992. Worldwatch Institute, Washington, DC.

Santiago Ron, R., and A. Merino. 2000. Amphibian declines in Ecuador: Overview and first report of chytridiomycosis from South America. FROGLOG 42:4.

Saunders, D. A., and R. J. Hobbs. 1991. The role of corridors in conservation: What do we know and where do we go? Pp. 421–427 *in* D. A. Saunders, and R. J. Hobbs, editors. Nature Conservation 2: The Role of Corridors. Surrey, Beatty and Sons, Chipping Norton, New South Wales, Australia.

Sayler, A. 1966. The reproductive ecology of the red-backed salamander, *Plethodon cinereus*, in Maryland. Copeia 1966:183–193.

Scadding, S. R., and M. Maden. 1986a. Comparison of the effects of vitamin A on limb development and regeneration in the axolotl, *Ambystoma mexicanum*. Journal of Embryology and Experimental Morphology 91:19–34.

Scadding, S. R., and M. Maden. 1986b. Comparison of the effects of vitamin A on limb development and regeneration in *Xenopus laevis* tadpoles. Journal of Embryology and Experimental Morphology 91:35–53.

Schell, S. C. 1985. Trematodes of North America North of Mexico. University Press of Idaho, Iowa City, IA.

Schindler, D. W., P. J. Curtis, B. R. Parker, and M. P. Stainton. 1996. Consequences of climate warming and lake acidification for UV-B penetration in North American boreal lakes. Nature 379:705–708.

Schlaepfer, M. A., and T. A. Gavin. 2001. Edge effects on lizards and frogs in tropical forest fragments. Conservation Biology 15:1079–1090.

Schrope, M. 2000. Aquarium group fights "cyanide fishing." Nature 408:8–9.

Schuler, J. L., and R. D. Briggs. 2000. Assessing application and effectiveness of forestry best management practices in New York. Northern Journal of Applied Forestry 17:125–134.

Scott, N. J. 1993. Postmetamorphic death syndrome. FROGLOG 7:1–2.

Scott, A. F., and A. Bufalino. 1997. Dynamics of the amphibian communities at two small ponds in Land Between the Lakes over the past decade. P. 117 *in* A. F. Scott, S. W. Hamilton, E. W. Chester, and D. S. White, editors. Proceedings of the 7th Symposium on the Natural History of Lower Tennessee and Cumberland River valleys. Austin Peay State University, Clarksville, TN.

Scott, D. E. 1990. Effects of larval density in *Ambystoma opacum*: An experiment in large-scale field enclosures. Ecology 71:296–306.

Scott, D. E. 1994. The effect of larval density on adult demographic traits in *Ambystoma opacum*. Ecology 75:1383–1396.

Scott, D. E., and M. R. Fore. 1995. The effect of food limitation on lipid levels, growth, and reproduction in the marbled salamander, *Ambystoma opacum*. Herpetologica 51:462–471.

Scott, J. M., H. Anderson, F. Davis, S. Caicoo, B. Csuti, T. C. Edwards, Jr., R. Noss, J. Ulliman, C. Groves, and R. G. Wright. 1993. Gap analysis: A geographic approach to protection of biological diversity. Wildlife Monographs 0(123):1–41.

Scott, N. J., and C. A. Ramotnik. 1992. Does the Sacramento Mountain salamander require old-growth forests? Pp. 170–178 *in* M. R. Kaufmann, W. H. Moir, and R. L. Bassett, technical coordinators. Old-growth Forests in the Southwest and Rocky Mountain Regions. USDA Forest Service, General Technical Report RM-213.

Seabrook, W. A., and B. E. Dettmann. 1996. Roads as activity corridors for cane toads in Australia. Journal of Wildlife Management 60:363–368.

Seale, D. B. 1980. Influence of amphibian larvae on primary production, nutrient flux, and competition in a pond ecosystem. Ecology 61:1531–1550.

Semlitsch, R. D. 1983. Structure and dynamics of two breeding populations of the eastern tiger salamander, *Ambystoma tigrinum*. Copeia 1983:608–616.

Semlitsch, R. D. 1987. Relationship of pond drying to the reproductive success of the salamander *Ambystoma talpoideum*. Copeia 1987:61–69.

Semlitsch, R. D. 1998. Biological delineation of terrestrial buffer zones for pond breeding salamanders. Conservation Biology 12:1113–1119.

Semlitsch, R. D. 2000a. Principles for management of aquatic breeding amphibians. Journal of Wildlife Management 64:615–631.

Semlitsch, R. D. 2000b. Size does matter: The value of small isolated wetlands. Environmental Law Institute January–February 2000:5–6, 13.

Semlitsch, R. D. 2002. Critical elements for biologically-based recovery plans for aquatic breeding amphibians. Conservation Biology 16:619–629.

Semlitsch, R. D., and J. R. Bodie. 1998. Are small, isolated wetlands expendable? Conservation Biology 12:1129–1133.

Semlitsch, R. D., C. M. Bridges, and A. M. Welch. 2000. Genetic variation and a fitness tradeoff in the tolerance of gray treefrog (Hyla versicolor) tadpoles to the insecticide carbaryl. Oecologia 125:179–185.

Semlitsch, R. D., M. Foglia, A. Mueller, I. Steiner, E. Fioramonti, and K. Fent. 1995. Short-term exposure to triphenyltin affects the swimming and feeding behavior of tadpoles. Environmental Toxicology and Chemistry 14:1419–1423.

Semlitsch, R. D., and J. W. Gibbons. 1990. Effects of egg size on success of larval salamanders in complex aquatic environments. Ecology 71:1789–1795.

Semlitsch, R. D., and J. B. Jensen. 2001. Core habitat, not buffer zone. National Wetlands Newsletter 23:5–6.

Semlitsch, R. D., D. E. Scott, and J. H. K. Pechmann. 1988. Time and size at metamorphosis related to adult fitness in Ambystoma talpoideum. Ecology 69:184–192.

Semlitsch, R. D., D. E. Scott, J. H. K. Pechmann, and J. W. Gibbons. 1993. Phenotypic variation in the arrival time of breeding salamanders: Individual repeatability and environmental influences. Journal of Animal Ecology 62:334–340.

Semlitsch, R. D., D. E. Scott, J. H. K. Pechmann, and J. W. Gibbons. 1996. Structure and dynamics of an amphibian community: Evidence from a 16-year study of a natural pond. Pp. 217–248 in M. L. Cody, and J. A. Smallwood, editors. Long-term Studies of Vertebrate Communities. Academic Press, San Diego, CA.

Sessions, S. K. 1997. Evidence that abnormal amphibians are caused by natural phenomena. 18th Annual Meeting of the Society of Environmental Toxicology and Chemistry, San Francisco, CA. Abstract.

Sessions, S. K., and S. V. Bryant. 1988. Evidence that regenerative ability is an intrinsic property of limb cells in Xenopus. Journal of Experimental Zoology 247:39–44.

Sessions, S. K., R. A. Franssen, and V. L. Horner. 1999. Morphological clues from multi-legged frogs: are retinoids to blame? Science 284:800–802.

Sessions, S. K., A. Franssen, V. Horner, L. Hecker, and G. Stopper. 2001. Update on abnormal amphibian research at Hartwick College. Pp. 99–116 in M. S. Adams, editor. Catskill Ecosystem Health. Purple Mountain Press, Fleischmanns, NY.

Sessions, S. K., and S. B. Ruth. 1990. Explanation for naturally occurring supernumerary limbs in amphibians. Journal of Experimental Zoology 254:38–47.

Sexton, O. J., and J. R. Bizer. 1978. Life history parameters of Ambystoma tigrinum in montane Colorado. American Midland Naturalist 99:101–118.

Shave, C. R., C. R. Townsend, and T. A. Crowl. 1994. Antipredator behaviors of a freshwater crayfish (Paranephrops zealandicus) to a native and an introduced predator. New Zealand Journal of Ecology 18:1–10.

Shea, K., and P. Chesson. 2002. Community ecology theory as a framework for biological invasions. Trends in Ecology and Evolution 17:170–176.

Sih, A., L. B. Kats, and R. D. Moore. 1992. Effects of predatory sunfish on the density, drift, and refuge use of stream salamander larvae. Ecology 73:1418–1430.

Simberloff, D. 1981. Community effects of introduced species. Pp. 53–81 in M. H. Niteki, editor. Biotic Crises in Ecological and Evolutionary Time. Academic Press, New York, NY.

Simberloff, D., and P. Stiling. 1996. How risky is biological control? Ecology 77:1965–1974.

Sinsch, U. 1990. Migration and orientation in anuran amphibians. Ethology, Ecology, and Evolution 2:65–79.

Sinsch, U., and D. Seidel. 1995. Dynamics of local and temporal breeding assemblages in a *Bufo calamita* metapopulation. Australian Journal of Ecology 20:351–361.

Sjogren, P. 1991. Extinction and isolation gradients in metapopulations: The case of the pool frog (*Rana lessonae*). Biological Journal of the Linnean Society 42:135–147.

Skelly, D. K. 1996. Pond drying, predators, and the distribution of *Pseudacris* tadpoles. Copeia 1996:599–605.

Skelly, D. K., E. E. Werner, and S. Cortwright. 1999. Long-term distributional dynamics of a Michigan amphibian assemblage. Ecology 80:2326–2337.

Smith, C. K., and J. W. Petranka. 2000. Monitoring terrestrial salamanders: Repeatability and validity of area-constrained cover object searches. Journal of Herpetology 34:547–557.

Smith, D. C. 1983. Factors controlling tadpole populations of the chorus frog (*Pseudacris triseriata*) on Isle Royale, Michigan. Ecology 64:501–510.

Smith, D. C. 1987. Adult recruitment in chorus frogs: effects of size and date at metamorphosis. Ecology 68:344–350.

Smith, G. R., M. A. Waters, and J. E. Rettig. 2000. Consequences of embryonic UV-B exposure for embryos and tadpoles of the plains leopard frog. Conservation Biology 14:1903–1907.

Smith, L. L., K. G. Smith, W. J. Barichivich, C. K. Dodd, Jr., and K. Sorensen. In Press. Roads and Florida's herpetofauna: A review and mitigation case study. In W. E. Meshaka, Jr., and K. J. Babbitt, editors. Status and Conservation of Florida Amphibians and Reptiles. University Press of Florida, Gainesville, FL.

Smith, T. B., S. Kark, C. J. Schneider, R. K. Wayne, and C. Moritz. 2001. Biodiversity hotspots and beyond: The need for preserving environmental transitions. Trends in Ecology and Evolution 16:431.

Smith, W. 1994. Use of animals and animal organs in schools: Practice and attitudes of teachers. Journal of Biological Education 28:111–119.

Snodgrass, J. W., M. J. Komoroski, A. L. Bryan, Jr., and J. Burger. 2000. Relationships among isolated wetland size, hydroperiod, and amphibian species richness: Implications for wetland regulations. Conservation Biology 14:414–419.

Snyder, D. H. 1991. The green salamander (*Aneides aeneus*) in Tennessee and Kentucky, with comments on the Carolinas' Blue Ridge populations. Journal of the Tennessee Academy of Sciences 66:165–169.

Snyder, N. F. R., S. R. Derrickson, S. R. Beissinger, J. W. Wiley, T. B. Smith, W. D. Toone, and B. Miller. 1996. Limitations of captive breeding in endangered species recovery. Conservation Biology 10:338–348.

Sodhi, N. S., and L. H. Liow. 2000. Improving conservation biology research in Southeast Asia. Conservation Biology 14:1211–1212.

Southerland, M. T. 1986. Behavioral interactions among four species of the salamander genus *Desmognathus*. Ecology 67:175–181.

Spackman, S. C., and J. W. Hughes. 1995. Assessment of minimum stream corridor width for biological conservation:species richness and distribution along mid-order streams in Vermont, USA. Biological Conservation 71:325–332.

Sparling, D. W., C. A. Bishop, and G. Linder. 2000. The current status of amphibian and reptile ecotoxicological research. Pp. 1–13 in D. W. Sparling, G. Linder, and C. A. Bishop, editors. Ecotoxicology of Amphibians and Reptiles. Society of Environmental Toxicology and Chemistry, Pensacola, FL.

Sparling, D. W., G. M. Fellers, and L. L. McConnell. 2001. Pesticides and amphibian population declines in California, USA. Environmental Toxicology and Chemistry 20:1591–1595.

Speare, R. 1990. A review of the diseases of the cane toad, Bufo marinus, with comments on biological control. Australian Wildlife Research 17:387–410.

Speare R., and L. Berger. 2000a. Chytridiomycosis in amphibians in Australia. Available online at: http://www.jcu.edu.au/school/phtm/PHTM/frogs/chyspec.htm. Accessed 9 October 2001.

Speare R., and L. Berger. 2000b. Global distribution of chytridiomycosis in amphibians. Available online at: http://www.jcu.edu.au/school/phtm/PHTM/frogs/chyglob.htm. Accessed 11 November 2001.

Speare, R., L. Berger, P. O'Shea, P. W. Ladds, and A. D. Thomas. 1997. Pathology of mucormycosis of cane toads in Australia. Journal of Wildlife Diseases 33:105–111.

Spemann, H. 1967. Embryonic Development and Induction. Hafner Publishing Co., New York, NY. 401 p.

Spotila, J. R. 1972. Role of temperature and water in the ecology of lungless salamanders. Ecological Monographs 42:95–125.

Sredl, M. 2000. A fungus amongst frogs. Sonoran Herpetologist 13:122–125.

Stallard, R. F. 2001. Possible environmental factors underlying amphibian decline in eastern Puerto Rico: Analysis of U.S. government data archives. Conservation Biology 15: 943–953.

Stamps, J. A., M. Buechner, and V. V. Krishnan. 1987. The effects of edge permeability and habitat geometry on emigration from patches of habitat. American Naturalist 129: 533–552.

Starke, L., editor. 2001. State of the World 2001. W.W. Norton and Company, New York, NY.

Starnes, S. M., C. A. Kennedy, and J. W. Petranka. 2000. Sensitivity of southern Appalachian amphibians to ambient solar UV-B radiation. Conservation Biology 14:277–282.

Stearns, S. C. 1992. The Evolution of Life Histories. Oxford University Press, New York, NY. 249 p.

Stebbins, R. C. 1951. Amphibians of Western North America. University of California Press, Berkeley, CA. 539 p.

Stebbins, R.C. 1985. A Field Guide to Western Reptiles and Amphibians. 2nd edition. Houghton Mifflin, Boston, MA. 336 p.

Stewart, M. M. 1995. Climate driven population fluctuations in rain forest frogs. Journal of Herpetology 29:437–446.

Still, C. J., P. N. Foster, and S. H. Schneider. 1999. Simulating the effects of climate change on tropical montane cloud forests. Nature 398:608–610.

Stopper, G. F., L. Hecker, R. A. Franssen, and S. K. Sessions. 2002. How trematodes cause limb deformities in amphibians. Journal of Experimental Zoology (Mol. Dev. Evol.) 294:252–263.

Strahler, A. N. 1957. Quantitative analysis of watershed geomorphology. Transactions of the American Geophysical Union 38:913–920.

Stratman, D. 2001. Using micro and macrotopography in wetland restoration. USDA Natural Resources Conservation Service, Indianapolis, IN.

Strauss, R. T., and M. B. Kinzie. 1994. Student achievement and attitudes in a pilot study comparing an interactive videodisc simulation to conventional dissection. American Biology Teacher 56:398–402.

Stumpel, A. H. P. 1992. Successful reproduction of introduced bullfrogs *Rana catesbeiana* in northwestern Europe: A potential threat to indigenous amphibians. Biological Conservation 60:61–62.

Sutherst, R. W., R. B. Floyd, and G. F. Maywald. 1995. The potential geographical distribution of the cane toad, *Bufo marinus* L. in Australia. Conservation Biology 9:294–299.

Swett, F. H. 1926. On the induction of double limbs in amphibians. Journal of Experimental Zoology 44:419–473.

Tevini, M., editor. 1993. UV-B radiation and Ozone Depletion: Effects on Humans, Animals, Plants, Microorganisms, and Materials. Lewis Publishers, Boca Raton, FL.

Thomas, A. D., J. C. Forbes-Faulkner, R. Speare, and C. Murray. 2001. Salmonelliasis in wildlife from Queensland. Journal of Wildlife Diseases 37:229–238.

Thoms, S. D., and D. L. Stocum. 1984. Retinoic acid induced pattern duplication in regenerating urodele limbs. Developmental Biology 103:319–328.

Thornburgh, D. A., R. F. Noss, D. P. Angelides, C. M. Olson, F. Euphrat, and H. H. Welsh, Jr. 2000. Managing redwoods. Pp. 229–261 *in* R. F. Noss, editor. The Redwood Forest: History, Ecology, and Conservation of the Coast Redwoods. Island Press, Covelo, CA.

Thrall, B., and J. J. Burdon. 1997. Host-pathogen dynamics in a metapopulation context: The ecological and evolutionary consequences of being spatial. Journal of Ecology 85:743–753.

Thurman, E. M., and A. E. Cromwell. 2000. Atmospheric transport, deposition, and fate of triazine herbicides and their metabolites in pristine areas at Isle Royale National Park. Environmental Science and Technology 34:3079–3085.

Tietge, J. E., M. Lanoo, and V. Beasley. 1996. Discussion of Findings Relative To Meeting Objectives. North American Amphibian Monitoring Program III Conference. Available online at: http://www.im.nbs.gov/naamp3/naamp3.html.

Tilley, S. G. 1980. Life histories and comparative demography of two salamander populations. Copeia 1980:806–821.

Tilman, D., J. Fargione, B. Wolff, C. D'Antonio, A. Dobson, R. Howarth, D. Schindler, W. H. Schlesinger, D. Simberloff, and D. Swackhamer. 2001. Forecasting agriculturally driven global environmental change. Science 292:281–284.

Tilton, D. L. 1995. Integrating wetlands into planned landscapes. Landscape and Urban Planning 32:205–209.

Tiner, R. S., D. Petersen, K. Snider, K. Ruhlman, and J. Swords. 1999. Wetland characterization study and preliminary assessment of wetland functions for the Casco Bay watershed, southern Maine, USA. Maine State Planning House Paper. U.S. Fish and Wildlife Service, National Wetland Inventory, Northeast Region, Hadley, MA.

Tocher, M. D., C. Gascon, and B. L. Zimmerman. 1997. Fragmentation effects on a central Amazonian frog community: A ten-year study. Pp. 124–137 *in* W. F. Laurance, and R. O. Bieffegaard, Jr., editors. Tropical Forest Remnants: Ecology, Management, and Conservation. University of Chicago Press, Chicago, IL.

Tomlinson, G. H. 1990. Effects of Acid Deposition on the Forests of Europe and North America. CRC Press, Boston, MA. 281 p.

Touart, L. W. 1995. The Federal Insecticide, Fungicide, and Rodenticide Act. Pp. 657–669 *in* G.M. Rand, editor. Fundamentals of Aquatic Toxicology. 2nd edition. Taylor and Francis, Washington, DC.

Townsend, C. R. 1996. Invasion biology and ecological impacts of brown trout *Salmo trutta* in New Zealand. Biological Conservation 78:13–22.

Travis, J. 1994. Calibrating our expectations in studying amphibian declines. Herpetologica 50:104–108.

Travis, J., W. H. Keen, and J. Juiliana. 1985a. The effects of multiple factors on viability selection in *Hyla gratiosa* tadpoles. Evolution 39:1087–1099.

Travis, J., W. H. Keen, and J. Juiliana. 1985b. The role of relative body size in a predator-prey relationship between dragonfly naiads and larval anurans. Oikos 45:59–65.

Trenham, P. C., W. D. Koenig, and H. B. Shaffer. 2001. Spatially autocorrelated demography and interpond dispersal in the salamander *Ambystoma californiense*. Ecology 82:3519–3530.

Twery, M. J., and J. W. Hornbeck. 2001. Incorporating water goals into forest management decisions at a local level. Forest Ecology and Management 143:87–93.

Twisk, W., M. A. W. Noordervliet, and W. J. ter Keurs. 2000. Effects of ditch management on caddisfly, dragonfly and amphibian larvae in intensively farmed peatlands. Aquatic Ecology 34:397–411.

Tyler, M. J. 1999. Distribution patterns of amphibians in the Australo-Papuan region. Chapter 10. Pp. 541–563 *in* W. E. Duellman, editor. Patterns of Distribution of Amphibians: A Global Perspective. John Hopkins University Press, Baltimore, MD.

Tyler, T. J., W. J. Liss, L. M. Ganio, G. L. Larson, R. L. Hoffman, E. Deimling, and G. Lomnicky. 1998a. Interaction between introduced trout and larval salamanders (*Ambystoma macrodactylum*) in high elevation lakes. Conservation Biology 12:94–105.

Tyler, T. J., W. J. Liss, R. L. Hoffman, and L. M. Ganio. 1998b. Experimental analysis of trout effects on survival, growth, and habitat use of two species of ambystomatid salamanders. Journal of Herpetology 32:345–349.

U.S. Army Corps of Engineers. 2000. Civil Works Program Statistics. Information Paper CECW-ZP, 6 April 2000.

U.S. Congress. 1993. Harmful Non-Indigenous Species in the United States. Office of Technology Assessment, OTA-F-565, U.S. Government Printing Office, Washington DC.

U.S. Fish and Wildlife Service. 2000. Final rule to list the Santa Barbara County distinct vertebrate population segment of the California tiger salamander as an endangered species. Federal Register 65:57242.

UNEP (United Nations Environment Programme). 2001. Conference of the Plenipotentiaries on the Stockholm Convention on Persistent Organic Pollutants. Stockholm, Sweden, 22–23 May 2001.

UNEP World Conservation Monitoring Center. 1998. Significant Trade in Animals: Net Trade Outputs. Decision 10.79 of the Conference of the Parties Regarding the Implementation of Resolution Conf. 8.9.

UNEP World Conservation Monitoring Centre). 2001. A Global Overview of Forest Conservation. Available online at: http://www.unep-wcmc.org/forest/data/cdrom2/index.html.

USEPA (United States Environmental Protection Agency). 1995. Use of surrogate species in assessing contaminant risk to endangered and threatened fishes. EPA 600/R-96/029. Office of Research and Development, Resource Publication 160. Gulf Breeze, FL.

USEPA (United States Environmental Protection Agency). 1999. Assessing contaminant sensitivity of endangered and threatened species: Toxicant classes. EPA/600/R-99/098. Office of Research and Development, Washington, DC.

Vallan, D. 2000. Influence of forest fragmentation on amphibian diversity in the nature reserve of Ambohitantely, highland Madagascar. Biological Conservation 96:31–43.

Van Buskirk, J., and D. C. Smith. 1991. Density-dependent population regulation in a sala-
    mander. Ecology 72:1747–1756.
Van de Mortel, T., W. Buttemer, P. Hoffman, J. Hays, and A. Blaustein. 1998. A comparison
    of photolyase activity in three Australian tree frogs. Oecologia 115:366–369.
Van der Leun, J. C., X. Tang, and M. Tevini, editors. 1998. Environmental Effects of Ozone
    Depletion 1998 Assessment. Elsevier, Lausanne, Switzerland.
van Leeuwen, B. H. 1982. Protection of migrating common toad (Bufo bufo) against car
    traffic in the Netherlands. Environmental Conservation 9:1.
Van Valen, L. 1973. A new evolutionary law. Evolutionary Theory 1:1–30.
Vannote, R. L., G. W. Minshall, G. W. Cummins, J. R. Sedell, and C. E. Cushing. 1980. The
    river continuum concept. Canadian Journal of Fisheries and Aquatic Sciences 37:130–137.
Veith, M., J. Kosuch, R. Feldmann, H. Martens, and A. Seitz. 2000. A test for correct species
    declaration of frog legs imports from Indonesia into the European Union. Biodiversity
    and Conservation 9:333–341.
Vitt, L. J., J. P. Caldwell, H. M. Wilbur, and D. C. Smith. 1990. Amphibians as harbingers of
    decay. BioScience 40:418.
Vogl, R. J. 1973. Effects of fire on the plants and animals of a Florida wetland. American Mid-
    land Naturalist 89:334–347.
Vos, C. C., and A. H. P. Stumpel. 1996. Comparison of habitat isolation parameters in reloca-
    tion to fragmented distribution patterns in the tree frog (Hyla arborea). Landscape Ecology
    11:203–214.
Wake, D. B. 1991. Declining amphibian populations. Science 253:860.
Wake, D. B. 1993. Phylogenetic and taxonomic issues relating to salamanders of the family
    Plethodontidae. Herpetologica 49:229–237.
Wake, D. B. 1998. Action on amphibians. Trends in Ecology and Evolution 13:379–380.
Wake, D. B., and E. L. Jakusch. 2000. Detecting species borders using diverse data sets:
    Examples from plethodontid salamanders in California. Pp. 95–119 in R. C. Bruce,
    R. G. Jaeger, and L. D. Houck, editors. The Biology of Plethodontid Salamanders. Kluwer
    Academic/Plenum Press, New York, NY.
Wake, D. B., and H. J. Morowitz. 1990. Declining amphibian populations—a global phenom-
    enon? Report to Board on Biology, National Research Council, on workshop in Irvine,
    CA, 19–20 February 1990; reprinted 1991. Alytes 9:33–42.
Waldick, R. C., B. Freeman, and R. J. Wassersug. 1999. The consequences for amphibians of
    the conversion of natural, mixed-species forests to conifer plantations in southern New
    Brunswick. Canadian Field-Naturalist 113:408–418.
Ward, J. V., and K. Tockner. 2001. Biodiversity: Towards a unifying theme for river ecology.
    Freshwater Biology 46:807–819.
Warner, R. R., and P. L. Chesson. 1985. Coexistence mediated by recruitment fluctuations:
    A field guide to the storage effect. American Naturalist 125:769–787.
Warner, S. C., W. A. Dunson, and J. Travis. 1991. Interaction of pH, density, and priority
    effects on the survivorship and growth of two species of hylid tadpoles. Oecologia
    88:331–339.
Warner, S. C., J. Travis, and W. A. Dunson. 1993. Effect of pH variation on interspecific com-
    petition between two species of hylid tadpoles. Ecology 74:331–339.
Wassersug, R. J. 1975. The adaptive significance of the tadpole stage with comments on the
    maintenance of complex life cycles in anurans. American Zoologist 15:405–417.
Watkinson, A. R., R. P. Freckleton, R. A. Robinson, and W. J. Sutherland. 2000. Predictions

of biodiversity response to genetically modified herbicide-tolerant crops. Science 289: 1554–1557.

Weis, J. S., and A. A. Khan. 1990. Effects of mercury on the feeding behavior of the mummichog, *Fundulus heteroclitus,* from a polluted habitat. Marine Environmental Research 30: 243–249.

Welcomme, R. L. 1988. International Introductions of Inland Aquatic Species. Food and Agriculture Organization of the United Nations, Rome, Italy. Fisheries Technical Paper 294.

Wellborn, G. A., D. K. Skelly, and E. E. Werner. 1996. Mechanisms creating community structure across a freshwater habitat gradient. Annual Review of Ecology and Systematics 27:337–363.

Wells, K. D., and R. A. Wells. 1976. Patterns of movement in a population of the slimy salamander, *Plethodon glutinosus,* with observations on aggregations. Herpetologica 32: 156–162.

Welsh, H. H., Jr. 1990. Relictual amphibians and old-growth forests. Conservation Biology 4: 309–319.

Welsh, H. H., Jr., and S. Droege. 2001. A case for using Plethodontid salamanders for monitoring biodiversity and ecosystem integrity of North American forests. Conservation Biology 15:558–569.

Welsh, H. H., Jr., and A. J. Lind. 1988. Old growth forests and the distribution of the terrestrial herpetofauna. Pp. 439–455 *in* R. C. Szaro, K. E. Severson, and D. R. Patton, editors. Management of Amphibians, Reptiles, and Mammals in North America. USDA Forest Service, Rocky Mountain Forest and Range Experimental Station, Fort Collins, CO, General Technical Report RM-166.

Welsh, H. H., Jr., and A. J. Lind. 1991. The structure of the herpetofaunal assemblage in the Douglas-fir/hardwood forests of northwestern California and southwestern Oregon. Pp. 394–413 *in* L. F. Ruggiero, K. B. Aubry, A. B. Carey, and M. H. Huff, technical coordinators. Wildlife and Vegetation of Unmanaged Douglas-Fir Forests. USDA Forest Service, General Technical Report PNW-285.

Welsh, H. H., Jr., and A. J. Lind. 1992. Population ecology of two relictual salamanders from the Klamath Mountains of Northwestern California. Pp. 419–437 *in* D. R. McCullough, and R. H. Barrett, editors. Wildlife 2001: Populations. Elsevier Applied Science, London, UK.

Welsh, H. H., Jr., and A. J. Lind. 1996. Habitat correlates of the southern torrent salamander, *Rhyacotriton variegatus* (Caudata: Rhyacotritonidae), in northwestern California. Journal of Herpetology 30:385–398.

Welsh, H. H., Jr., and L. A. Ollivier. 1998. Stream amphibians as indicators of ecosystem stress: A case study from California's redwoods. Ecological Applications 8:1118–1132.

Welsh, H. H., Jr., T. D. Roelofs, and C. A. Frissell. 2000. Aquatic ecosystems of the redwood region. Pp. 165–199 *in* R. F. Noss, editor. The Redwood Forest: History, Ecology, and Conservation of the Coast Redwoods. Island Press, Covelo, CA.

Werner, E. E. 1986. Amphibian metamorphosis: Growth rate, predation risk, and the optimal size at transformation. American Naturalist 128:319–341.

Werner, E. E., and K. S. Glennemeier. 1999. Influence of forest canopy cover on the breeding pond distributions of several amphibian species. Copeia 1999:1–12.

Werner, E. E., and M. A. McPeek. 1994. Direct and indirect effects of predators on two anuran species along an environmental gradient. Ecology 75:1368–1382.

Werner, E. E., G. A. Wellborn, and M. A. McPeek. 1995. Diet composition in postmetamorphic bullfrogs and green frogs: implications for interspecific predation and competition. Journal of Herpetology 29:600–607.

Wetherald, R.T. 1991. Changes of temperature and hydrology caused by an increase of atmospheric carbon dioxide as predicted by general circulation models. Pp. 1–17 *in* R. L. Wyman, editor. Global Climate Change and Life on Earth. Routledge, Chapman & Hall, New York, NY.

Weygoldt, P. 1989. Changes in the composition of mountain stream frog communities in the Atlantic mountains of Brazil: Frogs as indicators of environmental deterioration? Studies of the Neotropical Fauna and Environment 243:249–255.

Wiest, J. A., Jr. 1982. Anuran succession at temporary ponds in a post oak-savanna region of Texas. Pp. 39–47 *in* N. J. Scott, Jr., editor. Herpetological Communities. Fish and Wildlife Service, U.S. Department of Interior, Washington, DC.

Wilbur, H. M. 1980. Complex life cycles. Annual Review of Ecology and Systematics 11:67–93.

Wilbur, H. M. 1984. Complex life cycles and community organization in amphibians. Pp. 195–224 *in* P. W. Price, C. N. Slobodchikoff, and W. S. Gaud, editors. A New Ecology: Novel Approaches to Interactive Systems. John Wiley and Sons, New York, NY.

Wilbur, H. M. 1987. Regulation of structure in complex systems: Experimental temporary pond communities. Ecology 68:1437–1452.

Wilbur, H. M., and J. P. Collins. 1973. Ecological aspects of amphibian metamorphosis. Science 182:1305–1314.

Wilbur, H. M., and J. E. Fauth. 1990. Experimental aquatic food webs: Interactions between two predators and two prey. American Naturalist 135:176–204.

Wilkins, R. N. and N. P. Peterson. 2000. Factors related to amphibian occurrence and abundance in headwater streams draining second-growth Douglas-fir forests in southwestern Washington. Forest Ecology and Management 139:79–91.

Williams, S. E., and J.-M. Hero. 1998. Rainforest frogs of the Australian Wet Tropics: Guild classification and the ecological similarity of declining species. Proceedings of the Royal Society of London 265B:597–602.

Williams, S. E., and J.-M. Hero. 2001. Multiple determinants of Australian tropical frog biodiversity. Biological Conservation 98:1–10.

Willson, M. F., S. M. Gende, and B. H. Marston. 1998. Fishes and the forest: Expanding perspectives on fish-wildlife interactions. BioScience 48:455–462.

Wilson, E. O. 1992. The Diversity of Life. Harvard University Press, Cambridge, MA.

Wilson, E. O. 1993. Biophilia and the conservation ethic. Pp. 33–34 *in* S. R. Kellert, and E. O. Wilson, editors. The Biophilia Hypothesis. Island Press, Washington, DC.

Wilson, L. D., and L. Porras. 1983. The ecological impact of man on the South Florida herpetofauna. University of Kansas Museum of Natural History, Special Publication Number 9.

Winter, R. M., S. A. S. Knowles, F. R. Bieber, and M. Baraitser. 1988. The Malformed Fetus and Stillbirth. John Wiley and Sons Ltd., New York, NY. 317 p.

Wolf, K., G. L. Bullock, C. E. Dunbar, and M. C. Quimby. 1968. Tadpole edema virus: A viscerotropic pathogen for anuran amphibians. Journal of Infectious Diseases 118:253–262.

Wolf, K., G. L. Bullock, C. E. Dunbar, and M. C. Quimby. 1969. Tadpole edema virus: Pathogenesis and growth studies and additional sites of virus infected bullfrog tadpoles. Pp. 327–336 *in* M. Mizell, editor. Biology of Amphibian Tumors. Springer-Verlag, New York, NY.

Woodward, B. D. 1982. Tadpole interactions in the Chihuahuan Desert at two experimental densities. Southwestern Naturalist 27:119–121.

Woodward, B. D. 1983. Predator-prey interactions and breeding pond use of temporary-pond species in a desert anuran community. Ecology 64:1549–1555.

World Commission on Dams. 2000. Dams and Development: A New Framework for Decision-Making. The Report of the World Commission on Dams. Earthscan Publications, London, UK.

World Resources Institute. 2000. World Resources 2000–2001. People and Ecosystems: The Fraying Web of Life. Elsevier Science, New York, NY.

Worrest, R. D., and D. J. Kimeldorf. 1976. Distortions in amphibian development induced by ultraviolet-B enhancement (290–310 nm) of a simulated solar spectrum. Photochemistry and Photobiology 24:377–382.

Wright, R. F., and D. W. Schindler. 1995. Interaction of acid rain and global changes: Effects on terrestrial and aquatic ecosystems. Water, Air, and Soil Pollution 85:89–99.

Wyman, R. L. 1988. Soil acidity and moisture and the distribution of amphibians in five forests of southcentral New York. Copeia 1988:394–399.

Wyman, R. L. 1991. Multiple Threats to Wildlife: Climate Change, Acid Precipitation, and Habitat Fragmentation. Pp. 134–155 in R. L. Wyman, editor. Global Climate Change and Life on Earth. Routledge, Chapman & Hall, New York, NY.

Wyman, R. L. 1998. Experimental assessment of salamanders as predators of detrital food webs: Effects on invertebrates, decomposition and the carbon cycle. Biodiversity and Conservation 7:641–650.

Wyman, R. L., and D. S. Hawksley-Lescault. 1987. Soil acidity affects distribution, behavior, and physiology of the salamander Plethodon cinereus. Ecology 68:1819–1827.

Wyman, R. L., and J. Jancola. 1992. Degree and scale of terrestrial acidification and amphibian community structure. Journal of Herpetology 26:392–401.

Yahner, R. H. 1988. Changes in wildlife communities near edges. Conservation Biology 2:333–339.

Yinfeng, G., Z. Xueying, C. Yan, W. Di, and W. Sung. 1997. Sustainability of wildlife use in traditional Chinese medicine. Technical Report No. 34 in J. MacKinnon, and W. Sung, editors. Conserving China's Biodiversity. China's Environmental Press, Beijing, China.

Young, B. E., K. R. Lips, J. K. Reaser, R. Ibañez, A. W. Salas, J. R. Cedeno, L. A. Coloma, S. Ron, E. La Marca, J. R. Meyer, A. Muñoz, F. Bolanos, G. Chaves, and D. Romo. 2001. Population declines and priorities for amphibian conservation in Latin America. Conservation Biology 15:1213–1223.

Young, M. D., and N. Gunningham. 1997. Mixing instruments and institutional arrangements for optimal biodiversity conservation. Pp. 123–135 in P. Hale, and D. Lamb, editors. Conservation Outside Nature Reserves. Centre for Conservation Biology, University of Queensland, Brisbane, Australia.

Zaga, A., E. E. Little, C. F. Rabeni, and M. R. Ellersieck. 1998. Photoenhanced toxicity of a carbamate insecticide to early life stage anuran amphibians. Environmental Toxicology and Chemistry 17:2543–2553.

Zhang, Q., Z. Li, Y. Jiang, S. Liang, and J. Gui. 1996. Preliminary studies on virus isolation and cell infection from diseased frog Rana grylio. Acta Hydrobiologica Sinica 20:390–392.

Zhang, Q.-Y., Z.-Q. Li, and J.-F. Gui. 1999. Studies on morphogenesis and cellular interactions of Rana grylio virus in an infected fish cell line. Aquaculture 175:185–197.

Zhang, Q.-Y., F. Xiao, Z.-Q. Li, J.-F. Gui, J. Mao, and V. G. Chinchar. 2001. Characterization of an iridovirus from the cultured pig frog (*Rana grylio*) with lethal syndrome. Diseases of Aquatic Organisms 48:27–36.

Zimmermann, E., and H. Zimmermann. 1994. Reproductive strategies, breeding, and conservation of tropical frogs: Dart-poison frogs and Malagasy poison frogs. Pp. 255– 266 *in* J. B. Murphy, K. Adler, and J. T. Collins, editors. Contributions to Herpetology, Volume 11. Captive Management and Conservation of Amphibians and Reptiles. Society for the Study of Amphibians and Reptiles, Ithaca, NY.

Zug, G. R., and P. B. Zug. 1979. The marine toad *Bufo marinus:* A natural history resume of native populations. Smithsonian Contributions to Zoology 284:1–58.

CONTRIBUTORS

Lisa K. Belden
Department of Zoology
Oregon State University
Corvallis, OR 9731-2914

Andrew R. Blaustein
Department of Zoology
Oregon State University
Corvallis, OR 9731-2914

Michelle D. Boone
U.S. Geological Survey, Columbia
    Environmental Research Center
4200 New Haven Road
Columbia, MO 65201

Christine M. Bridges
U.S. Geological Survey, Columbia
    Environmental Research Center
4200 New Haven Road
Columbia, MO 65201

R. Bruce Bury
U.S. Geological Survey, Forest and
    Rangeland Ecosystem Science Center
3200 S.W. Jefferson Way
Corvallis, OR 97331

Jesse L. Brunner
Department of Biology
Arizona State University
Tempe, AZ 85287-1501

Aram J. K. Calhoun
Department of Plant, Soil, and
    Environmental Sciences
University of Maine
Orono, ME 04469-5722

Carlos D. Camp
Department of Biology
Piedmont College
Demorest, GA 20535

Cynthia Carey
Department of Environmental, Population
    and Organismic Biology
University of Colorado
Boulder, CO 80309-0334

James P. Collins
Department of Biology
Arizona State University
Tempe, AZ 85287-1501

Paul Stephen Corn
U.S. Geological Survey, Aldo Leopold
  Wilderness Research Institute
P.O. Box 8089
Missoula, MT 59807

Martha L. Crump
Department of Biological Sciences
Northern Arizona University
Flagstaff, AZ 86011

C. Kenneth Dodd, Jr.
U.S. Geological Survey, Florida Caribbean
  Science Center
7920 N.W. 71st Street
Gainesville, FL 32653

J. Whitfield Gibbons
University of Georgia's Savannah River
  Ecology Laboratory
P.O. Drawer E
Aiken, SC 29802

Audrey C. Hatch
Department of Zoology
Oregon State University
Corvallis, OR 9731-2914

Jean-Marc Hero
School of Applied Science
Griffith University Gold Coast
PMB 50, Gold Coast MC
Queensland 4217
Australia

Malcolm L. Hunter, Jr.
Department of Wildlife Ecology
University of Maine
Orono, ME 04469-5755

Erin J. Hyde
U.S. Geological Survey, Forest and
  Rangeland Ecosystem Science Center
3200 S.W. Jefferson Way
Corvallis, OR 97331

John B. Jensen
Georgia Department of Natural Resources
Nongame-Endangered Wildlife Program
116 Rum Creek Drive
Forsyth, GA 31029

Joseph M. Kiesecker
Department of Biology, 208 Mueller Lab.
The Pennsylvania State University
University Park, PA 16802

Verma Miera
Department of Biology
Arizona State University
Tempe, AZ 85287-1501

Matthew J. Parris
Department of Biology
University of Memphis
Memphis, TN 38152

Angela D. Peace
Department of Environmental, Population
  and Organismic Biology
University of Colorado
Boulder, CO 80309-0334

Joseph H. K. Pechmann
Department of Biological Sciences
University of New Orleans
New Orleans, LA 70148

Allan P. Pessier
University of Illinois Zoological Pathology
  Program
Loyola University Medical Center, Room
  0745, Building 101
2160 South First Street
Maywood, IL 60153

Betsie B. Rothermel
Division of Biological Sciences
University of Missouri
Columbia, MO 65211-7400

Erin Scheessele
Department of Zoology
Oregon State University
Corvallis, OR 9731-2914

Danna M. Schock
Department of Biology
Arizona State University
Tempe, AZ 85287-1501

Raymond D. Semlitsch
Division of Biological Sciences
University of Missouri
Columbia, MO 65211-7400

Stanley K. Sessions
Department of Biology
Hartwick College
Oneonta, NY 13820

Lora L. Smith
U.S. Geological Survey, Florida Caribbean
   Science Center
7920 N.W. 71st Street
Gainesville, FL 32653

Andrew Storfer
School of Biological Sciences
Washington State University
Pullman, WA 99164-4236

Richard L. Wyman
Edmund Niles Huyck Preserve and
   Biological Research Station
P.O. Box 189
Rensselaerville, NY 12147

INDEX

Page numbers with *f* and *t* indicate figures and tables.